Samuel Davies

Samuel Davies

Apostle to Virginia

Dewey Roberts

SOLA FIDE PUBLICATIONS

Copyright © 2017 Dewey Roberts

All rights reserved. No part of this book may be reproduced, scanned,
or distributed in any printed or electronic form without permission.

First Edition: 2017

Cover Illustration:
Based on a map from United States Digital Map Library
http://usgwarchives.net/maps/virginia/statemap/1751virginia.jpg
showing the "most inhabited part of Virginia" drawn by Joshua Fry and Peter Jefferson, 1751, reproduced with the permission of Special Collections, John D. Rockefeller Library, Colonial Williamsburg Foundation

© Used with permission

Book design and cover by www.greatwriting.org

ISBN: 978-0-9972666-1-0 (paperback)
ISBN: 978-0-9972666-2-7 (clothbound)

Chapter Contents

Appreciations 7
Acknowledgements 11
Foreword 13
Preface 16
1   The Son of Prayer 18
2   Behold, He Is Praying 36
3   Blair's Academy at Fagg's Manor 56
4   The Great Awakening Comes to Virginia 80
5   Set Apart for the Gospel 103
6   First Year at Hanover 120
7   Opposition to the Gospel 142
8   John Todd Comes to Virginia 162
9   Preaching That Aroused a Colony 184
10 The College of New Jersey 200
11 Fund Raising in London 220
12 North to Scotland 240
13 Charity and Truth United 261
14 The French and Indian War 276
15 Hanover Presbytery 289
16 Evangelizing the African Slaves 307
17 Virginia's Danger and Remedy 325
18 Mission to the Overhill Cherokees 342
19 The Call to Nassau Hall 361
20 President of the College of New Jersey 376
21 The Pamphlet War among Presbyterians 396
22 Davies' Last Sickness and Death 407
Select Bibliographies 421
Index 432

To Jane, my Chara

Unless indicated otherwise, Scripture quotations are taken from the New American Standard Bible®, Copyright © 1960, 1962, 1963, 1968, 1971, 1972, 1973, 1975, 1977, 1995 by The Lockman Foundation
Used by permission.

SOLA FIDE PUBLICATIONS
Destin, Florida

Appreciations

Samuel Davies is one of the lesser known men God used in that period of American history known as the Great Awakening. But being lesser known today does not mean his ministry was not strong and effective in his time. Davies as been referred to as the founder of Southern Presbyterianism, and as the "Apostle" of Virginia. He planted congregations throughout central Virginia and south into North Carolina. Dewey Roberts provides us with a new and fresh history of Samuel Davies that will engage us in reviewing his life and ministry as well as this period of eighteenth-century America. After reading this book I believe you will agree with what Dr. Martyn Lloyd-Jones said of Samuel Davies: "You Americans do not know one of your greatest preachers." But we will know and appreciate him after reading this book.

Dr. Dominic A. Aquila,
President, New Geneva Theological Seminary, Colorado Springs, Colorado

Dewey Roberts introduces his readers to the great Samuel Davies, providing a robust historical and biographical account where there was so little before. Davies' all-round ministry is made known as a renowned preacher, an earnest minister to African slaves and Overhill Cherokees, and as the president of early Princeton. Roberts describes the phases of Davies' life in which an apprehension of God's grace moved such a gifted man from potential to reality.

Dewey Roberts is a fine biographer, describing Samuel Davies' Christian experience with such pastoral precision that we are able to appreciate the best of the Great Awakening's influence on him and learn from worst of trials he faced. Roberts sounds his conclusion with admiration and wisdom: "We know in part and we saw in part something of what those uncommon gifts were, but, for reasons known only to God, he was called to his heavenly home before all his gifts were manifested to the world. Yet, here is where Davies was perhaps best—he was arguably the best combination of evangelist, preacher, and theologian in the whole

Appreciations

history of the church. With his passing, the American church lost her greatest preacher ever and one of the most astounding all-around ministers to ever grace an American pulpit.

Dr. Robert Davis Smart,
Senior Pastor of Christ Church (PCA), Bloomington-Normal, Illinois

I read Reverend Dewey Roberts' *Samuel Davies* with an eagerness to learn more about one of the most important but underappreciated figures in American Presbyterian history. The Samuel Davies story is nothing short of amazing grace. That a man is able, in the short span of thirty-seven years, and with the relatively limited communication resources of the mid-eighteenth century, to produce so varied a record of service is a testimony to the prodigious subject of this new book, as well as to the gracious intent of the God whom Davies preached.

As Reverend Roberts demonstrates with remarkably fresh and readable prose and well-documented footnotes (that form their own enticing footpath begging to be followed) Davies was not merely an evangelist (in a day when Whitefield roamed the Colonial coast), or an academic, or a college president (following Jonathan Edwards); he was a pastor, a writer, a patriot, a hymn-writer, and an administrator. He was quintessentially *American* and in a real way forged those peculiar traits that mark out the strong, optimistic spirit that the world thinks of today as the indomitable youthful spirit of our people. Yet, Davies was an unabashed Calvinist. He was not *rigid* as some imagine Calvinists—indeed, he chastised those whose theology made them brittle and inhuman—but, was unashamed to confess that *the Westminster Confession of Faith* was essential for ordination in the Presbyterian Church of his day.

Dewey Roberts should be commended for this generous work in bringing this great American Presbyterian clergyman back to the vanguard of spiritual giants (where Davies belongs). For this Samuel Davies who stirred the spirit of a young Patrick Henry, may well be the one who stirs the spirit of some young person, now, to serve God in a new day. Perhaps—shall we not pray—the Lord who brought revival then might even grace us with even the minutest dewdrop of spiritual renewal in our land. Oh, what a joy that would be for this country that Davies helped to found! For as I read this new book on Samuel Davies, I could not help but pray the words of his hymn for our generation (On Thee, O Lord our God, we call):

"Lord, we repent, we weep, we mourn,
To our forsaken God we turn;
Oh, spare our guilty country, spare
The church thine hand hath planted here!"

Without reservation and with the greatest enthusiasm possible I commend *Samuel Davies* by Rev. Dewey Roberts to the Church with my prayer for personal and corporate revival.

Dr. Michael A. Milton, PhD, MPA
James Ragsdle Chair of Missions and Evangelism, Erskine Theological Seminary
President, D. James Kennedy Institute
Fourth Chancellor, Reformed Theological Seminary
Chaplain (Colonel), US Army Reserve

I have been waiting for years to read a thorough, well-documented and enlightening biography on Samuel Davies, the greatest preacher our nation has seen. Thanks to Dewey Roberts we now have this important work on Davies. Read this book for your edification and motivation for ministry.

Al Baker
Evangelist with Presbyterian Evangelistic Fellowship (PEF)
Director of Samuel Davies Conference on Evangelism

Dewey Roberts was born in Cleveland, Mississippi, and raised in the southeastern states of the USA. He studied Bible and English at Belhaven College and earned his Master of Divinity from Reformed Theological Seminary (both institutions in Jackson, Mississippi). He is the founding pastor of Cornerstone Presbyterian Church in Destin, Florida, where he has served since 1995. He was an Army Reserve chaplain for twenty-four years and served three tours on active duty. He retired in the rank of Colonel in 2011 and spent the last eight years of his chaplain career as a writer / instructor at the US Army Chaplain School and Center in Fort Jackson, SC. In addition to his pastoral duties, he also serves as Executive Director of Church Planting International (CPI) which promotes reformed indigenous missions in Russia, Uganda, Myanmar, India, and Portugal. CPI was founded by Rev. Donald Dunkerley in 1993.

Samuel Davies: Apostle to Virginia is the first full-scale biography ever produced on Samuel Davies, America's greatest ever preacher. It is a meticulously researched work which presents the story of Davies' life from cradle to grave. With the publication of this biography, the great Samuel Davies will no longer be an obscure figure from the past. It deserves a place on the bookshelves of those who have read the biographies of Whitefield, Spurgeon, McCheyne, Edwards, Lloyd-Jones, and other great Christian ministers.

Samuel Davies: Apostle to Virginia is Dewey Roberts' second book. In 2016 he published *Historic Christianity and the Federal Vision: A Theological Analysis and Practical Evaluation*.

Dewey and his wife, Jane, have two children and four grandchildren.

Acknowledgements

The research for this book began in earnest in October of 1978 with a visit to the Presbyterian Historical Center at Montreat, North Carolina. I was thankful to find several primary source materials on Samuel Davies, but was dismayed that there was so much of his life shrouded in mystery. It was, nonetheless, my conviction from the beginning of this project that Davies deserved to have his story told from cradle to grave. Thus, I undertook years of tireless research and have tried to leave no stone unturned in my effort to uncover the details of his life. Thirty-nine years is a long time to work on a book, but those years were not all spent on this one project.

A twenty-four year career as an Army Reserve/Army chaplain often left me little time to devote to the writing of this book. I always tried to redeem the time and studied at major libraries in every city where Providence placed me in hopes of finding some hidden treasure about Davies. Yet, the most important developments for completing this book came because of the Internet. Google books now has millions of books which can be studied online. The Evans Collection of Early American Imprints (including numerous materials concerning the Colonial era) has made many of those documents available online. Formerly, they were accessible only by using a microdot reader and could be found only in major libraries. Then, JSTOR has numerous magazine and periodical articles available online which once could be found only in certain libraries. In the past three years, I have been able to do a great deal of in-depth research on Samuel Davies from the confines of my office at the church I pastor. It has also been easier to access the materials and much faster to do so.

There are several libraries where I have studied that I especially want to acknowledge: the Firestone Library at Princeton University in Princeton, New Jersey; the Princeton Theological Seminary Library in Princeton, New Jersey; the Presbyterian Historical Society in Philadelphia, Pennsylvania; the Historical Society of Pennsylvania—Library Company of Philadelphia in Philadelphia, Pennsylvania; the Library of Congress in Washington, D.C.; the Virginia Historical Society in Richmond, Virginia; and, the Beinecke Rare Book and Manuscript Library at Yale University in New Haven, Connecticut. The staff at each of these libraries was most helpful to me in locating materials that aided my research on Davies. Additionally, there are other libraries that have answered enquiries and

Acknowledgements

sent me photocopies of documents about Davies. I particularly want to thank the staff at the Library of Union Presbyterian Seminary.

My editor, Jim Holmes of Taylors, South Carolina, has always been available to answer my questions or help me to think through an issue. His suggestions for the organization of the chapters has been invaluable as has his work on editing the whole manuscript, formatting it for print, and designing the dust jacket of the book.

In writing 126,000 words, there are numerous typographical, punctuation, and grammatical errors that find their way into the text. I am very thankful for the assistance given to me by several people who proofread the manuscript and offered valuable suggestions: Jane Roberts, Kathy Orr, Bob Good, Chuck Stoyer, Rich Rogers, Gail Rogers, Linda Wohleber, Sally Maddox, and Ed Maney. This book is much better as a result of their help. If any errors remain, they are wholly my fault.

Dewey Roberts,
Pastor, Cornerstone Presbyterian Church
Destin, Florida

Foreword

The Puritan Conference took place annually at Westminster Chapel and for nineteen years the much anticipated closing address was given by the chairman, Dr. Martyn Lloyd-Jones. I was privileged to hear many of them, and in 1964, in his address entitled "John Calvin and George Whitefield," Dr. Lloyd-Jones spoke of George Whitefield's preaching saying:

> Take the way his ministry is described for us by the author of the great hymn which begins with the words:
>
> *Great God of wonders, all Thy ways*
> *Are matchless, godlike, and divine.*
>
> Samuel Davies himself was an astonishing preacher and a great intellect also. He had been involved in a great revival in the eighteenth century. He had been made principal of a college and one year Samuel Davies and Gilbert Tennent were sent over to this country to collect money for that college. They arrived after a terrible voyage during which they thought they were going to be shipwrecked many times over. They at last arrived in London on a Saturday morning, and the first question they asked was this—"Is Mr. Whitefield in town?"
>
> To their delight they were told he was and that he was due to preach the next morning; I think it was in Moorfields. So they made certain that they would be there in very good time to listen to him. Samuel Davies writes the account of the service and this is what he says. He says, "It became clear to me quite soon in the service that Mr. Whitefield must have had an exceptionally busy week; obviously he had not had time to prepare his sermon properly." He adds, "From the standpoint of construction and ordering of thought it was very deficient and defective; it was a poor sermon. But," said Samuel Davies, "the unction that attended it was such that I would gladly risk the rigours of shipwreck in the Atlantic many times over in order to be there just to come under its gracious influence." That is preaching, my friends. Poor sermon, but tremendous preaching! What do we know about this?[1]

Here we have one of the most discerning and helpful preachers of the twentieth century, Martyn Lloyd-Jones, writing about the impact that

---

[1] (Dr D. Martyn Lloyd-Jones, 'John Calvin and George Whitefield', "The Puritans: Their Origins and Successors" Banner of Truth, pp. 123&124, 1987).

Foreword

one of the greatest preachers of the eighteenth century, George Whitefield, had upon another preacher who himself had displayed those rarest of homiletic qualities so evident in the New Testament apostles, an awakening ministry allied to much discernment, a keen intellect and powers of poetic expression, Samuel Davies. Doesn't this whet your appetite to know more about him? Until now we have been dependent for our knowledge of this American preacher with his Welsh forebears upon the reprint volumes of his sermons, and also the brief sketch of his life in the standard work on revival written by Iain Murray entitled "Revival and Revivalism" (Banner of Truth). Now our friend Dewey Roberts has come to our deliverance and has provided for us this rich biography of Davies' life.

Of course it is a "fascinating read" and a page turner. It will thus be widely enjoyed and appreciated, but its ultimate value does not lie in the engaging nature of its style, nor in any romanticized view of the eighteenth century. Indeed, when Davies and Tennent walked about London and even met the diminutive Wesley brothers, they were disturbed by the carnality and degradation they saw everywhere in the metropolis, and that was at a time some decades after the Great Awakening had begun. The book is not nostalgic; it is not looking back to a utopia that never existed. It is valuable because Samuel Davies is approached with four crucial questions in mind:

> How did Samuel Davies become the mighty preacher he was?
> What did he preach and do?
> Were his sermons biblical and how did they become an awakening ministry?
> What can we learn from his life and witness today?

We are living in remarkable days when we are being given the fruits of the studies of many men from all over the world of the greatest preachers of the past, and these books are of great potential importance for the church. The long-ignored writings of Reformers, Puritans, and the leading preachers of the Evangelical Awakening are being reprinted, and these books have reached the ends of the earth with the strange discovery of their unexpected relevance for today and in every place of the stand they took and what they said. They expose much weakness of contemporary preaching, and they assist us in our controversy with new movements that have emerged in conservative evangelical circles. Reading the life of Samuel Davies is a practical enterprise, not something theoretical or archaeological. Remembering him is to honor one who stood fast for the central important truths of the Christian religion. His life and opinions can encourage our own generation to believe in God and His glorious grace.

Geoffrey Thomas,
Pastor Emeritus of Alfred Place Baptist Church, Aberystwyth, Wales

Preface

Samuel Davies has suffered in obscurity, unknown to many Christians today, because there was no full-scale biography written about him during the eighteenth century. That oversight by his peers and those who knew him best has resulted in many facts about his life being lost to posterity. It has also proven to be the greatest challenge to me in trying to do his memory justice with the writing of this new biography. Where direct information about his life was not available, I have had to supplement it with facts from secondary sources.

A diary which he started keeping in his youth has apparently been lost for all time. That diary was mentioned by Samuel Finley at the funeral service of Davies in 1761 and was last known to be viewed by Dr. Jonathan Witherspoon who was one of the successors of Davies as president of Princeton College. If it were available it would provide valuable insights into the circumstances of his conversion, his education, his church membership, his assurance of salvation, and numerous other details. It is very likely that this diary was burned in the fire that nearly destroyed Nassau Hall in 1802.

There are several people who have written partial or brief biographies of Davies—Ashbel Green, John Holt Rice, William Henry Foote, Albert Barnes, Enoch Pond, William B. Sprague, B. B. Edwards, George H. Bost, George W. Pilcher, and Iain H. Murray. Each of those biographies, biographical notices, or unpublished manuscripts covers the same general facts while leaving much of his life untouched. There are some interesting anecdotes communicated by the older biographers—Green, Rice, Foote, Barnes, Edwards, and Sprague—but very little information on the first twenty-three years of his life.

It would have been a much easier task for me to write a biography of Samuel Davies using primary source materials only. Such a biography would have added little new information about this great man. Instead, I chose the more difficult task of writing a full-scale biography. One of his earlier biographers, B. B. Edwards, suggested the need of such a work 180 years ago:

> The individual who shall undertake this work will deserve well of the church and of his country. He should make a personal investigation of the places where Davies resided—Newcastle in Delaware, Princeton in New Jersey, and the scenes of the labors of Davies in Virginia—examining the records of the college of New Jersey, and of the ecclesiastical bodies with which the president was connected. Something might possibly be found

in Nottingham, Pa., and among the papers of Dr. Gibbons of London. It is not honorable to the country, that while the memorials of her greatest general are carefully prepared and elegantly published, many memorials of one of her most distinguished pulpit orators, should be left to decay and utter loss.[1]

The Scripture teaches us that every fact must be confirmed by two or three witnesses. Secondary source materials have sometimes provided irrefutable documentary evidence of some fact pertinent to Davies' life. Thus, I decided long ago to write a new and fresh biography of Davies instead of a romanticized retelling of the same facts already known about him. I especially wanted to show that Davies was a child of the Great Awakening and one of the greatest evangelists in that exciting period of church history. Therefore, this book is being sent forth to the Christian public with the hope that it will inspire a new generation of believers to pray and labor for a fresh awakening of God's Spirit in our day.

Dewey Roberts

---

[1] B. B. Edwards, "Memoir of President Davies," *American Quarterly Register*, Vol. IX, No. 4 (May, 1837), 324.

-1-

The Son of Prayer

"The greatest preacher you have ever produced in this country was Samuel Davies, the author of the hymn, 'Great God of wonders, all thy ways/Are matchless, godlike, and divine', and the man who followed Jonathan Edwards as president of Princeton."[1]
~*Dr. D. Martyn Lloyd-Jones*~

The birthplace home of Samuel Davies near Glasgow, Delaware

---

[1] D. M. Lloyd-Jones, *Knowing the Times* (Edinburgh, Scotland and Carlisle, Pennsylvania: The Banner of Truth Trust, 1989), 263.

The Son of Prayer

Patrick Henry awoke early in the morning on March 20, 1775, which was a day of great importance for Virginia and the American colonies. A light snow was falling as he mounted his horse for the twenty-mile ride to Richmond.[2] Henry was the delegate for Hanover County to the second meeting of the Virginia Convention that would debate the issue of waging war with Great Britain. Many of the delegates were Tories who opposed any rebellion against the Crown. Recently bereaved of his wife, Sallie, after twenty years of marriage, the impending crisis at this convention weighed heavily on Henry's heart.

When Henry arrived in Richmond, the sky was clearing and the delegates were gathering outside St. John's Parish Church. There was a flurry of excitement with horses, gigs, and carriages everywhere, according to witnesses. St. John's, which sat conspicuously on Church Hill, was the only building in the city that could seat the one-hundred-and-thirty delegates and friends from sixty-one counties. Suddenly, a howling March wind swept through the church grounds, upsetting the horses and sending the delegates scurrying for seats. The foul weather further depressed an already downcast assembly, particularly Henry, who quickly repaired to the third pew.

Peyton Randolph, speaker of the Virginia House of Burgesses, was elected President of the Convention, which made the cause of rebellion appear hopeless. Little was accomplished the first day. The following day, Henry made a resolution to arm the colony which passed the convention with ease. His second motion, to declare war with Great Britain, was hotly debated and vigorously opposed by delegates Edmund Pendleton, Robert Carter Nicholas, Richard Bland, Benjamin Harrison, and George Wythe. Much of their opposition focused on Henry himself with some delegates ready to oppose any measure which he championed.

On the epoch fourth day of this convention, March 23, Henry passed "through the westerly gate in the brick wall surrounding the churchyard and . . . into the little wooden building."[3] The weather was balmy and the church windows were opened to let in the refreshing breeze.[4] Randolph called the convention to order at 10 a.m. and the ironic prayer for the King

---

[2] Norine Dickson Campbell, *Patrick Henry: Patriot and Statesman* (New York: Devin-Adair, 1969), 123. Most of the information for the first six paragraphs is taken from this work.
[3] Robert Douthat Meade, *Patrick Henry, Practical Revolutionary* (Philadelphia: Lippincott, 1969), 23.
[4] Ibid.

The Son of Prayer

was read by Reverend Miles Selden, rector of the St. John's Church. A motion from the Jamaican Assembly[5] was read to the convention by Pendleton, the delegate from Caroline County. That resolution wished for "a speedy return to those halcyon days" of British rule as "a free and happy people."[6] This sentiment aroused the patriotic spirit of Henry who quickly presented amendments which were vigorously opposed by several influential members of the Convention.

Rising from his seat, Henry spoke in favor of his amendments without attacking the patriotism of the opponents to his motion. In the audience were John Mason, Thomas Jefferson, and George Washington. The time for action was now, in Henry's opinion. Before he finished, Henry gained immortality for his speech with the final sentence:

> I know not what course others may take; but as for me, give me liberty or give me death!

As the delegates reflected on his words, liberty and freedom wafted through the assembly like the balmy breeze that blew in the open windows. Colonel Edward Carrington, a delegate from Virginia to the Continental Congress in 1786-1788, was so overcome with emotion as he listened by an open window that he exclaimed, "Let me be buried on this spot!"[7]

Henry dramatically held up an ivory letter-opener as he exclaimed, "Give me liberty . . . ," and feigned stabbing his heart as he uttered the word "death."[8] This speech stunned the convention into silence for a few minutes before Richard Henry Lee rose to second Henry's motion. Jefferson, who called Henry the "greatest orator ever," spoke in favor of the motion with great eloquence. Henry's speech carried the day. His amendment was passed, and the colony of Virginia prepared for war with Great Britain.

Where did Henry, the former tavern keeper and planter whom some considered to be illiterate, acquire such oratorical powers? As a youth, he drove his mother and sisters by carriage over Hanover County's back

---

[5] Jamaica was a British colony.
[6] Meade, *Patrick Henry, Practical Revolutionary*, 23.
[7] Campbell, *Patrick Henry: Patriot and Statesman*, 131.
[8] Meade, *Patrick Henry, Practical Revolutionary*, 35.

roads from their home at Studley to hear the great Samuel Davies preach.[9] On the ride home, he was required to recite as much of the sermon as he could remember, which was undoubtedly the source of his education in oratory. Henry repeated the sermons word for word and mimicked the gestures of the man he esteemed as "the greatest orator he ever heard."[10] Two decades before his speech to the Virginia Convention at Richmond, Henry had heard several of Davies' war sermons, particularly "Religion and Patriotism the Constituents of Good Soldiers," which was preached at Hanover Courthouse on August 17, 1755 to the company raised by Captain Samuel Overton for the French and Indian War. There are no phrases in Davies' sermons that exactly match Henry's immortal words, but the ideas of fighting for liberty and preparing for death are interspersed throughout them. Many of the ideas in Henry's speech were inimical to Davies' thoughts and style of oratory.

Who was Samuel Davies, whose preaching prowess was the model for one of the most important speeches in American history? Known by few today, Davies was, in the opinion of D. Martyn Lloyd-Jones, former pastor of Westminster Chapel in London, "the greatest preacher you ever produced in this country."[11] The man who inspired some of the most important words in the history of the United States and who championed religious toleration in Virginia well deserves our study.

Without Davies' example, Patrick Henry might never have become the orator and statesman he was. Without Henry's moving speech before Virginia's convention in March of 1775, that colony might not have voted in favor of the Revolutionary War. Without Virginia's support in the cause of freedom, her favorite son, George Washington, might not have led the Continental Army through all the difficult days and losing battles to eventual victory over the British in the Revolutionary War. Perhaps independence would have come at a later date through different circumstances, but the place of Davies in the prelude to the Revolution is but one of the reasons he is worthy of this book.

There are several other reasons Davies is worthy of our attention. First, he was a champion of religious toleration and freedom. He was the first

---

[9] Campbell, *Patrick Henry: Patriot and Statesman*, 17.
[10] Ibid., p. 19.
[11] Lloyd-Jones, *Knowing the Times*, 263.

Presbyterian minister east of the Shenandoah and Appalachian Mountains to be lawfully licensed in Virginia, and he was intimately involved in efforts to secure the freedoms guaranteed by the Act of Toleration in 1689 for other Dissenters. Second, he was active in promoting the flames of revival throughout Virginia for over a decade. Third, he was one of the first American ministers to actively labor among the African slaves, and received many of them into membership in his Hanover congregation. Fourth, he started a mission to the Overhill Cherokees along the western borders of North Carolina and South Carolina. Fifth, his sermons were among the most popular in print for nearly a century after his death. Finally, he was the fourth President of the College of New Jersey (later Princeton College or Princeton University), succeeding the venerable Jonathan Edwards upon his unexpected death. All these reasons commend his life to us as worthy of our interest and study.

Morgan David's Family Flees Religious Persecution

The hand of God can be seen in preparing Samuel Davies to be a champion of liberty and religious toleration through providential events on both sides of his family. Both his paternal and maternal ancestors were subject to religious persecution in Wales. His paternal grandparents, Morgan[12] and Catherine David[13] and their three sons—Shionn, Evan, and David—fled the persecution of Quakers (the Society of Friends) in Wales and emigrated to America in the spring of 1684. Almost all of the Welsh who emigrated to Pennsylvania in the 1680s were Quakers by religious conviction.

The persecution came as a result of the Act of Uniformity of 1662 which denied the rights of religious freedom for all Nonconformists except those who would worship according to the Church of England's *Book of Common Prayer*. Quakers, though, were more persecuted than almost any other religious group. Their very presence could cause Anglicans and Dissenters alike to become distempered. They held several distinctive doctrines which were repugnant to most Protestants: they took the Scriptural and Protestant principle of the priesthood of all believers to an extreme; they

---

[12]Morgan David was born in 1622–23 and was several years older than his wife, Catherine.
[13]The Davies family name, typical of the period, is alternately spelled David, Dafid, Dafis, Dafydd, or Davis.

rejected creeds; they held to the doctrine of the "inner light" that believers could be guided by the Holy Spirit apart from the Word of God which would cause their hearts to tremble or quake (hence their nickname); they also rejected the sacraments, war, and taking oaths in law courts. The Quakers were among the first to flee to America to be a part of William Penn's "Holy Experiment" which was envisioned as a safe haven for all those who were persecuted for their faith. In 1682, twenty-three ships brought two thousand Quakers or Quaker sympathizers to Pennsylvania, with ninety more ships coming over the next three years.

Leaving their Welsh homeland in 1684, Morgan David and his family boarded the *Vine* at Merionethshire and ventured their future on a new start in the colonies. The master of the *Vine* was fifty-four-year-old William Preeson of Liverpool, and virtually all his passengers were Quakers. Such passenger ships as the *Vine* were almost always overcrowded. Food was constantly in short supply which caused some to arrive at their destination malnourished while others died from the ravages of sickness and disease during the voyage. Nearly thirty passengers on the *Welcome*, which carried William Penn and the first wave of Quaker emigrants to America in 1682, died from small pox. Similarly, an account by Edward Foulke of his voyage on the *Robert and Elizabeth* in 1698 records that a fatal illness of dysentery broke out on their ship resulting in forty-five deaths, including three ship's crewmen and numerous children. As Foulke commented:

> The distemper was so mortal that two or three corpses were cast overboard every day while it lasted. But through the *favour and mercy of divine providence* I, with my wife and nine children, escaped that sore mortality, and arrived safe at Philadelphia.[14]

Then, there were dangers from oceanic storms that drenched passengers in sea water, that frequently caused the dreadful ordeal of seasickness, and that terrified the stoutest of hearts. Shipwrecks, though infrequent, were another danger for passenger ships and the Atlantic Ocean has numerous Colonial era vessels buried on her floor.

David Davies was a boy of four at the time of this transatlantic voyage and apparently survived the ordeal without any difficulties. After nearly

---

[14] "A Short Genealogy of Edward Foulke (1651–1741)", *Bulletin of Friends' Historical Society of Philadelphia*, Vol. 6, No. 1 (November 1914), p. 7, Published by: Friends Historical Publishers.

three months at sea, the *Vine* entered the mouth of the Delaware Bay in the middle of July and harbored at Philadelphia on July 17, 1684. Morgan David[15] there received a grant of one hundred acres in Merion Township,[16] a part of William Penn's Welsh Tract,[17] which was northwest of Philadelphia across the Schuylkill River. Merion, Radnor, and Haverford Townships were settled exclusively by Welsh Quakers who envisioned establishing their self-government in that part of the colony. Thomas Glenn describes the land where the Welsh settled as follows:

> These lands, comprising what are now the Townships of Merion, Haverford, and Radnor, possessed, indeed, many natural advantages. There were amongst other desirable features, an abundance of excellent streams, plenty of good timber, and fine building stones, and the fair rolling country, reminding colonists of their native Wales, had much to commend itself to their eyes.[18]

The David family soon began attending the Merion Meeting (Quaker), the oldest Friends' church in Pennsylvania, a simple but elegant structure of stone in the shape of a cross which was erected in 1695. There were several other families with the surname of David or Davies in the Merion Meeting and some of them may have been relatives of Morgan David inasmuch as the Friends were a close-knit religious group that frowned on marriage outside of their fellowship. When Morgan David died in December of 1694, he was buried in the Merion Meeting cemetery.[19] His will was probated by Catherine on July 18, 1695, and it divided his property equally between his two older sons, Shionn and Evan, while leaving legacies to his other children (David, Catherine, and Elizabeth).

Samuel's father most likely never had the opportunity to attend school. An old desk from the school founded at the Merion Meeting has a crudely cut date of 1711, but there are no records of a school before that date. Quaker educational ideas were dynamic at the time of the first Welsh set-

---

[15] Morgan and Catherine David became parents of two daughters in America: Catherine and Elizabeth.
[16] Merion Township was in Philadelphia County, northwest of Philadelphia, Pennsylvania.
[17] The Welsh Tract was a vast acreage on the west side of the Schuylkill River and the city of Philadelphia.
[18] Thomas Allen Glenn, *Merion in the Welsh Tract: With Sketches of the Townships of Haverford and Radnor* (Norristown, Pennsylvania: 1896), 46.
[19] http://www.lowermerionhistory.org/burial/merion/d.html accessed on March 18, 2016.

tlement in Pennsylvania and for several years afterwards. The idea that most prevailed was that education should be practical in the apprenticeship of boys and girls. It is likely that David and his brothers were taught to work a trade, to labor as a carpenter, or to farm, but were not given the rudiments of a classical education or even taught to read.[20]

Almost nothing is known of the daily life of the David family until David Davies' marriage to Sarah Dickinson, of Plymouth Township, Pennsylvania, on March 31, 1716. The wedding was held at the Plymouth Meetinghouse, a native limestone structure built in 1708, with some fifty people in attendance. Their marriage was short-lived, though, due to the untimely death of the bride a few weeks later from complications unknown. In June of 1716, Shionn and David sold their interest in the family farm to their brother, Evan, and moved to a new Welsh Tract[21] in New Castle County, about forty miles south of Philadelphia. Other family members who migrated south to New Castle County with the two brothers included Shionn's wife, Ann Thomas Davies, and their sisters, Catherine and Elizabeth Davies. They settled in that part of the Welsh Tract known as the Pencader Hundred where the two brothers jointly purchased four hundred acres on May 21, 1717 from David Evans and William Davis of Radnor Township. Ann Davies' relatives already lived in this new Welsh Tract and that was probably the impetus for this move.

Persecution of Baptists and Protestants in Wales

Samuel's maternal ancestors fled to America when a new wave of persecution broke out in the late seventeenth century. For over a century, Dissenters in Great Britain had been uneasy concerning their religious freedoms. The brutal killing of as many as 70,000 Huguenots (French Reformed Protestants) in the bloody St. Bartholomew's Day Massacre on August 24, 1572, carried out with the approval of Catherine de Medici and the French court, had made them very apprehensive. In his *History of the Presbyterian Church in Kentucky*, Robert Davidson was certainly correct when he wrote:

> In England, ever since the memorable St. Bartholomew's day, all eyes had

---

[20] Thomas Woody, *Early Quaker Education in Pennsylvania* (New York: Columbia University, 1909), 102.
[21] The Welsh Tract in New Castle County, Pennsylvania—later Delaware—consisted of 30,000 acres of land granted by William Penn.

been anxiously directed to the Transatlantic settlements, notwithstanding they were as yet a wilderness; and while some fled to Holland, a great number, together with many of the ejected ministers, betook themselves to New England, Pennsylvania, and other American plantations.[22]

As a result of the previously mentioned Act of Uniformity under King Charles II, ministers and churches in England were required to conform to the *Book of Common Prayer* by St. Bartholomew's Day, 1662. That day, a Sunday in 1662, became infamously known as "Black Bartholomew's Day" because it resulted in at least 2,000 Nonconformist ministers being immediately ejected from their pulpits. The event came to be known as the Great Ejection. It was not an isolated, temporary event and the main issue was more than just conformity to a form of worship. As Iain Murray wrote in an introductory article to *Sermons of the Great Ejection*, it was a watershed moment when a "wider issue, namely, what is true Christianity"[23] was being decided wrongly. Murray then quotes from an evangelical Anglican author, J. B. Marsden, who assessed the damage done by the Great Ejection as follows:

> If it be presumptuous to fix upon particular occurrences as proofs of God's displeasure, yet none will deny that a long, unbroken course of disasters indicates but too surely, whether to a nation or a church, that His favour is withdrawn. Within five years of the ejection of the two thousand Nonconformists, London was twice laid waste, first by pestilence and then by fire. . . . But other calamities ensued, more lasting and far more terrible. Religion in the Church of England was almost extinguished and in many of her parishes the lamp of God went out.[24]

John Charles Ryle, the nineteenth-century evangelical Anglican, described the Great Ejection as:

> An injury to the cause of true religion in England which will probably never be repaired. . . a more impolitic deed never disfigured the annals of a Protestant church.[25]

Some of the ministers who lost their positions within the Church of

---

[22] Robert Davidson, *A History of the Presbyterian Church in Kentucky* (New York: Robert Carter, 1847), 15.
[23] *Sermons of the Great Ejection* (London: The Banner of Truth Trust, 1962), 8.
[24] Ibid., 8–9.
[25] Ibid., 9.

England included Thomas Watson, Thomas Manton, John Flavel, Richard Baxter, Edmund Calamy, and Thomas Brooks. In 1662, August 24th fell on a Sunday, so the last sermon for these ministers was August 17, a day filled with gloominess and heaviness of heart. Other ministers who were already Nonconformists, such as John Bunyan, were also punished for their refusal to conform. Bunyan spent twelve years in the Bedford jail where he wrote *The Pilgrim's Progress* and other works.

While some ministers eagerly sought religious freedom in the American colonies, others were exiled to the New World only after being marched as criminals through the streets of London in manacles, two-by-two. In 1685, one hundred such "criminals" were banished to America on a ship sailing from Newcastle. Since they could not pay their own passage, their fares were paid by a wealthy gentleman for whom they would be indentured servants until their debt was repaid. Not everyone on this ship made it to the New World. The ravages of the sea took its toll and over sixty of the passengers died before they reached New Jersey, including the man who had paid their fares. In America, they were declared free men by a jury gathered by the Governor, and most of them settled in New England. For those who survived the dangers of the sea, their new life in America was worth the risk. Having been imprisoned for their religious convictions in Great Britain, they were willing to be exiles for the Word of God.

The Founding of the Pencader Meeting (Baptist)

It was during such a time of persecution that a small colony of believers from the Rhydwilyn Baptist Church in Wales determined to flee to America. They were constituted as a church at Milford Haven, Wales, under the spiritual leadership of Rev. Thomas Griffith. Boarding the *James and Mary* in June of 1701, they embarked for the New World where they arrived in Philadelphia on September 8th. Elisha and Mary Thomas, along with their small daughter, Martha, were among the fourteen other members of this new church on board that ship.

On their arrival in the New World, this colony of emigrants first settled in Philadelphia County where they were warmly welcomed by the Pennepack Baptist Church, located northeast of Philadelphia. This new congregation from Wales insisted on the practice of the laying on of hands as confirmation to the newly baptized which led to a sharp disagreement with the Pennepack Baptists who considered the practice a matter of indifference.[26] The Welsh emigrants, though, believed that the laying on of hands was such an essential New Testament ordinance that they soon decided they could no longer fellowship with the Pennepack Church in the Lord's Supper[27] or worship with them. The *History of the Welsh Tract Baptist Church* records their reasons for this separation:

> After landing, we were received in a loving manner (on account of the gospel) by the congregation meeting in Philadelphia and Pennepek who held the same faith with us (excepting the ordinance of Laying-on-of-hands on every particular member) with whom we wished much to hold communion at the Lord's table; but we could not be in fellowship with them in the Lord's supper; because they bore not testimony for God touching the forementioned ordinance. There were some among them who believed in the ordinance: but it was neither preached up, nor practiced in that church: for which cause we kept separate from them for some years. We had several meetings on this account, but could not come to any agreement; yet were in union with them (except only in the Lord's-supper, and some particulars relative to a church).[28]

In *The Doctrine of "Laying on of Hands," Examined and Vindicated*, David Jones (1736-1820), a Baptist minister and son of the Pencader Meeting, wrote the following:

> We believe that the laying on of hands, with prayer, upon baptized believers, as such, is an ordinance of Christ, and ought to be submitted unto by all such persons, that are admitted to partake of the Lord's Supper; and that the end of this ordinance is not for the extraordinary gifts of the Spirit, but for a farther reception of the Holy Spirit of promise; or for the addition of the graces of the Spirit and the influences thereof, to confirm, strengthen, and comfort them in Christ Jesus; it being ratified and established by extraordinary gifts of the Spirit in the primitive times.[29]

---

[26] Horatio Gates Jones, *Historical Sketch of the Lower Dublin (or Pennepek) Baptist Church* (Morrisania, New York, 1869), 11.
[27] Morgan Edwards, "History of the Baptists in Delaware" in *The Pennsylvania Magazine of History and Biography*, Vol. IX (Philadelphia: The Historical Society of Pennsylvania, 1885), 52.
[28] http://www.newrivernotes.com/other_states_delaware_religion_welshtractbaptistchurch.htm, accessed on March 18, 2016.
[29] David Jones, *The Doctrine of the "Laying on of Hands," Examined and Vindicated* (Philadelphia: Francis Bailey, 1786), 2.

In tying the further reception of the Holy Spirit to the actions of men within an alleged scriptural ordinance, this doctrine of the laying on of hands by the Pencader Meeting was entangled in an element of superstition. Though Jones disclaims that the laying on of hands confers the extraordinary gifts, he contends that an additional gift of the Spirit subsequent to the new birth is bestowed through such. Interestingly, his position comes perilously close to teaching that the imposition of hands bestows a second blessing experience.

Having fled the intolerance of their religious freedom in Wales, the Pencader Meeting was now intolerant of a sister church over what is judged by many Christians to be a matter of indifference. This difference no doubt contributed to the decision of this congregation to migrate to New Castle County in 1703. Before doing so, there were twenty-two additions to their membership from Philadelphia and Bucks counties, some of whom had recently emigrated from Wales while others were converts from other denominations. In New Castle County, the church acquired some property on a promontory known as Iron Hill and took the name of the Pencader Meeting (Baptist), later changing that name to the Welsh Tract Baptist Church. In 1710, there was a large influx of members to the church from Pembrokeshire and Caermarthonshire, Wales. Despite this division over a non-essential matter, the Pencader Meeting was the first Baptist congregation south of present-day Pennsylvania and became the mother church of a number of other Baptist congregations as far south as the Pee Dee River in South Carolina.

Marriage of David Davies and Martha Thomas

Martha Thomas was the oldest of the six siblings of Elisha and Mary Thomas. She was born during the last decade of the seventeenth century and would have been a toddler or an adolescent when her parents made their transatlantic voyage to America. Along with her sister, Mary, and two brothers, William and John, she joined the Pencader Meeting in 1712 by believer's baptism. She was probably about fifteen years old at the time. Martha's paternal grandparents, Thomas and Mary Thomas, had emigrated to America in 1695 and settled in Cecil County, Maryland, before joining the Welsh Baptist colony in 1702 by transfer of their membership.

David Davies' first encounter with his new bride was probably on some occasion when Martha's family visited Shionn and Ann Thomas Davies at their home near Merion township. Since David was fifteen to twenty years older than Martha, he would have taken little notice of her at first.

The Son of Prayer

In the intervening years, Martha would have blossomed into a young lady with all the attendant female charms. A whirlwind courtship between them was followed by the exchanging of wedding vows before February 4, 1717, when David and Martha signed the confession of the reorganized Baptist congregation with an "X" as husband and wife.

The following year, Martha Davies gave birth to a daughter[30] who died in infancy. Moved by the loss of her first child, Martha prayed fervently over the next five years for a son whom she could dedicate to the Redeemer's service. Her faith was exercised in "waiting for the divine answer to her petition,"[31] and her patience was rewarded. On November 3, 1723,[32] Martha gave birth to her son, Samuel, at Summit Ridge in New Castle County on Lums Pond,[33] about twelve miles southeast of Newark, Delaware. In later years, Samuel commented on the circumstances of his birth:

> I am a son of prayer, like my name-sake *Samuel* the prophet; and my mother called me *Samuel* because, she said, I have asked him of the Lord. . . This early dedication to God has always been a strong inducement to me to devote myself to Him by my own personal act; and the most important blessings of my life I have looked upon as the immediate answers to the prayers of a pious mother. But, alas! what a degenerate plant am I. How unworthy of such a parent, and such a birth.[34]

David Davies was a modest farmer of average intelligence who never received any formal education. He was evidently industrious and a man of great character whom Foote described as having "a blameless, religious life."[35] He built a substantial two-story brick home with five bays, one room deep, which is still standing.[36] The living area and kitchen were

---

[30] "An Appendix," in Samuel Davies, *Sermons on Important Subjects* (New York: J & J Harper, 1828), I, 27. The author of this appendix is unknown, but it was someone who lived in Princeton, New Jersey during Davies' term as President of the College of New Jersey.
[31] Ibid.
[32] Samuel Davies' tombstone in the Princeton cemetery gives 1724 as the year of his birth. However, an Old Testament in the Virginia Historical Society in Richmond, VA, which once belonged to Davies, states: "Born in New-Castle County, Pennsylvania Nov. 3, 1723."
[33] A state park by this name is across the highway from the house where Davies was born.
[34] Thomas Gibbons, "Divine Conduct Vindicated," in Davies, *Sermons on Important Subjects*, I, 32. Gibbons quotes from a letter from Davies in this sermon on the occasion of his death.
[35] William Henry Foote, *Sketches of Virginia: Historical and Biographical*, First Series (Philadelphia: William S. Martien, 1850), 157.
[36] The home is located on state highway 73 in Delaware, about three miles east of state high-

downstairs with the bedrooms upstairs.[37] Both floors were heated by fireplaces.

While Martha Davies was uneducated in the English language at the time of Samuel's birth, she was probably not illiterate. Welsh was her native tongue and the services at the Pencader Meeting were in that language. She was probably unable to read and write in English, but she possessed numerous talents. She was also a woman of unblemished character and great piety.[38] Samuel once wrote "that he was blessed with a mother whom he might account, without filial vanity or partiality, one of the most eminent saints he ever knew upon the earth."[39] She provided Samuel with his early education, and he inherited most of his extraordinary talents from her.

Pencader Meeting Censures Martha Davies

Few facts about the Davies' family are known until a distasteful and regrettable incident in 1732. Martha Davies adopted some differences with the Baptists, apparently over the doctrine of baptism. Thus, she sought information from the local Presbyterian minister, Thomas Evans, concerning this issue for which she was disciplined for her rebellion and excommunicated from the Pencader Meeting[40] on March 4, 1732. The record of "The Case of Martha David" gives the following details:

> The rebellion of Martha David against the Church appeared.
> (1) In opposing the truth which she once professed to the church according to the commandment of Christ and the practice of the Apostles under the ministry of the New Testament.
> (2) In refusing instruction, and despising advice tho' offered many a time by the brethren in particular, and by the church, in general.
> (3) In breaking covenant with the church by carrying unconnected pieces of what was talked in the church to the Presbyterians to have their opinion upon them, tho' the church charged her beforehand not to do so.
> (4) In being so false and unfaithful in carrying her tales so that she has cur-

---

way 896. A road sign marks it as the birthplace of Samuel Davies. The original structure has been expanded and the present building is very dilapidated.
[37] The inside of the house is off limits to visitors, so my observation was from outside.
[38] Foote, *Sketches of Virginia: Historical and Biographical*, First Series, 157.
[39] Gibbons, "Divine Conduct Vindicated," in Davies, *Sermons on Important Subjects*, I, 32.
[40] This congregation changed its name to the Welsh Tract Baptist Church at a later date.

tailed the truth and increased her falsehoods; and thereby hath wronged the church by her change of opinion, and putting a false gloss on what was said to her—and putting it in the power of the enemies to blaspheme—also to renew the varience between us and the Presbyterians, for which causes she was put out of the church Mar. 4, 1732.[41]

In light of the above censure, the reason for Martha Davies' visits to Thomas Evans, the Presbyterian minister, almost certainly included discussion of the doctrine of baptism since she was accused of "opposing the truth she once professed" and having a "change of opinion." The issue was neither simple gossip nor a fundamental difference with the truth of the gospel. Rather, it was a discussion with the Presbyterian minister about "truth" she had once professed over an issue where the Baptists and Presbyterians differed. Her meeting with Evans probably began innocently enough since she was primarily concerned about her son's education, a precocious child with a great thirst for learning. Martha was also cognizant of the vows she made in praying for a son and earnestly desired to prepare him for the ministry. Yet, she was not literate in English and was incapable of teaching her son without first being educated herself. The only school in the Welsh Tract at this time was the academy under the tutelage of Thomas Evans, pastor of the Welsh Tract Presbyterian Church. Academies were intended for those who had already gained the rudiments of an education from an English grammar school. Martha probably wanted Evans to tutor her so she could instruct her son. The ensuing conversations may have led to discussion of the differences between Presbyterians and Baptists concerning covenant theology and infant baptism. Both congregations held to Calvinistic doctrine at this time and baptism was one of the very few areas where they differed with one another. It is disappointing, but not surprising, that the Pencader Meeting, which had previously denied fellowship to a sister congregation over a non-essential matter of order, should discipline a member with the censure of excommunication for doctrinal discussions with a Presbyterian minister. They should have considered the words of Rupertus Meldenius, the German Lutheran theologian, who wrote dur-

---

[41] "Records of the Welsh Tract Baptist Meeting, Pencader Hundred, New Castle County, Delaware, 1701–1828", *Papers of the Historical Society of Delaware*, V, no. xlii, pt. 1 (Wilmington, Delaware: 1904), 26.

ing the Thirty Years War (1618-1648):

> In essentials, unity; in non-essentials, liberty; in all things, charity.[42]

Those words have been called by the great church historian, Philip Schaff, "the watchword of Christian peacemakers."[43] In the incident of Martha Davies, the Pencader Meeting, then pastored by Enoch Morgan, was guilty of neither permitting liberty in non-essentials nor being charitable in all things. Instead, the congregation imposed the highest censure on Martha Davies despite her numerous relatives in the congregation. Moreover, Martha's father, Elisha Thomas, had served as the second pastor of this congregation from 1725 until his death on November 7, 1730. Fifteen months afterwards, Elisha's oldest daughter was put out of the congregation. On June 9, 1733, another relative, Esther Thomas, who had joined the church in 1702, was also removed from the membership for having her grandchildren baptized at the Presbyterian church. After Martha's ouster, the Davies family soon began attending the Welsh Tract Presbyterian Church in Glasgow.[44] Samuel was only eight at the time of this upheaval in his family. He never mentioned this incident in later life, but it undoubtedly had a great impact on teaching him to be a peacemaker and to have a charitable spirit toward the religious views of others.

Samuel's Childhood

Samuel's childhood, otherwise, was typical of most farm boys on the Welsh Tract. He was a normal child with a docile temperament who enjoyed the games played by other children. The boys in the Welsh Tract would often wrestle, jump, run, or throw the discus. It is easy to imagine Samuel joining in contests of skill along with the other children. He and his father surely took trips to the nearby coast where they would go crabbing or fishing. In the fall and winter, they probably hunted squirrel, rabbit, deer, and other wildlife. On other occasions, they would travel to Wilmington, about seventeen miles away, to buy and sell at the markets

---

[42] Philip Schaff, *The History of the Christian Church*, Volume VII (Grand Rapids, Michigan: Wm. B. Eerdmans Publishing Company, 1980), 650.
[43] Ibid.
[44] Glasgow was about six miles from the Davies' home, situated between the Pencader Meeting and Summit Ridge.

that flourished along that river city. There were numerous chores—planting crops and tending livestock—on the family farm to keep him busy, but Samuel quickly wearied of such tasks. His real love was education and learning.

Young boys reared in farming communities were at a great disadvantage in acquiring an education. The towns and villages of the northern colonies provided greater opportunities for education than the agrarian colonies to the south. In farming areas, the rudiments of an education, particularly reading, were almost always taught by one of the parents. Frequently, the children learned little more than to write their names and spell out the catechism. Some families used a standard text, like Edmund Coote's *The English Schoole-Maister*, while the poorer class simply taught the alphabet and a few syllables that combined a consonant with a vowel.[45] Samuel's mother, who had abundant reasons to consider him as an answer to her prayers and a blessing of God, began to teach him to read herself since there was no English school in the area. He soon made so much progress that it surprised everyone who heard him read.[46]

It was an unwritten rule that each person who learned to read was to teach another one to do the same. Samuel's own adherence to this rule resulted in an interesting anecdote concerning his youth. David Davies used various workers in the farming of his land. One of his helpers was a young man named John Campbell.[47] The elder Davies would send his son and Campbell to the fields to work, but was quickly disappointed in their efforts. On investigation of their progress, he found the boys sitting in the fields, with open books, involved in lessons. Samuel, though ten years younger than his friend, was the teacher! David Davies scolded the boys, returned home and complained to his wife that their son would never make a farmer. Martha replied that if he would not make a farmer perhaps he would make a scholar, and she determined from that day to send him away to a grammar school.[48]

---

[45] Lawrence A. Cremin, *American Education: The Colonial Experience*, 1607–1783 (New York: Harper and Row, 1970), 129.
[46] "An Appendix" in Davies, *Sermons on Important Subjects*, I, 27.
[47] John Campbell (1713–1753) later studied at the Log College and became a Presbyterian minister before dying of palsy at the age of 40.
[48] J. L. Vallandigham, Mrs. J. Wilkins Cooch, W. T. Skinner, and George A. Blake, *History of the Pencader Presbyterian Church* (Glasgow, Delaware: The Woman's Missionary Society, 1899), 42.

Conclusion

There is always the danger that both individual Christians and churches will fail to distinguish between essentials and non-essentials, will refuse to allow Christian liberty to other believers in non-essential matters, or will neglect to practice charity towards others in all things. The Pencader Meeting fled the persecutions of their native Wales, but often treated others in America with the same intolerance with which they had been treated. They separated from the Penepack Baptist Church over a difference concerning the ordinance of the laying on of hands. They excommunicated the daughter of one of their former pastors over a difference concerning baptism. Yet, it must be stated that this problem is not confined to this Welsh Baptist congregation only. Their real issue was deeper than any differences over baptism. The harsh disciplinary procedure of the Pencader Meeting has been exercised by numerous congregations of all denominations both before and after this event.

Christian charity requires us not to make everything we consider to be a scriptural principle as a term of communion among Christians. The body of Christ is wider than our convictions. The reformed faith is a greater bond of unity than the different practices concerning baptism among Presbyterians and Baptists. None of us has yet attained to the mature man and the unity of the faith. We only see through a glass dimly and we only know in part while we dwell in houses of clay. True Christian toleration is not learned by circumstances or trials alone, but by the Holy Spirit.

The Pencader Meeting/Welsh Tract (Baptist) Church in Delaware

-2-

Behold, He Is Praying

"The first twelve years of his life were wasted in the most entire negligence of God and religion, which he often afterwards bitterly lamented, as having 'too long wrought the will of the flesh.' But about that time the God to whom he was dedicated by his word and Spirit awakened him to serious thoughtfulness, and anxious concern about his eternal state. He then saw sufficient reason to dread all the direful effects of divine displeasure against sin. And so deeply imprinted was the rational sense of his danger, as to make him habitually uneasy and restless, until he might obtain satisfying scriptural evidence of his interest in the forgiving love of God."[1]

~Samuel Finley, Fifth President of the College of New Jersey (Princeton)~

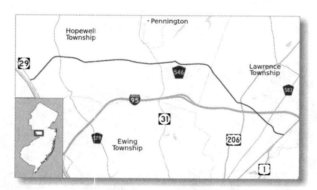

Location of Hopewell and Pennington, New Jersey where William Robinson taught an English school attended by Samuel Davies

---

[1] Samuel Finley, "Sermon, on the Death of Rev. Samuel. Davies", in Samuel Davies, *Sermons on Important Subjects*, Vol. I (New York: J. & J. Harper, 1828), 20.

W illiam Henry Foote, one of Davies' biographers, stated about his early education:

At about ten years of age he had the opportunity of attending an English school, some distance from home.[2]

Colonial education was very different from modern education. Children learned to read and write at home with a few of the best students being sent to English schools from the ages of seven to ten. These schools provided an elementary education that placed a strong emphasis on religion. According to Lawrence A. Cremin, an expert in Colonial education, the Bible was "the single most important cultural influence in the lives of the Anglo-Americans."[3] For instance, the *New England Primer* was based on both the Bible and the *Westminster Confession of Faith*. These schools also provided a rudimentary education in Latin using a standard textbook such as Lily's *Latin Grammar*, which had been a mainstay of grammar school education in Great Britain—and later in the Colonies—for two-hundred years. These schools usually held classes six days a week for nine to ten hours a day with discipline being rigorously maintained by a wooden rod, if necessary. They were generally private, tuition-based schools which placed higher education beyond the reach of most Colonial children. Yet, some English schools, like the one founded by the Anglican Church in Northumberland County, Virginia, were required "to teach free four or five poor children of the parish and to give them their diet, lodging, and washing."[4] The tuition fee was usually paid to the schoolmaster, with lodging and board being additional fees. Parents in farming communities, such as the Welsh Tract, would place their sons under the care of these schoolmasters, who became surrogate parents responsible for the discipline, manners, and religious instruction of their pupils.

Numerous colonial leaders were educated in this manner. Benjamin Franklin was sent to a boarding school at the age of eight in his father's

---

[2] William Henry Foote, *Sketches of Virginia: Biographical and Historical*, First Series (Philadelphia: William S. Martien, 1850), 158. Foote's comment is confirmed also by: "An Appendix," in Samuel Davies, *Sermons on Important Subjects*, Vol. I (New York: J & J Harper, 1828), 27.

[3] Lawrence A. Cremin, *American Education: The Colonial Experience, 1607–1789* (New York, Evanston, and London: Harper and Row, 1970), 40.

[4] Louis B. Wright, *The Cultural Life of the American Colonies* (Mineola, New York: Dover Publications, 2002), 100.

hope that his son would become a minister. John Rodgers (1727-1811), who became a Presbyterian minister and one of Samuel's closest friends, boarded at a school in Neshaminy, Pennsylvania, under the care of Rev. John Roan (1717-1775). Benjamin Rush (1746-1813), one of the Signers of the Declaration of Independence and the first Surgeon General of the United States, was sent at the age of eight to a school fifty miles from his mother's home in Philadelphia. The school where Rush boarded was taught by his uncle, Rev. Samuel Finley (1715-1766), and was justly acclaimed as "the most respectable and flourishing of any in the middle colonies of America."[5] Most of Finley's students were from neighboring communities, but some came from as far away as South Carolina. Rush wrote that Finley "obliged all the boys who lodged in his house to commit the Shorter Catechism of the Church of Scotland to memory, and to repeat it every Sunday evening. Upon each of the answers, he made pertinent and instructing or pious remarks."[6] While it might seem strange for Samuel's parents to send him to a school one hundred miles from the Welsh Tract, it was common in eighteenth-century America for intellectually talented youth to be sent to schools that far from home.

Hopewell Presbyterian Church's English School

John Holt Rice[7] and Archibald Alexander[8] are agreed that Samuel studied under William Robinson in his youth and this period of his childhood is the only time it could have been.[9] According to Samuel Blair[10]

---

[5] George W. Corner, ed., *The Autobiography of Benjamin Rush: His "Travels Through Life" Together with His Commonplace Book for 1789–1813* (Westport, Connecticut: Greenwood Press, 1970), 29.

[6] Ibid., 31.

[7] John Holt Rice (1777–1831) was a Presbyterian minister in Virginia who wrote some brief biographical articles about Davies.

[8] Archibald Alexander, *The Log College* (London: The Banner of Truth Trust, 1968), 194.

[9] Robinson studied at the Log College after his conversion which was probably sometime in 1736. He came under care of New Brunswick Presbytery on April 1, 1740; was licensed to preach May 27, 1741; and, was ordained on August 4, 1741. He spent the next five years in itinerant evangelism from the Carolinas to New York. He did not become a settled pastor at St. George's Presbyterian Church until a few months before his death in 1746. Cf. William Henry Foote, *Sketches of Virginia: Biographical and Historical*, First Series (Philadelphia: William S. Martien, 1850), 125 ff.

[10] Samuel Blair (1712–1751) was a graduate of the famous Log College, prepared Davies for the ministry, and preached Robinson's funeral service on August 3, 1746. It is not likely that Blair

and several others,[11] Robinson conducted this English school at Hopewell (Pennington),[12] New Jersey from 1729 to 1739.[13]

Since there was no such English or grammar school in the vicinity of the Welsh Tract,[14] David and Martha Davies made the difficult decision to board[15] their son at Robinson's school, a hundred miles north of their home, sometime in 1733 or 1734. This decision represented a great sacrifice for the Davies family because their income had always been small and Samuel's labor was essential to help run the family farm.

It is most likely that Thomas Evans, pastor of the Welsh Tract Presbyterian Church, informed the Davies family about the church school in New Jersey. Evans had known the pastor at the Hopewell Presbyterian Church, Rev. Joseph Morgan (1671-1742), for at least twenty years through their denominational connections. On October 20, 1715, they both had been members of the commission of presbytery that ordained

---

could have been mistaken about such an important matter of where Robinson taught this English school with Davies in the audience.

[11] Foote, Richard Webster, and Samuel Miller also affirm that Robinson taught school at Hopewell, New Jersey from 1729–1739. Davies would have either studied under Robinson at the English school in Hopewell, New Jersey in the 1730's or not at all. Archibald Alexander is primarily responsible for the confusion about Davies's studies under Robinson when he conjectured in the *Log College* (p. 194) that Robinson probably taught Davies in the Welsh Tract. Alexander evidently was not familiar with Blair's sermon at Robinson's funeral. Cf. *Log College*, p. 209: "We are also entirely ignorant of the circumstances of his (Robinson's–DR) death." See also the next footnote.

[12] Samuel Blair, *A Sermon Preach'd at George's-Town, in Newcastle County at the Funeral Service of the Reverend Mr. William Robinson, late Minister of the Gospel there, who departed this Life, August 3, 1746* (Philadelphia, Pennsylvania: William Bradford, n.d.), 21. A photocopy of this sermon is in the archives of the Princeton Theological Seminary Library in Princeton, New Jersey. "After he came to this country, he took up his residence about Hopewell, in New Jersey . . ." (p. 21). Cf. William B. Sprague, *Annals of the American Presbyterian Pulpit*, Volume One (Birmingham, Alabama: Solid Ground Christian Books, 2005), 92. Cf. Thomas Murphy, *The Presbytery of the Log College; or, The Cradle of the Presbyterian Church in America* (Philadelphia: Presbyterian Board of Publication, 1889), 102. Cf. Samuel Miller, *Memoir of the Rev. John Rodgers, D. D.* (Philadelphia: Presbyterian Board of Publication, 1813), 36–7. Miller states in a footnote about Robinson: "Soon after his arrival in America he had recourse for teaching a school in New Jersey in the bounds of the Presbytery of New Brunswick."

[13] George H. Ingram, "Biographies of the Alumni of the Log College: William Robinson," *Journal of the Presbyterian Historical Society*, Vol. 13. No. 6 (1929), 255.

[14] Foote, *Sketches of Virginia*, First Series, 158.

[15] Cf. Samuel Miller, *Memoir of the Rev. John Rodgers, D.D.* (Philadelphia: Presbyterian Board of Publication, 1813), 22.

Robert Orr, Morgan's predecessor at the Hopewell Presbyterian Church. It is likely that this connection between Morgan and Evans permitted Samuel to attend Robinson's school at a reduced cost, especially since he was a prospective Presbyterian minister.

William Robinson was reared in a wealthy Quaker family near Carlisle, England where his father's medical practice provided handsomely for the household. He was given a liberal education at his father's expense, including the knowledge of Greek and Latin, as well as other branches of learning. When he attained adulthood, he had a strong desire to launch out on his own. He left Carlisle to visit an aunt in London where he became ensnared in the dissipations of that city and acquired numerous debts through his foolish extravagance. He was unable to repay his debts, his aunt refused to do so, and he knew his father would never stand good for them. "Fearing to return home, and unable to remain longer in London, he determined to quit his native country, and seek his fortune in America."[16] His aunt finally lent him a small sum of money for this purpose. Arriving in America, he put his education to good use by teaching the English school at Hopewell, New Jersey, but he continued in a state of unbelief for several years afterwards[17] while maintaining an outward profession of religion. Foote further elaborates on where and why Robinson began his teaching career:

> Taking his abode in New Jersey, he commenced teaching school as an honourable means of support and regaining his character.[18]

A few sentences later in that book, Foote identifies the place of Robinson's residence as Hopewell, New Jersey, which was within the bounds of New Brunswick Presbytery. Hopewell was a farming community in the western part of the colony, about forty-five miles north of Philadelphia. When Joseph Morgan became pastor of the Hopewell Presbyterian Church in 1729, subscriptions were also collected to purchase one hundred acres for a parsonage or, as they called it, "a plantation to be a

---

[16] Alexander, *Log College*, 193. The other information about Robinson in this paragraph is derived from this source.
[17] William B. Sprague, *Annals of the American Presbyterian Pulpit*, Volume One (Birmingham, Alabama: Solid Ground Christian Books, 2005), 93.
[18] Foote, *Sketches of Virginia*, First Series, 125.

dwelling-place at all times"[19] for their minister. If the subscriptions were sufficient, there was also to be a Latin school erected on that land. Morgan, despite being one of the first six graduates of Yale in 1702, possessed neither the intellectual attainments nor the spiritual industry to undertake the daily instruction of a grammar school as he readily acknowledged to Cotton Mather, the Puritan minister of Boston's North church, in a letter written in September of 1721:

> I spent only three years in the study of languages and the arts, and, for twenty-five years I have labored almost constantly with my hands. A Latin, Greek, or Hebrew book I have sometimes not had in my hands for a whole year. I have scarcely any books: possess no dictionary but an imperfect Rider. I have no commentaries, nor theological systems, nor histories. I have no leisure for reading, nor for writing discourses for the church, and often know not my text before the Sabbath.[20]

Thus, Robinson, an accomplished scholar, soon thereafter became the first teacher of the school founded by the Hopewell Presbyterian Church in rural Pennington. Yet, it says something about the low spiritual condition of Morgan at this period of his life that he would entrust the teaching of this school, founded by his congregation, to a Quaker who was still a stranger to grace for the first several years of his engagement in this work.[21] Robinson continued as the teacher of this school for four years before uniting with the Hopewell Presbyterian Church on August 31, 1733,[22] along with twenty-one other new members. The records of this church indicate that new members were received in groups which would suggest that they were given some sort of formal catechetical training before their reception into church membership.

Estranged from God

Though a child of the covenant and a son of prayer, Samuel "appeared to have no remarkable impressions of a religious kind"[23] when he enrolled

---

[19] John Hall, *History of the Presbyterian Church in Trenton, N. J.: From the First Settlement of the Town* (New York: Anson D. F. Randolph, 1859), 50.
[20] Ibid., 46–47.
[21] Alexander, *Log College*, 193.
[22] Edwin G. York, *The Pennington Area Presbyterians, 1709–1984* (Pennington, New Jersey: Pennington Presbyterian Church, 1985), 22.
[23] "An Appendix," Samuel Davies, *Sermons on Important Subjects* (New York: J. & J. Har-

at Robinson's school. Additionally, a later acquaintance stated that "for want of the pious instruction with which [Samuel] was favored at home, he grew somewhat more careless of the things of religion."[24] Despite his formal membership in the Hopewell Church, it is likely that the veil of unbelief had not yet been removed from Robinson's eyes when Samuel began his studies at there.

Neither was the trifling Joseph Morgan capable of being a true shepherd to Samuel's soul. Philadelphia Presbytery had been cautious in receiving Morgan into membership in 1710 when he transferred from New England and almost immediately investigated a mysterious affair involving him and Rev. Paulus Van Vleck, minister of the Dutch Presbyterian congregation at Neshaminy, Pennsylvania. Within two years, Van Vleck "was found guilty of bigamy and other offenses"[25] for taking a wife in America while still having a wife in Holland. Morgan was also suspected of scandalous conduct, but nothing substantial was brought against him until 1728 when seven charges (including practicing astrology, countenancing promiscuous dancing, and intemperance in drinking)[26] were laid before Philadelphia Presbytery by his congregation at Freehold, New Jersey, and adjudicated by the Synod of Philadelphia. Concerning the charge of intemperance, the Synod determined that it was a "groundless prosecution against one who has ever been esteemed a temperate man."[27] He was then permitted by the Synod to move to the united congregations at Hopewell and Maidenhead. Despite these questions concerning his morality, Morgan had appeared for many years to faithfully adhere to orthodox doctrine and expressed his views in a letter to Cotton Mather in 1722:

> Of all the engines Satan has formed against our salvation, the most effectual is Arminianism; especially so, because, while it owns most of the great articles of faith, it goes less feared and mistrusted, and under the

---

per,1828), I:27.

[24] Ibid. This statement could not have been made about either Abel Morgan in the Welsh Tract or William Robinson after his conversion, but was true of Robinson when he first started teaching school at Hopewell, New Jersey.

[25] Hall, *History of the Presbyterian Church in Trenton*, 47–48.

[26] Richard Webster, *A History of the Presbyterian Church in America: From Its Origin Until the Year 1760* (Philadelphia: Joseph M. Wilson,1857), 338.

[27] Hall, *History of the Presbyterian Church in Trenton*, 48–49.

specious pretext of vindicating God's benevolence and encouraging virtue, and such like, it privately strikes the work of regeneration under the fifth rib, and it is usually followed by Socinianism, and that by Deism.[28]

Yet, not everyone was convinced that Morgan combined true piety with orthodox doctrine. The suspicions of Philadelphia Presbytery and the charges against him by his congregation testify that there was a dark cloud hanging over him. One pastor who knew him well, but not in commendable way, was Theodore Jacobus Frelinghuysen (1691-1747). Frelinghuysen, the Dutch Reformed pastor in the Raritan Valley of New Jersey, considered Morgan to be a formalist in the ministry because he would promiscuously baptize the children of disaffected former members of Frelinghuysen's congregation. Morgan had not always been so careless about spiritual matters. In 1722, he had written a pamphlet emphasizing the "Necessity of the Anointing of the Spirit to guard us from Error" and insisted on "examining candidates for the ministry on their experience of a saving change."[29]

Whether his spiritual declension had its roots in an unhealthy association with ministers like Van Vleck or in the neglect of diligent study, Morgan was obviously a minister in a backslidden state in the 1730s. Four years after moving to Hopewell and Maidenhead, Morgan's wife, Sarah, died in 1733. The loss of his spouse combined with his own spiritual declension probably sunk him into a deep depression wherein he resorted to further intemperance to drown his sorrows. Such a minister was unqualified to be a spiritual mentor to Samuel in the years between 1733 and 1736.

Morgan was a new widower, whereas Robinson was a lifelong bachelor. Morgan was given to excessive alcohol and Robinson was escaping his profligacy in London. Neither could provide the spiritual encouragement that an aspiring young ministerial student needed. Nor could either impart to Samuel the tender spirit of his mother with whom he had been so favored at home. As Rush testified, "The comfort and reputation of a boarding school depends so much on the conduct of the wife of its master."[30] While Rush was accustomed at his uncle's school to

---

[28] Webster, *History of the Presbyterian Church*, 337.
[29] Ibid.
[30] Corner, *Benjamin Rush*, 32.

feasting on "a plentiful table of country food dressed in a pleasant manner,"[31] it is much to be doubted that Samuel found either Robinson's or Morgan's cooking equal to what he had enjoyed at home. For these reasons, we can imagine Samuel being overcome with homesickness and shedding a tear in the evening when he lay down to sleep. Samuel apparently continued in this state of unbelief for most of his time at this English school. Thus, he later acknowledged that "the first twelve years of his life were wasted in the most entire negligence of God and religion, which he often afterwards bitterly lamented, as having 'too long wrought the will of the flesh.'"[32]

The Winds of Heaven in 1736

Providentially, the period when Samuel studied under Robinson was the beginning of the Great Awakening in America. The first decades of the eighteenth century were a period of great religious declension in the colonies which Cotton Mather lamented in his great work, *Magnalia Christi Americana*:

> It is confessed by all who know anything of the matter. . . that there is a general and horrible decay of Christianity, among professors of it. . . The modern Christianity is too generally a spectre, scarce a shadow of the ancient. . . So notorious is this decay of Christianity, that whole books are even now and then written to inquire into it.[33]

Yet, "[t]he winds of heaven had begun to blow upon America"[34] by the fourth decade of the eighteenth century. A revival had broken out in the congregation of Jonathan Edwards at Northampton, Massachusetts, in December of 1734 with five or six people suddenly converted, which led to the awakening of numerous other residents of the town. The reports of this amazing work of the Spirit soon spread to other parts of New England. As Joseph Tracy stated:

---

[31] Ibid.
[32] Samuel Finley, "Sermon on the Death of Rev. Samuel Davies," in Davies, *Sermons on Important Subjects*, I, 20.
[33] Thomas Prince, *The Christian History, Containing Accounts of the Revival and Propagation of Religion in Great-Britain and America, For the year 1743* (Boston: S. Kneeland and T. Green, 1744), 104.
[34] Arnold Dallimore, *George Whitefield: The Life and Times of the Great Evangelist of the Eighteenth Century Revival*, Volume 1 (London: Banner of Truth Trust, 1970), 413.

About the same time there was an awakening in New Jersey, principally in connexion with the labors of William and Gilbert Tennent.[35]

Gilbert Tennent (1703–1762) at this time was pastor at New Brunswick, New Jersey, about twenty-two miles northeast of Hopewell, where he had witnessed an outpouring of God's grace on his congregation in 1729. For the first three years of his ministry, his preaching was barren of conversions. About that time, he underwent an unusual period of sickness. As he crept back from the dead, he sought the Lord with great earnestness to give him seals of his ministry in the conversion of souls. Tennent described his thoughts during this sickness as follows:

> I was then exceedingly grieved that I had done so little for God, and was very desirous to live one half year more, that I might stand upon the stage of the world as it were, and plead more faithfully for His cause, and take more earnest pains for the salvation of souls.[36]

Tennent was also encouraged and stimulated by the example of Frelinghuysen with whom he often held joint services. Frelinghuysen had already experienced an outpouring of the Holy Spirit on the dry bones of his congregation, who were orthodox but cold-hearted. Of all the sons of William Tennent, Sr., Gilbert was the one who was a true Boanerges, a son of thunder. His elder brother, William, Jr., was much more pacific, preferring to weep and pray than to confront. William, Jr. was also pastor of the Freehold congregation where Morgan had previously labored. Thus, both Tennent brothers were aware of the rumors of Morgan's moral failings.

1736 was a year of crisis in many respects for the Hopewell and Maidenhead churches. It was also a time of crisis for Joseph Morgan who had been under suspicion for infidelity to his calling as a minister for a quarter of a century. By November of 1736, those suspicions were confirmed and the too benevolent judgments of him by the Synod of Philadelphia in 1728 and the Presbytery of Philadelphia in 1710 proved to be wrong. The charges against him were proved to the satisfaction of the court and Morgan was suspended from the ministry in 1737.

---

[35] Joseph Tracy, *The Great Awakening: A History of the Revival of Religion in the Time of Edwards and Whitefield* (Edinburgh, Scotland and Carlisle, Pennsylvania: The Banner of Truth Trust, 1976), 13–14.
[36] Dallimore, *George Whitefield*, 416–417.

1736 was a time of crisis for the Presbyterian denomination as well. A cauldron was boiling just below the surface and it would soon erupt into a division that would split the denomination into two separate branches. When the Tennent brothers, Gilbert and William, Jr., learned of the troubles in the Hopewell and Maidenhead churches, they took it upon themselves to engage in itinerant ministry to those churches. Their actions in this case, and probably in other cases as well, resulted in the Synod of Philadelphia adopting the Act of Itineration in 1737 which forbade itinerant ministers from preaching in the parishes of other ministers without their consent. On the surface, the Presbyterian Church seemed to be simply upholding the rights of church courts to govern those under their care. As Charles Hodge wrote:

> This act is not so much an illustration of the power of the synod, as it is a declaration, and enforcing the rights of presbyteries. It is merely provided that no man should preach in any congregation against the will of the presbytery under whose care such congregation was placed. This is a principle fully recognised in our present constitution.[37]

Yet, there were more important issues at stake. Gilbert Tennent was the principal figure to lead the opposition to this Synodical Act. He would have certainly agreed that anyone who preached in the parish of a converted minister or created a division within the bounds of such was guilty of a schismatic offense. Tennent did not view the situation at Hopewell and Maidenhead in that light. Morgan was a trifling, injudicious, and intemperate minister who gave little evidence of a gracious spirit or a true call to his office at this time in his life. In such a situation, Tennent felt an obligation to preach to those who were suffering under such a barren ministry. No court on earth could have persuaded him to act otherwise. Thus, Hodge agreed that Tennent's principle was correct:

> In this he was clearly right, as far as the principle is concerned. There are obligations superior to those of mere ecclesiastical order; and there are times when it is a duty to disregard rules, which we admit to be legitimate both in their own nature, and in respect to the authority whence they proceed. It was on this principle that the apostles and the reformers acted. It is analogous to the right of revolution in civil communities; and

---

[37] Charles Hodge, *The Constitutional History of the Presbyterian Church in the United States of America*, Part I, 1705–1741 (Philadelphia: William S. Martien, 1839), 248.

consequently the cases are very rare in which it can be resorted to, with a good conscience.[38]

The primary case which justifies the actions of Tennent is the very situation he envisioned to exist in Morgan's case. Tennent would certainly have agreed with John Owen's definition of schism:

> The schism, then, here described by the apostle, and blamed by him, consists in causeless differences and contentions amongst the members of a particular church, contrary to that [exercise] of love, prudence, and forbearance, which are required of them to be exercised amongst themselves, and towards one another. . . And he is a schismatic that is guilty of this sin of schism.[39]

The differences that Tennent had with Morgan and other such ministers were not causeless, but concerned the essentials of the gospel. He was not guilty of schism, therefore. He was simply spreading the flame of the gospel while the winds of heaven were blowing. Moreover, the Synod of Philadelphia had recently established the Presbytery of New Brunswick with the Hopewell and Maidenhead churches falling within the boundaries of that ecclesiastical body. It could rightly be argued that the Tennents had acted correctly in rescuing congregations within the bounds of their presbytery.

Samuel's Conversion

1736 was a year of spiritual crisis for Samuel Davies also. His night of darkness was almost over and his day of grace was nigh. Even before Gilbert Tennent's itinerant preaching at Hopewell and Maidenhead, God was preparing Samuel for the reception of the Gospel. He was a son of prayer and his mother's prayers were not in vain. The first work that God initiated in Samuel's heart was to cast him on his knees. Separated from family and fearful for his salvation, Samuel then took up the long-neglected "practice of secret prayer, especially in the evening. The reason . . . why he was so punctual in the evening was, that 'he feared lest he should die before morning.'"[40] Samuel Finley gives us further

---

[38] Ibid., 248–249.
[39] William H. Goold, ed., *The Works of John Owen*, Volume XIII (London: The Banner of Truth Trust, 1967), 108.
[40] "An Appendix," in Davies, *Sermons*, I, 28

insight into Samuel's spiritual experiences during this period:

> But about this time the God to whom he was dedicated by his word and spirit awakened him to solemn thoughtfulness and anxious concern about his eternal state. He then saw sufficient reason to dread all the direful effects of divine displeasure against sin. And so deeply imprinted was the rational sense of danger, as to make him habitually uneasy and restless, until he might obtain satisfying scriptural evidence of his interest in the forgiving love of God.[41]

There was a nighttime prayer taught in the *New England Primer* that has survived in several slightly different forms: "Now I lay me down to sleep, I pray the Lord my soul to keep. If I should die before I wake, I pray the Lord my soul to take. Amen." The earliest version of this prayer was probably written by Joseph Addison who, along with his friend Richard Steele, founded *The Spectator* magazine in London which enjoyed a very brief publication life. On March 8, 1711, the following prayer appeared in that magazine: "When I lay me down to sleep, I recommend myself to his care, when I awake, I give myself up to his Direction."[42] It is almost certain that young Samuel learned such a prayer at some point in his youth or at Robinson's school.

While that child's prayer may have contributed to Samuel's fear of dying in an uncertain spiritual state, there were other factors that also impressed that thought on the minds of colonial youth. In Colonial America, almost one out of every three children died before the age of ten—the age at which Samuel began his studies under Robinson. Cotton Mather lost thirteen of his fifteen children to various sicknesses. It was common, therefore, for godly parents to teach their children that sleep was somewhat like death and they should pray for God's protection throughout the night. Life was precarious in colonial America with dangers from sickness and barbarism. Thus, a fear of the torments of eternal separation from God was often impressed on young children by their parents and pastors. Jonathan Edwards' father, Timothy Edwards (1669-1758), would query his congregants in his sermons, thusly: "Can you bear to live half an hour in a fire, and if not how can you bear to live in hell to all eternity?"[43] That question

---

[41] Finley, "Sermon on the Death of the Rev. Samuel Davies," in Davies, *Sermons*, I, 20.
[42] http://en.wikipedia.org/wiki/Now_I_Lay_Me_Down_to_Sleep, accessed on January 29, 2016.
[43] George M. Marsden, *Jonathan Edwards: A Life* (New Haven, Connecticut and London, Eng-

is reminiscent of the famous sermon of his son, "Sinners in the Hands of an Angry God." It was in such a world that Samuel Davies lived where the awful separation of God for all eternity was deeply and daily impressed on young children. Thus, at some point during his study under Robinson, Samuel came under a conviction of his sinful condition through the work of the Holy Spirit and began to implore the God of heaven for mercy. With this awakening of his conscience, Samuel "very sincerely inquired for the way of salvation."[44]

We do not know how long he had to wait for the sun of righteousness to rise with healing in its wings (Malachi 4:2), but we do know the year of his conversion. Richard Webster, who wrote a history of the Presbyterian Church in America, tells us when and, most probably, by whom Samuel was converted:

> The great event took place in 1736, probably under the preaching of Gilbert Tennent, whom he called his spiritual father.[45]

Years later, Samuel referred to Gilbert Tennent as "my spiritual Father"[46] in his travel diary for his trip to Great Britain. While the circumstances of Samuel's conversion are shrouded in mystery, that notation in his travel diary was more than likely an indication of the source of his conversion rather than merely a term of endearment. The great change for Samuel, therefore, happened when he was twelve. In adulthood, he referred to his conversion in a letter to Thomas Gibbons:

> When I consider that I set out about twelve years old, and what sanguine hopes I then had of my future success, and yet that I have been almost at a stand ever since, I am quite discouraged.[47]

Once converted, Samuel was also mindful of his mother's dedication of him to the gospel ministry. Thus, "he was more ardent in his supplica-

---

land; Yale University Press, 2003), 27.
[44] Enoch Pond, *Memoir of the Rev. Samuel Davies* (Boston: Massachusetts Sabbath School Society, 1832), 7.
[45] Richard Webster, *A History of the Presbyterian Church in America: From Its Origin Until the Year 1760* (Philadelphia: Joseph M. Wilson, 1857), 549.
[46] George Pilcher, *The Reverend Samuel Davies Abroad: The Diary of a Journey to England and Scotland, 1753–55* (Urbana, Chicago, London: University of Illinois Press, 1967), 13, 28.
[47] Thomas Gibbons, "Divine Conduct Vindicated," in Davies, *Sermons on Important Subjects*, I, 37.

tions for being introduced into the gospel-ministry, than for any other thing."[48]

From the time of his spiritual awakening, Samuel began keeping a diary[49] of his spiritual experiences. Richard Webster was conversant with this diary, and said it was "a record of great distress relieved by large measures of heavenly comfort."[50] Samuel earnestly sought relief from his sins, according to Finley:

> While thus evidenced he clearly saw the absolute necessity, and certain reality of the gospel-plan of salvation, and what abundant and suitable provisions it makes for all the wants of a sinner. No other solid ground of hope, or unfailing source of comfort could he find, besides the merits and righteousness of him, "whom God set forth to be a propitiation for sin, through faith in his blood." On this righteousness he was enabled confidently to depend; by this blood his conscience was purged from guilt; and "believing he rejoiced with joy unspeakable, and full of glory."[51]

One of the chief characteristics of Samuel's conversion was his deep, abiding sense of sin. He saw both the magnitude of his sin and the gospel remedy for his depravity in the blood of Christ. In future years, he would call sinners to cease trusting in their false hopes inasmuch as he had learned to put no trust in the arm of flesh. What Robert Murray McCheyne wrote about the conversion of children a century later was certainly true of him:

> The greatest want in the religion of children is generally *sense of sin*. Artless simplicity and confidence in what is told are in some respects natural to children; and this is the reason why we are so often deceived by promising appearances in childhood. The reality of grace in a child is best known by his sense of sin.[52]

---

[48] "An Appendix," in Davies, *Sermons on Important Subjects*, I, 28
[49] This diary, not to be confused with his travel diary to Great Britain in 1753–55, passed into the hands of Samuel Finley at Davies' death and was last known to be seen by Ashbel Green. To our knowledge, all that remains of this diary are the few brief quotes from his intimate friends.
[50] Webster, *History of the Presbyterian Church in America*, 549.
[51] Finley, "Sermon on the Death of the Rev. Samuel Davies," in Davies, *Sermons on Important Subjects*, I, 21.
[52] Andrew A. Bonar, *Memoir and Remains of Robert Murray McCheyne* (London: The Banner of Truth Trust, 1968), 560.

When gospel light flooded his soul, Samuel quickly set his mind on heavenly things and was "watchful over all his thoughts, words, and actions."[53] He was not free from youthful sins, but he did resist them mightily. Finley further elaborates:

> Did any censure his foibles, or juvenile indiscretions? They would have done it compassionately, had they known how severely he censured them himself. The tribunal daily erected in his bosom was critical in scrutinizing, and more impartial and severe in passing sentence, than either his friends or enemies could be.[54]

William Robinson's Conversion

Robinson himself became a subject of grace at some point during the 1730s. Samuel Miller relates the experience that opened Robinson's heart to the gospel:

> He was riding at a late hour one evening, when the moon and stars shone with unusual brightness, and when everything around him was calculated to excite reflection. While he was meditating on the beauty and grandeur of the scene which the firmament presented, and was saying to himself, "How transcendently glorious must be the Author of this beauty and grandeur!" the thought struck him with the suddenness and force of lightning, "But what do I know of this God? Have I ever sought his favour, or made him my Friend?" This happy impression, which proved by its permanency and its effects, to have come from the best of all sources, never left him until he took refuge in Christ as the hope and life of his soul.[55]

Samuel Blair[56] informs us that Robinson's "earnest solicitude about the case of his soul, put him upon the reading of Mr. Allein's *Alarm to the Unconverted*, and other good books of that nature."[57] As Robinson read,

---

[53] Finley, "Sermon on the Death of the Rev. Samuel Davies," in Davies, *Sermons on Important Subjects*, I, 21.
[54] Ibid.
[55] Samuel Miller, *Memoir of the Rev. John Rodgers, D. D.* (Philadelphia: Presbyterian Board of Publication, 1813), 37.
[56] Samuel Blair (1712–1751) was pastor of the Presbyterian congregation at Fagg's Manor, Pennsylvania. He opened a school for training ministers and Samuel Davies studied under him. There was a remarkable revival in his congregation in 1740–1.
[57] Blair, *A Sermon Preach'd at George's-Town at the Funeral of the Rev. Mr. William Robinson*, 21.

his convictions deepened until the happy moment when God was pleased to reveal His Son in him. "And so he came to have *Joy and Peace in believing*."[58] His conversion proved to be genuine, and he manifested all the marks of a sincere Christian.

Robinson came into contact with some Presbyterian ministers about this time—undoubtedly Gilbert Tennent and William Tennent Jr[59]—who encouraged him to continue his education with a design for the ministry. He began his studies at the Log College[60] taught by William Tennent, Sr. at Neshaminy, Pennsylvania sometime in the latter part of the 1730's.[61]

The Log College at Neshaminy, Pennsylvania

The Log College was a school begun by Rev. William Tennent, a native of Ireland, who had come to America in 1716. Tennent was educated at Trinity College in Dublin, Ireland, and ordained in the Protestant Episcopal Church of Ireland. After his arrival in America, he applied to the Synod of Philadelphia to become a Presbyterian minister due to his rejection of the Arminian doctrines of the Irish Church. The Synod deliberated over his case and asked him to put in writing his reasons for leaving the Episcopal Church. Being satisfied with his answers, Synod voted affirmatively to admit him as a member on September 17, 1718. In 1721, Tennent received a call to a small Presbyterian congregation in Bensalem, Pennsylvania, where he remained until he received a call in 1726 to the Presbyterian Church at Neshaminy in Bucks County, some twenty miles north of Philadelphia. At Neshaminy, he erected a small log building next to his house for the education of three of his sons—John, William, Jr., and Charles—as gospel ministers. While Tennent's eldest son, Gilbert, was educated by him before the erection of the Log College, he

---

[58] Ibid., 22.
[59] Both Tennents pastored churches in New Jersey not far from Hopewell and Pennington during the 1730s and were very active in promoting revival throughout that colony.
[60] The Log College was started by William Tennent Sr. for the education of his own sons as ministers. Tennent could not afford to send his sons to Harvard, Yale, or one of the universities in Great Britain. There is more about this college in a later chapter.
[61] Robinson was received under care of New Brunswick Presbytery on April 1, 1740; was licensed on May 27, 1740; and was ordained as a minister on August 4,1741. Students at the Log College often spent five years in preparation for the ministry. Robinson was already classically educated and may have been able to finish sooner than others, but he probably began his theological studies sometime between 1737–1739.

can "without impropriety be classed among the pupils of the institution."[62] The Log College was located on the main highway between Philadelphia and New York and was observed by numerous travelers between those cities, including such colonial leaders as Benjamin Franklin. One of the best descriptions of it is given by that flaming evangelist George Whitefield:

> It happens very providentially that Mr. Tennent and his Brethren are appointed to be a Presbytery by the Synod, so that they intend breeding up gracious youths, and sending them out from Time to Time into our Lord's Vineyard. The place wherein the young Men study now is in contempt call'd the *College*. It is a Log-House, about Twenty Feet long, and near as many broad; and to me it seemed to resemble the Schools of the old Prophets. . . . From this despised Place Seven or Eight worthy Ministers of Jesus have lately been sent forth; more are almost ready to be sent, and a Foundation is now laying for the Instruction of many others. The Devil will certainly rage against them, but the Work, I am persuaded, is of God, and therefore will not come to naught. Carnal ministers oppose them strongly; and because People, when awaken'd by Mr. Tennent, or his Brethren, see through, and leave their Ministry, the poor Gentlemen are loaded with Contempt, and look'd upon (as all faithful Preachers will be) as Persons that turn the World upside down.[63]

Other students who attended the Log College included Samuel Blair[64], John Blair[65], Samuel Finley[66], John Rowland[67], and Charles Beatty[68], all of whom became useful and mighty servants of the Lord.

---

[62] Archibald Alexander, *The Log College* (London: The Banner of Truth Trust, 1968), 23.
[63] *George Whitefield's Journals* (London: The Banner of Truth Trust, 1973), 44–45.
[64] Samuel Blair (1712–1751) was pastor of the Presbyterian congregation at Fagg's Manor, Pennsylvania. He opened a school for training ministers and Samuel Davies studied under him. There was a remarkable revival in his congregation in 1740–1.
[65] John Blair (1719–1771) pastored several churches, including Fagg's Manor, after his brother's death. Upon the death of Samuel Finley, he became professor of divinity and acting President of the College of New Jersey before the arrival Dr. John Witherspoon.
[66] Samuel Finley (1715–1766) was pastor at Nottingham, Maryland where he taught a classical school. He became the fifth president of the College of New Jersey after Davies died in 1761.
[67] John Rowland was pastor of the Hopewell and Maidenhead congregations in New Jersey (1738–1741). He later removed to a church near Norristown, Pennsylvania. He witnessed revivals in both churches. He died early, but his age at death is unknown.
[68] Charles Beatty died on August 13, 1771, but little is known about his life. He labored for awhile among the Indians as a missionary.

Samuel Returns to the Welsh Tract

After two years under Robinson's tutelage, therefore, Samuel returned to his home in the Welsh Tract of Delaware. In spiritual matters, he continued to struggle with doubts about his salvation for several years after his conversion before he attained full assurance. Concerning his struggles in attaining assurance, Finley stated:

> Yet he was afterwards exercised with many perplexing doubts for a long season, but at length, after years of repeated self-examination, he attained to a settled confidence of his interest in redeeming grace, which he retained to the end.[69]

The Westminster Confession of Faith 18.3 surely had such people as Samuel in mind when it stated:

> This infallible assurance doth not so belong to the essence of faith, but a true believer may wait long, and conflict with many difficulties, before he be partaker of it: yet, being enabled by the Spirit to know the things which are freely given him of God, he may without extraordinary revelation, in the right use of ordinary means, attain thereunto.

Due to this lack of assurance about his salvation, Samuel did not immediately unite with any congregation, but slowly things changed for him. After waiting long and conflicting with many doubts, he was then able to profess his faith at about the age of fifteen[70] and joined the Welsh Tract Presbyterian Church. Thus, this "son of prayer" had become one about whom it could be said, "he is praying" (Acts 9:11).

Conclusion

First, the situation of Joseph Morgan is a lighthouse to other ministers, lest they abandon their posts and make shipwreck of their faith. The Christian faith must be cultivated in a warm, lively heart which issues forth in evangelistic fervor for the lost. Bad companions corrupt good morals, as the apostle Paul taught. Close friendships with those who are in a state of spiritual declension generally has a deadening effect on one's soul. Neglect of diligent study will make us worse at the end of our

---

[69] Finley, "Sermon on the Death of the Rev. Samuel Davies," in Davies, *Sermons on Important Subjects*, I:21.
[70] Foote, *Sketches of Virginia*, First Series, 158.

days than we were in the beginning. The scriptural standard is to press on to know the Lord and to study to show ourselves approved to God.

Second, there are things that are more important than adherence to manmade rules of church order. There are times when those rules must give way so that we can be obedient to Christ. The Tennents were right in spreading the flames of the Great Awakening in the parishes of slumbering ministers in order to rescue the perishing. Our eternal obligation is to preach the gospel in season and out of season. No judicatory on earth, whether the Sanhedrin or a church court or a civil government, has the authority to compel our disobedience to the Great Commission. As Peter and the apostles told the Sanhedrin, so must we say, "We must obey God rather than men" (Acts 5:29). Any judicatory that tries to silence the faithful preaching of the gospel is usurping authority that belongs only to God. Any judicatory that sanctions or permits false doctrine by rules of church government is acting contrary to the faith.

-3-

Blair's Academy at Fagg's Manor

"Some men accomplish more by those whom they educate than by their personal labors... If they are so favored as to be the means of bringing forward a few pious youth, and preparing them for the ministry, they may do more good than if their whole lives had been spent in doing nothing else than preaching the Gospel."[1]
~*Archibald Alexander in* **The Log College**~

Samuel Blair (1712-1751), Samuel's teacher at Fagg's Manor Academy

---

[1] Archibald Alexander, *The Log College* (London: The Banner of Truth Trust, 1968), 22.

After his return to the Welsh Tract in 1736, Samuel enrolled in the Pencader Academy which had been founded by Thomas Evans of the Welsh Tract Presbyterian Church. That academy was now under the tutelage of Abel Morgan, the son of Enoch Morgan, pastor at the Pencader Meeting. Samuel's biographer, William Foote, unequivocally states that he studied "under the tuition of an estimable and learned Welsh minister, a Mr. Morgan, a pupil of the Rev. Thomas Evans of the same nation,"[2] "The incomparable Morgan,"[3] as some called him, combined "unusual literary attainments" with a "sound judgment"[4] which preeminently qualified him as a tutor to young scholars. This arrangement was to be short-lived, though.

In the latter part of 1738, Morgan accepted a call to the Middletown Baptist Church[5] near Shrewsbury along the coastal plain of the New Jersey shore, 125 miles north of the Welsh Tract. Morgan's move left a serious void in Samuel's education. At this juncture of his life, Samuel had completed only four or five years of formal education and was suddenly forced to find another tutor or school where he could continue his preparation for the gospel ministry. His options were few, but God's providence would make clear his path of duty.

There were several factors working together to point Samuel in the direction of God's will for his education. First, there was an act passed by the Synod of Philadelphia in 1738 that all ministerial candidates must produce a diploma from Harvard, Yale, or one of the British institutions before being ordained. That option was not financially feasible for the Davies family. Second, the spiritual deadness that had spread across the colonies would soon be transformed by the revival known as the Great Awakening. Samuel was a son of the Great Awakening and that revival had the greatest influence on his ministry. Third, the Great Awakening caused a rift in the Presbyterian Church between those who were friends or foes of the revival. The former were called Old Lights and the latter were called New Lights.

---

[2] William Henry Foote, *Sketches of Virginia: Historical and Biographical*, First Series (Philadelphia: William S. Martien, 1850), 158.
[3] http://baptisthistoryhomepage.com/morgan.abel.tbe.bio.html, accessed on January 30, 2015.
[4] Ibid.
[5] This congregation had been formed in 1688 and held to a version of the *London Confession of Faith* of 1688.

The Synodical Act on Ministerial Education

This act by the Synod of Philadelphia in 1738 decreed that any ministerial candidate who was devoid of a diploma from Harvard, Yale, or one of the British schools would have to be examined by a committee of the Synod, rather than presbytery, before his ordination examination was approved. It was vigorously opposed by those ministers who supported the Great Awakening, particularly the members of New Brunswick Presbytery, as an intrusion on the rights of presbytery. One of the effects of this act was to move the Presbyterian Church closer to a hierarchical form of government. As Joseph Tracy said about this particular act:

> This act was also opposed as an infringement on the rights of presbyteries, to whom, it was contended, the great Head of the church has committed the entire power of licensing and ordination. And this brought up another controversy, which related to the legislative power of church courts. The "Old Side" claimed the right to enact rules, not contrary to the laws of Christ, which would be binding on the conscience, and must be obeyed on pain of ecclesiastical censure. The "New Side" contended that church courts have no legislative power whatever; that they are authorized only to administer the laws that Christ has made; and that any additional rules that they may enact, are mere recommendations, which every one is bound to observe so far as he can with a clear conscience, and not further.[6]

This act was obviously an attempt to undermine William Tennent's Log College where many of the supporters of the revival had been trained. Yet, another such institution was soon to be formed by one of the graduates of the Log College, Samuel Blair, for the purpose of training students for the gospel ministry. Samuel would not have been encouraged to attend either the Log College or any New Light institution by Thomas Evans, pastor at the Welsh Tract Presbyterian Church. Evans had several gifts and was widely read, but he was not among the friends of the revival that was spreading through New England and the Middle Colonies, especially among the Presbyterians. Therefore, it was through different people and circumstances that Samuel Blair and Samuel Davies came to know each other.

---

[6] Joseph Tracy, *The Great Awakening; A History of the Revival of Religion in the time of Edwards and Whitefield* (Edinburgh, Scotland and Carlisle, Pennsylvania: The Banner of Truth Trust, 1976), 62–3.

Fagg's Manor Presbyterian Church

The special providence that led Abel Morgan to leave the Welsh Tract in 1738 was working mysteriously in favor of Samuel Davies, though it was not immediately apparent. Events were to prove what the Puritan author, John Flavel, set forth as his first proposition concerning God's conduct towards His people:

> That the affairs of the saints in this world are certainly conducted by the wisdom and care of special providence.[7]

Samuel Blair (1712-1751) was laboring at Middletown and Shrewsbury, New Jersey, under difficult circumstances in 1738, but things were soon to change. A native of Ireland, Blair became a student at William Tennent, Sr.'s Log College at the age of fifteen. He completed his course in five years and was licensed by the Presbytery of New Castle in 1733. In May of 1734, he accepted a call to Middletown and Shrewsbury[8] where he labored for five years with little success. Richard Webster describes the members of both congregations as "being very irreligious."[9] In 1739, Blair petitioned the Presbytery of New Brunswick to release him of this charge due to the discouragements of the work and the feebleness of his health. Blair soon thereafter received a call to the Fagg's Manor Presbyterian Church which he submitted to Presbytery for their counsel:

> After mature deliberation, they advised him to accept the call, as they were of the opinion it would introduce him into a wider field of usefulness.[10]

Thus, presbytery released Blair from his pastorate at Middletown and Shrewsbury on September 6, 1739; he moved to Fagg's Manor, Pennsylvania, in November; and he was formally installed as pastor in April of 1740. Blair's new congregation would soon experience times of refreshing from the Lord and that season of grace would leave an indelible impression on Davies for the rest of his life. Under Blair's powerful minis-

---

[7] *The Works of John Flavel*, Volume IV (London: The Banner of Truth Trust, 1968), 350.
[8] These communities are situated along the coast of New Jersey about 40 miles south of New York City.
[9] Richard Webster, *A History of the Presbyterian Church in America: From Its Origin Until the Year 1760* (Philadelphia: Joseph M. Wilson,1857), 426.
[10] Alexander, *Log College*, 154.

try, the Fagg's Manor congregation would be a stark contrast to the Welsh Tract Presbyterian Church where Thomas Evans labored in opposition to the revival.

Declension of Christianity in the Colonies

When Blair began his ministry at Fagg's Manor, the congregation was in the throes of a spiritual slumber. There had been a horrible declension of Christianity throughout America in the first four decades of the eighteenth century. Religious formalism dominated almost every denomination, even those that held to a Calvinistic creed or confession. The Presbyterian Church was guilty of this formalism just as much as less evangelical denominations were. Lawrence E. Brynestad describes why this was so:

> Natural religion was prevalent. The rule of life was that of conventional morality, rather than Christianity...
> Theologically, Christianity had degenerated from an inner experience of the grace of God to a mere external observance of the sacraments, and a superficial morality. This was clearly evident in the theological controversies of the day. Originally, the New England Puritans placed great stress upon being "born again."[11]

At the same time, there were civil ordinances in many communities and Colonies that granted civil rights only to church members and required all citizens to financially support the established churches through taxation. The effect of these civil ordinances was to undermine true Christianity. Solomon Stoddard, the grandfather of Jonathan Edwards, devised the 'half-way covenant' which lowered the standards to permit children whose parents were not church members to be baptized if one or more grandparents were members. In 1702, the Synod of Boston modified this covenant even more, so that:

> "Persons baptized in infancy, understanding the doctrines of faith, and publicly professing their assent thereto, not scandalous in life, and solemnly owning the covenant before the Church wherein they give themselves and their children up before the Lord, and subject themselves to the government of Christ in the Church" might have their children bap-

---

[11] Lawrence E. Brynestad, "The Great Awakening in the New England and Middle Colonies," *Journal of the Presbyterian Historical Society*, Vol. XIV (1930–1), 84.

tized. Such baptism could take place even though the parents were unregenerated and excluded from the Lord's Supper. This removed the requisite of a definite spiritual experience to enjoy the privileges of the Church.[12]

Experimental religion was further damaged by Stoddard's position that "sanctification is not a necessary qualification to the partaking of the Lord's Supper, for the Lord's Supper is a converting ordinance."[13] It is difficult, if not impossible, to retain the truth of the gospel where the love of the truth is not in the hearts of the members of the church. And thus, that proved to be the case in New England and the Middle Colonies. Religious formalism was promoted by these actions, however well-intentioned they were to relieve the oppressions of civil ordinances.

An Awakening in the Fagg's Manor Congregation

Blair was the first regularly installed pastor of this congregation which was formed in 1730 from mostly Irish immigrants. The congregation derived its name from the plot of land known as Sir John Fagg's manor, near the township of New Londonderry. Their first building was a simple log structure, completely unadorned inside or out, but its glory would soon be the presence of Christ within. Some of the members were hopefully pious when Blair assumed their pastoral oversight, but formality had replaced spirituality in most hearts. In Blair's words, "The mass of the people were satisfied with the rind without ever tasting the rich meat of the gospel ordinances."[14] Sinners under concern for their souls were thought to be suffering from "melancholy, trouble of mind, or despair" which were considered evils to be avoided.

Many of those at Fagg's Manor who professed faith in Christ were indifferent to heart religion, were careless about public ordinances, and profaned the Lord's Day with "unsuitable, worldly discourse." Blair lamented that public occasions, such as weddings, resulted in a 'vain and frothy lightness. . . in the deportment of many professors." "In some places very extravagant follies, as horse running, fiddling and dancing,

---

[12] Ibid, 85.
[13] Ibid.
[14] Foote, *Sketches of Virginia*, First Series, 109.

pretty much obtained."[15] The result was, in Blair's opinion, that "religion lay dying, and ready to expire its last breath of life in this part of the visible church."[16]

Blair's preaching over the winter of 1739-40 was calculated to convince unregenerate sinners of their dangerous state outside of Christ. His labors resulted in four or five people being "brought under deep convictions," but most church members remained unmoved by the truth. In March of 1740, Blair made a journey to East Jersey, probably to gather the rest of his belongings at his former residence. In his absence from Fagg's Manor, he asked a neighboring minister[17], who was a warm advocate of revivals, to preach for him the next Sabbath. This visiting pastor's sermon from Luke 13:7 produced such a torrent of emotions in many hearts that "some burst out with an audible noise into bitter crying; a thing not known in these parts."[18] The news of this strange happening reached Blair a hundred miles away, causing him to rejoice and to hasten his return home.

Blair preached the next Lord's Day from Matthew 6:33, "Seek ye first the kingdom of God and his righteousness."

While he was pressing the unconverted with reasons why they should seek the kingdom and righteousness of God, he offered as one reason "that they had neglected too—too long—to do so already"—many could not contain themselves but burst out into the most bitter mourning. Checking this outburst of feeling he finished his discourse.[19]

One of the first converts of this spiritual awakening was a young man, a "light merry youth", who had listened to the message from Luke 13:7 with great unconcern. He described to Blair what happened to him the following day at work:

> He went to his labor which was grubbing, in order to clear some new ground; the first grub he set about was a pretty large one, with a high top, and when he had cut the roots, as it fell down, these words came instantly to his remembrance, and as a spear in his heart,—Cut it down, why cumbereth it the ground—so thought he must I be cut down by the justice

---

[15] Ibid., 110.
[16] Ibid.
[17] Possibly the neighboring minister was Alexander Craighead.
[18] Foote, *Sketches of Virginia*, First Series, 110.
[19] Ibid.

of God, for the burning of hell, unless I get into another state than I am in now.[20]

After suffering such great distress of soul, this young man came to a saving acquaintance of Christ which was apparent to all who knew him. He was the first among many others in Blair's congregation who were transferred from the kingdom of darkness into the realm of gospel light. Many were moved by Blair's preaching over the course of the next several months and a large number of them came to him for spiritual counsel. Soon thereafter, Blair started a Friday evening meeting throughout the spring and summer of 1740 where he took pains to explain saving faith and the new birth. A summary of the type of sermons Blair preached during this period are given in his own words:

> I treated much on the way of sinners closing with Christ by faith and obtaining a right peace to an awakened conscience; showing that persons were not to take peace to themselves on account of their repentings, sorrows, prayers, and reformations; nor to make these things the grounds of their adventuring themselves upon Christ and his righteousness, and of their expectations of life by him; and that neither were they to obtain or seek peace in extraordinary ways, by visions, dreams, or immediate inspirations, but by an understanding view, and believing persuasion of the way of life as revealed in the gospel, through the suretyship, obedience and sufferings of Jesus Christ.[21]

Samuel Finley described Blair's preaching in the following words:

> As a preacher, [he] was very eminent. There was a solemnity in his very appearance which struck his hearers with awe before he opened his mouth. And his manner of preaching, while it was truly evangelical and instructive, was exceedingly impressive. He spoke as in the view of eternity, as in the immediate presence of God.[22]

Another person who was awakened during this early period of Blair's ministry was a man named Hunse Kirkpatrick who was nearly fifty at the time of his conversion. He emigrated to America about the time when the Great Awakening had begun and was puzzled by accounts of it. He told Blair that he had various religious convictions in his youth,

---

[20] Ibid., 111.
[21] Alexander, *Log College*, 161.
[22] Ibid., 174.

but it seemed to Blair that he had stifled his conscience by a legal and formal conformity to religious duties. His outward conduct was sober, but he was troubled by such books as Cotton Mather's *Dead Faith Anatomized*. Meanwhile, he continued to worship at Blair's congregation and a few Sundays later he was powerfully convicted of his sinfulness while listening to a sermon. He traveled to Philadelphia for a Synod meeting, hoping that one of the sermons preached there would relieve his great distress. As he walked through the city, he was afraid that the streets would open up and swallow whole such a wretched creature as himself. But soon his fears were relieved with very lively impressions of the freeness of the gospel and his soul found satisfaction in Christ as his righteousness. Kirkpatrick was subsequently elected to the office of ruling elder by Blair's congregation before dying of a consumptive illness with which he had suffered for a long time.[23]

The Great Awakening in 1740

The time when Samuel was searching for an academy where he could complete his education for the ministry was the beginning of a great spiritual change in the colonies. The revival in the Fagg's Manor congregation was soon to be followed by similar outpourings of the Spirit in other towns and villages. 1740 was to prove to be the year that this religious phenomenon known as the Great Awakening reached its zenith. Prior to this year, there had been revivals in the colonies which were generally restricted to particular congregations or regions, but 1740 was like the bursting forth of a great geyser. The prelude to this great revival had begun the previous fall under the preaching of George Whitefield. In November of 1739, Whitefield was preaching to great throngs in Philadelphia. One of those who went to hear the great evangelist was a young boy named John Rodgers.

> As the famous evangelist preached from the courthouse steps, the boy pressed near to him to hold a lantern for his convenience. As the Whitefieldian eloquence heightened, the youth became so engrossed that the lantern slipped from his hand and was dashed in pieces. Under these

---

[23] Samuel Blair, "A Short and Faithful Narrative of a Remarkable Revival of Religion in the Congregation of New Londonderry," prefixed to *The Doctrine of Predestination Truly and Fairly Stated* (Baltimore: R. J. Matchett, 1836), 84–86.

influences, John came early to what he hoped was a saving knowledge of Jesus Christ and resolved to devote himself to the ministry.[24]

This event took place when Rodgers was twelve years old, and it resulted in his call to the ministry. Thus, he began preparatory studies under Blair at Fagg's Manor in 1743 where he and Samuel Davies developed an intimate friendship which lasted throughout their lives. From the latter part of 1739 and throughout 1740, Whitefield preached to thousands of people in the vicinity of Samuel's home—at Wilmington, New Castle, Christiania Bridge, White Clay Creek, and Bohemia. At Bohemia, there were about 2,000 people gathered to hear Whitefield in later November of 1739. Though Samuel never mentions hearing Whitefield, he certainly would not have absented himself while thousands of others traveled long distances to hear the great evangelist. In after years, Davies referenced those times of revival as one who was an eye-witness to them.

The outbreak of the Great Awakening in the Middle Colonies was stoked by Whitefield's preaching in the latter part of 1739, but the bursting forth of the flames of revival took place almost simultaneously in the Fagg's Manor and Nottingham Churches in Pennsylvania. March of 1740 was the month when the Holy Spirit lit the flame that spread rapidly throughout the colonies in that wondrous year of God's grace. About the time that revival broke out in Blair's congregation, the same thing happened in the nearby Nottingham congregation. On March 8, 1740, Gilbert Tennent preached at the Nottingham Presbyterian Church on the subject of "The Dangers of an Unconverted Ministry" from Mark 6:34: "And Jesus when he came out, saw much people and was moved with compassion towards them, because they were as sheep not having a shepherd." Much of his sermon is simply faithful exposition of the text against which no one could rightly object without contesting Scripture itself. What made his sermon so reprehensible to many people in his day was his close application of this passage to the controversies then brewing in the Presbyterian Church—particularly, itinerant preaching, private academies for training ministers, and his insistence that ministers should be strictly examined concerning experimental religion. Tennent was of a naturally vehement temperament and did not

---

[24] Robert T. Handy, "John Rodgers, 1727–1811: 'A Life of Usefulness on Earth,'" *Journal of the Presbyterian Historical Society*, Vol. XXXIV, No. 2 (1956), 70.

shy away from cryptically referring to some within the Presbyterian Church as "Pharisee teachers, having no experience of a special work of the Holy Ghost upon their souls, . . . therefore neither inclined to, nor fitted for, discoursing, frequently, clearly, and pathetically upon such important subjects."[25] Tennent made the mistake of aiming his sermon at his opponents in the ministry rather than allowing the Holy Spirit to make the application.

Yet, Tennent was not alone in sounding a warning against unconverted ministers. Both Tennent's mentor, Theodore Frelinghuysen, and his father, William Tennent, Sr., had opposed an unconverted ministry for more than twenty years. George Whitefield also stood firmly on the same side of that issue and preached several sermons to that same effect. Indeed, ministers on both sides of the issue were guilty of referring to the other side as being unconverted. Thus, if there were excessive denunciations concerning this matter, all parties shared in the blame.

The topic of an unconverted ministry was a major issue at that time. Whitefield found that there was a principle among the New England churches that said, 'A converted minister is best, but an unconverted one cannot fail to do some good.'[26] Some of this sentiment was due, no doubt, to the views of church membership which developed out of the halfway covenant mentioned earlier. It is not difficult to see how such a doctrine could influence the church to think that an unconverted minister could do good. As Joseph Tracy wrote concerning that system:

> It is easy to see, that this system favored the entrance of unconverted men into the ministry. If one was fit to be a member of the church; if he was actually a member in good standing; if he was living as God requires such men to live, and pressing forward, in the use of the appointed means, after whatever spiritual good he had not yet attained; if conversion is such a still and unobservable matter, that neither the candidate nor any one else can judge whether he has yet passed that point or not; and if his mental qualifications are found sufficient; why should be excluded from the ministry? It could not be. The form of examining candidates as to their piety was still retained, but the spirit of it was dying away; and though it was

---

[25] Archibald Alexander, comp., *Sermons of the Log College* (Ligonier, PA: Soli Deo Gloria Publications, 1993), 381.
[26] *George Whitefield's Journals* (London: The Banner of Truth Trust, 1965), 470.

esteemed improper to fasten the charge upon individuals by name, nobody doubted that there were many unconverted ministers.[27]

While both Tennent and Whitefield later publicly apologized for their intemperate speech on this issue, Tennent is the one who is infamously remembered for his "Nottingham" sermon. Whitefield's biographer, Arnold Dallimore, opined that Tennent's sermon was a double-edged sword. He preached "with an urgency that befitted the occasion" but also with "something of the sword-brandishing."[28] Joseph Tracy wrote that Tennent's "Nottingham" sermon was a watershed moment in the history of both Presbyterianism and evangelical Christianity in America:

> It was doubtless Tennent's duty to write and preach and print on that subject; and if this sermon had been completely faultless, there is no reason to believe that it would have given any less offence. Yet he was angry, and that we may not justify; but let him who would have kept his temper better, cast the first stone at him. . . And though he spoke with an anger that debased his style and wrought evil, yet he spoke truth, mainly from good motives. He spoke it in a style which he knew would command attention, and cause it to be understood and remembered. The sermon was widely circulated, and was a topic of discussion for years. Neither friends nor enemies would let it rest. It turned the tide of popular opinion against unconverted ministers; and to no other agency, probably, so much as to this sermon, is it owing that Presbyterian ministers at the present day (1842) are generally pious men.[29]

Tennent's sermon was published by Benjamin Franklin and, no doubt, was read by tens of thousands of people throughout the colonies. Prior to this sermon, itinerant preaching was considered an evil intrusion into the ministries of others (and certainly was viewed that way by the Synod of Philadelphia), but things quickly changed. Following Tennent's message, thousands of people flocked to hear these itinerant ministers who labored to fan the flames of revival. Tennent's sermon was only one contributor to the Great Awakening, but a very significant one nonetheless. Almost simultaneous with what was happening at Fagg's Manor and Nottingham, a new revival broke out in Jonathan Edwards' congre-

---

[27] Tracy, *Great Awakening*, 7.
[28] Arnold Dallimore, *George Whitefield: The Life and Times of the Great Evangelist of the 18th Century*, Volume 1 (London: The Banner of Truth Trust, 1970), 552.
[29] Tracy, *Great Awakening*, 70.

gation in the spring of 1740. The winds of revival spread to other places as well. William Tennent, Jr. was involved in a revival in the highlands of New York in the early part of 1740. James Davenport waded through snow to preach at Easthampton where many were under deep concern for their souls. At Elizabethtown, New Jersey, Jonathan Dickinson witnessed the whole town under conviction of their sins in the winter of 1739-40 before a revival erupted in June of 1740 by means of a single sermon. Similar things were taking place through the preaching of John Rowland at Hopewell and Maidenhead in New Jersey.

Of course, Whitefield was the greatest spark for the revival and helped to carry it across denominational lines. In 1740 alone, he preached in Presbyterian, Baptist, Moravian, and Dutch Reformed congregations. He also was hosted on several occasions by Quakers in Pennsylvania. On May 15, 1740, he preached to nearly 12,000 people[30] at Blair's congregation which he described in his *Journal* as follows:

> Preached at Fagg's Manor, three miles from Blair's house, where he had earnestly invited me to come. The congregation was about as large as that at Nottingham. As great, if not a greater commotion was in the hearts of the people. Most were drowned in tears. The Word was sharper than a two-edged sword. The bitter cries and groans were enough to pierce the hardest heart. Some of the people were as pale as death; others were wringing their hands; others were lying on the ground; others were sinking into the arms of friends; and most lifting up their eyes to Heaven and crying to God for mercy. I could think of nothing, when I looked upon them, so much as the Great Day. They seemed like persons awakened by the last trump, and coming out of their graves to judgment.[31]

Whitefield returned to Fagg's Manor in November of that year and preached "to many thousands, when God was pleased to own His Word"[32] and two days later, on November 24, was in the vicinity of Samuel's home at a place called Bohemia in Maryland. He alluded to

---

[30] This number was the estimate of Whitefield as the following footnote shows. There are a couple of sights near the church which would have provided a natural amphitheater for such a large crowd of people. The area is still a remote farming community even as it was in the eighteenth century.
[31] *Whitefield's Journals*, 425–426.
[32] Ibid., 497.

these times of revival sixteen years later in a sermon on "The Happy Effects of the Outpouring of the Spirit":

> It is my happiness to be able to furnish you with an instance of the like nature, in the view of my own short life. About sixteen years ago, in the northern colonies, when all religious concern was much out of fashion, and the generality lay in a dead sleep in sin, having at best but the form of godliness, but nothing of the power; when the country was in peace and prosperity, free from the calamities of war, and epidemical sickness; when, in short, there were no extraordinary calls to repentance; suddenly a deep, general concern about eternal things spread through the country; sinners started out of their slumbers, broke off from their vices, began to cry out, What shall we do to be saved? and make it the great business of their life to prepare for the world to come. Then the gospel seemed almighty, and carried all before it. It pierced the very hearts of men with an irresistible power. I have seen thousands at once melted down under it; all eager to hear as for life, and hardly a dry eye to be seen among them.
>
> Many have since backslidden, and all their religion is come to nothing, or dwindled away into mere formality. But blessed be God, thousands still remain shining monuments of the power of divine grace in that glorious day. The harvest did not continue very long; and now, in the same places, and under the same ministry, or a better, there are hardly any appearances of it; though Providence has given them so many alarms of late, and such loud calls to repentance.[33]

Fagg's Manor Academy

This mighty revival that was taking place in the colonies urgently necessitated more schools of the prophets to shepherd the thousands of souls who were pressing into the kingdom of God. Blair's congregation was in the vanguard of meeting this need, following the example of William Tennent's Log College. Whitefield's two successful visits to their area in 1740 and the revival within the Fagg's Manor congregation convinced the session at Fagg's Manor that the congregation needed to support promising ministerial students with an education. The sessional records of December 8, 1740 give the reason for their decision as follows:

---

[33] Samuel Davies, *Sermons on Important Subjects*, IV (London: W. Baynes and Sons, 1824), 49–50. This sermon was preached at Hanover, Virginia on October 16, 1757.

> The Session, viz., the minister & Elders of ye Presbyterian congregation of New Londonderry, being sensible yt that the coming of godly men into ye ministry, such as are experientially acquainted wt the renewing & sanctifying grace of God in their own souls, has ye most helpful aspect upon ye interests of Christ's Kingdom & true vital godliness amongst us; and that, upon ye other hand, the receiving men of a contrary character into that sacred office is ye great Bane of ye church of Christ, and ye great reason for ye sad decay of true lively experimental Religion. . . We think the yielding them our Assistance by contributing to their support for their carrying on & obtaining their pious, & so very needful as well as useful Design, one of the best ways in wc our charity can be bestow'd: and therefore, being ready to contribute our own mite, we heartily recommend it all such of our christian Brethren to whom these may come, to joyn us in the same, promising, yt upon their giving what they allow this way, to any one of us, it shall be apply'd to ye fores purpose. And in so doing we hope the Blessing of many souls ready to perish will come upon the givers, an ye interest of our Glorious redeemer be promoted in ye World.[34]

Blair probably learned of John Rodgers through George Whitefield and possibly learned of Samuel through the Tennent brothers—William, Jr., and Gilbert—who had preached in the Hopewell and Maidenhead area of New Jersey in 1736 where the lad had studied under William Robinson. Robinson himself also might have been the source of Blair's information about Samuel and his call to the gospel ministry. Indeed, there were many ways in which Samuel could have become connected to Blair.

The exact time when the Fagg's Manor school was started cannot be known for sure, but it was probably in 1741. Fagg's Manor, or New Londonderry, Pennsylvania, was only about thirty-five miles northwest of the Welsh Tract and Samuel Davies certainly became one of Blair's first students. Others who studied under Blair were John Rodgers, Alexander Cummings, James Finley[35], Hugh Henry, and Robert Smith—all of whom became useful ministers of the gospel.

Blair built a plain log structure, twenty feet by thirty feet, at the front of his small farm which was about three miles north of the church. He furnished his students with a sound theological education and a thor-

---

[34] "Records of the Old Londonderry Congregation, Now Faggs Manor, Chester Co., PA.", *Journal of the Presbyterian Historical Society*, Vol. 8, No. 8 (June 1916), 345–6.
[35] James Finley was Samuel Finley's younger brother.

ough preparation for the work of the ministry. It was the observation of Samuel Finley that Blair had "a very considerable store of critical learning and was especially conversant with the Scriptures in the original languages."[36] The course of study at Blair's academy was similar to what had been taught at the Log College. Davies later described the curriculum at Fagg's Manor Classical School as follows:

> We had a regular education in a private academy. . . which private method we were obliged to take for want of a convenient college. . . and have acquired the Latin and Greek Languages, studied Philosophy, particularly Logic, Ontology, Pneumatology; and read sundry approven Systems of Theology, besides various Writings on particular important Subjects; as, on Natural and Revealed Religion in Opposition to Atheism, Deism, etc. Most of them have learn'd Hebrew, and some of them have read Physics[37] and Ethics, or Natural and Moral Philosophy; besides what Progress they made in sundry Branches of Mathematics. This I have known by *personal Acquaintance* with them.[38]

Old Light—New Light Division

Satan is never more active in sowing tares than when the gospel is being planted in good hearts. That would certainly prove to be the case during the Great Awakening. Samuel's first year at Blair's academy witnessed a terrible division of the Presbyterian Church in America into two separate Synods. Though he was only a ministerial student during these events, Samuel was decidedly in agreement with the New Lights in all the matters that resulted in this schism. Moreover, these matters helped shape him into the minister he became.

The New Lights / New Side and the Old Lights / Old Side had been divided in their sentiments for over a decade on issues affecting the nature of the gospel. The doctrine which the "New Lights" endorsed is summed up in Whitefield's description of his own conversion upon reading Henry Scougal's, *The Life of God in the Soul of Man*:

---

[36] Alexander, *The Log College*, 147.
[37] Davies' ordination sermon before the Presbytery of New Castle on "Man's Primitive State; and the First Covenant" revealed an accurate knowledge of human physiology which would be an unusual course of study for modern theological students.
[38] Samuel Davies, *The Impartial Trial, Impartially Tried, and Convicted of Partiality* (Williamsburg, Virginia: William Parks, 1748), 17.

> God soon showed me. . . that, "true religion is a union of the soul with God, and Christ formed within us", a ray of Divine light was instantaneously darted in upon my soul, and from that moment, but not till then, did I know that I must become a new creature.[39]

A large majority of the Old Light Presbyterians, according to Joseph Tracy, taught regeneration was not even essential for ministers of the gospel. This view was a chief reason for Tennent's Nottingham sermon. Concerning this state, Archibald Alexander observed:

> Under such a state of things, it is easy to conceive that in a short time vital piety may have almost deserted the church, and that formality and "dead orthodoxy" have been all that was left of religion.[40]

The New Lights, on the other hand, believed regeneration was essential for ministers and church members alike. Most of the controversies between these factions, according to Archibald Alexander, "grew out of this fundamental difference, and all were more or less directly related to it."[41] In other words, many of the Old Lights superficially appeared to be orthodox because they proclaimed the *objective grace* of redemption through Christ's atonement. Yet, in denying regeneration, they were also denying the *subjective grace* of the Holy Spirit. Their views were heterodox at best, erroneous at worst, in that respect. Thus, many of the Old Lights also opposed the inner witness of the Spirit, the assurance of salvation, and the New Lights' emphasis on vital piety. The Old Lights' formal adherence to the Westminster Confession of Faith notwithstanding, the fundamental difference between them and the New Lights concerned the work of the Holy Spirit and what is called subjective grace. While not all the Old Lights imbibed these errors, this issue concerning subjective grace was the fundamental difference between the two parties.

Sometimes it is mistakenly taught that the primary difference between the Old Lights and New Lights was that the former were more rigid in their adherence to the Westminster Standards while the latter were looser about doctrine and more evangelistic. That is a false caricature. The New Lights were as strictly orthodox as any ministers in the history of the church, but they combined objective grace (what Christ has

---

[39] Dallimore, *George Whitefield*, I, 73.
[40] Alexander, *Log College*, 17.
[41] Ibid., 61.

done for me or the accomplishment of redemption) and subjective grace (what the Spirit has done in me or the application of redemption) in their proper balance. On the other hand, some of the Old Light ministers emphasized objective grace to the neglect or exclusion of subjective grace and the work of the Holy Spirit. Some of the New Lights, such as Gilbert Tennent, became uncharitable and judgmental in their denunciations of fellow ministers. Others of them went to excess in promoting emotional outbursts as signs of conversion. Despite those excesses, such New Lights as Samuel Finley, Samuel Blair, Samuel Davies, John Rodgers and others maintained the right balance throughout their ministries. Yet, uncharitable judging was not confined to the New Lights. Both before Tennent's Nottingham sermon and afterwards, the Old Light Presbyterian ministers accused their New Light counterparts of delusion and fanaticism. One of the most virulent of the Old Light ministers was George Gillespie who wrote several books and pamphlets to that effect.[42]

These differences between the New Lights and the Old Lights were also stoked by two acts of the Synod of Philadelphia in 1737 and 1738. The first act forbade itinerant preaching (which was covered in the previous chapter) and the second act was a requirement concerning the education of all ministerial candidates. Both acts have been mentioned previously and were direct attacks on the labors of the New Light ministers and their schools for training ministers—the Log College and Blair's Academy. The New Lights also believed that these acts of the Synod were in opposition to the Great Awakening which was then at its height. At the 1740 meeting of Synod, both Gilbert Tennent and Samuel Blair responded to the actions of the Synod. Blair defended the New Lights against the charge of intruding into the parishes of other ministers by turning the tables on their opponents within the Synod.

> Our design, I hope, was to attempt to propagate the kingdom of our Lord Jesus, and save the souls of men. . . It is a vain shift for any of them, in or-

---

[42] *Remarks Upon Mr. George Whitefield, Proving Him a Man Under Delusion* (Philadelphia: B. Franklin, 1744); *A Letter to the Rev. Brethren of the Presbytery of New York* (Philadelphia: B. Franklin, 1740). The first title needs no explanation. The second book was written to justify the action of the Synod of Philadelphia in illegally dismissing the Presbytery of New Brunswick in 1741 and trampling on their rights of due process. He probably also had a hand in a volume titled, *The Querists* (Philadelphia: B. Franklin, 1741), which was written in response to Tennent's sermon.

der to clear themselves from the charge of having made an opposition to the late revival of religion, to say that they have opposed things that were evil and irregular, which ought to be opposed.[43]

Tennent also spoke to this meeting of the Synod of Philadelphia and brought out a matter that has mostly been overlooked in evaluation of this controversy. In his words to that court, Tennent said:

> Our protesting brethren have quite omitted any mention of the late extraordinary canon framed by the Presbytery of Donegal, which *ipso facto* excommunicates, or deprives of church privileges, all of their people that go to hear any of the itinerary preachers.[44]

However highhanded such an action of the Presbytery of Donegal may appear to us today, this became the standard policy of those presbyters who opposed the Great Awakening and who hoped by such actions to blunt its effectiveness. What this action reveals is that when church courts usurp the authority of Christ and begin to legislate according to their whims, there are scarcely any limits to which they will not go to exercise their authority over others.

This matter continued to boil until the next year when the Old Lights overplayed their hand. At the Synod of Philadelphia meeting in 1741, the members of New Brunswick Presbytery (New Light) were not allowed to take their seats and the Presbyterian Church in America was divided into two branches. On June 1, Robert Cross, the pastor of the First Presbyterian Church of Philadelphia, presented a "Protestation" which was signed by twelve ministers and twelve elders. The effect of this "Protestation" was to compel the New Lights to accede to the positions of the Old Lights in order to remain in the Synod. Clearly, the Old Lights had marshaled their forces well. The New Brunswick party spoke in their defense, but to no avail. Some commissioners were absent (including all those from the Presbytery of New York); others were disgusted with both sides; still others silent and refused to take sides. Yet, this left the supporters of this "Protestation" in the majority and their position carried the day. These actions by the Old Lights were the greatest miscarriage of justice in the history of American Presbyterianism. All the rights

---

[43] Tracy, *Great Awakening*, 72.
[44] Ibid., 74.

of due process of the New Brunswick ministers were violated by the Synod of Philadelphia.

The ringleader of the Protesters, Robert Cross, had at one time permitted Whitefield to preach in his pulpit during a snow storm, but later became an enemy of the Great Awakening. Whitefield was opposed both by Cross and other Old Light Presbyterian ministers who printed their objections instead of speaking directly with him. One of the charges made against the great evangelist was that his doctrine was Antinomianism—a scurrilous charge that was also made against the New Light Presbyterians. For instance, Jedidiah Andrews, stated clerk of Synod, wrote to John Pierson, pastor at Woodbridge, New Jersey, on June 25, 1741, as follows:

> The prevailing opinion among that party is, that the moral law is no rule to believers. They freely declare they don't do any good, or bring forth any fruit, or avoid any evil, on consideration of any law obliging or forbidding them, or from any fear of God at all.[45]

Andrews misrepresented the views of the New Light Presbyterians. They never held that the moral law is no rule to believers for their obedience. What they believed was that obedience to the moral law could never be the basis of a person's justification before God, but they held just as thoroughly that good works are the evidence of a saving change in a believer. In every age, formalists or legalists have accused those who hold to free grace and justification by faith alone of being guilty of antinomianism.

After this "Protestation" by Cross and others, the New Light Presbytery of New Brunswick withdrew from the assembly hall where the Synod of Philadelphia was in session. Ironically, the tumult was so great that a vote was never officially taken on the matter. While the New Lights immediately met to form themselves into two Presbyteries, they did not form a new Synod until 1746. Despite the intemperate way in which they were treated, the New Lights still hoped to avoid a division of the Presbyterian Church. This fact is brought out even more by the remarks of Gilbert Tennent to Jonathan Dickinson on February 12, 1742:

> I have many afflicting thoughts about the debates which have subsisted in our synod for some time. I would to God the breach were healed, were it

---

[45] Webster, *History of the Presbyterian Church in America*, 178.

the will of Almighty. As for my own part, wherein I have mismanaged in doing what I did, I do look upon it to be my duty, and should be willing to acknowledge it in the openest manner. I cannot justify the excessive heat of temper which has sometimes appeared in my conduct.[46]

The great problem for people like Tennent, who sometimes exhibit more heat than grace, is that they later tend to repent overmuch also. Tennent was certainly wrong for losing control of his passions and for the excessive heat of his temper, but he was also quick to take measures to heal the breach—a fact which is almost never mentioned by those who criticize the great man for his Nottingham sermon. On the other hand, the Old Lights in 1742 were far from wanting a reunion unless the New Light ministers conceded every point included in the "Protestation" and desisted from itinerant preaching. Rather, they commissioned members of their body to defend their "Protestation" and their actions in print. In a rehearsal of the ecclesiastical issues involved, it is easy to forget that God honored the itinerant preaching of the New Lights with a mighty revival.

Even though Samuel was not professionally involved in these events as an ordained minister, it is beyond question that he agreed with the New Lights and the Synod of New York in their controversy with the Synod of Philadelphia. At a later date, he expressed his displeasure with the acts of 1737 and 1738 as follows:

> Being fired with resentment at our conscientious non-compliance with these Acts, and, we fear, at the success of our ministry, thro' the Divine blessing, in various parts, these members magnified or misrepresented matters of fact, brought in unproven accusations against us; and ripened every thing into a lamentable separation;—and at length excluded us by a shocking protestation, without any regular previous trial.[47]

Davies' Struggles to Complete His Education

Due to financial difficulties, Samuel was unable to complete his course of study at Fagg's Manor in successive order. There were times he had to interrupt his studies in order to help his father on the farm and to save enough money to continue his instruction under Blair. Yet, help was soon to come from an unusual and unexpected source to aid his educa-

---

[46] Ibid., 189.
[47] Davies, *Impartial Trial, Impartially Tried, and Convicted of Partiality*, 11.

tion. In striving to finish his education as soon as possible, he developed the practice of studying for such long periods each day that he nearly ruined his health.

> His slender frame became enfeebled, and, at the time his course of preparatory studies was completed, his health was very delicate.[48]

The interesting times in which Samuel studied under Blair helped form his ministerial character for the fields where the Lord would have him labor. He was fired with a holy zeal, anxious for the conversion of sinners, but also gracious to all. No doubt, he learned from the mistakes of others and determined not to be a son of thunder like Gilbert Tennent. Samuel Blair was a much more pacific person than Tennent, though he was just as zealous for the truth. As such, he was the right person to train one of the holiest ministers to ever adorn the Presbyterian Church.

Conclusion

In the controversy concerning Gilbert Tennent's Nottingham sermon, it has sadly been overlooked or ignored that his warning against unconverted ministers was heeded by thousands of church members. Thousands met in the open air or in tents erected for the occasion to hear the revival preachers. Many of them were the subjects of God's redeeming grace. Their willingness to seek Christ outside the camp was particularly honored by God in 1740 with the greatest year of revival in the history of America. Evangelical Christianity ever since Tennent's sermon has held it to be a duty of God's people to leave churches where the pure gospel is not being preached. While there were certain flaws to the Great Awakening, the good accomplished far outweighed the bad effects of it. Thus, those ministers who opposed that revival were guilty of opposing the God who was answering by fire in the conversions of multitudes. As a result of the Great Awakening, evangelical Christianity has been the predominant type of Christianity in America for most of her history.

Yet, evangelical Christianity must be continually nourished by revivals and evangelism. Church history clearly shows that whenever church members trust in sacramental works of righteousness, such as baptism and the Lord's Supper, religious formalism increases and morality de-

---

[48] Foote, *Sketches of Virginia*, First Series, 159.

clines. The practical effect is always that sound doctrine vanishes and heresy abounds. Such was the case in New England in the early part of the eighteenth century. Brynestad, therefore, wrote about the ministers:

> The clergy were as a rule ignorant and indifferent to true Christianity. Arianism and Socinianism spread widely within and without the Church.[49]

The only cure for such spiritual deadness is an outpouring of God's Spirit, in a way similar to what happened in the Great Awakening.

Samuel Blair's grave in the cemetery across the road from the Fagg's Manor Presbyterian Church

---

[49] Brynestad, "Great Awakening in the New England and Middle Colonies.," 84.

Fagg's Manor Presbyterian Church in 2016, built on the same site as the original building where Samuel Blair preached. In 1740, George Whitefield preached to 12,000 people in the fields nearby.

-4-

The Great Awakening Comes to Virginia

"The history of the world shows, that there are times, when the public mind is readily turned to religion; and, if in such times, the gospel be presented in its purity and simplicity, the concerns of the soul become the all absorbing subject. One of those happy times was enjoyed in Hanover in common with many other parts of the world, both in Europe and America."[1]

~*William Henry Foote*, Sketches of Virginia~

Hanover Tavern in Hanover, Virginia, opened circa 1733

---

[1] William Henry Foote, *Sketches of Virginia: Historical and Biographical*, First Series (Philadelphia: William S. Martien, 1850), 120.

The Great Awakening Comes to Virginia

The Great Awakening in America was an outpouring of the Holy Spirit that revived various Presbyterian, Congregational, and Baptist churches, but left the Anglican churches in New England and the Middle colonies virtually unchanged. Indeed, many of the Anglican clergy bitterly opposed it. Soon after George Whitefield, the Anglican minister from Great Britain, began his first preaching tour of the colonies, there was a pamphlet written by an American Anglican clergyman, Jonathan Arnold, and printed in New York on November 17, 1739. In that pamphlet, "To the Inhabitants of New-York," Arnold sounded a dire denunciation of Whitefield:

> I therefore Warn you in Christ's Name, in Faithfulness to your Souls, to Shun him as an open Enemy to religion, whatever may be his specious pretenses, a Violator of all Rule and Order, disobeying those who have the Rule over him, and dispising (sic) his Betters. Don't suffer yourselves to be imposed upon or drawn away by this Deceiver, but Watch and Pray that you enter not into Temptation.[2]

Arnold's poisoned pen sparked a debate between the friends and foes of the Great Awakening that found its way into print in such newspapers as the *Boston Evening-Post*, the *New York Gazette*, the *Boston Weekly News-Letter*, and the *American Weekly Mercury* of Philadelphia. From 1739 to 1745, nothing was more of a boon to Colonial publications than the revival. One third of all newspaper stories during that period were concerning it, both for and against, with notifications of the time and place where revival ministers were scheduled to preach. Additionally, the printing business thrived from the numerous pamphlets, sermons, and books which were printed by both sides. Advertisements of such works were found in all the newspapers of that period, as well as many Puritan books which were recommended by the supporters of the revival. The practice of that day was for newspapers to borrow from one another and to print reports of important events in other colonies. Thus, the citizens of Virginia were able to read the reports of the surprising work which the Lord was doing in the colonies to the north of them.

---

[2] Lisa Smith, *The First Great Awakening in Colonial American Newspapers: A Shifting Story* (Lanham, Maryland; Boulder, Colorado; New York, New York; Toronto, Canada; and Plymouth, United Kingdom: Lexington Books, 2012), 1.

The Great Awakening Comes to Virginia

When those reports of the Great Awakening in New England and the Middle Colonies began to reach Virginia in the late 1730s, "reflecting men . . . inquire[d] respecting the nature of these things and their consequent importance."[3] The colony of Virginia, then dominated by the Church of England, was hostile to this revival and intolerant of religious freedom. The Anglican clergy of Virginia, especially, were opposed both theologically and practically to the Great Awakening. As Samuel Miller opined in *Memoir of the Rev. John Rodgers., D.D.* concerning them:

> The established clergy were . . . notoriously profligate in their lives, and very few among them preached, or appeared to understand, the Gospel of Christ.[4]

One of the ways this opposition manifested itself was through intolerance. The Act of Toleration of 1689[5] granted certain rights to Dissenters in Great Britain which had been denied them in the Act of Uniformity of 1662. Yet, the governing officials of Virginia, at the behest of the Anglican clergy, were reluctant to recognize the extension of that law to her territories. The effect was to deny, as Foote states, "whether the minority had any rights of conscience."[6]

Four Gentlemen from Hanover County Converted

The Great Awakening was a work of God, though, and it spread to the Old Dominion despite the opposition of men. There are various accounts of this revival in Virginia. The period of 1739-40 was an important marker for the beginning of the Great Awakening in this colony just as it was in New England and the middle colonies. John Holt Rice tells us how the work of grace began in Virginia without the direct instrumentality of the preached word:

---

[3] Foote, *Sketches of Virginia*, First Series, 120.
[4] Samuel Miller, *Memoir of the Rev. John Rodgers, D.D.* (New York: Presbyterian Board of Publication, 1813), 31.
[5] The Act of Toleration provided Protestant Dissenters in Great Britain and her colonies—primarily Congregationalists, Baptists, and Presbyterians—the freedom to worship without having to subscribe to the *Book of Common Prayer* of the Church of England. This Act restored the freedom they had lost in the Act of Uniformity in 1662.
[6] Foote, *Sketches of Virginia*, First Series, 119.

The Great Awakening Comes to Virginia

> Four gentlemen. . . at the same time became convinced that the Gospel was not preached by the minister of the parish; and that it was inconsistent with their duty to attend on his ministrations.[7]

While there is no documentary evidence to show that these four gentlemen knew of Gilbert Tennent's Nottingham sermon, their actions in leaving their parish were quite unusual if they were totally ignorant of it. It is very likely that among the numerous reports they had heard of the Great Awakening they also learned that large numbers of people in New England had left their congregations to hear the revival preachers. Each of the men had been officers at St. Paul's Parish in Hanover County under the Rev. Patrick Henry, Sr., who was accused by Alexander White, a fellow Anglican minister in Virginia, of being an irascible fellow who was "incapable of true friendship."[8] Since they were all absent from church on the same day, their court hearings were scheduled for the same day, wherein they discovered the similar sentiments of one another.

Samuel Morris, a bricklayer and planter, was one of those who refused to attend Henry's services. Morris providentially acquired a copy of Martin Luther's *Commentary on the Galatians*, which he read with great eagerness and approval.

> He there found representations of Gospel truth, such as he had never met with before, and widely different from what he had been accustomed to receive from the pulpit.[9]

Morris continued to read and pray until he came to a full understanding and acceptance of Christ as his Savior and Lord.

John White and John Hunt were two of the other men who absented themselves from the parish services, with the other person probably being Roger Watkins. One of these men, a wealthy planter, found a few pages of Thomas Boston's *Fourfold State*, which had been owned by a pious Scottish woman. On his next shipment of tobacco to Great Britain, he put in an order for a copy of this book.

---

[7] John Holt Rice, "The Origin of Presbyterianism in Virginia," *The Virginia Evangelical and Literary Magazine*, II (1819), 346.
[8] Joan Gundersen, *The Anglican Ministry in Virginia, 1723–1766: A Study of a Social Class* (New York and London: Garland Publishing, Inc., 1989), 187.
[9] Miller, *Memoir of the Rev. John Rodgers*, 32.

He obtained it; and the more he read, the more he found himself interested in its contents; until he was brought . . . to a saving acquaintance with the truth as it is in Jesus.[10]

All four men believed their actions were right and were determined not to go to St. Paul's Parish regardless of the fines or punishment. Instead, "they agreed to meet every sabbath, alternately, at each other's house, and spend the time with their families, in prayer and the reading of the scriptures, together with Luther's commentary on the Galatians."[11] They were soon joined by numerous other families who heard reports of this new society.

An additional account of the beginning of this revival is given by David Rice, who was reared in Hanover. Two of Rice's uncles, James Rice and John Symms, became deeply impressed with salvation through the reading of Scripture. David's grandmother and a neighbor, James Hooper, began to meet in the homes of Rice and Symms for religious conversation every Lord's Day rather than attend the local parish church. When James Rice visited some relatives in the country, he found some works by the Puritans as well as a copy of Luther's *Commentary on Galatians*. James Rice made such a careful study of Luther and the Puritans that he could quote them almost verbatim to all who visited him.

The Morris Reading Room

A meetinghouse was soon thereafter built on land owned by Morris, and it quickly became known as the "Morris Reading House" or the "Morris Reading Room." Morris himself would generally read such works as Luther's *Commentary on Galatians*, his *Tabletalk Discourses*, and several of the works of John Bunyan to the attentive crowds that gathered in his small building. The works of other Puritans such as Bolton, Baxter, and Flavel were also read in private by several of the people converted during this period. In a short time, the number of people meeting at the Morris Reading Room became so numerous that three additional meetinghouses were erected. Morris's narrative gives further information about these times:

---

[10] Ibid., 32–33.
[11] Foote, *Sketches of Virginia*, First Series, 121.

> My dwelling house was at length too small to contain the people, whereupon we determined to build a meeting house merely for *reading*. And having never been used to social prayer, none of us durst attempt it. By this single means several were awakened, and their conduct ever since is a proof of the continuance and happy issue of their impressions. When the report was spread abroad, I was invited to several places, to read these sermons, at a considerable distance, and by this means the concern was propagated.[12]

Some people, like John Hunt, had probably had religious convictions for years prior to this period of awakening. James W. Alexander describes an experience which Hunt had as a young man which remained with him until his conversion around the time of the beginning of the Morris Reading Room:

> He had a notion that when a young man God had called him by name, it is believed in Williamsburg. Sitting up till midnight he heard a voice from above distinctly calling him, James Hunt, James Hunt! Contrary to what is usual in such visitations, the voice was distinctly heard by two women who were ironing in a room near at hand. From that time he had very serious thoughts about religion, but was ignorant of its nature, until the famous "reading" commenced at Mr. Morris's house, in the neighborhood of which he lived.[13]

James Hunt, the son of John Hunt, provides a supplementary account of how God blessed the Morris Reading Room to further the work of grace in Hanover:

> Curiosity prompted the desire to be among them,—one and another begged for admission, till their houses, on Sabbath, were crowded. And here a new scene opened upon their view. Numbers were pierced to the heart,—the word became sharp and powerful, —"what shall we do," was the general cry. What to do or say the principal leaders knew not. They themselves had been led by a still small voice, they hardly knew how, to an acquaintance with the truth; but now the Lord was speaking as on Mount Sinai, with a voice of thunder, and sinners, like that mountain itself, trembled to the centre. And it was not long before they had the happiness to see a goodly little number healed by the same word that had wounded them, and brought to rejoice understandingly in Christ.[14]

---

[12] Ibid.
[13] James Waddell Alexander, *Life of Archibald Alexander, D.D.* (New York: Scribner, 1854), 138.
[14] Ibid., 122.

The Great Awakening Comes to Virginia

George Whitefield Visits Williamsburg in 1739

During the winter of 1739-40, George Whitefield visited Virginia on his second missionary trip to America. Prior to this visit to Virginia, Whitefield had spent nearly forty days preaching in Pennsylvania, New Jersey, and Maryland to great crowds which immediately aroused the opposition of Jonathan Arnold, who was mentioned earlier. At Williamsburg, Whitefield dined with Governor William Gooch on Saturday, December 15. Afterwards, he was received joyfully by the Commissary of Virginia, the Rev. Mr. James Blair (1656-1743), whom he said was "by far the most worthy clergyman I have yet conversed with in all America."[15] Whitefield's assessment of Blair was probably a comparison of him to the Anglican clergy in other colonies who had mostly treated him as an enemy. He was also impressed with Blair's work in the establishment of William and Mary College at Williamsburg. Blair, a moderate Arminian, had preached 117 sermons on the Sermon on the Mount which were then printed in four volumes as *Our Saviour's Divine Sermon on the Mount*. Though Blair's work was praised by the English non-conformist, Philip Doddridge, it was more legalistic than evangelical. In a sermon from Matthew 6:33, Blair set forth his view that heaven is gained by a sincere though imperfect obedience:

> The Evangelical Righteousness consists in a hearty Endeavour to obey the Laws of the Gospel; and in a diligent applying to God for Grace to do it; and a quick and sincere Repentance after Lapses. . . God looks chiefly after the Sincerity of the Heart, and if that be right with him, he is ready to Pardon many Failings.[16]

With those words, Blair indicated his agreement with the neonomian[17] view of salvation; i.e., that the gospel is a new law which requires sincere obedience as the condition of gaining eternal salvation. Neonomianism and all other legalistic views of salvation have been the bane of the Church for centuries. Blair's view of the method of obtaining

---

[15] *George Whitefield's Journals* (London: The Banner of Truth Trust, 1965), 371.
[16] James Blair, *Our Saviour's Divine Sermon on the Mount* in Four Volumes, Volume III (London: J. Brotherton and J. Oswald, 1740), 400–401.
[17] Neonomian means 'new law.' It is a view held by those who teach that the Gospel provides a new and easier law for us to obey than the Old Testament law. This 'new law' is a works based scheme of salvation which makes the terms of salvation easier.

grace is the same view that every natural person has. Outside of Christ, every person hopes to gain heaven through sincere obedience and the natural man is confident that he is capable of such obedience.

The following day, Sunday, December 16, Whitefield preached for Commissary Blair, who was also the rector at the Bruton Parish Church in Williamsburg, from the text, "What think ye of Christ?" The *Virginia Gazette* contained the following report about the services:

> There was a numerous Congregation, and 'tis thought there would have been more, if timely Notice had been given of his Preaching. His extraordinary Manner of Preaching, gains him the Admiration and Applause of most of his Hearers.[18]

Despite the reputed admiration and applause of many, there was one person who was apparently displeased with Whitefield's message and that was Blair himself. Following Whitefield's visit to Williamsburg, he learned that the Bishop of London had proscribed Whitefield because of his evangelical doctrines. Thus, Blair wrote a letter of apology to the Bishop for his actions and inquired further concerning the Bishop's opinion of the great evangelist. Yet, Blair probably discerned the difference between his own neonomian views and the evangelical views of Whitefield while listening to the latter's message at Bruton Parish. He likely had buyer's remorse before Whitefield concluded his sermon. Whereas Blair taught that evangelical righteousness is comprised of our own sincere obedience, Whitefield proclaimed that the only righteousness that can save any person is the imputed righteousness of Christ:

> What think ye then, if I tell you, that ye are to be justified freely through Jesus Christ, without any regard to any work or fitness foreseen in us at all? . . . Our righteousness, in God's sight, are but as filthy rags: he cannot away with it. Our holiness, if we have any, is not the cause, but the effect of our justification in God's sight. . . The righteousness, the whole righteousness of Jesus Christ, is to be imputed to us, instead of our own.[19]

Blair surely discerned the difference between his doctrine and that of Whitefield. These doctrinal differences underscored the essential prob-

---

[18] *Virginia Gazette*, December 7–14, (Williamsburg, VA: William Parks, 1739).
[19] George Whitefield, *Seventy-Five Sermons on Various Important Subjects* in Three Volumes, Volume I (London: W. Baynes, 1812), 355–356.

lems that the New Light Presbyterians would soon face from the ecclesiastical and civil authorities in Virginia. The real opposition that the established church had against the Morris Reading Room and New Light Presbyterians was their adherence to the gospel. The Anglican clergy in Virginia, like many of their counterparts elsewhere, taught that salvation is gained both by moral works of righteousness and ceremonial works of righteousness; both through sincere obedience to God's requirements and partaking of the sacraments. Such legalism has always had a deadening effect on the morals of both clergy and laity, while the free grace that Whitefield preached has been productive of true holiness.

After this sermon in Williamsburg, Whitefield was invited by several men from the nearby town of York to preach there on Monday. He regretfully declined this invitation because he intended to leave the colony that same day.[20] Yet, Whitefield was hopeful from this visit that a work of grace would some day begin in Virginia. He considered the colony to be "more dead to God, but far less prejudiced than in the northern parts"[21] of America. Regrettably, the colony would soon manifest the same prejudice against the gospel as those in the northern parts had evidenced. Before leaving Virginia, Whitefield arranged for the printer to publish his *Journals* and *Sermons* with the hope and prayer that:

> God who loves to work by the meanest instruments, will be pleased to bless them to the conviction and edification of these His people. Visit them, O Lord, with Thy salvation.[22]

Whitefield abruptly left the colony before Morris and others in Hanover, fifty miles northwest of Williamsburg, heard about his visit. The people at Hanover were also unaware that the public printer, William Parks, had published some of Whitefield's sermons which could be purchased at the bookshop in Williamsburg.

Civil Punishments for Absenting Worship in the Anglican Churches

In the meantime, the civil authorities of Virginia were increasingly alarmed when large numbers of people at Hanover ceased attending the

---

[20] *Whitefield's Journals*, 372.
[21] Ibid.
[22] Ibid.

established church. To prevent further defections, the authorities cracked down with the strong arm of the law. Samuel Morris's account of this period states:

> Our absenting ourselves from the church contrary as was alleged to the laws of the land, was taken notice of, and we were called upon by the court to assign reasons for it, and to declare what denomination we were of.[23]

The narrative of James Hunt supplements Morris's account at this point:

> They were no longer considered as individual delinquents whose obstinacy might be sufficiently punished by the civil magistrate; but as a malignant cabal, that required the interposition of the executive. They were accordingly cited to appear before the Governor and Council. The exaction of frequent fines for non attendance at church they bore, with patience and fortitude, for the sake of a good conscience, but to be charged with a crime, of the nature and extent and penalty, of which they had but indistinct conceptions, spread a gloom over their minds, and filled them with anxious forebodings more easily conceived than described.[24]

Considering themselves to be Lutherans, Samuel Morris, John Hunt, John White, and their other friend hastened to Williamsburg for an interview with Governor William Gooch and the Council. One member of their party was compelled to travel alone and was overtaken by a violent rainstorm. He sought shelter in a nearby farmhouse and began to peruse the library of his gracious host where he found an old volume which exactly represented his sentiments. He offered to buy the book, but the gentleman kindly gave it to him instead. The book was the *Confession of Faith* of the Church of Scotland.[25] Arriving in Williamsburg, he showed this volume to his three friends, who likewise expressed their agreement with it.

The four men then presented the Scottish *Confession of Faith* to the Governor and the council as representative of their views. Governor Gooch, who was of Scottish origin, perused the book and declared them to be Presbyterians. They were then granted toleration under the laws of

---

[23] Foote, *Sketches of Virginia*, First Series, 123.
[24] Ibid.
[25] Ibid., 124. Also, Rice, "The Origin of Presbyterianism in Virginia", 349.

Virginia as Presbyterians and were allowed to continue meeting together. The Governor's only admonition was for the men to be careful not to cause any disturbances.

People continued to meet at the Morris Reading Room over the next few years until a young Scottish gentleman in 1743 brought to Hanover a volume of Whitefield's sermons preached in Glasgow, Scotland. This book was lent to Morris who carefully read the sermons for himself and then invited his neighbors and friends to hear them, with this result:

> The plainness and fervency of these discourses being attended with the power of the Lord, many were convinced of their undone situation, and constrained to seek deliverance with the greatest solicitude. A considerable number met to hear these sermons every Sabbath, and frequently on week days. The concern of some was so passionate and violent, that they could not avoid crying out, weeping bitterly, etc.[26]

William Robinson Visits Virginia and Hanover

It was during the winter of 1742–43, that William Robinson was sent out by the Presbytery of New Castle (New Light) to evangelize the Shenandoah Valley, the south side of the James River in Virginia, and the settlements along the Haw River in North Carolina. Shortly after entering Virginia, "he was seized near Winchester by the sheriff of Orange County . . . and was sent on his way to Williamsburg to answer to the Governor for preaching without a license."[27] Yet, the sheriff released him before he arrived at Williamsburg and Robinson was free to pursue his mission.

Robinson spent that winter in North Carolina where he contracted smallpox, a particularly deadly and contagious disease in Colonial America, from which he never fully recovered.[28] When he returned to Virginia, he "preached with great success to the Presbyterian settlements in Charlotte, Prince Edward, Campbell and Albemarle"[29] counties. All those counties were west or southwest of Hanover County and provided little cause of concern for the governing officials in Williamsburg. Through his labors, a congregation was founded in Lunenberg County.

---

[26] Foote, *Sketches of Virginia*, First Series, 122.
[27] Ibid., 126.
[28] Ibid.
[29] Ibid.

Robinson intended to travel up the Shenandoah Valley and evangelize that region, but the news of his visit to the colony was conveyed to someone in Hanover by a man from Augusta County who had come into the area in search of supplies. A deputation from Hanover was quickly dispatched and they overtook Robinson near Rockfish Gap in Amelia County. The group was instructed, though, not to extend an invitation to Robinson without first hearing him preach. The deputation was divided in their opinions about him for reasons summed up by James Hunt:

> Already differences of opinion had arisen which threatened the most serious evils. Some of their number, carrying some of the peculiar and distinguishing doctrines of the gospel to a licentious extreme, began to deny, not only the merit of good works, but their necessity— not only the means, but their expediency, so that it was made a serious question among them, whether it was right to pray, as prayer could not, as it would be impious to desire it should, alter the divine purposes.[30]

Some members of this group thought Robinson was evangelical, but others thought he insisted too much on good works. They finally agreed to extend a cordial invitation to Robinson to visit Hanover. Robinson initially declined their offer, but afterwards accepted it as the will of God and followed the men to Hanover.

Arriving at Hanover, Robinson stopped at Shelton's Tavern, across the road from the Hanover Court House, the evening before he was to preach at the Morris Reading Room. Foote records what happened next:

> The tavern keeper was a shrewd, boisterous, profane man. When uttering some horrid oaths, Mr. Robinson ventured to reprove him for his profanity; and although it was done in a mild way, the innkeeper gave him a sarcastic look, and said—"Pray sir, who are you to take such authority upon yourself?" "I am a minister of the gospel," says Mr. Robinson. "Then you belie your looks very much" was the reply.[31]

Robinson's looks had been badly marred by the smallpox, and he had lost the use of one of his eyes. Yet, he extended an invitation to this tavern owner to attend his preaching and observe for himself that he was a minister. The tavern owner agreed on the condition that Robinson

---

[30] Ibid., 127.
[31] Ibid., 131.

preach from the text, "For I am fearfully and wonderfully made," to which he gladly agreed. Foote records what happened next:

> The man was at Mr. Robinson's meeting, and that text was the theme of one of his sermons. Before it was finished, the wicked man was made to feel that he was the monster, and that he was fearfully and wonderfully made. It is said that he became a very pious and useful member of the church. . . Thus this good man cast the gospel net and caught of every sort, gathering whom his Lord called.[32]

Robinson's first sermon at Hanover on July 6, 1743, was from Luke 13:3, "I tell you, no, but, unless you repent, you will all likewise perish." The crowd that attended the first day was large and grew even larger on the following three days of his visit to Hanover. The effect of these sermons was such that Morris described them as "these glorious days of the Son of Man."[33] Robinson also corrected the Hanover group's habit of meeting without engaging in prayer and encouraged them to include the singing of Psalms in their worship. Morris describes the effect of those sermons on the hearers:

> Many that came through curiosity were pricked in the heart, and but few in the numerous assemblies on those days appeared unaffected. They returned alarmed with apprehensions of their dangerous condition, convinced of their former entire ignorance of religion, and anxiously inquiring what they should do to be saved. And there is reason to believe there was as much good done by those sermons as by all the sermons preached in these parts before or since.[34]

The tavern owner was not the only profane person drawn into the gospel net during the four days of Robinson's visit. There was a man named David Austin at Hanover who was one of the most wicked sinners in the region. Austin's wife learned that a traveling preacher intended to deliver a sermon in the area and desired to hear him preach. He absolutely refused to let her go, but told her that he would hear this man himself. When the congregation assembled for Robinson's sermon, Austin was fast asleep underneath a tree outside the building.

---

[32] Ibid.
[33] Ibid., 130.
[34] Archibald Alexander, *The Log College* (London: The Banner of Truth Trust, 1968), 199.

And thus he lay until the preacher took his text, which he uttered in a thundering voice, 'Awake, thou that sleepest.' Austin sprang to his feet as if pierced with a dart, and fixing his eyes on the preacher, never removed them, but drew nearer and nearer the stand, until at the close he was observed standing at the preacher's feet, and the tears streaming from his eyes. After a few days of pungent conviction, he received comfort by faith in Christ, and became one of the most eminent Christians in all the land.[35]

After his conversion, Austin became very useful in counseling with others under spiritual distress. On one occasion, he was "sent for as far as thirty miles, to converse with a lady under spiritual darkness and distress of mind."[36]

One of the most amazing conversions during Robinson's visit was a man named Isaac Oliver, who had been deaf and dumb since birth. Oliver lived with Samuel Morris and Davies described him in a letter to Joseph Bellamy in 1751:

> I have the utmost reason to believe he is truly gracious, and also acquainted with most of the doctrines, and many of the historical facts of the Bible. I have seen him represent the crucifixion of Christ in such significant signs, that I could not but understand them... So much, however, I know of him, that I cannot but look upon him as a miraculous monument of Almighty grace, that can perform its purposes on men, notwithstanding the greatest natural or moral impediments; and I submit it to the judgment of others, whether a person so incapable of external instructions, could be brought to know the mysteries of the kingdom of Heaven any other way than by immediate revelation.[37]

Robinson remained at Hanover long enough to correct some of the group's doctrinal errors concerning the relationship of the sovereignty of God and prayer, and the necessity of good works as evidence of God's grace. When he departed, he left them a volume of sermons by Ralph Erskine which they eagerly read. As a result of these improvements, their

---

[35] Ibid., 196.
[36] Ibid. Alexander related that a pious lady told him Austin was more useful in relieving distressed souls than even Samuel Davies, James Waddell or the Smith brothers—John Blair Smith and Samuel Stanhope Smith.
[37] John Gillies and Horatius Bonar, *Historical Collections of Accounts of Revival*, 2 Volumes in One, (Edinburgh, Scotland and Carlisle, Pennsylvania: The Banner of Truth Trust, 1981), 336.

meetings soon increased greatly, according to David Rice. Morris found it necessary to travel fifteen, twenty, and thirty miles away to read Erskine's sermons to anxious crowds at the various reading rooms.

To show their gratitude for Robinson's ministry, the people of Hanover took up a considerable sum of money which they presented to Robinson as an offering, but he refused their gift. The committee then secretly placed it in his saddlebag during the last night of his stay in Hanover. He already had begun his journey the next morning when he stopped to refresh himself. He discovered the gift in his saddlebag and returned to Hanover. He entreated the people to keep the money, but they refused. He then told them:

> I see you are resolved. I shall have your money; I shall take it; but as I told you before, I do not need it; I have enough, nor will I appropriate it to my own use; but there is a young man of my acquaintance of promising talents and piety, who is now studying with a view to the ministry, but his circumstances are embarrassing, he has not funds to support and carry him on without much difficulty; this money will relieve him from his pecuniary difficulties: I will take charge of it and appropriate it to his use; and as soon as he is licensed we will send him to visit you; it may be, that you may now, by your liberality, be educating a minister for yourselves.[38]

The young man Robinson had in mind was Samuel Davies. Samuel Blair said Robinson gave forty pounds on one occasion and twenty pounds on another to assist in Davies' education. These gifts enabled Davies to finish his course sooner than he would have otherwise. The Hanover group found such agreement with Robinson's ministry that they applied for membership in New Castle Presbytery.

Robinson proceeded from Hanover to the Shenandoah Valley, according to his original plan. A report that he was to be arrested by the civil magistrate for preaching at Hanover without a license made him leave the area very suddenly.

Other Ministers Sent by New Castle Presbytery

New Castle Presbytery sent other ministers on short preaching tours to Hanover after Robinson left the area. John Blair, Samuel Blair's brother, and a fellow graduate of the Log College, was the next to come to Virgin-

---

[38] Foote, *Sketches of Virginia*, First Series, 129.

ia, and his preaching was blessed to many hearts. Blair was newly ordained on December 27, 1742 as the pastor of a three church field in Cumberland County, Pennsylvania when New Castle Presbytery sent him to Virginia. Samuel Morris tells us the results of his ministry there:

> Truly he came to us in the fulness of the blessings of the gospel of Christ. Former impressions were ripened, and new ones made on many hearts. One night, in particular, a whole house full of people was quite overcome with the power of the word, particularly of one pungent sentence that dropped from his lips; and they could hardly sit or stand, or keep their passions under any proper restraints, so general was the concern during his stay with us; and so ignorant were we of the danger persons in such a case were in of apostasy, that we pleased ourselves with the expectation of the gathering of more people to the divine Shiloh, than now seem to have actually been gathered to him; though there still be the greatest reason to hope, that sundry bound themselves to the Lord in an everlasting covenant, never to be forgotten.[39]

John Blair was followed in the winter of 1744–45 by John Roan, newly licensed by New Castle Presbytery, who supplied Hanover for a longer period than either of his predecessors. Roan was sometimes intemperate in his remarks about the Anglican clergy, which caused troubles for the Dissenters in Hanover. Morris reports that on one occasion, "a perfidious wretch deposed he heard Mr. Roan utter blasphemous expressions in his sermons."[40] Roan preached on January 7–9, 1745, at the home of Joshua Morris in James County, where he was accused of making defamatory statements about the established church such as:

> "At church you pray to the devil"—and "That your good works damn you, and carry you to hell,"—"That all your ministers preach false doctrine, and that they, and all who follow them, are going to hell"—and "The church is the house of the Devil,—that when your ministers receive their orders they swear that it is the spirit of God that moves them to it, but it is the spirit of the Devil, and no good can proceed out of their mouths."[41]

---

[39] Joseph Tracy, *The Great Awakening: A History of the Revival of Religion in the Time of Edwards and Whitefield* (Edinburgh, Scotland and Carlisle, Pennsylvania: The Banner of Truth Trust, 1976), 381.
[40] Foote, *Sketches of Virginia*, First Series, 134.
[41] Wesley Marsh Gewehr, *The Great Awakening in Virginia: 1740–1790* (Durham, NC: Duke University Press, 1930), 56.

Governor Gooch became concerned when affidavits were presented to him concerning Roan's preaching in Hanover and James counties. On information received from James Axford, the grand jury drew up an indictment against him on April 19, 1745, but Roan had already left the colony. The Governor issued an order that Moravians, Muggletonians[42], and New Light Presbyterians were forbidden to meet and gave his reason as follows:

> Without a breach of charity, we may pronounce that 'tis not liberty of conscience, but freedom of speech, they so earnestly prosecute.[43]

In those words, the Governor indicated that he thought it was within the power of his administration to grant liberty of conscience to its citizens which would also mean that he thought that the government could withhold the same. If liberty of conscience does not carry with it freedom of speech, then it is simply a matter of the secret thoughts of an individual's mind. Liberty of conscience is nothing without freedom of speech. No power on earth can prevent a person from entertaining his own thoughts.

Gooch's attitude towards the New Light Presbyterians was in stark contrast to what he had written several years earlier to the Synod of Philadelphia on November 4, 1738:

> Sir, by the hands of Mr. Anderson[44] I received an address signed by you[45], in the name of your brethren of the Synod of Philadelphia. And as I have been always inclined to favour the people who have lately removed from other provinces, to settle on the western side of the great mountains, so

---

[42] Muggletonianism was a small movement of a general Protestant nature that was started in 1651 when two London tailors, John Reeve and Lodowicke Muggleton, came to the conviction that they were the last two prophets of the book of Revelation. Their basic belief was that God does not intervene in the everyday affairs of life until He brings the world to an end. Thus, their position is the opposite of Quakerism which taught the "inner light." Muggleton and his followers believed that there is no inner light possible.

[43] Richard Webster, *History of the Presbyterian Church in America: From Its Origin Until the Year 1760* (Philadelphia: Joseph Wilson, 1857), 499.

[44] James Anderson (1678–1740) was the pastor of Donegal Presbyterian Church along the Susquehanna River in Lancaster County, Pennsylvania at that time.

[45] This letter of Governor Gooch was addressed to Richard Treat, the Moderator of the Synod of Philadelphia in 1738. Treat was pastor at Abingdon Presbyterian Church in Pennsylvania and was initially supportive of the majority opposed to the Great Awakening. In 1739, he became convinced of his formality in religion through hearing a sermon of Whitefield and sided with the New Lights in the division of 1741.

you be assured, that no interruption shall be given to any of your profession who shall come among them, so as they conform themselves to the rules prescribed by the act of toleration in England, by taking the oaths enjoined thereby, and registering the places of their meeting, and behave themselves peaceably toward the government. This you may communicate to the Synod as an answer of theirs. Your most humble servant.
William Gooch.[46]

In this communication, Governor Gooch set forth several things that are instructive concerning the difficulties that the New Light Presbyterians encountered in Virginia. First, Gooch promised his favor to those who settled on the western side of the great mountains of Appalachia. The clear implication is that no such favor was promised to those who settled east of the mountains in the areas of the colony populated mostly by the Anglicans. Second, he acknowledges that the rules of the Act of Toleration in England were in force in Virginia. Third, he promised that ministers who took the oaths required by the Act of Toleration and registered their meetinghouses would not be interrupted.

In the midst of these accusations against Roan, Patrick Henry wrote to the Rev. William Dawson, the new Commissary of Virginia, on February 13, 1745. This letter was prejudicial to the New Light Presbyterians in Hanover and the representatives from the Synod of New York. John Thomson, the Old Light Presbyterian minister and initiator of the 1729 Act of Subscription, was then laboring in western Virginia.[47] Thomson aided Henry in his preparation of a prejudicial report against the New Lights as a result of what he considered a snub by the Presbyterians in Hanover County. Roan and the Dissenters at Hanover had refused to let Thomson preach at the "Morris Reading House," so he preached for Henry at St. Paul's Parish. Henry gave the Commissary the following account of his conversation with Thomson:

He entertained me with a distinct account of these new light men, their

---

[46] *Records of the Presbyterian Church in the United States of America: Embracing the Minutes of the Presbytery of Philadelphia, From A.D. 1708 to 1716; Minutes of the Synod of Philadelphia, From A. D. 1717 to 1758; Minutes of the Synod of New York, From A.D. 1745 to 1758; Minutes of the Synod of Philadelphia and New York, From A. D. 1758 to 1788* (Philadelphia: Presbyterian Board of Publication, 1841), 145.

[47] Presbyterians were more tolerated west of the mountains in Virginia because they provided a buffer against the Indian populations. Thompson was extended all the privileges of the Act of Toleration of 1681 while the Hanover Presbyterians were denied those same rights.

particular tenets, and practices, their rise and progress to this time. He is, in my opinion, a man of learning and good sense, a strenuous opposer of these new preachers and Whitefield, having published two small treatises against them[48] . . . and I believe he is a man of piety and veracity.[49]

Henry, particularly, objected to the New Lights' insistence "that a minister being unconverted hath no call or authority from God to preach the Gospel and such a minister's preaching, tho' he preach sound doctrine, can be of no saving use to the hearers."[50] Even in Virginia, Tennent's sermon on "The Dangers of an Unconverted Ministry" became a lightning rod for criticism of the New Lights. Henry also gave the Commissary a one-sided account of the events that led to the disruption of the Synod of Philadelphia in 1741 while clearly siding with the Old Lights. He leveled the charge against Robinson, Blair, and Roan that they were gathering an immoral group of people and teaching them to boast of their assurance of salvation while still being guilty of lying, cheating, theft, and gross immoralities.[51] Part of Henry's missive was taken up in castigating the laymen who were involved in this revival. In addition to Samuel Morris, Roger Shackleford and Thomas Green were singled out for criticism in this letter. Shackleford had allegedly accused Henry of being graceless and preaching "Damnable doctrine," while Green supposedly spoke against the Liturgy of the Anglican Church. Interestingly, Henry seemed to want the Act of Uniformity to still be in force in the colony and Dissenters to be compelled to worship according to the *Book of Common Prayer*. Thus, he wished to limit the Act of Toleration to Great Britain and to not extend it to the British colonies where earlier ministers had fled when persecuted because of the Act of Uniformity. In conclusion, Henry solicited the aid of Commissary Dawson in preventing the representatives from the Synod of New York from administering the sacraments in Hanover the following month.[52]

---

[48] Those works were *The Government of the Church of Christ* and *The Doctrine of Conviction Set in a Clear Light*. The latter was in opposition to Gilbert Tennent's Nottingham sermon.
[49] "Letters of Patrick Henry, Sr., Samuel Davies, James Maury, Edwin Conway and George Task," from Dawson Manuscripts, Library of Congress, *William and Mary Quarterly*, Second Series, I (October 1921), 261.
[50] Ibid., 263.
[51] Ibid., 264.
[52] Ibid, 265–266.

The case was docketed for the October meeting of the General Court. In May, Samuel Morris and three other representatives from Hanover attended the spring meeting of the Synod of New York where they were successful in gaining the support of that body. Thus, the Synod sent Gilbert Tennent and Samuel Finley to represent the cause of the Presbyterians in Hanover before the governor and to officiate a few days among them.[53] When Tennent and Finley arrived in the colony, they immediately met with Governor Gooch, who assured them that members of their body would be protected under the Act of Toleration as long as they qualified themselves according to law. Despite Henry's efforts, Tennent and Finley were able to proceed to Hanover which revived the wilting spirits of the people and they continued there for about a week. Morris' account of that week is as follows:

> The people of God were refreshed, and sundry careless sinners were awakened. Some that had confided before in their moral conduct and religious duties, were convinced of the depravity of their nature, and the necessity of being renewed in the spirit of their mind.[54]

On May 28, 1745, the Synod of Philadelphia sent a letter to Governor Gooch to prejudice him against the New Light Presbyterian ministers, to which he replied on June 20th, as follows:

> And in answer to your present address, intended to justify yourselves and members from being concerned in a late outrage committed against the purity of our worship, and the sacred appointment of pastors for the service of the altar of the established church, which some men calling themselves ministers, were justly accused of in my charge to the grand jury...
>
> As the wicked and destructive doctrines and practices of itinerant preachers ought to be opposed and suppressed by all who have concern for religion, and just regard to public peace and order in church and state, so your missionaries producing proper testimonies, complying with the laws, and performing divine service in some certain place appropriated for that purpose... may be sure of the protection...[55]

In that letter, Gooch revealed his prejudice against the New Light

---

[53] Gewehr, *Great Awakening in Virginia*, 56.
[54] Tracy, *Great Awakening*, 382.
[55] *Minutes of the Synod of Philadelphia, From A. D. 1717 to 1758* in *Records of the Presbyterian Church in the United States of America*, 183

Presbyterians and in favor of the Old Lights, his promises to Tennent and Finley notwithstanding. Gooch's future interactions with the New Lights would manifest this primal prejudice against them. Despite the machinations of the Synod of Philadelphia, Patrick Henry, and others, the indictment eventually came to nothing. The primary witness fled the colony when he heard that Tennent and Finley were dispatched by the Synod of New York, and the six witnesses cited by the attorney general could not testify that Roan had uttered such statements. The more immediate concern, though, was that "all circumstances seemed to threaten the extirpation of religion among the dissenters in these parts."[56]

William Tennent, Jr., Samuel Blair, and George Whitefield Visit Hanover

Following the uproar occasioned by Roan's visit to Virginia, every New Light minister thereafter sent to that colony by the Synod of Virginia was punctilious in observing the admonition of Governor Gooch to qualify himself according to the law. Some time afterwards, both William Tennent, Jr. and Samuel Blair were sent to Virginia and, passing through Williamsburg, humbly petitioned the Governor's permission to officiate in the colony. They spent about two weeks in Hanover with evidence of many blessings. Morris's narrative continues:

> They administered the sacrament of the Lord's Supper among us before their departure; which was the first administration of that heavenly ordinance among us since our dissent from the Church of England; and we have reason to remember it till our last moments, as a most glorious day of the Son of man. The assembly was large, and the novelty of the mode of administration did peculiarly engage their attention. The children were abundantly fed, and others were brought to thirst after righteousness. It appeared as one of the days of heaven to some of us; and we could hardly help wishing we could, with Joshua, have delayed the revolutions of the heavens, to prolong it.[57]

In October of 1744, Whitefield had returned to America for his third missionary tour; and, for the first time with a wife. The great evangelist had married the widow, Elizabeth James, and this was her first trip to

---

[56] Tracy, *Great Awakening*, 382.
[57] Ibid., 383.

The Great Awakening Comes to Virginia

the colonies. Almost as soon as he arrived in America, Whitefield became sick and even he anticipated that this sickness would result in his death. Yet, he recovered slowly. At the time, Great Britain was in the midst of a war which pitted the British Crown, the Dutch Republic, and Austria against France and Germany. Whitefield himself was in a different war. The excesses and fanaticism of the Great Awakening were unjustly being blamed on him. Whatever excesses had taken place in New England and the middle colonies, the Old Dominion was relatively free of such. The revival there was less tainted with detrimental features. Thus, it is not surprising that Whitefield paid a visit to Hanover of a few days which was reported by Morris as follows:

> Mr. Whitefield came and preached four or five days in these parts; which was the happy means of giving us further encouragement, and engaging others to the Lord, especially among the Church people, who received his doctrines more readily than they would have from ministers of the Presbyterian denomination.[58]

Whitefield's visit was especially troubling for Henry. Both men were ministers in the Church of England, but they were opposites in doctrine and spirit. Arriving in Hanover on a Friday, Whitefield requested the opportunity to preach for Henry on the next Lord's Day. Henry then notified Whitefield that an interview would be necessary before he could offer him the use of his pulpit. In a letter to Commissary Dawson on October 14, 1745, Henry described what happened that Sunday:

> Next day I set out for Church and was told by the way that he was to preach either in the Church or Churchyard. I found a great multitude waiting for him at Church, and after consulting some of my friends, I thought it advisable to give him leave to preach in the Church, on this condition that he read the common prayer etc. before sermon, which when he came, he consented to do and accordingly read prayers and preached.[59]

James Allen was converted through that sermon by Whitefield, according to Archibald Alexander, and afterwards joined in with the Presbyterians at the Morris Reading Room:

> While Whitefield was preaching, Mr. Allen fell at full length, as suddenly

---

[58] Ibid., 382.
[59] "Letters of Patrick Henry, Sr., et. al.," 267.

as if shot through the heart, and lay for the remainder of the evening as one dead.[60]

When Allen regained consciousness, he had undergone a hopeful conversion to the gospel. Such scenes of the power of the gospel were hard to endure for cold, formal ministers like Henry and his Anglican brethren in Virginia.

In his report to Dawson, Henry ignored all mention of Allen's conversion, but stated that Whitefield encouraged the Dissenters to return to the Anglican Church. Morris's account of Whitefield's visit, though, makes no mention of any such advice by the great evangelist. It is more likely that Henry was trying to justify his actions in allowing a warm friend of the New Light Presbyterian to preach in his pulpit.

After Whitefield's departure, the people at Hanover were without any other ministerial supply from the Presbytery of New Castle for nearly eighteen months. Yet, God began this important work and He would perfect it in His own time through the instrument of His choosing.

Conclusion

The Great Awakening began in Virginia at nearly the same time that it was at its zenith in the northern colonies. In its outset, the revival in Virginia was not the result of itinerant preaching, though a succession of ministers helped spread the flames after it had begun. Where human instruments were used in many instances in the New England and the Middle colonies, there were no such instruments that initiated the religious outbreak in the Old Dominion. The common bond was the Holy Spirit who works in wondrous ways according to the will of God. Without the Holy Spirit, all the most passionate words of Whitefield, Edwards, Gilbert Tennent, Samuel Blair, and others would have proved powerless to convert a single soul. Thus, it is not surprising that the Holy Spirit used the written word, rather than the spoken word, to effect spiritual conviction in the hearts of Morris and others at Hanover. Revival is God's extraordinary work and He alone is sovereign in all the results of it.

---

[60] Alexander, *Life of Archibald Alexander*, 178.

-5-

Set Apart for the Gospel

"No man may intrude into the sheepfold as an under-shepherd; he must have an eye to the chief Shepherd, and wait his beck and command. Or ever a man stands forth as God's ambassador, he must wait for the call from above; and if he does not do so, but rushes into the sacred office, the Lord will say to him and others like him, 'I sent them not, neither commanded them; therefore they shall not profit this people at all, saith the Lord.' Jer. Xxiii.32."[1]

~*Charles Haddon Spurgeon in* Lectures to My Students~

Marker for Wicomico Presbyterian Church in Somerset County, Maryland, where Davies preached in the winter of 1746-7

---

[1] C. H. Spurgeon, *Lectures to My Students* (Grand Rapids, Michigan: Associated Publishers and Authors, Inc., n.d.), 19.

On August 1, 1746, William Robinson—Davies' teacher, mentor, benefactor, pastor, and friend—departed this world at St. George's in New Castle County, Delaware for his heavenly mansion. His funeral sermon was preached by Samuel Blair on August 3rd from Psalm 112:6, "The righteous shall be in everlasting remembrance," and Robinson was buried in the cemetery near the St. George's Presbyterian Church. On March 19, 1746, New Brunswick Presbytery had released Robinson to the care of New Castle Presbytery so that he could become pastor of the St. George's congregation. Five years of intensive preaching as an itinerant evangelist from New York to North Carolina had so weakened his constitution that he was unable "to bear much sickness" and, thus, he became "an easy Prey for Death."[2] He died before being installed as pastor of the congregation he had established in 1742 with the help of George Whitefield. His last days were spent in "serenity and peace," while his earnestness for the salvation of others was described by Blair:

> With what Importunity and vehement Desire would he plead with God, for the Life of perishing Sinners! He bore such a Sense of the deplorable Case of the Unregenerate upon his Heart, and was so full of tender Compassions for them, that it seem'd many Times, as if he knew not how to leave off insisting on the Subject, when imploring God on their Account. And in what a solemn pathetick manner would he deal with them in his Sermon![3]

Samuel Davies was among those grieving friends who visited Robinson in his last hours. After completing his studies at Blair's academy in the spring of 1746, he immediately returned to his parents' home at Summit Ridge, Delaware. David and Martha Davies were attending St. George's, and Samuel's name was on the membership records of the church during this period. Webster records that "on his deathbed [Robinson] left it as his last request to Davies to go to Hanover. To him he bequeathed most of his books, having previously aided him with money."[4]

---

[2] Samuel Blair, *A Sermon Preached at the Funeral of the Reverend Mr. William Robinson*, (Philadelphia: William and Bradford, 1746), 24. The original MS is in the Princeton Theological Seminary Library, Princeton, New Jersey.
[3] Ibid.
[4] Richard Webster, *A History of the Presbyterian Church in America*, (Philadelphia: Joseph M. Wilson, 1857), 477, footnote.

The esteem in which Davies held Robinson is revealed in his own words some years later:

> [T]hat favoured man, Mr. Robinson, whose success whenever I reflect upon it, astonishes me. Oh, he did much in a little time! — and who would not choose such an expeditious pilgrimage through the world![5]

The esteem in which Blair and Davies held Robinson was shared by Archibald Alexander who wrote about him:

> Probably Mr. Robinson during the short period of his life was the instrument in the conversion of as many souls as any minister who ever lived in this country.[6]

Davies spent the days after graduation from Fagg's Manor in final preparations for his licensure examination before the Presbytery of New Castle. His habits of study at Blair's Academy had greatly weakened his health and he was already suffering from the first stages of tuberculosis.[7] When Presbytery met on July 30, Davies was licensed to preach for the customary period of six months. Two days later, Robinson completed his course just as Davies was beginning his. Following licensure, Davies immediately began supplying the vacant pulpits in Pennsylvania, Maryland and Delaware where his efforts were received with great approval. Samuel Finley gives us the following information:

> When he was licensed to preach the gospel, he zealously declared the counsel of God, the truth and importance of which he knew by happy experience; and did it in such a manner as excited the earnest desires of every vacant congregation, where he was known, to obtain the happiness of his stated ministrations.[8]

Marriage to Sarah Kirkpatrick

Graduation from Blair's academy at Fagg's Manor, licensure by New Castle Presbytery, and the death of Robinson were not the only great

---

[5] William Henry Foote, *Sketches of Virginia: Historical and Biographical*, First Series (Philadelphia: William S. Martien, 1850) 124–125.
[6] Archibald Alexander, *The Log College* (London: The Banner of Truth Trust, 1968), 209.
[7] Thomas Jefferson Wertenbaker, *Princeton: 1746–1896* (Princeton: Princeton University Press, 1974), 45. Wertenbaker suggests Davies died from tuberculosis.
[8] Samuel Finley, "Sermon on the Death of the Rev. Samuel Davies," in Samuel Davies, *Sermons on Important Subjects*, I (New York: J & J Harper, 1828), 21.

events in 1746 for Davies. Soon to follow was his marriage to his childhood sweetheart, Sarah Kirkpatrick, the daughter of John and Elinor Kirkpatrick[9] of Chester, Pennsylvania. John was a ruling elder in the Nottingham Presbyterian Church who had emigrated to the colonies from Scotland around 1711 along with his first wife, Margaret, and an infant son, Hugh. In the New World, Margaret quickly gave him a daughter named after herself, but she died either in childbirth or shortly thereafter. John remarried a year later and his new wife, Elinor, gave him five additional progeny—Elenor, John, William, Sarah, and Jane. Sarah's half-brother, Hugh, spent several years in the Presbyterian ministry before his death at Chester in 1768 at the age of 58.

In the eighteenth century, courtship and marriage were quite different from today. The bride's parents were more actively involved in the process of selecting a suitable spouse for their daughter, who was expected to marry between the ages of twenty to twenty-three for optimal child-bearing. Social occasions were, therefore, provided by the parents for young men and women to meet and court one another. Whirlwind courtships leading to marriage were the norm in those days. It is not known when Samuel first met Sarah Kirkpatrick, but the arrangements for such a meeting were undoubtedly made through two Presbyterian ministers, Samuel Blair and Samuel Finley, with the consent of Sarah's parents. Blair and Finley were both graduates of the Log College, and their congregations were only a few miles from one another.

The Kirkpatrick-Davies wedding was celebrated on Sunday, October 23, 1746, at the Nottingham Presbyterian Church with Finley performing the service. The bride was twenty-one at the time of the wedding and was a good match for the aspiring minister with her strong religious background. There are no records of the guest list for this wedding, but it is not hard to imagine that one hundred or more people witnessed it. In addition to the extended Kirkpatrick family, there were many friends in both the Nottingham and Fagg's Manor churches who would have been present to witness this union. Samuel's parents and relatives lived forty miles to the south of Chester, Pennsylvania, and a large number of them

---

[9] Samuel A. Gayley, *An Historical Sketch of the Lower West Nottingham Presbyterian Church* (Philadelphia: Alfred Martien, 1865), 10. Further genealogical information is at: http://www.geni.com/people/John-Kirkpatrick/6000000003613958254, accessed on August 4, 2016.

would have attended as well. Samuel Blair and his family were no doubt gathered with the congregation on this date and Blair might have assisted Finley in the service. Following the ceremony, the newlyweds lived with Samuel's parents in Delaware while he preached at vacant pulpits and prepared for his ordination examination.

Set Apart for the Gospel
After his probationary period of licensure, Davies' was examined for ordination by presbytery on February 19, 1747, which trials of the court he passed with extraordinary approval. He was then ordained as an evangelist to the vacant congregations in Virginia, particularly the Hanover congregation. "His prudence and piety were of that order called for in difficult posts in the Lord's vineyard. All these things designated him as the proper person to send to the interesting, yet perplexing field of Hanover County, Virginia."[10]

About six weeks later, Davies left his pregnant wife and parents behind to fulfill this order of presbytery. He traveled down the eastern shores[11] of Maryland and Virginia, crossed the Chesapeake Bay by ferry, and immediately rode to Williamsburg, the Capitol of Virginia. Waiting on the General Court of Virginia on Friday, April 14, 1747, Davies laid before them his petition to officiate at four meetinghouses in the vicinity of Hanover. Governor Gooch was impressed by Davies' dignified and courteous appearance, but the court hesitated.

> Davies in after years may have appeared more grand, but he never appeared more interesting than when he modestly asked of the court, and finally obtained by the influence of the Governor, permission to preach the gospel unmolested, to the vexed and harassed people of God, in Hanover.[12]

Davies' petition was granted by the court before the end of the day with the stipulation that the Dissenters must behave themselves peaceably. With license in hand, he hastened to Hanover to share the glad news and preach for them on Sunday, April 16. This surprising turn of events

---

[10] Foote, *Sketches of Virginia*, First Series, 159.
[11] The eastern shores of Maryland and Virginia are bordered on the west by the Chesapeake Bay and on the east by the Atlantic Ocean.
[12] Foote, *Sketches of Virginia*, First Series, 160.

came at a time when many of the Dissenters were confused and discouraged. The doors of the Morris Reading Room had been shut by order of the civil magistrate on the previous Lord's Day to all itinerant ministers under threat of penalty. Several people at Hanover were also scheduled to appear before the court for their failure to attend the Established Church and some of them had already been heavily fined. William Henry Foote tells us that:

> The coming of Dr. Davies, with his license, was like a visit from the angel of mercy. His ardent sermons refreshed the congregation, and his legal protection turned the enmity of the opposers to their own mortification.[13]

Davies' account of those days is as follows:

> I preached frequently in Hanover and some of the adjacent counties; and though the fervour of the late work was considerably abated, and my labours were not blessed with success equal to that of my brethren, yet I have reason to hope they were of service in several instances. The importunities they used with me to settle with them were invincible; and upon my departure, they sent a call for me to the Presbytery.[14]

Six weeks of his preaching convinced the people at Hanover that Davies was the man of God's choosing for them.

> The month of April, 1747, in Hanover county, Virginia, was one of those times in which, the current of human events, running on with increasing bitterness, takes an unexpected turn; the waters of Mara are sweetened, and the night of clouds and thick darkness has its morning of brightness and joy.[15]

While in Virginia, Davies subscribed in a general way to the Thirty-Nine Articles of the Church of England, according to the requirements of the Act of Toleration. It was permissible to dissent from any article not striking at the vitals of the faith and he gave his reasons in writing for dissenting to any part thereof. On April 21, 1747, Davies wrote to the Reverend Clergy of the Anglican Church in Virginia and directed his letter to Rev. Patrick Henry, the rector of St. Paul's Parish in Hanover. Davies subscribed to thirty-four of the articles without reservation. His dif-

---

[13] Ibid., 162.
[14] Ibid.
[15] Ibid., 157.

ferences with the other five Articles were as follows:

> 1. Concerning Article Three, the phrase "He went down into Hell," Davies understood not to be a reference to a "local Descent into the place properly called Hell where the damned are, but either being in a State of the Dead; or his enduring extreme Misery & great Distress; or his lying in the Grave."[16]
> 2. Concerning Article Six, he dissented from "the Reading of the Apocryphal Books in publick Religious Assemblies."[17]
> 3. Concerning Article Twenty, he differed with the idea that the "Church hath Power to decree Rites & Ceremonies."[18] Davies held to the Regulative Principle that Scripture alone governs worship and man does not have authority to introduce new practices.
> 4. Concerning Article Twenty-One, he expostulated that the Church can call general councils to decide matters of doctrine or great importance without the command of the civil magistrate.[19]
> 5. Concerning Article Thirty-Seven, he denied that the civil magistrate is the head of the church. Thus, he denied the Erastian idea that the state can exercise control of the church. He clearly believed that Christ alone is the head of the church.[20]

Davies' differences with the Thirty-Nine Articles were mostly minor, which legally qualified him under the Act of Toleration to serve as a Dissenting minister in an Anglican colony. Yet, Patrick Henry was alarmed by this New Light minister who had gained a license to preach within the bounds of his parish. In a letter to Rev. William Dawson on June 8, 1747, he complained concerning Davies that "all of his Fraternity were disturbers of the societies of Christians of all Denominations, by declining to settle in any place" and that he was "confirmed in that opinion. . . by Mr. Davies's conduct."[21] It apparently never occurred to Henry that Presbyterians could never be more than itinerants in Virgin-

---

[16] "Letters of Patrick Henry, Sr., Samuel Davies, James Maury, Edwin Conway and George Trask," from the Dawson manuscripts, Library of Congress, William and Mary Quarterly, Second Series, I (October 1921), 268.
[17] Ibid.
[18] Ibid.
[19] Ibid.
[20] Ibid., 269.
[21] "Letters of Patrick Henry, Sr., Samuel Davies, James Maury, Edwin Conway and George Trask," 272.

ia as long as they were forbidden licenses to officiate at particular congregations!

Davies left Hanover around June 8, 1747 and set out on a preaching circuit which took him as far as Roanoke, nearly 175 miles southwest of Hanover. His first stop was at Goochland, thirty miles west of Hanover, where he preached on Thursday, June 11. An advertisement announcing Davies' preaching plans was placed on the doors of the Goochland Court House where it was "seen by hundreds" to the exasperation of Henry. Printed circulars of the times and places of his other meetings were distributed widely, and anxious crowds gave attention to his services. Preaching appointments were probably arranged in Amelia, Lunenberg, Cumberland, and Augusta counties. Robinson had labored in this region four years earlier with great success and the Presbytery of New Castle appointed Davies to cultivate the fruit of his labors. Henry's complaint about Davies' activities, though, had some merit because the General Court had only licensed him to preach to the four meetinghouses in and around Hanover County.

After completing this circuit, Davies returned to the Welsh Tract in Delaware where he arrived sometime in the late summer. By this date, Sarah Davies was in the seventh or eighth month of her pregnancy with their first child. His joy was soon turned to gloom, though, when Sarah died in labor and their son was stillborn. Samuel's only reference to this matter is a single sentence in his Bible: "Separated from her by Death & bereaved of an abortive Son Sep. 15."[22] His own consumptive illness, coupled with the deaths of his wife and infant son, sunk him into a melancholy state from which he only slowly recovered.

Preaching in Somerset County, Maryland

After burying mother and child, Davies spent the next six months in preaching tours to several places in Pennsylvania and Maryland. Two months were spent in Somerset County, Maryland, where a considerable revival had flourished through Robinson's preaching in 1745. Davies described the beginning of this revival to a friend in 1751:

> The most glorious display of Divine grace in Maryland has been in and

---

[22] Samuel Davies' Old Testament. Samuel Davies MS in Virginia Historical Society, Richmond, Virginia.

about Somerset county. It was begun, I think, in 1745, by the ministry of Mr. Robinson, and was afterwards carried on by several ministers that preached transiently there. I was there about two months, when the work was at its height, and I never saw such a deep and spreading concern: the assemblies were numerous, though in the extremity of a cold Winter, and unwearied in attending the word; and frequently there were very few among them that did not give some plain indications of distress or joy. Oh! those were the happiest days that ever my eyes saw. Since that, the harvest seems over there, though considerable gleanings, I hear, are still gathered.[23]

Thomas Gibbons gives additional information about Davies' preaching in Maryland:

> Finding himself upon the borders of the grave, and without any hopes of recovery, he determined to spend the little remains of an almost exhausted life, as he apprehended it, in endeavoring to advance his Master's glory in the good of souls. Accordingly he removed from the place where he was to another, about a hundred miles distance,[24] that was then in want of a minister. Here he laboured in season and out of season; and as he told me preached in the day, and had his hectic fever by night, and that to such a degree as to be sometimes delirious, and to stand in need of persons to sit up with him.[25]

Somerset County had earlier been the scene of the labors of Francis Makemie (1658-1708), the father of American Presbyterianism. Makemie was ordained by the Laggan Presbytery of Ireland in 1681 and sent to the American colonies as a missionary in response to the urgent appeal of Colonel William Stevens of Maryland in December of 1680. In Somerset County, Makemie founded the Snow Hill and Rehoboth Presbyterian churches, but his labors were not restricted to the Eastern Shore of Maryland. He traveled from South Carolina to New England, like a flying angel, preaching the everlasting gospel. His industry was greatly blessed of the Lord and he was prominent in forming the first Presbyterian judicatory in the colonies in 1706, the Presby-

---

[23] John Gillies and Horatius Bonar, *Historical Collections* (London: The Banner of Truth Trust, 1983), 337–338.
[24] Somerset County, Maryland is almost exactly 100 miles south of Summit Ridge, Delaware on the peninsula of the eastern shores of Maryland and Virginia.
[25] Thomas Gibbons, "Divine Conduct Vindicated," in Samuel Davies, *Sermons on Important Subjects*, I (New York: J & J Harper, 1828), 32–33.

tery of Philadelphia, serving as its Moderator in December of that same year.

In Somerset County, God gave Davies the first-fruits of his ministry in the remarkable conversion of two gentlemen whom he afterwards had "good reason to believe. . . were saints indeed" and who yielded "the fruits meet for repentance in a holy and well-ordered conversation."[26] Thomas Gibbons described what happened next:

> One of the Gentlemen. . . came into the assembly where Mr. Davies preached, with the greatest signs of contempt imaginable, but before the assembly was broken up, appeared to be indeed pricked to the heart under a Sermon from these words, Matt. xxii. 5. *But they made light of it*. The other gentleman. . . under the character of a *dark, bewildered, doubtful, anxious soul*. . . had been for some time in such a condition . . . but Mr. Davies's endeavors for his illumination and comfort were not only employed on his behalf, but. . . *were not in vain in the Lord*.[27]

There are no extant sermons dated from Davies' time at Somerset County, but an undated sermon on Matthew 22:5, "The Nature and Danger of Making Light of Christ," was concluded with these words:

> I cannot but fear, after all, that some of you as, usual, will continue careless and impenitent. Well, when you are suffering the punishment of this sin in hell, remember that you were warned and acquit from being accessory to your ruin. And when we all appear before the supreme Judge, and I am called to give an account of my ministry: when I am asked, "Did you warn these creatures of their sin? Did you lay before them their guilt in making light of these things?" you will allow me to answer, "Yes, Lord, I warned them in the best manner I could, but they would not believe me; they would not regard what I said, though enforced by the authority of thy awful name, and confirmed by thine own word." O Sirs, must I give in this accusation against any of you? No, rather have mercy upon yourselves, and have mercy upon me, that I may give an account of you with joy, and not with grief.[28]

Whether that sermon was first preached in some form during the days of Davies' itineration in Somerset County or not, the sentiments ex-

---

[26] Ibid.
[27] Ibid., cv.
[28] Samuel Davies, *Sermons on Important Subjects*, I (New York: J & J Harper, 1828), 157.

pressed in it were certainly similar to the thoughts he must have expressed on that occasion. In addition to his labors in Somerset County, Davies also preached at Church Hill in Queen Anne's county, Maryland, along the eastern shore of the Chesapeake Bay, which was about thirty miles from his parents' home. His preaching at Church Hill supplemented the earlier ministry of Robinson to these same people and produced a great blessing. In Baltimore County, Maryland, there was such an extensive revival in 1746-7 that it seemed to Davies "like the first planting of religion there."[29]

After two months in Somerset County, Davies returned to the Welsh Tract and slowly began to recover from the sickness which "he then looked upon. . . only as the intermission of a disorder that would finally prove mortal."[30] During his convalescence, he had additional opportunities to supply the St. George's congregation and was preparing to "settle in ease near my native place."[31] Additionally, the churches he had supplied in Maryland were vacant and very anxious for his permanent services, as well as others in Pennsylvania. As Davies later wrote:

> Sundry congregations in Pennsylvania, my native country, and in other northern colonies, most earnestly importuned me to settle among them, where I should have had at least an equal temporal maintenance, incomparably more care, leisure, and peace, and the happiness of the frequent society of my brothers.[32]

Before Davies could accept a call to St. George's, or one of the other calls before him, a messenger from Hanover arrived with an urgent request for his services "signed by about one hundred and fifty heads of families." This latest effort by the Hanover congregation, aided by a living voice that represented their earnest desires, moved his heart and he determined to accept their call. At a later time, he described his decision as follows:

> I put my life in my hand and determined to accept their call, hoping I might live to prepare the way for some more useful successor, and willing

---

[29] Webster, *History of the Presbyterian Church in America*, 653.
[30] Foote, *Sketches of Virginia*, First Series, 163.
[31] Samuel Davies, *Sermons on Important Subjects*, IV (London: W. Baynes and Son, 1824), 455.
[32] Webster, *History of the Presbyterian Church in America*, 551.

to expire under the fatigues of duty rather than in voluntary negligence.[33]

Davies' call to Hanover was prosecuted before the Presbytery of New Castle on April 13, 1748, twelve months after he had visited the colony of Virginia. His only condition for accepting this call was that his close friend, John Rodgers, be permitted to assist him for several months, which was most agreeable with Presbytery. Davies' sermon before Presbytery became his first printed work, "A Sermon on Man's Primitive State; and the First Covenant. Delivered Before the Reverend Presbytery of New Castle, April 13th 1748." It was a model exposition of covenant theology, particularly the covenant of works. Taking Genesis 1:27; 2; 16, 17 as his text, he shows that imperfect obedience of the covenant can never be acceptable to God:

> There was the same Reason that he should *obey it perfectly*, as there was that he should *obey it at all*; for if *imperfect* Obedience was allowable, no Obedience at all, or perfect Disobedience might be so too; for as far as Obedience is imperfect, it is no Obedience at all; it is *perfect Disobedience*.[34]

By choosing this subject for his ordination sermon, Davies proved himself to be a sound theologian and knowledgeable of the essential elements of the gospel. In one sentence, he demolished the whole basis of legalism, or neonominism, by showing that so-called sincere obedience is no obedience or simply perfect disobedience. As Wilhelmus a' Brakel once stated:

> Whoever errs or denies the existence of the covenant of works, will not understand the covenant of grace, and will readily err concerning the mediatorship of the Lord Jesus. Such a person will very readily deny that Christ by His active obedience has merited a right to eternal life for the elect.[35]

Davies and John Rodgers Travel to Virginia

Immediately following this meeting of presbytery, Davies and Rodgers set out on horseback for Hanover. Along the way, they were overtaken

---

[33] Foote, *Sketches of Virginia*, First Series, 163.
[34] Samuel Davies, *A Sermon on Man's Primitive State; And the First Covenant* (Philadelphia: William Bradford, 1748), 28.
[35] Bartel Elshout, trans., Wilhelmus a' Brakel, *The Christian's Reasonable Service*, Vol 1 (Ligonier, Pennsylvania: Soli Deo Gloria Publications, 1992), 355.

in a densely wooded part of Virginia by a sudden and violent thunderstorm, miles from the shelter of the nearest house, after darkness had descended. Rodgers suffered with an extreme phobia of thunder and lightning for several years which "neither reason, philosophy, nor religion availed anything" in overcoming and which he feared would hinder his own usefulness as a minister. Samuel Miller gives additional information about that storm:

> The storm came up with great rapidity; the lightning and thunder were violent beyond all description; and the whole scene such as might be supposed to appal the stoutest heart. Their horses, terrified and trembling, refused to proceed. They were obliged to alight; and standing by their beasts, expected every moment to be precipitated into eternity by the resistless element. Providentially, however they escaped unhurt: and the consequence was as wonderful, as the preservation happy. From that hour Mr. Rodgers was entirely delivered from the infirmity which had long given him so much distress! . . . during the whole of his after life, he displayed an unusual degree of composure and self-possession amidst the severest thunder storms.[36]

After the storm passed, they proceeded to Hanover where they rested from their journey. When the Lord's Day arrived, both Davies and Rodgers preached to the eager people at the meetinghouses. Regrettably, Rodgers did not take the necessary steps to qualify himself according to law to preach in Virginia before speaking to the Hanover congregation. The following week, the two young ministers rode to Williamsburg for the purpose of obtaining a license for Rodgers. In the Capitol, Governor Gooch received the two ministers with great kindness and expressed support for their application. The Council, though, was alarmed with the prospects of having another Dissenting minister in the colony and the Anglican clergy were actively opposed to these proceedings.

Rodgers produced his testimonials before the meeting with the Governor and the Council, requesting they be read. Refusing to hear these testimonials, the Council demanded, instead, a private session with the Governor. When the clerk refused his orders to read Rodgers' testimonials, the Governor repeated his demand. Peyton Randolph, the Attorney General,

---

[36] Samuel Miller, *Memoirs of the Rev. John Rodgers, D.D.* (New York: Whiting and Watson, 1813), 26–27.

and some other members of the Council were equally insistent the matter should be considered in private. At this turn of events, Governor Gooch gave in to the Council and, bowing to the ministers, said, "Gentlemen, you shall hear from us in a day or two." As they left the Council that day, it was apparent that most of the members were opposed to Rodgers' application. "They immediately withdrew to their lodgings, shut themselves in their chamber, and poured out their hearts unto God. A separation seemed inevitable, or Virginia must be abandoned."[37]

On the following afternoon, the Governor invited Davies and Rodgers to his residence. Three members of the Council who were friendly to their petition also waited upon them. After exchanging polite introductions, Sir William Gooch addressed Davies as follows: "Sir, it has been with the greatest difficulty that we have been able to prevent the court from revoking your license, and sending you out of the colony. This, however, we have been happy enough to prevent." The Governor had sadder news for Rodgers, though: "I am extremely sorry to inform you, Sir, that the gentlemen of the court will by no means consent to your qualifying, as the law directs, for preaching in the colony."[38] Davies and Rodgers insisted that they were not asking for a privilege but a right granted under the Act of Toleration. The Governor acknowledged the legality of their position, but he pled that his hands were tied.

That same evening, the Governor sent Davies and Rodgers a message advising them to prepare a memorial on their position which they could present to the Court the next day. "Upon this suggestion they prepared a respectful but spirited memorial, which they signed, and presented the next day to the court."[39] The Governor, fearing that his presence would not be helpful, absented himself from that session of the Court. In the Governor's absence, the senior member of the Court presided and ended discussion of the matter with the impassioned declaration: "We have Mr. Rodgers out, and we are determined to keep him out."[40]

The injustice and inconsistency of the Court's decision concerning Rodgers was observed by Davies in a letter to Joseph Bellamy, the Congregational minister at Bethlehem, Connecticut, in 1751:

---

[37] Foote, *Sketches of Virginia*, First Series, 165.
[38] Both Miller and Foote give ample information about these proceedings.
[39] Miller, *Memoirs of Rev. John Rodgers*, 51.
[40] Ibid.

> My dearest Brother, the Rev. Mr. *John Rodgers*, was sent along with me to *Hanover*, to assist me for a few Sabbaths at my first Settlement. But when he offer'd himself in the General Court to take Qualifications enjoined by the Law, he was rejected, under Pretence that his Certificate not being granted by the Synod, and particularly that of *Philadelphia*, but only by the Presbytery, was insufficient, (tho', by the Bye, it was as sufficient as mine, which they had admitted; and given according to universal President among Presbyterians) whereupon he was obliged to return without preaching but one Sermon.[41]

The decision of the General Court was a mockery of justice, as Davies observed. There was nothing in the Act of Toleration which limited tolerance only to the Old Light Synod of Philadelphia since the Presbyterian Church in the colonies was not even established until seventeen years after that Act. Yet, one reason is as good as another when governing officials are determined to act contrary to the law. In reality, the Court was concerned about the growth of the Presbyterian Dissenters in Virginia and was determined to deny them their legal rights.

Patrick Henry, Sr. of St. Paul's Parish in Hanover County followed Davies and Rodgers to Williamsburg for their meeting with the court. His purpose was to complain to Gov. Gooch that Rodgers had preached in Hanover without a license. When he requested that the Governor punish Rodgers, Sir William Gooch revealed the liberality of his own religious sentiments:

> Mr._____, I am surprised at you! You profess to be a minister of Jesus Christ, and you come to me to complain of a man, and wish me to punish him, for preaching the Gospel! For shame, Sir! Go home and mind your own duty! For such a piece of conduct, you deserve to have your gown stript over your shoulders.[42]

The trials against some of the Dissenters in Hanover had been adjudicated only a few days before Rodgers presented himself to the Court. On April 18, 1748, Isaac Winston appeared before the Council and was fined twenty shillings in addition to court costs. Samuel Morris was rendered the identical verdict that same day, but the case of Edward Wat-

---

[41] Samuel Davies, "The State of Religion among the Protestant Dissenters in Virginia; in a letter to the Rev. Mr. Joseph Bellamy, of Bethlem, in New England" (Boston: S. Kneeland, 1751), 21.
[42] Ibid., 54.

kins was unexpectedly dismissed. Both Winston and Morris were fined for having invited John Roan to preach in their meetinghouses without a license. These trials, no doubt, affected the attitude of the General Court towards Rodgers and the Dissenters.

Rodgers and Davies Separate

Since the Court refused his license, Rodgers was strictly forbidden to preach in the colony under the threat of a fine of five hundred pounds and a year's imprisonment. Rodgers "lamented, however, afterwards, that he had not appealed to the King in council; as such a measure would not only, in all probability, have secured proper redress in his own case; but also have done good, in subsequent cases of a similar kind.."[43] Nevertheless, Rodgers left Virginia in May of 1748. He crossed the Chesapeake Bay, traveled up the Eastern Shore of Maryland, and visited the scenes of Francis Makemie's[44] earlier labors.

In Somerset County, Rodgers was greatly used during the summer of 1748 in the winning of souls. One gentleman converted through Rodgers' ministry was William Winder, Esq., of Wicomico; a man of "wealth, worth and high standing." Upon hearing Rodgers preach, Winder cast off his Arminian notions and became an exemplary Christian as well as a faithful elder in the Presbyterian Church. "At Church Hill, in Queen Anne's… [Rodgers] baptized twenty-nine adults on the same day in which many others were admitted to the communion."[45]

While at Wicomico, Rodgers stayed at the home of Captain Joseph Venable, a Presbyterian elder, who had donated the land for the local meetinghouse. After "the most enjoyable summer of his life," Rodgers was invited in the fall to become the pastor of the Wicomico and Monokin churches. At nearly the same time, he received calls from churches at Pequa[46], Pennsylvania, St. George's, Delaware, and Conecocheague. Of these churches, St. George's was the weakest, but Rodgers accepted it at the urging of the Presbytery of New Castle. On March 16, 1749, Rodgers was ordained and installed at St. George's with

---

[43] Ibid, 55–56.
[44] Makemie was the first Presbyterian minister in the colony of Virginia and labored with success along the peninsula of Maryland and Virginia.
[45] Webster, *History of the Presbyterian Church in America*, 578.
[46] The modern spelling is Pequea for this township in Pennsylvania.

Samuel Finley preaching the sermon.

Three years after Rodgers was forced to leave Virginia, Davies wrote to Joseph Bellamy the following assessment of that ordeal:

> The Hon. Sir William Gooch, our late governor, always discovered a ready disposition to allow us all claimable privileges, and the greatest aversion to persecuting measures; but considering the shocking reports spread abroad concerning us by officious malignants, it was no great wonder the council discovered considerable reluctance to tolerate us. Had it not been for this, I persuade myself they would have shown themselves the guardians of our legal privileges, as well as generous patriots to their country, which is the character generally given them.[47]

Thus, Davies assumed the difficult responsibilities of laboring in the colony of Virginia with neither a helper nor a helpmeet, but with the help of the Lord.

Conclusion

Probably the most important lesson to be learned from this chapter is the way Davies waited on the Lord to lead him rather than to choose his own path apart from that leading. Instead of settling in ease near his parents or accepting a call to a church in the middle colonies, he chose the path of duty. His acceptance of a call the Hanover is an example of his submission to the will of God in all things.

The Governor's House in Colonial Williamsburg, Virginia

---

[47] John Gillies, *Historical Collections Relating to the Remarkable Periods of the Success of the Gospel*, 2 vols. in one, (Kelso, Scotland: John Rutherford, 1845), 224.

-6-

The First Year at Hanover

"Almost all the intelligent men in the colony [of Virginia—DR] and amongst the rest several who afterwards became distinguished as the champions of an unqualified freedom in everything relating to the human mind,—and even the venerable name of Pendleton, appear in the class of persecutors; a proof that liberality and toleration are not instinctive qualities, the growth of an hour; but the result of wisdom and experience."[1]
~Edmund Burke~

A sign for the Polegreen Church in Hanover County where Davies preached

---

[1] William Henry Foote, *Sketches of Virginia: Historical and Biographical,* First Series (Philadelphia: William S. Martien, 1850), 166.

The First Year at Hanover

On November 11, 1747, William Parks, the public printer in Virginia, reprinted a sermon preached by John Caldwell at New Londonderry, Pennsylvania, on October 14, 1741 and titled, "An Impartial Trial of the Spirit of God. . ." Patrick Henry, Sr., who was alarmed at the numerous losses from his parish in Hanover County to the New Light Presbyterians, wrote the preface to this edition. The reasons for this reprint were given as follows:

> The following sermon, preached by a Presbyterian minister in New England, is now published in this colony, chiefly with a design to open the eyes of some deluded people among us, who are imposed upon by the itinerants, who have frequently preached here of late, and let the world see, what the Presbyterians, in the Northern Provinces, think of these men, who, tho' they pass here for Presbyterian ministers are in reality, a set of incendiaries; enemies not only to the Established Church, but also common disturbers of the peace and order of all religious societies where ever they come.[2]

Caldwell's text was 1 John 4:1: "Beloved, believe not every spirit, but try the spirits whether they are of God: because many false prophets are gone out into the world." It was originally preached to refute Gilbert Tennent's oft-maligned sermon, "The Dangers of an Unconverted Ministry." Caldwell's discourse was preached in the same area where Davies attended the Fagg's Manor school taught by Samuel Blair and during the period he was a student there. A more improvident defense of the indefensible could not have been published by Parks since God had chosen Davies to be the first New Light Presbyterian pastor regularly installed in Virginia.

In that sermon, Caldwell revealed he was a rationalist concerning God's revelation and ignorant of the free grace of the gospel. In one part of his message, he entertained the notion that it was possible for a person to be saved while still in a state of spiritual darkness:

> Suppose ye not, that if a master should send forth two servants in quest of something he had lost, if the one should search diligently, use all possible means he could conceive of to find the same, but could not; and the other

---

[2] John Caldwell, *An Impartial Trial of the Spirit Operating in this Part of the World: By Comparing the Nature, Effects, and Evidences of the Present Supposed Conversion, with the Word of God* (Williamsburg, VA: William Parks, 1747), 5.

neglect all enquiry, yet accidently find what he should have sought for; suppose ye not that he would approve the former more than the latter? Tis not to be doubted. And will not "the" judge of all the earth do what is right?[3]

Thus, Caldwell denied the Scripture that says, "You will seek the LORD your God, and you will find Him if you search for Him with all your heart and all your soul" (Deuteronomy 4:29). The promise of Scripture is that all who sincerely seek the Lord will find Him. There are no accidental discoveries of grace in God's kingdom. Caldwell turned that promise on its head when he exclaimed that God would reward with salvation those who sincerely sought Him, even if they could not find Him. For him, salvation is a reward dispensed by God to those who are sincere seekers even if they fail of their quest despite all their diligence.

He also censured all bodily effects in response to the preaching of the Gospel — such as crying, tears, and various emotional outbursts — which he caricatured as "strange" commotions:

> Alas! why should so great stress be laid upon shedding Tears, and convulsive motions? Are these true Evidences of good Dispositions? Do they not spring from mechanical Causes? Are they not the Effect of sudden Motion of the Blood and Animal Spirits in Persons of Abounding Fluids and weak Nerves? The aptness of Children and Women to weep easily and in greater Abundance than Persons and Men is a plain proof of this; Anatomy convincing us that their Fluids are more numerous in Proportion to their Solids, and their Nerves weak.[4]

Davies was reluctantly drawn into this controversy at the outset of his ministry at Hanover because he felt silence on his part would be interpreted as guilt which would confuse multitudes of Virginians. He felt duty-bound to defend the gospel and the New Light Presbyterians against these incendiary attacks. In the fall of 1748, therefore, he went to print with a work aptly titled, "The Impartial Trial, Impartially Tried, and Convicted of Partiality." Davies revealed Caldwell's real name was Thornton and he satirically stated that he should have taken the name 'Cald-ill' because of his infamous reputation:

---

[3] Ibid., 9.
[4] Ibid., 14.

Mr. Caldwell was a minister for some time in Ireland, if I remember rightly in Dublin.—Being reputed a gentleman of tolerable sense and learning, he flourished there for sometime; but went on in a course of pilfering and stealing.—His theft being discovered he fled to New England; and having changed his name, imposed upon some of the ministers there, and was received by them for sometime as a Presbyterian minister: During which time he distinguished himself in virulent opposition to the religious concern which then prevailed in the land.[5]

The true character of Caldwell was discovered quite providentially. Some Irish immigrants settled in the neighborhood where Thornton (Caldwell) preached and gave an account of his scandalous conduct to the proper authorities. Being unmasked, he took up the practice of medicine in Pennsylvania under his real name. He later made an open confession of his sins in the congregation of Rev. Alexander McDowell[6], but New Castle Presbytery did not permit him to resume his office as a minister. He then applied to the Church of England for ordination, but did not meet with success in that communion either.

In an appendix, Davies defended the New Light Presbyterian ministers against their illegal expulsion by the Synod of Philadelphia without charges being proffered against them and without a regular trial. One of the primary differences between the Old Lights and New Lights was the matter of ordination. The New Lights insisted that ordination alone did not make a man a true minister of the gospel, but the grace of God was required to do so. As he wrote:

> And because we contended, that *Grace* and *Piety* are very necessary *Prerequisites to that Office*; and that there is little Reason to expect, that the Ministry of *unconverted* ministers, especially when they act as *such*, will be of *much* Service to the Souls of Men.[7]

Caldwell's (Thornton's) opposition to the saving grace of the gospel and his open immorality brought reproach on his ministry. It was against just such ministers that Gilbert Tennent's sermon, "The Dangers of an Unconverted Ministry," had warned. Tennent's sermon came un-

---

[5] Samuel Davies, *The Impartial Trial, Impartially Tried, and Convicted of Partiality* (Williamsburg, VA: William Parks, 1748), 34.
[6] McDowell was the minister at the White Clay Creek and Elk River churches in New Castle Presbytery of the Synod of Philadelphia.
[7] Davies, *Impartial Trial, Impartially Tried, and Convicted of Partiality*, 12.

der attack by numerous people, but the "Son of Thunder" was not alone in his belief. The seraphic and pacific Davies was just as committed to this idea as Tennent. Others who joined them in this conviction included George Whitefield, Samuel Blair, Samuel Finley, Jonathan Edwards, and countless others. In more recent years, Dr. D. Martyn Lloyd-Jones has a wonderful explication of this principle in his two volume set, *Studies in the Sermon on the Mount*. Indeed, every part of Scripture sounds a warning against false prophets and wolves in sheep's clothing. While Tennent's message was tinctured with a measure of anger and name-calling, his basic principle was scriptural to the core. Thus, Davies did not hesitate to defend a principle of such great importance.

While acknowledging the Great Awakening was not free from error, Davies asserted in his reply to Caldwell's sermon that "the enemy is never so busy sowing tares, as when the Son of man is sowing good seed"[8] and further defended bodily effects as follows:

> Scripture often makes use of bodily effects, to express the strength of holy and spiritual affections. . . I can't think God would commonly make use of things which are very alien from spiritual affections. . . and are shrewd marks of the hand of Satan, and smell strong of the bottomless pit, as beautiful figures, to represent the high degree of holy and heavenly affections.[9]

Caldwell had asserted in his message that the trembling of the Philippian jailer was the fear of temporal punishment only. Davies' reply pointed out the jailer trembled *after* all the reasons to fear temporal punishment were removed:

> The earthquake was over;—the Apostle had assured him, the prisoners were all there; his bloody design of self-murder was frustrated, and all those were causes of joy. And did they, contrary to their nature produce sorrow? Did he tremble to find himself safe? And was he afraid, because he found all expected grounds of fear removed? Or was his enquiry about temporal salvation? But what need had he of it, when he saw himself safe already? And how impertinent the Apostle's answer, "Believe in the Lord Jesus Christ, and thou shalt be saved."[10]

---

[8] Ibid., 41.
[9] Ibid., 52.
[10] Ibid., 53.

In defense of the bodily effects which sometimes accompany sound conversions, Davies queried his readers:

> Must we conclude a sinner's conviction of his sin and danger irrational because it is so affecting to his soul that it affects his body too? Must we pronounce his sense of condemnation under the penalty of the violated law delusive or diabolical because it is attended with such commotions as would not be thought strange in one that sees himself condemned to death at a human bar, as weeping, crying, swooning?[11]

Yet, Davies neither endorsed all bodily effects as sure signs of an outpouring of the Holy Spirit nor did he discount them as evidences of delusion. He would surely have agreed with Rev. Jonathan Parsons, the Congregational minister at Lymes, Massachusetts, who wrote to Thomas Prince the following words:

> I am humbly of the opinion that it is not reasonable for any to conclude persons to be under the influence of the Holy Spirit, either in convincing of sin, or sanctifying the soul, merely because they cry aloud, faint away, or the like; even though they may be observed under the faithful preaching of religion... Nor, 2, Is it reasonable, I think, for any to conclude, persons are not under the convincing or sanctifying influences of the Holy Spirit, because they tremble, cry out aloud, fall down as dead, or have great bodily disorders of such a nature.[12]

Caldwell was obscuring the real issues by his attacks on bodily effects in response to the preaching of the gospel. The real issues for Davies were twofold: First, he strongly believed that a revival could not be wrought through the instrumentality of unconverted ministers because they would be deficient in preaching the unchanging gospel. Second, he insisted on the necessity of a supernatural regeneration. The theory of baptismal regeneration which predominated in the Old Dominion[13] at that time was not true regeneration at all.

In another part of his sermon, Caldwell asserted that the preaching of wrath is a strange work which God seldom does in Scripture. Davies responded that the Bible is full of warnings to the impenitent because the

---

[11] Ibid., 40–41.
[12] John Gillies, *Historical Collections Relating to Remarkable Periods of the Success of the Gospel* (Kelso, Scotland: John Rutherford, 1845), 383.
[13] Old Dominion, or Ancient Dominion, is a nickname for Virginia.

generality of mankind are lost in their sins. As Davies stated:

> And to hope the contrary, however natural it is to a generous soul, is blasphemously to hope, that God will be a liar.[14]

One of the lessons learned from Davies' ministry is how he responded to criticism. When the criticism was aimed at him personally, he accepted it meekly. When the criticism was really an attack on the gospel, he responded in an appropriate and necessary manner in order to uphold the truth of Scripture. Certainly, he could have hoped for a more peaceful beginning to his ministry in Virginia, but he was not going to shy away from a vigorous defense of the gospel.

Gaming, Cock-Fighting, and Horse Racing

There were other challenges that awaited Davies in Virginia. The colony of Virginia in 1748 was largely a society of elitists who had an abundance of time for leisure and amusements. The aristocrats and wealthy planters of eighteenth century Virginia were fascinated with numerous worldly pursuits, according to an account Davies wrote concerning the state of religion among the Dissenters in that colony:

> Gaming, cock-fighting, horse-racing and all the fashionable methods of killing time are indulged as the most important and serious business of life.[15]

Horse races were the preferred form of amusement in the Tidewater region of Virginia. A straight quarter-mile track tested both the speed of the horses and the skill of the riders. The riders would jockey for position at the starting line and make every effort to dismount their opponent while their horses bolted down the track at the firing of the starter's pistol.[16] Horse racing resulted in heavy betting with anxious spectators lining the track. The winner was greeted with a resounding applause when he crossed the finish line. By the 1750s, course racing on an oval track in

---

[14] Davies, *Impartial Trial*, 44.
[15] Samuel Davies, "The State of Religion Among the Dissenters in Virginia," *The Biblical Repertory and Princeton Review*, Vol. XI (1840), 202.
[16] Rhyss Isaacs, *The Transformation of Virginia, 1740–1790* (Chapel Hill, NC: The University of North Carolina Press, 1982), 101. This work provides the background information on the social life in Colonial Virginia which is the factual basis for many of the statements in the following paragraphs.

the English tradition was also gaining popularity as a rival to the quarter race.

Another amusement was the monstrous sport of cockfighting. It began as a favorite pastime of the common planters, but soon became popular with the wealthy gentry as well. It was a duel to death between two cocks placed in a pit and surrounded by cheering, fanatical spectators. A Yankee businessman, Elkanah Watson, once described the scene of attending a cockfight in Southampton County, Virginia with one of the local gentleman:

> The moment the birds were dropped, the bets ran high. The little heroes appeared trained to the business, and not the least disconcerted by the crowd and shouting. They stepped about with great apparent pride and dignity; advancing nearer and nearer, they flew upon each other. . . the cruel and fatal gaffs being driven in to their bodies, and, at times, directly into their heads. Frequently one, or both, were struck dead at the first blow, but they often fought after being repeatedly pierced, as long as they were able to crawl, and in the agonies of death would often make abortive efforts to raise their heads and strike their antagonists.[17]

Hanover County was not immune to this frivolity which presented an obstacle for Davies' efforts to establish an evangelical ministry there. One of the first notices in Hanover County of such worldly distractions was on October 7, 1737 in an advertisement in *The Virginia Gazette*:

> Williamsburg, October, 7: We have advice from Hanover County, that on St. Andrew's Day, being the 30th of November next, there are to be Horse Races and several Diversions, for the Entertainment of the Gentlemen and Ladies, at the Old Field near Capt. John Bickerton's in that County.[18]

Some of the diversions alluded to in this notice were: a horse race around a three-mile course; a 112-yard dash by twelve year old boys; a wrestling match for the prize of two silver buckles by "brisk young men"; and numerous "other Whimsical and Comical Diversions." The subscribers were required to "discountenance all Immorality with the utmost Rigour."[19]

---

[17] Ibid., 102.
[18] Robert Bolling Lancaster, *A Sketch of the Early History of Hanover County Virginia and Its Large and Important Contributions to The American Revolution*, (Richmond: Whittet and Shepperson, 1976), 14.
[19] Ibid., 15.

The intense interest in such diversions was in sharp contrast to the trifling levity with which most Virginians attended religious worship. While the formalities of Christianity were interspersed throughout the common life of the people, too often they did not penetrate the heart. Virginians would pray before their meals; they were taught to read from the pages of the Bible; they learned the catechism of the Anglican Church; and, they were required by law to attend the parish church once in every four weeks. Yet, Philip Frithian, a Presbyterian from New Jersey who tutored in Virginia at a later date, described the way many Virginians observed the Sabbath day:

> Three grand divisions of time at the Church on Sundays, Viz. Before Service giving & receiving letters of business, reading Advertisements, consulting about the price of Tobacco, Grain &c.& settling either the lineage, Age, or qualities of favorite Horses. 2. In the Church at Service, prayers read over in hast, a Sermon seldom under & never over twenty minutes, but always made up of sound morality, or deep studied Metaphysicks. 3. After Service is over three quarters of an hour spent in strolling round the Church among the Crowd... [when one might be] invited by several different Gentlemen home with them to dinner.[20]

Virginia was like most of the other American colonies before the Great Awakening. They had a form of godliness, but they denied the power thereof. The same spiritual deadness that Cotton Mather had decried in New England was present in the Old Dominion as well. Davies knew that the only cure for this attachment to trifling amusements and dead formality in worship was an outpouring of the Holy Spirit.

The Doctrine and Life of the Virginian Clergy

The generally loose morals of the Anglican clergy in Virginia were another obstacle to the spread of the gospel. Formalism and legalism invariably lead to loose morals and low spiritual standards. It is not surprising that the aristocrats in eighteenth-century Virginia would spend their idle time in frivolous pursuits, but it was disappointing that they were often joined by numerous members of the Anglican clergy. William Meade, the third bishop of the Protestant Episcopal Church of Virginia, may have overreached a century later when he described the colonial clergy

---

[20] Isaacs, *Transformation of Virginia.*, 60.

as "for the most part... the refuse or the more indifferent of the English, Irish, and Scottish Episcopal Churches, who could not find promotion at home,"[21] but he was certainly correct about many of them. Despite the view of John Boles that "tales of their immorality, drunkenness, and arrogance have surely been exaggerated,"[22] the contemporary testimony indicates otherwise.

Two Dutch missionaries to America, Jasper Dankers and Peter Sluyter, traveled through Virginia in 1699 and were distressed at the conduct of the Anglican ministers because "a scandalously large number of them took to drinking, horse racing, and gambling at cards."[23] Devereux Jarratt (1733 – 1801) was born into an Anglican family in New Kent County where, he says, he never heard from the Virginian clergy "any serious conversation respecting God and Christ, Heaven or Hell."[24] Numerous others have recorded their agreement with such an assessment of the Anglican ministers in Virginia, including Albert Barnes who wrote a brief biographical notice of Davies. Of course, the greatest problem was the doctrinal views of these Colonial Anglican ministers. As Davies himself wrote in a letter to Joseph Bellamy, the Congregational pastor at Bethlehem, Connecticut:

> Had the doctrines of the Gospel been solemnly and faithfully preached in the established church, I am persuaded there would have been but few dissenters in these parts of Virginia; for their first objections were not against the peculiar rites and ceremonies of that church, much less against her excellent articles, but against the general strain of the doctrines delivered from the pulpit, in which these articles were opposed, or (which was the more common case) not mentioned at all; so that at first they were not properly dissenters from the original constitution of the Church of England, but the most strict adherents to it, and only dissented from those who had forsaken it.[25]

---

[21] Quoted in David L. Holmes, *A Brief History of the Episcopal Church: with a chapter on the Anglican Reformation and an appendix on the annulment of Henry VIII* (Valley Forge, Pennsylvania: Trinity Press International, 1993), 36.
[22] John Boles, "The Beginning of the Southern Bible-Belt," in Kenneth Kaulman, ed., *Critical Moments in Religious History* (Macon, Georgia: Mercer University Press, 1993), 122.
[23] Thomas Andrew Bailey, ed., *The American Spirit: United States History As Seen By Contemporaries*, Volume 1 (Boston: D. C. Heath and Company, 1963), 14.
[24] J. W. Smith, "Devereux Jarratt and the Beginnings of Methodism in Virginia," *The John P. Branch Historical Papers of Randolph-Macon College* (June 1901), 6.
[25] Samuel Davies, "The State of Religion among the Protestant Dissenters in Virginia; in a letter

Yet, it was this failure of ministers to preach the doctrine of the gospel—not only in Virginia, but throughout the colonies—that necessitated the Great Awakening. The issue in every generation is the same which Paul inculcated on Timothy: "Pay close attention to yourself and to your teaching" (1 Timothy 4:16). Doctrine and life are always the standards for gospel ministers. When pastors defect from the gospel by living according to either antinomian principles or legalism, they indicate that they have never received the love of the truth in their hearts. Doctrine is for the purpose of promoting godliness, and the Anglican communion in colonial Virginia was generally defective in both. Bishop J. C. Ryle made the same observation of the parochial clergy on the other side of Atlantic during the eighteenth century:

> The vast majority of them were sunk in worldliness and neither knew nor cared about their profession. . . They hunted, they shot, they farmed, they swore, they drank, they gambled. They seemed determined to know everything except Jesus Christ and Him crucified.[26]

Such indifference to the truth is almost always evidence that those ministers have not experienced the new birth which alone can issue forth in saving faith. The Anglican church, both in America and Great Britain, was overrun at that time with the Laudian[27] principles which emphasized baptismal regeneration rather than the new birth through the Holy Spirit. An error at the fountainhead of truth inevitably leads to other errors in both doctrine and life. Thus, the Old Dominion of Virginia was in great need of a revival in the middle of the eighteenth century, but the clergy of the established church were incapable of providing such spiritual leadership.

A Different Kind of Ministry

From the beginning of his ministry in Hanover, Davies preached regularly at the four meetinghouses which were then licensed—three in Hanover county and the other one in Henrico county—and rotated his preach-

---

to the Rev. Mr. Joseph Bellamy, of Bethlem, in New England," (Boston: S. Kneeland, 1751), 6.
[26] J. C. Ryle, *Five Christian Leaders* (London: The Banner of Truth Trust, 1960), 14.
[27] Bishop William Laud was Archbishop of Canterbury from 1633 to 1640. Before his arrest in 1640 he was very active in persecuting the Puritans. He was chiefly responsible for eroding the Reformation foundations of the Church of England in contradiction to its doctrinal standards, the Thirty-Nine Articles of Religion, and for advocating baptismal regeneration.

ing in proportion to the number of Dissenters among them. Davies was tall and thin with a "manly and graceful" appearance whom Samuel Finley described as:

> Genteel, not ceremonious; grave, yet pleasant... he was an open, conversable, and entertaining companion, a polite gentleman, and devout Christian.[28]

Yet, it was not Davies' naturally sweet temper or tender spirit that was the secret of his success at Hanover and throughout Virginia. Rather, it was his zealous preaching of the gospel with manifest love both for God and his hearers. Concerning those sermons, Finley stated:

> His messages were tender, solemn, pungent, and persuasive... A certainty dignity of sentiment and style, a venerable presence, a commanding voice, and emphatical delivery, concurred both to charm his audience, and overawe them into silence and attention.[29]

The solemn, dignified, commanding, and emphatic delivery of Davies can be gathered from his printed sermons, even if the unction of the Spirit is missing from the printed page. Another description of Davies' gifts as a preacher is given by William Hill:

> [He] possessed naturally every qualification, both of body and mind, to make him an accomplished orator, and fit him for the pulpit. His frame was tall, well-proportioned, erect and comely;—his voice clear, loud, distinct, melodious, and well-modulated;—and his natural genius was strong and masculine; his understanding clear; his memory retentive; his invention quick; his imagination sprightly and florid, his thoughts sublime; and his language elegant, strong and expressive.[30]

The enthusiasm for this new kind ministry was so great that by "the summer of 1748, the people began to make long journeys to hear his teachings"[31] and "some of them rode through the forests twenty miles, some forty and some even sixty miles."[32] Foote also records:

---

[28] Samuel Finley, "Sermon on the Death of the Rev. Samuel Davies," in Samuel Davies, *Sermons on Important Subjects*, I (New York: J. & J. Harper, 1828), 22.
[29] Ibid.
[30] Albert Barnes, "Life and Times of the Author," in Samuel Davies, *Sermons on Important Subjects*, I (New York: Dayton and Saxton, 1841), xxxi.
[31] Henry Alexander White, *Southern Presbyterian Leaders* (Edinburgh, Scotland and Carlisle, Pennsylvania: The Banner of Truth Trust, 2000), 45.
[32] Ibid.

His preaching during the summer of 1748 was blessed. The desire to hear the gospel from the lips of the young dissenter spread in every direction; people rode great distances to attend upon his ministry, and became desirous to obtain some portion of his ministry in their more immediate neighborhood for the benefit of their families and neighbours.[33]

Like the Apostle Paul, he was in "far more labors" than those who were mere men pleasers, but that is not what attracted such great crowds Rather, he preached with scriptural authority, unlike most parish priests.

Despite Davies' best efforts, many members of his wider congregation were regularly deprived of a sermon on the Lord's Day. Additionally, several groups of Dissenters throughout the colony were also Davies' concern and sole responsibility. The Cub Creek congregation in Caroline county had been organized by William Robinson five years earlier. It was in a flourishing situation which required more oversight than Davies could devote. Presbyterians in Goochland and Louisa counties also needed a portion of his time. He resolved this dilemma by establishing chapels of ease after the pattern of the Anglican Church in the colony. Each Anglican parish consisted of a number of "chapels of ease" in addition to the local church in order to accommodate members who lived at the remote parts of the parish. Sermons were then preached at the churches on Sundays and the chapels on weekdays which allowed all the members of the parish to attend worship near their homes.

Davies took advantage of the idea of chapels of ease and established preaching posts at all the locations where he was unable to minister on the Lord's Day. The governing officials of Virginia frowned on Davies' weekday preaching while they required a report from the established clergy concerning how often they conducted weekday services at such chapels of ease. For instance, Rev. John Brunskill of St. Margaret's Parish in Caroline County had been charged in 1735 by his vestry of neglecting to preach at a chapel of ease in that county, and the General Court of Virginia investigated the matter. Yet, Davies was accused of teaching Virginians to be idle or stealing members from the Anglican church when he availed himself of the established system of "chapels of ease." It must be remembered that in colonial Virginia every citizen was considered a member of the Anglican church and a part of the local parish un-

---

[33] Foote, *Sketches of Virginia*, First Series, 168.

less they objected to it. Some attended Davies' chapels of ease out of curiosity and others were sincerely seeking a better ministry than what they found at their local parish. In a letter to Joseph Bellamy in 1751, he described the success these chapels of ease were having:

> Many of the church people also attend when there is a sermon at any of these houses. This I looked upon at first as mere curiosity after novelty, but as it continues, and in some places seems to increase, I cannot but look upon it as a happy token of their being at length thoroughly engaged. And I have the greater reason to hope so now, as experience has confirmed my former hopes. Fifty or sixty families having thus been happily entangled in the net of the gospel by their own curiosity, or some such motive.[34]

Some of his meetinghouses had only fifteen to twenty families who were members, but the attendance at his services could approach 400 to 500, and sometimes twice as much.[35] The sight of so many Virginians gathering in the backwoods to hear this New Light Presbyterian preach the gospel was thoroughly exasperating to the Anglican clergy. Yet, Davies was not deluded by the sight of mere numbers, but was very discriminating in his judgment of the progress of the revival in Virginia. His thoughts concerning why the crowds were leaving the Anglican churches and clamoring to hear him preach are revealed in his letter to Bellamy:

> The whole System of what is distinguished by the Name of *experimental Religion,* was past over in Silence. The *Depravity of humane Nature,* the *Necessity of Regeneration, and it's Pre-requisites, Nature and Effects,* the *various Exercises of pious Souls according to their several Cases,* &c. these were omitted; and without these, you know Sir, the finest Declamations on moral Duties or speculative Truths, will be but wretched Entertainment to hungry Souls. Such a maim'd System is not the compleat Religion of JESUS, that glories in the amiable *Symmetry,* mutual *Dependency* and *Subserviency* of all its Doctrines, as its peculiar Characteristic. Had the *whole Counsel of God* been declared, had all the Doctrines of the Gospel been solemnly and faithfully preached in the established Church; I am perswaded there would have been but few Dissenters in these Parts of *Virginia.*[36]

---

[34] Gillies, *Historical Collections,* 435.
[35] Davies, "The State of Religion among the Protestant Dissenters in Virginia," 22–23.
[36] Ibid., 6.

Davies would have been happy with an Anglican ministry that eschewed the Laudian emphasis on baptismal regeneration and preached faithfully the doctrines contained in the Thirty-Nine Articles. Yet, he had no delight in accumulating followers who merely objected to ceremonialism while being devoid of saving grace.

> Yet as I am fully perswaded *the Kingdom of God is not Meat & Drink, but Righteousness and Peace and Joy in the Holy Ghost;* and that Persons of superior Piety and Judgment have used these Rites and Ceremonies with Approbation; I think the Alteration of Men's Principles and Practice with Respect to these Things *only,* without being born again of God, is a wretched Conversion; and it would inspire me with much greater Joy to see a *pious Church-man,* than a *graceless Presbyterian.*[37]

None of his printed sermons are dated from his first year at Hanover, but the types of sermons he preached is without doubt. He preached the great doctrines of the gospel, particularly 'the three R's'—Ruin by the fall, Regeneration by the Holy Spirit, and Redemption through Christ's blood—and there is every reason to believe that his early sermons dealt much with these scriptural truths. In a sermon on John 3:7, "The Nature and Author of Regeneration," Davies gave a definition of the new birth:

> It is the change of a thoughtless, ignorant, half-hearted, rebellious sinner, into a thoughtful, well-informed, tender-hearted dutiful servant of God. It is the implantation of the seeds or principles of every grace and virtue in a heart that was entirely destitute of them, and full of sin. The sinner that was wont to have no practical affectionate regard for the great God, is not made to revere, admire, and love him as the greatest and best of Beings; to rejoice in him as the supreme happiness, and cheerfully to submit to him as his Ruler. Formerly his conduct would better agree to the infidelity of an atheist than to the faith of a Christian; but now, he thinks, and speaks, and acts, as one that really believes there is a God; a God who inspects all his ways, and will call him to account.[38]

Davies also preached two undated sermons from Galatians 2:20, "The Divine Life in the Souls of Men Considered," which may be similar to

---

[37] Ibid., 7.
[38] *Sermons by the Rev. Samuel Davies*, Vol. 2 (Morgan, Pennsylvania: Soli Deo Gloria Publications, 1995), 486–7.

messages he preached during his first year at Hanover. He expressed the necessity of the new birth as follows:

> Now since a principal of spiritual life is in the spring and the beginning of all acts of holiness, it must be, in order of nature, prior to the first act of holiness: and consequently it is not gradually acquired by such acts, but precedes them all, and therefore must be instantaneously infused.
>
> Hence we may see the vanity of that religion which is gained in the same manner that a man learns a trade, or an uncultivated mind becomes knowing and learned, namely, by the repeated exercises of our natural powers in use of proper means, and under the aids of common providence. We have seen that a principal of spiritual life is not a good act, or a series of good acts, nor anything acquirable by them, but the spring and origin of all good acts. Let us then, my brethren, try whether our religion will stand this test.
>
> Hence also we may learn a considerable difference between what is commonly called morality and gospel-holiness. The one is obtained, as other habits are, by frequent and continued exercises; the other proceeds from a principal divinely implanted.[39]

The opposition by the Anglican clergy to this new kind of ministry made Virginia an improbable colony for advancing the gospel. Thus, Davies described to his congregation several years later the thoughts of his heart when he accepted their call to Virginia:

> It is known to no mortal but myself with what reluctance, fear and trembling, I accepted your call. The rawness and inexperience of my youth, and the formidable opposition then made both by church and state, when a dissenter was stared at with horror, as a shocking and portentous phenomenon, were no small discouragements in my way. For some years, I durst hardly venture to appear but in the pulpit, or in my study; lest, by a promiscuous conversation with the world at large, I should injure the cause of religion, by some instance of unguarded conduct. In short, my self-diffidence rose so high, that I often thought I had done a great exploit, when I had done no harm to this important interest, which I had a sincere desire, though but little ability, to promote.[40]

---

[39] Ibid., 523–4.
[40] Samuel Davies, *Sermons on Important Subjects*, IV (London: W. Baynes and Son, 1824), 455.

Marriage to Jane Holt

Davies' self-diffidence did not prevent him from finding a wife in Hanover, though. Within months of his move to Virginia, he courted and soon won the hand of Jane Holt, the daughter of David and Margaret (Didball) Holt[41] of Hanover County, as his second wife. Jane was one of nine children born to David and Margaret and was preceded in birth by Ann (b. 1713), Didball (b. 1717), and John (b. 1721). Born in 1726, she was three years younger than Samuel. Two of her siblings are known to have been younger than her—David, Jr. (b. 1728) and William (b. 1737)—while the birth dates of her other siblings—Sarah Truly, Mary, and Gazell—are unknown.

David Holt, Sr. was a landowner and planter who had migrated northwest from the Tidewater area of Virginia to New Kent County to Hanover County. The oldest Holt child, Ann, was born in New Kent County a year after David and Margaret married in 1712. All their other children were born in Hanover County (which was formed out of New Kent County). David Holt died sometime in 1748 at the age of 63 and he may not have lived long enough to see Jane marry the first New Light Presbyterian minister in Hanover County that fall.

The courtship of Samuel and Jane is shrouded in mystery, but it was just the tonic that he needed when he began his ministry in Virginia. Samuel was still suffering from the simultaneous deaths of his first wife, Sarah, and their son in childbirth. His heart naturally would have been sympathetic to Jane during the last days of her father. Their whirlwind courtship was consummated with the exchanging of nuptial vows at a ceremony on Tuesday, October 4, 1748. It is unknown whether the wedding vows were exchanged at the home of the bride's parents or at St.

---

[41] George William Pilcher and others assert that Jane came from a prominent Williamsburg family and that her father was named William who was also at one time a mayor of the Capitol city. There are no genealogical records cited to prove this assertion. William Holt served as mayor of Williamsburg in 1776–7 and 1782–3 and, was no doubt, the brother of Jane Holt. Cf. http://www.geni.com/people/David-Holt/6000000009023834558, accessed on February 13, 2016. Richard Webster in his *History of the Presbyterian Church in America* wrote: "Davies was married, October 4, 1748 to Jean, daughter of John Holt, of Hanover" (p.552). William Henry Foote in His *Sketches of Virginia*, First Series, wrote: "Mr. Davies entered the second time into the matrimonial state, being united in marriage October 4th, 1748, to Miss Jane Holt, of Hanover" (172). Both Webster and Foote agree that Jane Holt was from Hanover, but Webster is mistaken that she was the daughter of John Holt. John was her brother.

Paul's Parish in Hanover with the Rev. Patrick Henry, Sr. officiating. Jane was twenty-two at their wedding and Samuel turned twenty-five the following month. He found in Jane a young woman without pretense or guile. In her company, he was able to unburden himself and reveal his gentler side. His sonnet on "Conjugal Love and Happiness" casts light on the mysterious beginning of their courtship:

> I saw, I loved, I sought to gain,
> The blooming fair, nor fought in vain.
> Thy yielding bosom soon began to glow
> With the same flame thy charms taught me to know.
> Thy Soul, unskill'd in those inhumane Arts
> Thy Sex affect to torture captive Hearts,
> A constant Lover did disdain to vex,
> Or with unkind Delays and treach'rous Wiles perplex.
> Thy Soul, that knew not what dissembling meant,
> With modest soft Reluctance, blush'd Consent.
> In Transport lost the joyful News I heard;
> And vow'd my Life the favour to reward.
> A solemn Rite the willing Contract seal'd,
> To stand, 'till Death divide us, unrepeal'd.[42]

This union made both Samuel and Jane into "a finish'd one" by combining "the rougher virtues of a manly mind with her more tender female virtues" to "form a well-temper'd compound" and "a well-mix'd picture."[43] Jane's natural "mildness of... temper seem'd to court Masculine boldness for its kind support; unfit, alone, t'avert impending harms, and face life' terrors and outrageous storms."[44] Samuel's temptation was that his bride would become more important to him than God or leave Him "but the inferior part."[45] He, therefore, pleads with his wife to "help [him] restrain the wild Excesses of the Love you gain" and to "let Jesus reign unrivall'd."[46] The Holt-Davies union gave credibility to his claim that he was not guilty of sectarianism.

---

[42] Richard Beale Davis, ed. *Collected Poems of Samuel Davies, 1723–1761* (Gainesville, FL: Scholar Facsimiles and Reprints, 1968), 60.
[43] Ibid., 59. All of the quotes in this sentence are from this source.
[44] Ibid.
[45] Ibid., 61.
[46] Ibid., 62.

Petition for New Meetinghouses

A month after his wedding, in November of 1748, Davies petitioned the General Court of Virginia to license three new meetinghouses to be located on the properties of Joseph Shelton in Louisa County, Tucker Woodson in Goochland County, and John Sutton in Caroline County. The General Council, after some difficulty, approved these petitions which brought to seven the number of meeting places where he ministered.

About this same time, Davies was instrumental in helping another group of Presbyterians petition Governor Gooch for the right to assemble according to their consciences. Samuel Morris had a cousin, Thomas Morris, who lived in lower St. Margaret's Parish in Caroline County which bordered Hanover County on the north side. Thomas Morris probably became a Presbyterian through his family associations as a result of the "Morris Reading Rooms." Thomas was instrumental in the conversion of several of his neighbors and this group, sponsored by Davies, petitioned Governor Gooch in 1748 for authority to form a congregation. Gooch granted this request over the vigorous protest of Edmund Pendleton, who at the time was already a leading member of the Caroline bar. The congregation built a meetinghouse in Caroline County near "The Reeds," which was a famous plantation home owned by the Corbin family. The church was located about twenty miles from Davies' home to the west of the community called Point Eastern. While this meetinghouse did not become a part of his congregation, Davies probably supplied it on various occasions.

The granting of these new petitions for meetinghouses was an embarrassing defeat for Patrick Henry, Sr. and four of his colleagues who had sent a petition to the House of Burgesses of Virginia against itinerant preaching. The other four men were John Brunskill, Sr., rector at St. Margaret's Parish in Caroline County; David Mossom, rector at St. Peter's Parish in New Kent County; John Robertson, rector at the Northam and Southam Parishes in Goochland and Powhatan counties; and, Robert Barrett, rector at St. Martin's Parish in Hanover County. The two itinerants mentioned in the petition were Davies and John Cennick—a Methodist associate of George Whitefield who had lately preached in Albemarle and Amelia counties. The New Light Presbyterians were especially criticized by the petition as having been justly excluded by the Synod of Philadelphia in 1741 for errors which they had not yet recanted. The doctrine of the New Lights was alleged to be of "a dangerous consequence to Religion in general; and that the Authors and propagators thereof, are deservedly stigmatized with a name unknown, until of late in this part of the World."[47] The heart of the petition, though, was an attempt to persuade the House of Burgesses that the Act of Toleration did not apply to Virginia:

> That your Petitioners further humbly conceive, that tho' these excluded Members of the Synod of Philadelphia were really Presbyterians, or of any of the other sects tolerated in England, yet there is no Law in this Colony, by which they can be entitled to a License to preach; far less to send forth their Emissaries, or to travel themselves over several Counties (to many places without invitation), to gain proselytes to their way.[48]

This objection was really a slightly different form of the same complaint made by the Synod of Philadelphia against itinerant preaching in 1738. In this instance, these Anglican ministers argued that no one had a right to preach to anyone who was not already a member of their denomination. They viewed the whole of Virginia to be a parish of Anglicans which, in effect, it was by statutory law. Thus, they denied the extension of the Act of Toleration to that colony.

A Dissenting Minister

There were other criticisms which Davies faced early in his ministry which were closer to home. Davies' brother-in-law, John Holt, a staunch Episcopalian, could not understand why he insisted on being a Dissenter rather than seeking Episcopal ordination. Holt seemed displeased that his sister married a Presbyterian minister. On one occasion, Holt's mercantile business took him through Hanover County, but he passed by the Davies' family without stopping for a visit. When Davies learned of this slight, he questioned Holt about it in a letter dated February 10, 1749. In the same letter, he requested Holt's help in purchasing at a reasonable price a female slave[49] whom Governor Gooch was offering for sale. Their

---

[47] William Stevens Perry, ed., *Historical Collections Relating to the American Colonial Church*, Volume I—Virginia (Hartford, Connecticut: Church Press Company, 1870), 382.
[48] Ibid.
[49] The subject of slavery will be addressed in Chapter Seventeen. It was a pernicious evil of the eighteenth century which few people were able to avoid. Davies promoted the humane treatment of slaves and their Christian education. He was especially kind to the slaves who resided in his household, but was unable to overthrow an evil that permeated all of society at that

discussion of this matter gave Davies the opportunity to present the truths of the gospel to Holt. Having requested Holt to give him a summary of his views on the fundamentals of the faith, Davies responded in a letter of July 4, 1749:

> I believe sir, in the summary of fundamentals you sent me, that you make no express mention of the necessity of the renovation of our natures by special grace, as an essential article of the Christian faith. . . Ere we can be saved there must be new principles implanted.[50]

The Anglican ministers of eighteenth-century Virginia, like high churchmen always have, generally held to baptismal regeneration and salvation through the ceremonies of the church. Thus, they either denied or were silent concerning the need of regeneration by the Spirit. John Holt's failure to list spiritual regeneration as a fundamental article of the faith was to be expected, but it is one of the cornerstones of evangelical theology. Davies would not allow the neglect of regeneration without correcting it, but he, nonetheless, expressed to Holt his catholicity in this same letter:

> An Episcopal Christian shall always attract more of my esteem than a Pharisee or profligate of my own denomination. If I am conscious of my own temper, my greatest concern for myself, for you and for all mankind, is that our hearts may be right with God; that we may be quickened by grace who were dead in trespasses and sins; and that holiness may be implanted in our spirits by divine agency.[51]

Conclusion

Nearly a century later, Charles Bridges, an evangelical Anglican minister at Old Newton in Suffolk, England, gave a description of the type of minister who is signally blessed in his great work, *The Christian Ministry*, which helps to explain some of the secret of Davies' success:

> Those Ministers whom we observe specially honoured in their work, we shall mark generally to be distinguished by a consistent standard of profession and conduct. And doubtless with more spiritualized affections,

---

time. Only the Civil War could accomplish that.
[50] Davies to John Holt, July 4, 1749. MS letter in the Benjamin Rush MSS, Library Company of Philadelphia—Historical Society of Pennsylvania, Philadelphia, PA.
[51] Ibid.

with greater abstraction from the world, with more fervent love to the Saviour and zeal for his cause, with a higher estimate of the value of souls, and with a more habitual determination to live with and for God—we shall have a clearer and more effective testimony in the hearts of our people. We shall "magnify our office" among them; and they will gladly "receive us as angels of God, even as Christ Jesus."[52]

In the spirit of Bridges' words, Davies manifested an uncommon wisdom and zeal for lost souls from the outset of his ministry at Hanover which contributed greatly to his success in Virginia.

St. Paul's Parish Church (Episcopal) in Hanover, Virginia where Rev. Patrick Henry, Sr. was the rector

---

[52] Charles Bridges, *The Christian Ministry* (London: The Banner of Truth Trust, 1967), 183.

-7-

Opposition to the Gospel

"And for them, whether they listen or not—for they are a rebellious house—they will know that a prophet has been among them. And you, son of man, neither fear them nor fear their words, though thistles and thorns are with you and you sit on scorpions; neither fear their words, nor be dismayed at their presence, for they are a rebellious house. But you shall speak My words to them whether they listen or not, for they are rebellious."
~Ezekiel 2:5-7~

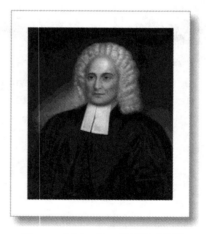

Samuel Davies (1723-1761)

Opposition to the Gospel

It was to be expected that the Anglican clergy in Virginia who opposed the Great Awakening would also oppose the ministry of Davies. Their real opposition was to the gospel, but some of their attacks on the youthful newcomer descended to the level of indecency and were altogether too personal. As Albert Barnes observed:

> Several scurrilous lampoons were written against him, and the sarcastic songs which were put into the mouths of drunkards to turn him into ridicule, are remembered by some old people to the present day. It was soon seen that such light weapons as these rather brought him into notice than did him any injury.[1]

Davies was by no means the first or only Dissenting minister to receive such treatment in America or Great Britain during the Great Awakening. George Whitefield had been ridiculed and belittled in a quite nasty manner by several people. False and filthy lies were sometimes spread about him. Other New Light Presbyterians in America faced the same kind of persecution as Whitefield endured. Like others before him, Davies responded to these criticisms and lies with Christian grace. He turned the other cheek, refused to respond in kind, and prayed for his enemies.

Our Lord had warned His disciples that they would suffer persecution at the hands of men. "A disciple is not above his teacher, nor a slave above his master. It is enough that he become like his teacher, and the slave like his master. If they have called the head of the house Beelzebub, how much more will they malign the members of his household!" (Matthew 10:24, 25). Usually such persecutors falsely malign the character of the servant of Christ or accuse him of breaking legalistic rules. The Pharisees accused Jesus of being born of fornication, of having a demon, of being a glutton and wine-bibber, and of promiscuous friendship with sinners. They also accused Him of breaking the Sabbath, of failure to keep the traditions, and of teaching without proper authority. What they did not do is directly refute His doctrine.

Likewise, the Anglican clergy in Virginia directed their first attacks against Davies in the same ways in which the Pharisees opposed Jesus. Just as the Pharisees questioned Jesus' authority to do what He did, the

---

[1] Albert Barnes, "The Life and Times of the Author," in Samuel Davies, *Sermons on Important Subjects*, I (New York: Dayton and Saxton, 1841), xxii.

Anglican clergy resented Davies exercising any of the functions of a licensed minister. Their primary opposition to him took the form of denying him the rights of other legally licensed ministers in the Colony.

Opposition to Davies Performing a Wedding

The opposition to Davies by the Anglican clergy was manifested early in his ministry concerning his innocuous performance of the marriage of a couple in Caroline County. Not knowing what legal privileges were afforded to Dissenters in the matter, he refused to perform the wedding for nearly a year before consulting with Governor Gooch in March of 1749. Gooch advised him that the appropriate procedure was to secure a license, post it at the meetinghouse where the couple intended to marry, and send the fee to the local Anglican minister. Davies followed this procedure in performing the marriage of a couple in Henrico County and sent the fee to the Anglican rector of St. Margaret's Parish in Caroline County, John Brunskill, whom he informed in writing:

> I had the Governour's Permission to warrant it,—That the Perquisites shou'd be always reserv'd for him, & I design'd never to take a Penny,— That I shou'd yield the readiest Submission to the first Intimation of the Pleasure of my Superior, particularly the Honorable President & Council, requiring me to desist, &c.[2]

Brunskill was, nevertheless, enraged that Davies performed that wedding and wanted him punished by the law. Surprised by Brunskill's reaction, Davies then wrote to the local Justice of the Peace on February 3, 1750 informing him of this matter and seeking his counsel. Davies' plea was:

> Without the Aid of a Judgement superior to my Own, I despair of convincing myself of the Illegality of my Conduct; & therefore humbly submit it to your Honour's Determination, requesting your Opinion of it, or rather (if it be obtainable by your condescending Interposition in my behalf) an Authoritative Order of Council, confirming or nullifying the Governour's License; to regulate & Indemnifie me in my future Conduct.[3]

---

[2] "Letters of Patrick Henry, Sr., Samuel Davies, James Maury, Edwin Conway and George Trask," *William and Mary Quarterly*, Volume 1, Series II (1921), 274.
[3] Ibid.

Davies also assured the Justice that "the Preaching of the Gospel is the Main End of my Function, &, I think, the principal object of my Zeal."[4] Performing marriages, in his view, was secondary to preaching the gospel and he was quite willing to relinquish that privilege upon a lawful order to do so and pledged himself to submit to the awful authority.

Application for a new Meetinghouse in New Kent County

In April of 1750, there was a petition signed by fifteen heads of houses for the licensing of an additional meetinghouse for Davies in New Kent County. Two of the signers were "gentlemen of good estates and excellent characters, who had been justices of the peace and officers in the militia."[5] Part of the petition read as follows:

> Whereas we are Protestant Dissenters of the Presbyterian denomination, under the ministerial care of the Rev. Samuel Davies,—and therefore humbly claim the liberties, and immunities granted to such by the Act of Toleration, upon our taking the qualifications therein imposed, which we are willing to do; and whereas our distance from the meeting-houses now licensed, renders our attendance on Public Worship,. . . sometime impracticable, your petitioners, therefore, pray that a place on the land of William Clopton, in this county, may be recorded, according to the direction of the said Act, and licensed for public religious use.[6]

The county courthouse approved this petition on April 12, 1750 and the petition was signed by the clerk of the county, John Dandridge. The court described them as "behaving in a peaceful manner and conforming themselves according to the provisions of the said Act of Parliament in that behalf made."[7] The licensing of this new meetinghouse to assemble on the land of William Clopton aroused the concern of the General Court because New Kent County was to the east of Hanover and Henrico counties and bordered James City County where Williamsburg was located. The rector at St. Peter's Parish in New Kent County, Rev. David Mossom (1690–1767), served that congregation for the last forty years of his life

---

[4] Ibid.
[5] William Henry Foote, *Sketches of Virginia: Historical and Biographical*, First Series, (Philadelphia: William S. Martien, 1850), 196–197.
[6] Ibid., 169
[7] Ibid., 169–170.

and was probably instrumental in persuading the General Court to overturn the decision of the county courthouse. Mossom was described by one of his former parishioners, Rev. Devereaux Jarratt, as a quarrelsome person who once railed against the clerk of the parish from the pulpit.[8] As a result, the religion and morals in that parish were very low. It is not surprising, therefore, that Mossom would be alarmed by a revivalist such as Davies.

When the Council took up the issue of this petition, they nullified the action of the county court on the premise that the Act of Toleration did not extend to the colony and that county courthouses could not license places of worship for Dissenters. Two primary factors contributed to the overturning of this license granted by the county court. First, Governor Gooch, who always showed leniency towards the Dissenters, returned to England in 1749 due to poor health. From September of 1749 to November of 1750, Colonel Thomas Lee served as the Council's president in the absence of a governor. Lee was not favorable to the New Light Presbyterians and he was responsible for pushing the Council to nullify the actions of the New Kent County Courthouse. Second, the close proximity of New Kent County to the Capitol of Williamsburg aroused greater concern among the Anglicans than any of the earlier petitions which were for additional meetinghouses in counties located away from Williamsburg.

Davies Represents the Petition before the General Court

John Holt Rice tells us what happened when Davies appeared before the General Court in Williamsburg in support of the Dissenters cause:

> On one occasion, by special permission, he spoke for himself. Captain John Morton of Prince Edward county, accompanied him at this time to Williamsburg. The circumstances of the case were often detailed by him with great satisfaction. From his narrative it would seem that the permission accorded, proceeded from an inclination in the king's officers to amuse themselves with the poor Dissenters, than from any other motive. The attorney-general was Peyton Randolph. He took the position that the act of toleration did not extend to the colony of Virginia; and delivered a speech of great legal learning. When Davies rose to reply, there was a

---

[8] William Meade, *Old Churches, Ministers and Families of Virginia*, Volume I (Philadelphia: J. B. Lippincott & Co, 1861), 386.

general *titter* through the court. His very first remark, however, discovered so intimate an acquaintance with the law on that subject, that marks of surprise were on every countenance. In a short while, the lawyers began to whisper, "The attorney-general has met his match to day, at any rate!" The position taken by Davies was that if the act of toleration did not extend to the colony of Virginia, then neither did the act of uniformity. That was illustrated with a force and ingenuity, and knowledge of law perfectly astonishing, and completely victorious. The general sentiment among the members of the Bar, as expressed in the hearing of captain Morton, was "There is a most capital lawyer spoiled." This display of talent called forth universal admiration, and Davies was treated in Williamsburg with great attention.[9]

Some of Davies' arguments on this occasion were:

That the desire of people to attend on his preaching was not. . . to be imputed to him as a crime:—That the ministers of the Established Church in Hanover and other counties had some two, and one three places of preaching,. . .That the members of his church, with the families connected , were sufficient to form two respectable congregations, were they located in the vicinity of each other, and the places of worship;—that they were however greatly scattered. . . and at distances too great to attend at two places, except by riding thirty or forty miles;—That the intention of the Act of Toleration was to enable the Dissenters from the Established Church to worship according to law, and under its provision;—that unless license was given for houses, in sufficient numbers, to accommodate the Dissenters, the intention of the Act of Toleration would not be followed out in its spirit;—and that the Dissenters would be compelled by the court to break the laws of the province which require citizens to be in the regular habit of attending the parish church;—and that it could not be the design of the court to compel the peaceable citizens to subject themselves to expensive and vexatious suits at law, or grieve their consciences.[10]

Davies' clarity of thought and intimate knowledge of the Act of Toleration marshaled forth such strong arguments in favor of the cause of the Dissenters that the General Court did not even attempt to refute his interpretation of it. Whenever courts are caught between what they want to do and what the law says, they resort to finding some technicality, ei-

---

[9] John Holt Rice, "Memoir of the Rev. Samuel Davies," *The Virginia Evangelical and Literary Magazine* (1851), 118.
[10] Foote, Sketches of Virginia, First Series, 171.

ther real or contrived, which will allow them to wiggle out of their dilemma. In this case, the General Court of Virginia decided that the Act of Toleration did not apply to Virginia, even though it had been made a part of the Virginia code in 1699. The law was on the side of Davies and the Dissenters and their efforts would not be for naught in this matter. The decision of the General Court would prove to be a pyrrhic victory at best and an inglorious defeat in the end.

Davies was truly dignified in his demeanor during this appearance before the Court. Someone observed him walking through the courtyard in Williamsburg on this occasion and remarked about him, "He looks like the ambassador of some great King!"[11] Yet, Davies was unimpressed with his performances on this and other occasions. Following an embarrassing situation some years later, he commented that it put him in remembrance of his "mortifications in the General Court in Virginia."[12] If he was mortified in defending the Dissenter cause against Peyton Randolph, he was undoubtedly the only one who realized it.

The General Court Appeals to the Board of Trade in London

Thomas Lee, on behalf of the Council, referred the matter of these additional petitions for licenses to the Board of Trade in London for advice in May of 1750. He described Davies as "a Presbyterian preacher [who] came hither to make proselytes" and whose interpretation of the Act of Toleration "gives great uneasiness to the clergy and people."[13] The answer of the Board of Trade was favorable to Davies' position, but he was counseled by them not to give the officials of Virginia just cause to complain against his behavior. The Lords of Trade responded in part:

> With regard to the affairs of Mr. Davies the Presbyterian: A Toleration and free exercise of Religion is so valuable a branch of true Liberty, and so essential to the improving and enriching of a Trading Nation, it should ever be held Sacred to his Majesty's Colonies. We must therefore

---

[11] Rice, "Memoir of the Rev. Samuel Davies," 118.
[12] George William Pilcher, *The Reverend Samuel Davies Abroad: The Diary of a Journey to England and Scotland, 1753–1755* (Urbana, Chicago, London: University of Illinois Press, 1967),
[13] George MacLaren Brydon, *Virginia's Mother Church and the Political Conditions Under which it Grew, 1727–1784*, II (Richmond, VA: Virginia Historical Society, 1952), 164.

earnestly recommend to your care that nothing be done which can in the least affect that great point.[14]

Before receiving this answer from the London Board of Trade, Commissary Dawson also wrote to the Bishop of London on July 27, 1750 for his advice concerning the New Kent situation. Though he declared his sentiments in favor of toleration, Dawson described the rise of the Dissenters as a "schism spreading itself through a colony which has been famous for uniformity of religion."[15] He unwittingly revealed that he was more in agreement with the Act of Uniformity than the Act of Toleration by this last statement. He also accused Davies of teaching his people to be idle and of preaching on weekdays to mostly poor people, "who, generally, are his only followers."[16] Only the charge of preaching on weekdays was true. Davies was obliged to preach weekday sermons because he was the only New Light Presbyterian licensed by the colony and those who desired his services were more than he could supply on the Sabbath. Dawson's complaint was evidently against Davies making use of the "chapels of ease" like all the Anglican ministers.

Davies then wrote a letter to Commissary Dawson, dated August 19, 1750, requesting a copy of that correspondence with the Bishop of London. He argued that "each party in such a case has a legal right to know the true state of it" and that he was not suspicious the Commissary had "knowingly or willfully given a partial and injurious representation of us."[17] Dawson was aware that he had indeed given an injurious report about the Presbyterians and, thus, refused to comply with Davies' request.

Davies waited for nearly three months on Dawson's reply before completing a letter to Thomas Sherlock, the Bishop of London, which he had begun on August 13, 1750. A copy of his letter to the Bishop was sent to Rev. Philip Doddridge and others for their advice. The advice of Doddridge was that "a minister licensed according to law has a right indifferently to preach in any licensed place whatsoever, and every licensed place is open to every qualified minister whom the proprietor or

---

[14] William Stevens Perry, ed., *Historical Collections Relating to the American Colonial Church*, I, (Hartford, CT: The Church Press, 1873), 380.
[15] Foote, *Sketches of Virginia*, First Series, 176–7.
[16] Ibid.
[17] Ibid., 174.

tenant will employ."[18] Yet, the Bishop of London took a different position in his response to Dawson's letter, wherein he stated:

> The Act of Toleration was intended to permit the Dissenters to worship in their own way, and to exempt them from penalties, but it never was intended to permit them to set up itinerant preachers, to gather congregations where there was none before.[19]

The Bishop wrote Doddridge on May 11, 1751 expressing his offense at Davies' conduct, "who under the colour of a toleration to his own conscience, is laboring to disturb the consciences of others, and the peace of a church acknowledged to be a true church of Christ."[20] Sherlock therein revealed that he also did not think the Act of Toleration extended to the colony. His Lordship also referred to Davies as an itinerant, which to him was the state of the question. Davies wrote again to the Bishop of London in 1751 which letter gave an unflattering account of the Anglican clergy in Virginia:

> They are more zealous and laborious in their attempts to regain those that have joined with other denominations, or to secure the rest from the contagion by calumniating the dissenters, than to convert men from sin to holiness.[21]

In another part of the letter, Davies further elaborated concerning the Anglican clergy:

> The plain truth is, a general reformation *must* be promoted in this colony by some means or other, or multitudes are eternally undone: and I see alas! but little ground to hope for it from the generality of the clergy here, till they be happily changed themselves; this is not owing to their being of the Church of England, as I observed before: for were they in the Presbyterian Church, or any other, I should have no more hopes of their success; but it is owing to their manner of preaching and behaviour.[22]

Bishop Sherlock undoubtedly resented Davies' description of the Anglican clergy in Virginia and might even have considered it a partisan

---

[18] Ibid., 175.
[19] Ibid., 177.
[20] Ibid., 178.
[21] Ibid., 204–205.
[22] Ibid, 205.

attack by a Dissenting minister who chafed at the restrictions placed on his ministry. Yet, Davies' description of the Anglican clergy in Virginia is supported by other reports which were sent to Bishop Sherlock's successors. A few years later, an anonymous layman wrote to the Bishop of London an account of the Anglican clergy in Virginia which castigated several of them. This correspondent said that "Mungo Marshall[23] was one of the most ignorant men (not to say Clergymen) I ever conversed with."[24] This anonymous writer also gave scathing accounts of two other Anglican clergymen: George Purdie of St. Andrew's Parish in Brunswick County and Robert McLaurin of Southam Parish in Cumberland County. Purdie was described as "both ignorant and immoral, to a Scandalous degree."[25] McLaurin was "remarkable only for his ignorance and folly."[26] Over twenty years later, John Lang, rector of St. Peter's Parish in New Kent County, VA, gave the Bishop of London a similar report about the Anglican clergy. He lamented:

> How dreadful is it to think that men authorized by the Church to preach repentance & forgiveness through Christ, should be the first in the very sin which they reprove: this is an infallible Means to keep the people in Infidelity & Impenitence, & to sooth them on to destruction.[27]

These testimonies over several decades from various sources legitimize the charge which Davies laid before Sherlock concerning the Anglican clergy. Virginia was a colony in great need of reformation and the Anglican clergy were a hindrance to the fulfillment of that need. In his letter to the Bishop of London, Davies took much the same position as Gilbert Tennent did in his infamous sermon, "The Danger of an Unconverted Ministry," preached in 1740, but he exhibited a more magnanimous spirit than Tennent.

Meanwhile, Patrick Henry, Sr. sent Commissary Dawson a letter on

---

[23] Mungo Marshall was rector of the St. Thomas' Parish in Orange County, VA.
[24] An anonymous letter to the Bishop of London, February 1, 1754. MS letter in the *Fulham Papers*, Lambeth Palace Library, Colonial Williamsburg Foundation Library, Williamsburg, VA.
[25] Ibid.
[26] Ibid.
[27] John Lang to the Bishop of London, February 7, 1776. MS letter in *Fulham Papers*, Lambeth Palace Library, Colonial Williamsburg Foundation Library, Williamsburg, VA.

August 22, 1751 concerning the New Kent petition and Brunskill's complaint against Davies. Henry stated the New Lights and Davies should be given "no Encouragement. . . which can be legally deny'd them."[28] Henry believed the Justices should reject this latest petition from the New Lights for the following reasons:

> That Mr. Davies perform'd several Parts of his pretended Ministerial Office, both here and in Henrico, before he was legally qualified. That, last May, he transgressed his Limits, by preaching &c. in the Southern Parts of this Colony. That he hath celebrated the Rites of Matrimony, in this, and a neighboring County. That many of his Hearers do, in their Meeting houses hold unlawful Assemblies, in Contempt of the Act of Toleration. That some of them have spoke reproachfully of the Liturgy, & officers of the Church. That they whom Mr. Davies married, joined with him in an illegal Act. These facts will, I hope, demonstrate that both Mr. Davies, and many of his Congregation have failed in giving Sufficient Evidence of their Fidelity to the civil Governments, and inoffensive Conduct.[29]

Henry was actually distraught that Davies had come to Virginia, particularly Hanover County. Davies contended he only wanted to turn men from sin to holiness to which Henry retorted that he then "should not waste his time preaching to those who were already cared for by the established church." "Why," asked Henry, "if Mr. Davies really wants to preach to the heathen, does he not go to the Indians or else to the area of North Carolina."[30] Yet, even Henry knew that Davies' preaching was decidedly different from the Anglican priests in Virginia. His real objection was to the planting of New Testament churches by the New Light minister. Davies' sermons were reaching the masses, which bothered the Anglican ministers in Virginia.

> The religious impressions on the minds of the people under such preaching were frequently attended not only with a copious flow of tears, but with faintings, and tremblings. Some person, therefore, under the signature of Artemas, undertook to lampoon Mr. Davies, whom he designated as the "Geneva Doctor." The writer of the satire, after giving a distorted account of evangelical doctrines, proceeded to describe, in ludicrous lan-

---

[28] Ibid., 275.
[29] Ibid.
[30] Frank Bell Lewis, "Samuel Davies, A Pattern for Preachers in Hanover Presbytery," *Minutes of Winter and Spring Meetings of Hanover Presbytery* (1958), 44.

guage, some of the bodily effects which accompanied the preaching. Mr. Davies immediately answered "the fool according to his folly," in a piece entitled, "A Pill for Artemas",[31] which evinced the power of his sarcasm.[32]

Davies was willing to turn the other cheek when it concerned himself, but he was bold to defend the cause of truth when it was necessary. The reception of Doddridge's communications evoked a lengthy reply to the Bishop from Davies on January 10, 1752. He sent this letter to friends in England whom he desired to present it to the Bishop if they thought it advisable. This letter was "evidence of the honesty and simplicity of Davies' heart, rather than his worldly wisdom," but "was never submitted to the Bishop's inspection."[33]

The charge of itinerancy greatly bothered Davies. He defended himself against this charge by asserting that his congregation was "but one particular church, though dispersed through so many counties and incapable of meeting at one place."[34] He additionally argued that "contiguity of residence" was not essential "to entitle dissenters to the liberties granted by the Act of Toleration."[35] Concerning Dawson's accusation that he was teaching people to be idle and preaching to masses of poor people, Davies responded that many of his "hearers are so well furnished with slaves, that they are under no necessity of confining themselves to hard labour; and that they redeem more time from the fashionable riots and excessive diversions of the age than they devote to this purpose."[36]

Davies never maligned the established clergy in his sermons, but his second letter to the Bishop of London gave a description of their character as follows:

> Instead of intense application to study, or teaching their parishioners from house to house, they waste their time in idle visits, trifling conversation, slothful ease, or at best, excessive activity about their temporal af-

---

[31] This work as well as the lampoon against Davies are not extant and nothing more than this brief notice is known about either.
[32] "A Recovered Tract of President Davies: Now First Published," *The Biblical Repertory and Princeton Review*, IX (1837), 363–364.
[33] Foote, *Sketches of Virginia*, First Series, 206.
[34] Ibid., 189.
[35] Ibid.
[36] Ibid., 198.

Opposition to the Gospel

fairs;—that sundry of them associate with the profane, and those that are infamous for the neglect of religion, not like their professed Master, to reform them, but without intermingling any thing serious in their discourse, or giving a solemn check to their guilty liberties; nay, that some of them are companions with drunkards, and partakers of their sottish extravagances.[37]

People flocked to his services, Davies asserted, because he preached the evangelical doctrines of the Bible with authority and conviction. In another part of this letter, Davies objected to being huddled with the Methodists as though he were motivated by a party spirit. He acknowledged his love for Whitefield, whom he considered a faithful minister of God, while objecting to certain aspects of his first conduct: "the eruptions of his first zeal were, in many instances, irregular; his regulating his conduct so much by impulses, etc., was enthusiastic, and his freedoms in publishing his experiences to the world, in his journals, were, in my opinion, very imprudent."[38]

Davies stated his opinion in this letter that a resident Bishop of the Church in England in the colony of Virginia would reform the morals of many of the clergy. This opinion was contrary to the sentiments of many of the ministers in New England and the Middle Colonies and did not find agreement with the Dissenters in England. Yet, Davies thought the clergy in Virginia were emboldened in their sinful habits because they feared no recourse from ecclesiastical sources. This correspondence to England was concluded in the latter part of 1752 when Davies received a letter from Dr. Benjamin Avery informing him that English dissenters could license as many places of worship as they desired. The opinion of Sir Dudley Ryder, the Attorney General of Great Britain, was also included to the effect that "this interpretation properly extended to Virginia."[39] These preliminary opinions did not lessen the immediate difficulties for Davies, but they gave the Dissenters hope for the future.

---

[37] Ibid., 204–205.

[38] Ibid., 199. Despite Davies' opinion of some parts of them, Whitefield's *Journals* have given spiritual comfort to many Christians.

[39] Ibid., 214.

The Virginia Pindar

Davies' poetry, which he began writing while a student at Blair's Academy, also became a subject of ridicule by a certain Anglican minister. After a few years at Hanover he had collected such a number that several of his intimate friends encouraged him to have them published. Many of these poems were originally "intended only as private Memorials of some Meditations or Occurrences"[40] with no view to publication. Yet, his poetry once in print caused Davies to be derisively called the "Virginia Pindar" by an opponent known only by the pseudonym of Walter Dymocke. Pindar was a Greek lyric poet who lived five centuries before Christ and was described by Quintilian "as by far the greatest of the nine lyric poets" of Ancient Greece.

In a letter dated March 2, 1751, Davies informed his brother-in-law, John Holt, of his desire to have sundry of his poems printed:

> I informed you in my last, that I had given but little heed to the importunity of some of my friends to publish some of my poems; but since that, they told me, that if I should consent to send the copy to the press, they would bear the trouble and expense: and this, with their arguments, has at length determined me to comply. My principal design is, the religious entertainment of ordinary capacities; for, however willing I am, I despair of ever pleasing the nice and judicious.[41]

A year later on April 18, Davies was in Williamsburg and stopped by the bookshop at the *Virginia Gazette* to purchase a copy of Aristotle's *Art of Poetry*. His business on that occasion was probably one of his meetings with Governor Dinwiddie wherein he was soliciting permission for an assistant to relieve him of him of some of his many pastoral duties. In the bookshop, Davies' *Miscellaneous Poems* was also for sale, having been recently published by William Hunter, the publisher of the *Gazette*.[42]

Davies was aware of his deficiencies as a poet and that "the critical and impartial Reader [would] soon discover. . . many imperfections"[43] in

---

[40] Richard Beale Davis, ed., *Collected Poems of Samuel Davies* (Gainesville, Florida: Scholars Facsimiles and Reprints, 1968), iii.
[41] *The General Assembly's Missionary Magazine; or Evangelical Intelligencer: For 1805*, (Philadelphia: Fry and Kammerer, 1805), 539.
[42] Davis, *Collected Poems of Samuel Davies*, xi. Davis quotes from the *Virginia Gazette* Day Book which is the property of the Manuscript Division, Alderman Library, University of Virginia.
[43] Ibid., iii.

them. Thus, he probably would have agreed with Richard Beale Davis that "one may never call his verse great poetry and by no means all of it good poetry."[44] He studied numerous authors in order to develop a better style. Edward Young, Alexander Pope, Isaac Watts, Philip Doddridge, John Milton, the Bible, and the classics were carefully perused in the forming of the Pindaric ode[45] which he used.

Most of the poems in Davies' *Miscellaneous Poems* dealt with sacred subjects. Polyhymnia, or the muse of sacred poetry, had been championed by the Puritans and their successors. Some Christian leaders felt that it was wrong to use verse for anything other than religious purposes. The poems of pagan and profane authors were likewise condemned. Yet, Davies took a somewhat different view. His poetry included some poems in celebration of his love for his wife, Jane Holt Davies. "Conjugal Love and Happiness" dealt with their courtship. Davies expressed his reservations about including this poem in his letter to Holt:

> The Poem on Conjugal Love is wholly my own, not only as to Invention, but intention. If ever I writ anything with tender Emotion and Sincerity, it was this. My Tho'ts were turn'd towards it by Occasion of some pleuretic Symptoms I had not long since. . . if I should publish it in a Vol. with other Poems, its particular Reference to my own Circumstances would probably be discovered, which I would rather conceal.[46]

Davies did not want this poem to cause his enemies in Virginia to accuse him of New Light enthusiasm for indiscreetly revealing his personal circumstances to the world at large. Yet, after careful consideration, he included *Conjugal Love* among several others which spoke of his courtship of Jane Holt, his *Chara*, in the volume of poetry that was published.

The fifty poems in this volume were generally encouragements to self-examination and "variously celebrate[d] the joys and terrors and the hopes and fears of a Christian struggling to find spiritual consolation in God's temporal world."[47] Alexander Pope was frequently quoted by Davies and was the source of inspiration for his poem, "The Messiah's

---

[44] Ibid., xxiv.
[45] Loose irregular verse which were characteristic of the poet Pindar.
[46] Craig Gilborn, "Samuel Davies' Sacred Muse," *Journal of Presbyterian History*, Vol 41, No. 2 (June 1963), 72. Gilborn quotes from a letter from Davies to Holt, March 2, 1751. MS letter in the Library Company of Philadelphia—Historical Society of Pennsylvania, Philadelphia, PA.
[47] Ibid., 70.

Kingdom." Watts, Doddridge, Milton, Baxter, the classics, and the Bible were additional aids to him in the composition of his poems and hymns.

The polite society of eighteenth-century Virginia was charmed by Davies' poetry, but his hymns are best remembered today. These hymns were originally composed as complements to his sermon for that week as he sought "to improve a vacant Hour on Saturday Evening after Study; and to give [himself] a more lively Impression of the Subject of Discourse for the ensuing Day."[48] Presbyterians in Colonial America restricted the singing in worship services to the Psalms and Scripture put to meter. Thus, Davies was the first American hymnist, after the example of Isaac Watts in England.

Sixteen of the eighteen hymns which Davies composed were collected by his friend, Thomas Gibbons of London, and arranged in his *Hymns Adapted to Divine Worship* (London, 1769). The other two hymns were "variations of hymns of Dr. Doddridge."[49]

The most well-known of all Davies' hymns is "Great God of Wonders", based on Micah 7:18. There is no date to this hymn and none of the extant sermons of Davies seem to have suggested it. This hymn by 1892 had been published "in more than one hundred hymn books, in England alone."[50] Samuel Duffield, who wrote *English Hymns: Their Authors and History*, summed up the assessment of several hymnologists with this comment on "Great God of Wonders":

> There are few hymns of consecration which are finer than the one before us.[51]

"National Judgments deprecated, and National Mercies pleaded" was composed by Davies at the same time that he preached two discourses from Amos 3:1-6, "Virginia's Danger and Remedy," occasioned by the defeat of General Braddock and a severe drought in the summer of 1755. After appearing in several early American hymnbooks, "gradually it assumed the character of a fast-day hymn... appearing in prominent collections of the Lutheran, Congregational, Presbyterian, Dutch

---

[48] Ibid., iii.
[49] Louis F. Benson, "The Hymns of President Davies," *Journal of the Presbyterian Historical Society*, Vol. II. No. 7 (December 1904), 343.
[50] Louis F. Benson, "President Davies as a Hymn Writer," *Journal of the Presbyterian Historical Society*, Vol. II, no. 6 (September 1904), 282.
[51] Ibid., 283

and German Reformed Churches."⁵²

Another useful hymn was "Self-Dedication at the Table of the Lord," a sacramental hymn. It was probably composed in conjunction with his sermon from 1 Corinthians 6:19, 20, "Dedication to God Argued from Redeeming Mercy." This was the best known of Davies' hymns in America for over a century. It was printed in the hymnals of Baptists, Lutherans, Methodists, Congregationalists, and other Reformed churches. Charles S. Nutter, who annotated *The Hymnal of the Methodist Episcopal Church*, "described this hymn as 'a rich legacy to the Christian Church.'"⁵³

The Criticisms of Walter Dymocke

Though Davies' *Miscellaneous Poems* found an audience among Dissenters and Anglicans alike, it also opened him to criticism from some of the Anglican ministers who chose to attack him personally rather than critique his poetry. The first notice of Davies' poems for sale came in the January 17, 1752 issue of the *Virginia Gazette*. Two months later, on March 20, the first of eight criticisms of this book was carried by the *Gazette* and signed under the pseudonym of "Walter Dymocke."

The identity of Dymocke remained a mystery and Davies did not unmask him in the pages of the *Gazette*. It is likely, though, that the author of these letters was the Anglican clergyman, John Robertson. Robertson was rector at the Southam Parish in Powhatan County, just south of Hanover County, from 1747 to late 1751. He was among five Anglican priests who signed a petition to the General Assembly in 1748 complaining that "strolling pretended ministers," including "one Samuel Davies," were arousing the "common populace" in the counties in and around Hanover.⁵⁴ Patrick Henry, Sr. was another among the five petitioners. Robertson revived a petty theological dispute with a passage from Davies' poetry in 1753 under his own name which was published in the *Gazette*. In a published letter to Henry, Davies implied that Robertson was the author of the Dymocke letters:

---

⁵² Benson, "The Hymns of President Davies," 351.
⁵³ Ibid., 366
⁵⁴ Bishop William Meade, *Old Churches, Ministers and Families of Virginia* (Philadelphia: Lippincott, 1861), I, 429–430. Also quoted in Craig Gilborn, "Samuel Davies' Sacred Muse," *Journal of Presbyterian History*, Vol. 41, No. 2 (June 1963), 75. Some of this paragraph follows Gilborn's thoughts.

> Assure him [Robertson], I shall never take it ill, that a Gentleman of his Judgment and Moderation should freely make his Remarks upon my Writings or Conduct; especially when he attacks me in open Day in his *proper Name.*"[55]

Davies previously suggested Dymocke was a minister by stating:

> I am confident that I do not treat you out of Character, when I refuse you the Epithet Reverend.[56]

There was some justice in Dymocke's criticisms because not all of Davies' poems were good poetry "as Davies later acknowledged (July 3, 1752)."[57] It is not unusual to find many illustrations of "rough metrics and contrived rhymes"[58] in them. Yet, Dymocke overreached when he criticized Davies' character. The usefulness of Davies' poems was testified by newspapers and magazines publishing them on both sides of the Atlantic.

The last five[59] of the critical articles of Dymocke, published on June 5, 1752, "became less reasonable and more vicious and personal in their attacks,"[60] particularly his comments on Davies' intimacy with God:

> Indeed our Author's whole Treatment of God is such, that setting aside the Pre-conception of his Piety or of his talking to God, you may, without any Force upon his Words, easily imagine him a modern poet addressing himself to his Mistress; or more literally an ancient Bard, making love to his admired youth, or Male-Mistress.[61]

Davies remained silent until Dymocke descended to personal accusations against but he forthwith responded with his defense on June 10, published on July 3. His reason for not replying sooner was:

> Where I have found a scrap of wit unmingled with Prophaneness, I have joined the general Laugh as readily as any of his Readers. Where his criti-

---

[55] *Virginia Gazette*, March 2, 1753. Also, Gilborn, "Davies' Sacred Muse," 78.
[56] Gilborn, "Davies' Sacred Muse", 78.
[57] Craig A. Gilborn, "The Literary Work of the Reverend Samuel Davies," Unpublished Master's Thesis. University of Delaware, 1961, 71. Gilborn dedicates several pages to the discussion of this controversy between Dymocke and Davies and his insights are perceptive.
[58] Ibid., 72.
[59] They were printed on April 17, 30, May 8, June 5, 12.
[60] Gilborn, "Literary Work of Reverend Samuel Davies," 72.
[61] Ibid.

cisms have been just. . . I have without Reluctance resigned the Prey to his Teeth.[62]

Davies accused Dymocke of "putting such horrid Constructions upon the Language of divine inspiration[63], under the popular Pretence of exposing the Performance of a Dissenter."[64] He then revealed: "I am not ashamed to own, I transplanted most of those beautiful Flowers of Poetry, from which you have sucked Poison"[65] from Dr. Watt's *Lyric Poems*, Mrs. Rowe's *Writings*, and Dr. Young's *Night Thoughts*. Then, he concludes:

> When my moral Character is most grossly Aspersed; when I am accused of blasphemously transforming our adorable Immanuel, (to whom I owe all my Hopes of a glorious Immortality, and the Saviour of whose divine Name I would willingly diffuse among my Fellow-Sinners) into an Indian Idolater; when I am charged with undeifying the venerable Jehovah, and transforming him into a Mistress, a He-Mistress, (with pious Indignation and Horror I repeat it; and I hope will pardon my transcribing, thro' an ungrateful Necessity, what you must shudder to read;) when the Devotion of my Poems is represented as a criminal Amour, or Love-Intrigue; in short, when I am aspersed as the most horrendous Blasphemer in the infernal regions. . . I hope, Sir, you will permit me to appear for once in my own Defence.[66]

Another of Davies' replies was published the following week, July 10, 1752, and there were others who wrote in favor of both sides. Davies admitted the justice of some of Dymocke's criticisms, but defended his poetry on literary grounds. "The matter was temporarily laid to rest on August 4 with an anonymous sardonic mock-elegy on the death of Walter Dymocke."[67] Dymocke's criticisms of Davies did not have their intended result. Davies was already widely esteemed for his preaching before this controversy. Most Virginians had the good sense to see that

---

[62] Ibid., 73.
[63] Much of Dymocke's criticism of Davies was really an attack upon Scripture. The "divine inspiration" which Davies refers to is the inspiration of the Bible.
[64] Gilborn, "Literary Work of Reverend Samuel Davies," 73.
[65] Ibid., 73.
[66] *Virginia Gazette*, July 3, 1752.
[67] Richard Beale Davis, *Intellectual Life in the Colonial South, 1585–1763*, Vol. II (Knoxville: University of Tennessee Press, 1978), 375.

Dymocke was really attacking the Dissenters by ridiculing Davies' poetry. Dymocke's criticisms only made the poems of Davies more popular among Virginians.

Conclusion

The prophet Ezekiel was warned by the Lord not to be dismayed before the rebellious house of Israel to whom he was being sent—"neither fear their words not be dismayed at their presence, for they are a rebellious people" (Ezekiel 2:6). The great John Calvin, who knew his share of such opposition, commented on these verses as follows:

> We see, therefore, that the domestic enemies of God not only use threats against his servants, but at the same time bring many false pretences by which they load the true and faithful Prophets with envy and hatred. But, however such calumnies have some appearance of truth when its enemies unjustly press us, God orders us to proceed with unconquered fortitude.[68]

Davies was learning by experience what every true minister of the gospel is taught—that there will always be critics who attack godly ministers in various ways. Eminent holiness, instead of sparing one from critics and persecution, often provokes the wicked to it (cf. Matthew 5:8-11). Every true minister will be ridiculed, scorned, threatened, and falsely accused. The pupil is not above the teacher. He must prepare ahead of time not to give in to such threats. Davies was, therefore, learning to say with Nehemiah, "Should a man like me flee?" (Nehemiah 6:11).

---

[68] Thomas Myers, trans., John Calvin, *Commentaries on the First Twenty Chapters of the Book of the Prophet Ezekiel*, Volume First in *Calvin's Commentaries*, Volume XI (Grand Rapids, Michigan: Baker Book House, 2009), 121.

-8-

John Todd Comes to Virginia

"And you, My dear Brother, who after all your anxious Perplexities about the Place where duty called you to settle, among the many vacant Congregations so earnest to obtain your Labours. . . No doubt, Sir, you will meet with many Difficulties in the discharge of your office. . . You will meet with Opposition and unkind treatment from an ungrateful World."[1]
~*Samuel Davies in the installation sermon for John Todd*~

Jonathan Edwards (1703-1758) whom Davies unsuccessfully tried to call as an assistant to the work in Virginia

---

[1] Samuel Davies, *The Duties, Difficulties and Rewards of the Faithful Minister* (Glasgow: William Duncan, Jr., 1754), 105-6.

John Todd Comes to Virginia

On June 27, 1751, Davies wrote to the Congregational minister, Joseph Bellamy of Bethlehem, Connecticut, concerning the numerous Presbyterians in Virginia who were destitute of a settled minister. The Old Light Synod of Philadelphia had congregations in both Augusta and Albemarle counties, but New Castle Presbytery (New Light) was unable to keep pace with "the settlement of new places or the breaking out of religious concern in places where there was little before."[2] Some of those new places or scenes of religious concern were in areas which Davies tried to supply annually in his wider circuit of ministry. There were enough Presbyterians in those areas to form several new congregations according to his letter to Bellamy:

> There are as many of them as would form five distinct congregations, three, at least, in Augusta, one in Frederica, and one, at least, in Lunenberg and Amelia. Notwithstanding the supplies our presbytery have sent them, some of them, particularly Lunenberg, have been above a year together without one sermon. I hope one of them may soon be provided by a pious young man, Mr Todd, sent by New Brunswick presbytery, but I have no prospect as to the rest; for I can now count up to at least six or seven vacant congregations in Pennsylvania, and two or three in Maryland, besides the five mentioned in the frontier counties of Virginia, and a part of my own congregation, which I would willingly declare vacant, had they opportunity of obtaining another minister.[3]

Those counties were all west of Hanover County. Frederick County was 125 miles from Hanover County and Augusta County was 116 miles from there. Lunenberg and Amelia counties were closer, but altogether they represented a very difficult circuit for Davies in addition to his responsibilities to his Hanover congregation. The congregations in Augusta and Frederick counties were in the Shenandoah Valley with the Blue Ridge Mountains to the east and the Appalachian Mountains to the west. The Opequon meetinghouse near Winchester was certainly the congregation in Frederick County of which Davies wrote to Bellamy. This congregation was first visited by Samuel Gelston (1692-1782) of Donegal Presbytery in 1735, but favored the New Light ministers after the split in

---

[2] John Gillies, *Historical Collections Relating to Remarkable Periods of the Success of the Gospel* (Kelso, Scotland: John Rutherford,1754), 432.
[3] Ibid.

1741. Davies gave Bellamy some brief information about the work of grace in this congregation:

> In Frederick county there has also been (as I have been informed by my brethren who have been there) a considerable awakening some years ago, which has had a blessed issue in many, and the congregation have been seeking a minister for several years.[4]

Winchester is where William Robinson was arrested when he came to Virginia by order of New Brunswick Presbytery. Robinson also preached in Augusta County and the churches there probably owe their first planting to him. The first New Light congregations in Augusta County were Timber Ridge and Providence near Lexington and Falling Springs near Glasgow. Those congregations were planted and watered by the ministries of William Dean (1719-1748) and Eliab Byram (1718-1754). Both ministers were sent out by New Brunswick Presbytery in 1746 to visit Augusta County and the revival lasted there until 1751. As Davies wrote Bellamy:

> In Augusta there is a great number of solid lively Christians. There was a pretty general awakening there several years ago under the ministry of Messrs. Dean and Byram. I believe three ministers might live very comfortably among them.[5]

Davies' Preaching Tours

As the only New Light Presbyterian minister in Virginia, Davies made missionary tours as often as he could to areas where there were new settlements of Presbyterians who were without the services of a minister. In addition to his responsibilities to the seven preaching places in five counties which comprised his congregation, "Davies found time and strength and disposition to make frequent missionary excursions."[6] Most of these excursions were to the counties south and southwest of Hanover County. Davies gave the Bishop of London a report of their circumstances as follows:

> The frontier counties of this colony, about an hundred miles west and

---

[4] Ibid., 433.
[5] Ibid.
[6] William Henry Foote, *Sketches of Virginia, Historical and Biographical*, First Series (Philadelphia: William S. Martien, 1850), 214

south-west from Hanover, have been lately settled by people that came from Ireland originally, and immediately from the Northern colonies, who were educated Presbyterians, and had been under the care of the ministers belonging to the Synod of New York (of which I am a member) during their residence there. Their settling in Virginia has been many ways beneficial to it, which I am sure most of them would not have done, had they expected any restraint in the inoffensive exercise of their religion, according to their consciences.[7]

The counties to which Davies referred included Cumberland, Powhatan, Prince Edward, Charlotte, Nottoway, Augusta, Frederick, Lunenberg, and Amelia. By affirming that numerous of his hearers were Presbyterians before they immigrated to Virginia, Davies was contradicting the argument of the Bishop of London that he was causing a schism in the Episcopal Church by attracting converts from among them. There certainly were Anglicans who became Presbyterians under Davies' ministry, but many of his adherents were transplanted Presbyterians — especially in the western counties of the colony.

On his missionary tours towards the North Carolina border, Davies frequently preached in the woods and sparsely populated areas. Many of the citizens were disaffected to the "New Lights" and it was frequently difficult for Davies to find a place to stay. With few taverns to be found in those counties, "he found it necessary to send forward a messenger to procure a lodging"[8] whenever he was traveling. This practice often gave him the opportunity to be a witness for Christ to those who were opposed to the New Light ministers.

One of the earliest conversions through Davies' itinerant ministry was a land surveyor named Little Joe Morton (1709-1772).[9] Morton was employed by the Randolph family[10] and others to explore uninhabited lands in Virginia for the wealthy gentry who would then lay warrants on them for surveying. His home was near a spot known as Little Roanoke

---

[7] Ibid., 182.
[8] "A Recovered Tract of President Davies: Now First Published," *The Biblical Repertory and Princeton Review*, IX (July 1837), 362.
[9] Little Joe Morton's descendants include the Rev. Dr. Morton Howison Smith, my former professor of Systematic Theology at Reformed Theological Seminary and the first Stated Clerk of the Presbyterian Church in America.
[10] Peyton Randolph was the Attorney General of Virginia and his family was prominent in Williamsburg and the entire colony.

Bridge,[11] on the border between Prince Edward and Charlotte counties. It was said that Morton could track a horse for any distance even if the tracks were crossed by hundreds of other tracks. Like most Virginians, Morton was a member of the Anglican Church. Davies and his guide, John Morton, were overtaken by darkness in the area where Morton lived and had to find some place to reside for the night. John Morton was one of the converts to Christ through Davies' ministry and a cousin of Little Joe Morton. Realizing they were near Little Roanoke Bridge, the young man suggested to Davies that they try to spend the night at his cousin's log cabin.

John Morton then rode ahead to ask his relatives if a New Light minister could spend the night with them. Little Joe was working in the fields and his wife, Agnes Woodson Morton, was reluctant to agree to this request without his permission. Initially hesitant, Little Joe Morton acquiesced in this request and as Foote notes, "Christ and salvation came to that house."[12] James W. Alexander relates what happened next:

> Mr. Davies, by the dignity and suavity of his manners, made such an impression on both, that when he departed they accompanied him to Cumberland[13] to the administration of the sacrament. His wife had become deeply concerned from the first evening, and was anxious about partaking of the Lord's Supper. But she was afraid her husband would not agree to it. She however broke the matter to him on Sunday morning. Though surprised, he told her to do as she thought proper. In the intermission after the "action sermon," he called out Mr. Davies, and told him he wished to join in communion with the church. Mr. Davies, after a little conversation, gave him a token[14] of admission, and the husband and wife went together to the Lord's Table.[15]

---

[11] The Little Roanoke River (or Meherrin River) starts where the northeastern boundary of Charlotte County touches Prince Edward County and runs southeast to North Carolina. It was about 86–90 miles from Davies' home in Hanover County.

[12] Foote, *Sketches of Virginia*, First Series, 217.

[13] Cumberland was probably a 'chapel of ease' that Davies supplied in Prince Edward County where Morton lived. The Cumberland Presbyterian Church was founded at Farmville, Virginia in 1754. It was 10–15 miles north of where Morton lived.

[14] Communion tokens were usually made of metal and were given to those who were permitted to partake of the sacraments to prevent the communion table from being profaned by unbelievers or unholy people.

[15] James Waddell Alexander, *The Life of Archibald Alexander, D.D.* (New York: Charles Scribner, 1854), 179–181.

Little Joe Morton was soundly converted to Christ and soon united with the fellowship of the New Light Presbyterians. He was the first elder of the Briery Presbyterian Church in Prince Edward County which was started through Davies' efforts. Morton and some others joined together in forming the church, and the first church building was erected in 1755. When a preacher was unavailable, Morton frequently taught the people himself by reading a discourse and catechizing the children. He later became a justice of the peace in that area of Virginia and used all his energies in suppressing immorality and profaneness. A wealthy, profane acquaintance once visited Morton, but refused to cease swearing. Morton, after several warnings, fined him according to the law. Archibald Alexander stated he had been "in no neighborhood where any man had left on the minds of all a stronger impression of his integrity and piety."[16]

A very similar experience to Morton's conversion took place on one of Davies' visits to Lunenberg County.[17] Davies and his traveling companion were overtaken with darkness and lost their way while traveling to visit a "little knot of Presbyterians."[18] His companion found the home of a Swiss gentleman by the name of Tscharner DeGraffenreid[19] and obtained permission for Davies to spend the night there. Davies observed there were a large number of black servants about the house and "requested the privilege of having them collected, that he might address them on the subject of religion. By means of these religious exercises, this gentleman and his wife became converts, and joined the Presbyterian Church."[20] Davies' letter to Bellamy gave more information about his visits to Lunenberg and Amelia counties:

> Mr. Robinson was the instrument of awakening several in Lunenberg and Amelia, with whom I lately spent a fortnight, at their earnest desire; and there is a prospect of doing much service, were they furnished with a faithful minister.—I met with most encouragement in a part of Amelia

---

[16] Ibid., 181.
[17] This county was about 90 miles southwest of Hanover County and bordered Charlotte and Prince Edward counties to the east and southeast.
[18] Richard Webster, *A History of the Presbyterian Church: From Its Origin Until the Year 1760*, (Philadelphia: Joseph M. Wilson, 1857), 558.
[19] Ibid.
[20] "A Recovered Tract of President Davies," *The Biblical Repertory and Princeton Review*, 363.

county, where few had heard any of my brethren. The assemblies were large even on week-days, and sometimes there appeared much solemnity and affection among them. There appears great probability of success, if they had a faithful minister. It was really affecting to me that the necessity of my own congregation constrained me to leave them so soon.[21]

DeGraffenreid became a Presbyterian elder shortly thereafter and began to accompany Davies on some of his missionary tours. Yet, Davies continued to give his greatest efforts to Hanover and the surrounding area. By 1751, his congregation had grown to almost three hundred communicants. Davies was convinced most were sincere Christians "in the judgment of rational charity," though some of them were unwilling to seek admission to the Lord's Table due to "excessive scrupulousness." One such member was the mother of Colonel Stephen Trigg,[22] Mary Trigg of Lunenberg County, who was a woman of great piety and goodness. Many years later, she spoke reverently and affectionately of Davies to Archibald Alexander and William Graham.[23] Still evidencing excessive scrupulousness, she stated, "I have never attained to the faith of assurance, but only to the faith of reliance." Graham promptly answered, "If you know you have the faith of reliance, you have the faith of assurance also."[24]

There were also about a hundred Negro slaves who frequently attended the services of Davies at Hanover. Of this number, Davies had baptized forty of them over the previous three years. Some of these slaves later apostatized, but many of them gave credible evidences of a sound conversion until their deaths. Davies said concerning them, "their artless simplicity, their passionate aspirations after Christ, their incessant endeavors to know and do the will of God, have charmed me."[25]

Davies' greatest grief at this time was that "his charge was so extensive that he could not take sufficient pains for their instruction."[26] There

---

[21] Gillies, *Historical Collections of Accounts of Revival*, 337
[22] Stephen Trigg (1742–1782) was an officer in the Continental Army during the Revolutionary War who was killed during the Battle of Blue Licks in Robertson County, Kentucky. He was the son of John and Mary Trigg.
[23] William Graham (1746–1799) was a Presbyterian minister in Virginia and the founder and first President of Liberty Hall Academy, the forerunner of Washington and Lee University.
[24] Alexander, *The Life of Archibald Alexander*, 51.
[25] Gillies, *Historical Collections of Accounts of Revival*, 335.
[26] Ibid.

were cases of apostasy among his hearers, but there were also great numbers who were brought to a saving relationship with Christ. Davies was thankful for these evidences of genuine conversion, but he was apt to judge his efforts too harshly. Thus, he concluded a letter to Joseph Bellamy:[27]

> At present there are a few promising impressions; but, in general, a lamentable security prevails. Oh for a little reviving in our bondage![28]

It was not surprising that the General Court denied a new petition for the license of a meeting place in New Kent County in 1751, but it perplexed Davies nonetheless. Despite the repeated assurances by the governing officials that Dissenters who made the proper applications according to the Act of Toleration and behaved themselves appropriately would be accorded all the rights belonging to them, it was apparent that those rights were considered to be mere privileges which could be denied at the whim of the General Court.

Supply Pastors from the Synod of New York

The Synod of New York (New Light) had been keenly interested in the spreading revival in Virginia for several years even though they had been unable to adequately supply the needs there. In 1745, Synod had instructed William Robinson to return there for several months[29] because of the "wide door that is opened for the preaching of the gospel."[30] Robinson, who had visited Virginia in 1743, died before he could fulfill this request.

A year after Davies took charge of the Hanover congregation, he appealed to the Synod of New York for additional supply pastors. Synod then directed James Davenport, David Youngs, Elihu Spencer, and Ebenezer Prime to write to the Eastern Association of the Congregational Church in Fairfield County, Connecticut, with an urgent request for some ministers to supply the southern provinces of Virginia and Mary-

---

[27] Joseph Bellamy (1719–1790) was a Congregational minister in Bethlehem, Connecticut.
[28] Gillies, *Historical Collections of Accounts of Revivals*, 335.
[29] *Minutes of the Synod of New York, From A.D. 1745 to 1758* in *Records of the Presbyterian Church in the United States of America* (Philadelphia: Presbyterian Board of Publications, 1841), 233.
[30] Ibid.

land. Davenport was instructed to supply Virginia himself if his health was sufficiently recovered.[31]

Davies then wrote to Joseph Pomroy, a Congregational pastor in Connecticut, at the conclusion of that meeting of Synod. He informed Pomroy of numerous vacancies in the colony where large congregations gathered[32] though they were generally over a hundred miles from the nearest New Light Presbyterian minister. This letter described their response to the gospel as "thousands [who] pant for the preaching of the Word, & affect us with their repeated melting supplications to the Presbytery of New Castle."[33] The Presbytery of New Castle had only nine ministers to serve eighteen congregations and Davies considered it his "Duty to endeavor to excite the Consideration & Seek the Assistance of the Ministers of Christ in other Places."[34]

News of Davies' success in Virginia reached Jonathan Edwards in Northampton, Massachusetts in 1749. Edwards related to a correspondent on May 23 of that year the following information:

> I heard lately a credible account of a remarkable work of conviction and conversion, among whites and negroes, at Hanover, Virginia, under the ministry of Mr. Davies, who is lately settled there and has the character of a very ingenious and pious young man; whose support in his preparation for service, Mr. Robinson contributed much if not mostly to, and on his death-bed gave him his books.[35]

Despite the Synod's requests, the Congregational Association in Connecticut was unable to send any of their ministers to assist Davies in Virginia. A few transient visits from some of his own brethren were Davies' only assistance for the first few years of his ministry. In 1750 he again requested help from Synod, which recommended the Presbytery of New Brunswick "endeavor to prevail with Mr. John Todd, upon his being licensed, to take a journey thither; and also to the Presbytery of New York,

---

[31] Davenport had suffered from extreme enthusiasm bordering on madness during the height of the Great Awakening.
[32] Samuel Davies to Joseph Pomroy, May 18, 1749. MS letter in Beinecke Rare Book & Manuscript Division, Yale University Library, Yale University, New Haven, Connecticut.
[33] Ibid.
[34] Ibid.
[35] William Henry Foote, *Sketches of Virginia: Historical and Biographical*, First Series (Philadelphia: William S. Martien, 1850), 172.

to urge the same upon Messrs. Syms and Greenman."[36] James Davenport, who was incapable of traveling to Virginia in 1749, and Eliab Byram were both urged by Synod to visit "the numerous vacant and destitute congregations"[37] in Virginia.

Davenport hastened to Virginia in the summer of 1750 and spent two months assisting Davies. Davies described Davenport's usefulness to Joseph Bellamy in a letter the following year:

> Blest be God, he did not labor in vain. Some were brought under concern and many of the Lord's people much revived, who can never forget the instrument of it.[38]

Efforts to Secure Jonathan Edwards for Virginia

It was in the midst of his communications with Bellamy that Davies received a reply in the summer of 1751 informing him that Jonathan Edwards had been unceremoniously removed from his pulpit at Northampton by a vote of 220 to 23. Edwards preached his farewell sermon to that congregation on July 1, 1750. Davies' thoughts immediately turned to inviting Edwards to come to Virginia, so he hastily began raising the necessary subscriptions to issue a call to Edwards. He made the following observations in reply to Bellamy on July 4, 1751:

> Rev. and Very Dear Brother,—I never received any information of the kind in my life that afforded me so many anxious thoughts, as yours concerning the great Mr. Edwards. It has employed my waking hours, and even mingled with my midnight dreams. The main cause of my anxiety was the delay of your letter which I did not receive till about three weeks ago when I was in Lunenberg, about one hundred and thirty miles from home. This made me afraid lest Mr. Edwards had settled somewhere else, being weary of waiting for the invitation from Virginia.[39] Should this be the unhappy case, and should the obligation to his new people be deemed indissoluble, I shall look upon it as a severe judgment of incensed Heaven

---

[36] *Minutes of the Synod of New York, From A.D. 1745 to 1758* in *Records of the Presbyterian Church in the United States of America* (Philadelphia: Presbyterian Board of Publications, 1841), 240.
[37] Ibid.
[38] Gillies, *Historical Collections of Accounts of Revival*, 432.
[39] Evidently, Bellamy informed Edwards of the requests from the Synod of New York for pastoral supplies to Virginia, which gave him reason to expect a call to the colony.

on this wretched colony. What shall I say? I am lost in perplexity at the thought.[40]

The issues that led to Edwards's removal at Northampton were not a problem for the New Light Presbyterians, particularly his opposition to the Half-Way Covenant. The Half-Way Covenant permitted the baptism of infants on the profession of faith of one of the grandparents and their subsequent participation in the Lord's Supper without giving credible evidence of a saving change. Edwards's grandfather, Samuel Stoddard, who preceded him at Northampton, had influenced much of New England in these lax views of the requirements for worthily partaking of the Lord's Supper. Edwards himself was initially uncertain concerning the requirements of this sacrament. In time, he came to believe personal faith in Christ and satisfactory evidences of regeneration were required by Scripture. His new position, regrettably, aroused the opposition of certain influential members of his congregation and led to his dismissal from that pulpit. The New Light Presbyterians restricted communion to those who made a credible profession of faith by the use of communion tokens.

After his dismissal from Northampton, Edwards was "thrown upon the wide oceans of the world"[41] with no visible means of supporting his family. He continued to supply his former pulpit for several months after his dismissal despite the division in the congregation over his services. Some of his friends wanted to establish a second church in town and install him as the pastor, while his enemies bitterly opposed the idea. Edwards never gave serious consideration to this idea of his supporters.

Edwards had other opportunities to continue his ministry during this period. John Erskine, of Scotland, was interested in helping Edwards relocate across the ocean. He responded to Erskine's questions in a letter on July 5, 1750:

> You are pleased, dear Sir, very kindly to ask me, whether I could sign the Westminster Confession of Faith, and submit to the Presbyterian form of

---

[40] William Henry Foote, *Sketches of Virginia: Historical and Biographical*, Second Series (Philadelphia: J. P. Lippincott and Co., 1856), 44.
[41] Iain H. Murray, *Jonathan Edwards: A New Biography* (Edinburgh, Scotland and Carlisle, Pennsylvania: The Banner of Truth Trust, 1987), 355.

church government; . . . As to my subscribing to the substance of the Westminster Confession, there would be no difficulty; and as to the Presbyterian government, I have long been perfectly out of conceit of our unsettled, independent, confused way of church government in this land; and the presbyterian way has ever appeared to me most agreeable to the word of God, and the reason and nature of things.[42]

Davies was convinced of Edwards's qualifications to pass the trials of presbytery, and requested Bellamy to use his influence in securing his services:

> I assure myself, dear sir, of your most zealous concurrence to persuade him to come to Virginia. Do not send him a cold, paper message, but go to him yourself in person. If he be not as yet engaged to any place, I depend upon your word, and "make no doubt but he will come." If he is engaged, I hope he may be regularly dismissed upon a case of so great importance. Of all the men I know in America, he appears to me the most fit for this place; and if he could be obtained on no other condition, I would cheerfully resign him my place, and cast myself into the wide world once more. Fiery, superficial ministers, will never do in these parts. They might do good, but they would do much more harm. We need the deep judgment and calm temper of Mr. Edwards among us. Even the dissenters here, have the nicest taste of almost every congregation I know, and cannot put up with even the truths of the gospel in an injudicious form. The enemies are watchful, and some of them crafty, and raise a prodigious clamor about raving, injudicious preaching. Mr. Edwards would suit them both.[43]

The plan was to call Edwards to the meetinghouse in Lunenberg which would permit more regular supply to the whole field. Davies was prepared to resign his position at Hanover and use that as an enticement to Edwards, if necessary. The calm spirit and godly character of Edwards were considered by Davies as especially helpful to the Presbyterian cause in Virginia. Davies thought Edwards could "do much good by keeping an academy,"[44] which would also supplement his income.

The original subscriptions from Lunenberg amounted to 80 pounds, which Davies felt would increase by 30-40 pounds in the first year. His own salary was 100 pounds, and he was able to "make a shift to live up-

---

[42] Ibid., 346.
[43] Foote, *Sketches of Virginia*, Second Series, 41.
[44] Ibid.

on it."[45] He therefore believed this amount would be sufficient to support Edwards and his family. Davies delayed sending this letter to Bellamy for nine days by which time he learned that the total subscriptions for Lunenberg would be 97 pounds. Davies renewed his plea in a postscript for Bellamy's aid in persuading Edwards to come to Virginia:

> The people seem eager for him above all the men on earth, yet they request you by me, in case this attempt fails, to endeavor to send some other to settle among them.[46]

They needed "a popular preacher of ready utterance, good delivery, solid judgment, free from enthusiastical freaks, and of ardent zeal."[47] Davies felt both Edwards and Bellamy fit those requirements, and he hoped to secure one or the other for Lunenberg. He dispatched a courier, John Harris, who was well acquainted with the situation in Virginia to take this letter to Bellamy. Davies requested that Bellamy at least visit Virginia if their efforts with Edwards failed. Regrettably, Edwards was already installed at Stockbridge when the letter arrived, and Bellamy refused the offer for reasons unknown. Edwards wrote John Erskine the following year about the invitation from Virginia:

> I was in the latter part of the last summer applied to, with much earnestness and importunity, by some of the people of Virginia, to come and settle among them, in the work of the ministry; who subscribed handsomely for my encouragement and support, and sent a messenger to me with their request and subscriptions; but I was installed at Stockbridge before the messenger came.[48]

It is more than likely Edwards would have accepted this call if the letter had arrived in a timely manner. Yet, the hand of God can be seen in the matter. Stockbridge provided Edwards an opportunity to concentrate on his writing ministry more than Lunenberg would have permitted. Also, Edwards was retiring by nature and was probably not suited to the demands of a frontier ministry.

Davies and Edwards had a brief interview at the 1752 meeting of the

---

[45] Ibid.
[46] Ibid., 43.
[47] Ibid.
[48] Ibid.

Synod in Maidenhead, New Jersey. Edwards, who delivered a sermon before that body, was much pleased with this conversation and wrote to William McCulloch of Cambuslang, Scotland, that Davies appeared "to be a man of very solid understanding, discreet in his behaviour, and polished and gentlemanly in his manners, as well as fervent and zealous in religion."[49]

Death of Samuel Blair

The news of Samuel Blair's desperate sickness reached Davies during his efforts to entice Edwards to Virginia. Blair was only thirty-nine when he breathed his last on July 5, 1751, but he had suffered poor health the last few years of his life. Davies was unaware Blair had already died when he penned a poem on July 9, 1751, expressing his veneration for his former tutor:

> What melancholy news does distant fame
> To anxious crowds and my shock'd ears proclaim!
> With what strange panic is each bosom struck,
> As though some pillar of the Heav'ns were broke!
> Alas! is Blair, the great, unrivall'd Blair,
> Most dear to all, but oh! to me more dear;
> My father! Tutor! Friend! each tender name
> That can the softest, warmest passions claim!
> My faithful guide to science and to truth,
> In the raw years of unexperienced youth:
> Ah! is the heavenly man just on the wing,
> And to his native skies about to spring?
> About to leave us mourning here below,
> And 'mong us share the remnant of his woe.[50]

Davies was unable to visit Blair before his death or attend the funeral. His sadness at this providence is expressed in another part of this poem:

> Oh! did my cruel distance but allow,
> I'd pay the last sad offices I owe:

---

[49] Sereno E. Dwight, "Memoirs of Jonathan Edwards," in *The Works of Jonathan Edwards*, Volume One (Edinburgh, Scotland and Carlisle, Pennsylvania: The Banner of Truth Trust, 1974), cliv.
[50] Richard Beale Davis, ed., *Collected Poems of Samuel Davies* (Gainesville, FL: Scholars Facsimiles & Reprints, 1968), 131.

> With tender hand support thy fainting head,
> Wipe off thy mortal sweat, and weep around thy bed;
> I'd view thee struggling in the grasp of death,
> And share the anguish of thy parting breath.[51]

Samuel Finley, who was with Blair in his last hours, was chosen to preach the funeral sermon and took 2 Kings 2:12 as his text, "And Elisha saw it, and cried, My father, my father, the chariots of Israel and the horsemen thereof. And he saw him no more: and he took hold of his own clothes, and rent them in two pieces." Finley declared that faithful ministers, like Elijah the prophet, are worthy of the appellation, "Father." He supported this point from both Testaments, declaring Blair to be a faithful minister and a father of the colonial church. Davies also esteemed Blair as "my father, Tutor, Friend."[52] Finley described Blair's last days and hours:

> When he approached near to the end he expressed most ardent desires to depart and be with Christ; and especially the last three days of his life were taken up in this exercise. Many gracious words he spoke, gave an affectionate farewell to his most beloved, sorrowful consort, and dear children; tenderly committed them to the divine mercy, and faithfulness; and tenderly prayed, that the blessings of the Most High might be vouchsafed to them; which prayer, I trust, will be answered. His last words, a minute or two before his departure, were these, *"The bridegroom is come, and we shall now have all things."* And thus under a gleam of heaven he breathed out his last.[53]

Davies penned a poem, "Elegiac Verses on the Lamented Death of the Rev. Mr. Samuel Blair," when he received the news of Blair's death. Archibald Alexander said this "poem is more remarkable for pathos than for smooth versification," but it reveals "the opinion entertained of Mr. Blair by this first of American preachers."[54] Davies esteemed Blair as being "as rich a jewel as [this poor world] could boast,"[55] and described his preaching powers as follows:

---

[51] Ibid., 135.
[52] Ibid., 131.
[53] Samuel Finley, *Faithful Ministers the Fathers of the Church: A Sermon Preached at Fogs-Manor. On Occasion of the Death of the Rev. Mr. Samuel Blair* (Philadelphia: W. Bradford, 1752), 48.
[54] Archibald Alexander, *The Log College* (London: The Banner of Truth Trust, 1968), 151.
[55] Davis, *Collected Poems*, 147.

> Now in the sacred desk, I see him rise,
> And well he acts the herald of the skies,
> Graceful solemnity, and striking awe
> Sit in his looks and deep attention draw.
> His speaking aspect—in the bloom of youth
> Renewed—declares unutterable truth.
> Unthinking crowds grow solemn as they gaze,
> And read his awful message in his face.[56]

Alexander wrote a half century later that:

> Blair was truly a burning and shining light; but like many others of this description, while he warmed others, he himself was consumed.[57]

Ministerial Students

The summer of 1751 continued to be a time of remarkable ministry for Davies. One of his missionary excursions took him to Roanoke, Virginia, where he met a young man, Henry Patillo, who was then residing in North Carolina. Patillo had been the subject of converting grace sometime in 1750 which he described in his journal:

> Here, by what means I cannot tell, it being so gradual, I got such astonishing views of the method of salvation, and of the glorious Mediator; such sweetness in the duties of religion; such a love to the ways of God; such an entire resignation to and acquiescence in the divine will; such a sincere desire to see men religious, and endeavor to make those so with whom I conversed, that after all my base ingratitude, dreadfull backsliding, broken vows, frequent commissions of sin, loss of fervor, and frequently lifeless duties since that time, I must, to the eternal praise of boundless free grace, esteem it a work of the Holy Spirit, and the finger of God.[58]

Patillo began speaking to others at every opportunity about the method of salvation which brought him increasing delight. He soon had a desire to prepare for the ministry so that he could preach publicly. His diary records his delight in those experiences:

---

[56] Ibid.
[57] Alexander, *Log College*, 176.
[58] Manuscript Journal in the Patillo Papers, Special Collections, William Smith Morton Library, Union Presbyterian Seminary, Richmond, VA.

I can boast of little success in these endeavors, yet my feeble attempts produced in me an indescribable desire of declaring the same to all mankind to whom I had access; and as I could not do this in a private station, I was powerfully influenced to apply to learning in order to be qualified to do it publicly.[59]

John Thompson, an Old Light Presbyterian minister, was on a missionary excursion into North Carolina for the Synod of Philadelphia when he providentially met Patillo. Thompson persuaded Patillo to pursue his education at the academy taught by Francis Alison in New Londonderry, Pennsylvania. Patillo immediately set out for Pennsylvania, but progressed only twelve miles before he was struck in the night "with a dangerous pleurisy" which kept him "for eight days at the Gates of Death."[60] He experienced a dangerous relapse six weeks later and spent the winter and spring of 1750-51 recovering in Virginia. Patillo and another young man at this point appealed to Thompson to tutor them. The other student suddenly quit a short while later which made Patillo feel wretched and he questioned his call to the ministry. Patillo's journal gives us what happened next:

> But (astonishing the whole) just before this last perplexity, the Rev. Samuel Davies came to supply at Roneoak, and freely offered me his assistance as my Tutor, if I should think fit to come to Hanover, which at that time I would not accept, because of my Prearrangements to Mr. Thompson and said young man. But on the latter's disappointment, the thought of applying for Mr. Davies struck me in my perplexities, with a sudden sweet surprise; I complied with the impression, and in a few days set off for Hanover where I had a kind welcome, and have continued from the first of August in 1751.[61]

Patillo was the first student that Davies began to train for the ministry. He lived in the Davies' household for the next several years and "was sustained in part by the kindness of friends, and in part by spending some hours each day in teaching."[62] Davies also had a hand in training other ministerial students in addition to Patillo. David

---

[59] Ibid.
[60] Ibid.
[61] Ibid.
[62] William Henry Foote, *Sketches of North Carolina: Historical and Biographical*, (New Bern, NC: Owen G. Dunn Co., 1965), 216.

Rice, whose father was an elder at Hanover, was converted in 1753 at the age of twenty and began his studies under Davies. James Hunt, also the son of an elder, probably began his preparations for the ministry during this period. John Harris, who delivered by hand Davies' letter to Edwards in 1751, lived in Hanover County and was another student who studied under Davies. James Caldwell, who was born at Cub Creek in Charlotte County, began his studies under Davies' tutelage in the 1750s before finishing at the College of New Jersey. In several instances, these students lived in Davies' home. It was not his design to finish their education himself, but to prepare them for a college education.

Despite the many successes and disappointments of Davies' ministry in Virginia, the greatest need was for a fellow laborer with whom he could share the many responsibilities in ministering to the needs of the Dissenters. By the end of 1751, Davies had narrowed his search for a helper to John Todd who had supplied the colony for several months by order of New Castle Presbytery.

Seeking a License for John Todd

In the spring of 1752, Davies waited upon the new governor of Virginia, Robert Dinwiddie, to request a license for Todd as a Presbyterian minister in the colony. Dinwiddie took this opportunity to lecture Davies on the duties of a minister which the Governor said Davies was not discharging satisfactorily.[63] The Governor then wrote to the Bishop of London on June 5, 1752 an account of his interview with Davies. In part of that letter, Dinwiddie revealed that he chastised Davies because:

> He did not discharge these duties, which I conceived he could not do without a close residence with his hearers, I must look upon him as an itinerant preacher more out of lucrative view than the salvation of the people. After a long silence he desired I would not look upon him as an itinerant preacher, which character he [abhorred], but agreed with me that in the meeting houses already Licensed he could not discharge the essential duties of his ministry and therefore desired me to admit one Mr.

---

[63] William Steven Perry, comp., "Robert Dinwiddie to the Bishop of London, June 5, 1752," *Historical Collections Relating to the American Colonial Church*, I, (Hartford, CT: The Church Press, 1870), 396.

> Todd for his assistant. I told him I had a due regard for people of tender consciences, and . . . he was admitted to be his assistant.[64]

Governor Dinwiddie was manifestly wrong in accusing Davies of being more interested in lucrative gain than the spiritual needs of his flock. Few ministers have ever been more intently interested in the salvation of sinners than Davies. Such an accusation was no doubt difficult for the young New Light Presbyterian minister to bear, as evidenced by the "long silence" that followed. Yet, Davies' ability to hold his tongue and control his spirit in this situation ultimately gained the very thing in which he was most interested—a license for John Todd to be his assistant. Four years earlier, Governor William Gooch had been forced by the General Council to deny such a license for John Rodgers to labor with Davies in Virginia. Now a new Governor opened the door not only for Todd, but ultimately for additional Presbyterian ministers throughout the colony. Davies meekly bore the injustice of Governor Dinwiddie's remarks, and his humility won the day for the Dissenter cause in the Ancient Dominion. On March 2, 1752, Davies wrote Jonathan Edwards about Dinwiddie:

> We have a new governor; who is a candid, condescending gentleman. And, as he has been educated in the Church of Scotland, he has a respect for the Presbyterians; which I hope is a happy omen.[65]

Davies' assessment of the new governor proved to be accurate, despite the way this interview began. Dinwiddie was probably under a lot of political pressure at the outset of his term in Virginia and wanted to placate the Anglicans. In the end, he proved to be a friend to the Presbyterians and to religious freedom.

John Todd had immigrated to America from Ulster, Ireland, in 1740 and graduated from the College of New Jersey in 1749. On May 7, 1750, he was taken on trials by the Presbytery of New Brunswick, and was licensed six months later on November 13. After his licensure, a report was made to Synod that he was making haste to go to Virginia. Nothing is known about his visit to Virginia except that Davies was pleased enough to seek him as his first assistant. A call to Todd was laid before

---

[64] Ibid.
[65] Dwight, "Memoirs of Jonathan Edwards," in *Works of Jonathan Edwards*, I, cxlvi.

the Presbytery of New Brunswick on May 22, 1751, and was approved contingent on his ability to be licensed by the General Court of Virginia.

The original plan was for Todd to reside in either Prince Edward or Charlotte County, but the General Court refused to license any new meetinghouses for the New Light Presbyterians. Thus, Todd was called as an assistant at four of the seven meetinghouses initially licensed for Davies. Davies continued his ministry to the three congregations in Hanover County, and Todd assumed the meetinghouses in Henrico, Louisa, Goochland, and Caroline counties. This arrangement allowed Davies to more regularly supply the meetinghouses in Hanover County and to engage more frequently in the missionary journeys that were his delight. Also, it provided Todd valuable experience from the counsel and friendship of Davies.

Davies' disappointment concerning Edwards and the sadness of Blair's death were overcome, in part, by the reception of John Todd as an assistant who began his ministry in Virginia in the latter part of 1752. Davies preached a sermon on May 31, 1752, from 1 Thessalonians 2:19, 20 to the meetinghouse on Joseph Shelton's land in Louisa County. It included the following exhortation:

> Exert yourselves to obtain the minister you have in view, in prayer, in proper application to him, & in ensuring to him a competent maintenance, that he may attend upon his great work free from the encumbrance of the world. When you obtain him, take all means to make his ministry comfortable to him, & profitable to you—by loving & esteeming him—by receiving the Word from his mouth as the messenger of God—& by living in peace & love among yourselves.[66]

He concluded by bidding farewell to them and encouraging them to give their support to the new minister. He probably preached the same sermon to the other three meetinghouses soon to be under Todd's pastoral care.

Todd's installation sermon was preached by Davies on November 12, 1752, with the preface being a dedication "To the Rev. Clergy of the Established Church of Virginia." Professing to preach the doctrines of cath-

---

[66] Samuel Davies' MS sermon on 1 Thessalonians 2:19, 20. Samuel Davies Collection (C1042). Manuscripts Division, Department of Rare Books and Special Collections, Princeton University Library, Princeton, New Jersey.

olic Christianity, of the Church of England, of the Reformation, and of the Bible, Davies declared what was the source of the New Lights' success in Virginia:

> If you would know, reverend sirs, what has been the strange charm that has enchanted people in these parts to leave the stated communion of the established church, and to profess themselves dissenters; we can solemnly assure you, and our hearers of every denomination are our witnesses, that it has not been any public or private artifice of ours to expose the liturgy and clergy of the Church of England; but the plain, peaceable preaching of such doctrines as are mentioned in the following sermon, in weakness, and in fear, and in much trembling. And if we may believe the united testimony of our adherents, it was an eager thirst after these doctrines, rather than a dissatisfaction with the peculiar modes of worship in that church, which first induced them to dissent.[67]

The sermon Davies preached on this occasion was taken from Acts 20:24 and titled, "The Duties, Difficulties, and Rewards of the Faithful Minister." Prior to the message, the congregation sang Psalm 132 from Watt's *Psalms and Hymns*. Davies' purpose was to show "the joy resulting at last from the faithful discharge of it, is a sufficient Encouragement to break thro' all the Difficulties attending it."[68] The faithful minister is "to expose, in all its naked deformity and horror, the universal Depravity of mankind, and their liableness to the divine Displeasure."[69] Yet, this is not an end in itself. As Davies said:

> And when we have reduced him to this happy, dreadful dilemma, that he must either submit to Christ, or irrevocably perish, let us exhibit the Almighty Redeemer full to his View, in the Medium of Gospel Light.[70]

Davies thus declared that the single-minded purpose of catching sinners with the gospel net is the chief responsibility of the minister, even as it was exemplified in his own ministry.

Todd quickly met the approval of Davies as a faithful minister according to a letter from James Davenport to Joseph Bellamy:

---

[67] Foote, *Sketches of Virginia*, Second Series, 217.
[68] Davies, *Duties, Difficulties and Rewards of the Faithful Minister*, 13.
[69] Ibid., 16.
[70] Ibid., 23.

> The interests of religion are perceivably advancing, since Mr. Todd's settlement near him. The ministrations of the Word particularly have a more abiding effect & have less time to wear off, as the opportunities of preaching are more frequent in the several congregations.[71]

Todd made the Providence Presbyterian Church near Gum Spring in Louisa County his base of operation and supplied the other three meetinghouses according to his ability and opportunity. Davies finally had his first assistant in John Todd, after four years of laboring by himself. Todd would prove to be a valuable confidant, faithful friend, and worthy minister for the important work in Virginia.

Conclusion

By 1752, the authorities in Virginia had realized that Davies would continue to vigorously request the rights afforded Dissenters under the provisions of the Act of Toleration. They first tried to deny the Dissenters the right to have a sufficient number of ministers to supply the various meetinghouses that had been granted licenses. Then, they denied them the right to preach to more than one meetinghouse. Unwittingly, the decisions of the General Court of Virginia had moved them into an indefensible legal position. They were either going to have to allow the Dissenters the right to preach at more than one meetinghouse or they would have to permit additional New Light ministers to be licensed in the colony. Governor Dinwiddie's letter to the Bishop of London was an acknowledgement that the Act of Toleration did indeed extend to the colony of Virginia. The Dissenters were not immediately given all the rights of that Act, but they soon would be.

---

[71] James Davenport to Joseph Bellamy, May 29, 1753. MS letter in Joseph Bellamy Papers, Hartford Seminary Library, Hartford, Connecticut.

-9-

Preaching That Aroused a Colony

"Let us then bring them into the glorious light of the *Gospel*. Let us open up the Method of Salvation by free grace alone, thro' the Mediation of our great Redeemer. Let us exhibit the blessed Jesus to a guilty World in all the *Glories*, and in all the *Sufferings* of his mediatorial Character; the infinite Dignity of his *Divinity*, and the innocence of his *Humanity*, and the *Merit* of his Obedience refuting from both these Sources. Let us exert all the Power of language to represent the Agonies of *Gethsemane*, the Tortures of *Calvary*, and the guilty Cause and Benevolent Design of all these Sufferings."[1]

~Samuel Davies~

Briery Presbyterian Church in Prince Edward County, Virginia

---

[1] Samuel Davies, *A Sermon Preached before the Reverend Presbytery of New-Castle*, October 11, 1752 (Philadelphia: Franklin and Hall, 1753), 12-3.

I n his incomparable work, *The Christian Ministry*, Charles Bridges quotes from a Mr. Robinson[2] concerning the primacy of preaching:

> It is well to visit; it is well to show kindness; to make friendly; to instruct at home; to instruct at their houses; to educate the children; to clothe the naked. But the pulpit is the seat of usefulness; souls are to be converted and built up there; no exertion must be allowed, which may have the effect of habitually deteriorating this; whatever else is done should be with the design and hope of making this more effective.[3]

It is without doubt that Davies agreed with those sentiments. While he engaged in many activities useful to the spread of the gospel, he never allowed anything to deter him from his grand calling as a preacher of righteousness. Thus, the testimony to the usefulness of Davies' sermons comes from several different branches of the church. Albert Barnes[4], in an introductory essay to Davies' printed sermons[5], stated "he became, perhaps, the most eloquent and accomplished pulpit orator that this country has produced; and was more successful in winning souls to the Redeemer, than any other minister of the age in which he lived, if we except, perhaps, Whitefield and Edwards."[6] The *Methodist Quarterly Review*, in 1846, assessed Davies' sermons "as among the most eloquent and useful sermons ever issued by the American or English press."[7] William Jay[8] stated that "no discourses ever appeared to me so adapted to awaken the conscience

---

[2] Perhaps this is a reference to John Robinson (1575–1625) who was pastor of the Pilgrim Fathers before they sailed on the Mayflower to America in 1620.

[3] Charles Bridges, *The Christian Ministry, With An Inquiry Into The Causes Of Its Inefficiency* (London: The Banner of Truth Trust, 1967), 191, fn1.

[4] Albert Barnes (1798–1870) was a New School Presbyterian who was tried for heresy in 1830 and 1835 for denying original sin, justification by faith, and the imputation of Christ's righteousness. These trials resulted in the split of the Presbyterian Church into two branches, Old School and New School (not to be confused with the Old Light–New Light split of 1741).

[5] The sermons of Davies were collected by Thomas Gibbons of London and printed in multi-volume sets, titled "Sermons on Important Subjects." These sermons aroused immediate interest by the Christian public, both in America and in Great Britain, and were the most popular of any of his contemporaries, with the possible exception of the sermons of John Wesley, until the middle of the nineteenth century.

[6] Albert Barnes, "Life and Times of the Author," in Samuel Davies, *Sermons on Important Subjects*, Volume I, (New York: Dayton and Saxton, 1841), XL.

[7] George Pede, ed., *Methodist Quarterly Review*, 3rd Series, Volume VI (1846), 145.

[8] William Jay (1769–1853) was a Congregationalist minister at Argyle Chapel in Bath, England for 60 years.

and impress the heart. In reading them, one seems always to feel that they were written by a man who never looked off from the value of a soul and the importance of eternity."[9] John Angell James[10] was led, through the reading of Davies' sermons, to make "the conversion of the impenitent *the great end of my ministry*."[11] Charles Hodge of Princeton Theological Seminary considered that Davies' sermons "have certainly proved the most generally acceptable ever published in this country."[12]

Davies' printed sermons were also instrumental in the conversion of sinners long after his death. An anecdote given by William Henry Foote illustrates this point:

> A gentleman of high standing in Virginia became deeply impressed with a sense of religion, and was aroused to seek the salvation of his soul. He enquired of a bookseller for some religious books. Davies' printed sermons were offered to him; and at first refused. But recollecting to have heard his father recount the circumstances of a Mr. Davies coming in contact with the Attorney General at Williamsburg, while he was a student of law at that place, and remembering that his father esteemed him a most extraordinary man, he purchased the volumes. The reading was specially blessed to him, and he was led to rejoice in the hope of the gospel. He ever afterwards spoke of the sermons as his father had spoken of their author—as "most extraordinary."[13]

Davies' Sermon to New Castle Presbytery

Davies' views of preaching were eloquently unfolded to New Castle Presbytery in a sermon he preached on October 11, 1752. This sermon, later printed by Benjamin Franklin, expressed his views on the essential marks of true preaching and the success of the ministry. His main points are incomparable elements of what constitutes faithful preaching. He be-

---

[9] George Redford and John Angell James, eds., *The Autobiography of William Jay*, (Edinburgh, Scotland and Carlisle, Pennsylvania: The Banner of Truth Trust, 1974), 123.

[10] John Angell James (1785–1859) was a Nonconformist minister at Carrs Lane Independent Chapel in Birmingham, England for more than 50 years.

[11] John Angell James, *An Earnest Ministry the want of the Times*, (New York: M. W. Dodd, 1850), 40.

[12] Charles Hodge, "The Theological Opinions of President Davies," in *The Biblical Repertory and Princeton Review* (1842), 144.

[13] William Henry Foote, *Sketches of Virginia: Historical and Biographical*, First Series, (Philadelphia: William S. Martien, 1850), 294.

lieved an unmistakable relationship existed between personal holiness and success in the ministry. He declared that careful preparation of sermons should be "intermingled with frequent excursions of the heart to God in prayer."[14] In all his messages, the faithful preacher must discover such an earnestness of spirit that will affect the hearts of our hearers. As he proclaimed:

> Such is the Constitution of human Nature, that we will *speak* in earnest, when we *are* in earnest. If we observe the most unpolished Speakers, when they are in earnest, even in common Conversation, we will find that *Nature* teaches them such *Expressions*, such a modulation of the *Voice*, such *Looks* and *Gestures*, as bespeak their Earnestness with inimitable Eloquence. And certainly when we feel the Almighty Energy of eternal Things, we cannot but give evident Indications of it in our Delivery: Let us therefore throw off the Mask of so awkward an Hypocrisy, and discover the inward Ardour and passionate Concern of our Hearts, if we would act the *Orator*, the *Minister*, or the *Christian*.[15]

Preaching week by week with such earnestness is not an easy matter for any minister as Davies knew by experience. Thus, he assessed his own preaching efforts as follows:

> Once in three or four weeks I preach as I could wish; as in the sight of God and as if I were to step from the pulpit to the supreme tribunal. I feel my subject. I melt into tears, or shudder with horror, when I denounce the terrors of the Lord; I glow, I soar in ecstacies, when the love of Jesus is my theme.[16]

Preaching with Diligent Preparation

Davies' first rule was that ministers of the gospel must cast off laziness in sermon preparation and "make *proper Preparations* for our publick Ministrations."[17] Thus, he exhorted his fellow ministers to avoid "the fooleries of trifling Conversations" and not to "suffer the Affairs of this Life to engross their Time and Thoughts,"[18] but to be diligent students, as follows:

---

[14] John Holt Rice, ed., *The Virginia Evangelical and Literary Magazine*, Vol. IX (1826), 508.
[15] Davies, *Sermon Preached before the Reverend Presbytery of New-Castle*, 18.
[16] Richard Webster, *A History of the Presbyterian Church in America: From Its Origin Until 1760*, (Philadelphia: Joseph Watson, 1857), 558.
[17] Davies, *Sermon Preached before the Reverend Presbytery of New-Castle*, 8.
[18] Ibid.

> If any in the sacred Character are capable of so much Meanness, they will prove a Disgrace to their fashion; and they will have the Mortification of seeing themselves excelled by Persons inferior to them in Parts and Education; for a *barren* Genius, diligently *cultivated* will produce more useful Fruits, than the wild spontaneous Productions of a *luxurious* Genius, suffered to *run waste*; and the best Foundation of Learning laid in Youth will soon become a Scene of Desolation and Ruin, unless Structure be carried on, and the Wastes of Time repaired, by diligent Study during our Afterlife.[19]

Careful, painstaking study was the regular habit of Davies. As B. E. Edwards, one of Davies' biographers, said about his preparations for the pulpit:

> Nor was he one of those who boasted how easily and rapidly his sermons were composed. He is known to have declared, that "every discourse of his which he thought worthy of the name of a sermon, cost him four days' hard study in the preparation."[20]

Davies wrote out every sermon in full, despite his numerous pastoral duties. He then preached the same messages to the various meetinghouses under his care which practice he could observe "without much danger of any of his hearers having heard the same discourse twice"[21] because of the great distances between his preaching posts. He would take the completed manuscript—a small hand-stitched booklet[22] which he carried in his coat pocket—into the pulpit from which he would make more or less use in the delivery of the sermon. He was not tied to the actual words he had written but was free "to extemporize to very happy effect"[23] which he encouraged others to do as well:

> And let us not so scrupulously *confine* ourselves in Publick to the Path we have laid out for ourselves in our Studies, as to admit no extempore Amplifications, or occasional Excursions; for it is attested by the Experience of all that have made the Trial, that in the Fervour of our publick Ad-

---

[19] Ibid., 8-9.
[20] B. E. Edwards, *American Quarterly Register*, Vol. IX, No. 4 (May 1837), 323.
[21] Albert Barnes, "Life and Times of the Author," in Samuel Davies, *Sermons on Important Subjects*, I (New York: Dayton and Saxton, 1841), xxviii.
[22] The Presbyterian Historical Society in Philadelphia has some of these original sermon booklets of Davies.
[23] Barnes, "Life and Times of Davies," in Davies, *Sermons on Important Subjects*, I, xxix.

dresses, a Variety of tender and passionate, and in the mean time *pertinent*, Thoughts will occur to us, which we might have sought in vain in the Coolness of our private Studies.[24]

Davies' own ability and freedom to extemporize caused some people to question his use of a manuscript. Yet, he drew a distinction between the unction of the Spirit in applying the message in ways that had previously not been considered and preaching extempore without any prior study. He encouraged ministers to seek the former but to eschew the latter. One of his elders quizzed him very closely on this matter, to which Davies responded:

> I always thought it to be a most awful thing to go into the pulpit and there speak nonsense in the name of God. Besides, when I have opportunity of preparing, and neglect to do so, I am afraid to look up to God for assistance, for that would be to ask him to countenance my negligence. But when I am evidently called upon to preach, and have had no opportunity to make suitable preparation, if I see it clearly to be my duty, I am not afraid to try to preach extempore, and I can with confidence look up to God for assistance.[25]

Davies spent as much time as he could in sermon preparation and theological education. His personal library consisted of 550 volumes—most of them bequeathed to him by William Robinson—which included as many of the standard works of theology and commentaries on the Scripture as possible. His library was small by the standards of most ministers today, but it was large for his own time. His greatest challenge was finding the time to study amidst his other duties, but he learned to redeem the time in other ways. His frequent journeys through "the silent forests" of Virginia sometimes provided him with ample opportunities "for meditation and reflection, and lively mental action."[26] In some respects, this reflection was probably better than his usual studies. As a result, William Henry Foote stated about Davies:

> The few hours he could spend in study, or with his pen, he was prepared to use to the greatest advantage on some angelic theme that had been the subject of his solitary meditations; or some point in morals or theology forced

---

[24] Davies, *Sermon Preached before the Reverend Presbytery of New-Castle*, 10.
[25] Barnes, "Life and Times of Davies," in Davies, *Sermons on Important Subjects*, I, xxviii.
[26] Foote, *Sketches of North Carolina*, 301.

upon his attention by the necessities or passions of his fellow men.[27]

Yet, Davies was not one who studied only with an eye to the pulpit and the needs of others. He first fed his own soul with his studies. His secret power in preaching can be discovered by a perusal of the notes he left behind in both an English Bible and a Greek New Testament. He gave out to his people what first fed his own soul. In commenting on Paul's statement in Galatians 4:18, "I have all things; I abound; I am full," Davies noted:

> And what was the reason of this? Had the possession of a large estate fallen to him? or had the abundance of riches poured in upon him? No: the poor prisoner had only received a small collection from the Philippian Church, just to furnish him with food and raiment. And who, without his Spirit, would have thought this such a mighty matter? But his contented and self-satisfied soul puts a language into his mouth, that the Emperors would never reach. When did Caesar or Darius, or any of the monarchs of the Earth, cry out, "I have all things; I abound; I am full."[28]

In the great passage on the humiliation of Christ, Philippians 2:6-8, Davies suggested the following train of thought in his notes:

> The first step of his humiliation was his assuming human nature in its lowest & most servile form: and he continued descending lower & lower all his life, till at length he reached the lowest step possible, the ignominious & torturing death of the cross.[29]

On Galatians 6:1, the well-known passage which commands believers to restore the sinning brother, Davies commented:

> Katartidzete signifies to *set* or *replace* a dislocated joint: and here it emphatically signifies the painful situation of the fallen brother—the pain & loss the church sustains by his fall—especially the care & tenderness that should be urged for his restoration.[30]

These comments are the more remarkable because none of Davies' sermons are known to be from these passages or made use of these in-

---

[27] Ibid.
[28] Samuel Davies' MS Bible. Samuel Davies MS, Virginia Historical Society, Richmond, VA.
[29] Ibid.
[30] Samuel Davies' MS Greek New Testament. Rare Book Division, Department of Rare Books and Special Collections, Princeton University Library, Princeton, New Jersey.

sights. It is certainly possible, even likely, that they were interwoven in sermons which were never published, but the remarkable thing is that these notes were made in the margins of his Bible—not on scraps of paper which he might have used for sermon preparation. In other words, these thoughts first fed his own soul. Davies believed Scripture was to be studied for the spiritual value it brings to the individual. He drank deeply from the wells of grace for his own soul and invited thirsty souls to drink from that same cistern.

Preaching with Prayerfulness

Yet, study alone was not sufficient, as Davies acknowledged a little further in this sermon to New Castle Presbytery, and that leads to his second constituent element of true preaching—frequent, heartfelt prayer in all our studies. As he said:

> And, *by Study*, intermingled with frequent excursions of the Heart to God in Prayer, and solemn Applications of divine Subjects to ourselves, we may make such deep impressions upon our Minds, as will give our Discourses those *genuine* Indications of affectionate Earnestness, and adorn our Delivery with that natural Air of Solemnity, which is the most powerful Oratory to our Hearers; and which *Affectation* and *Grimace* attempts to counterfeit in vain.[31]

It is in this area where many ministers fail in their sermon preparation. Sermons well prepared but not bathed in prayer will fail to make a deep impression on the hearts of the hearers. As Robert Murray McCheyne wrote a century later concerning his own resolutions for personal reformation:

> I am persuaded that I ought never to do anything without prayer, and, if possible, special, secret prayer.[32]

The primacy of preaching must certainly be supported by diligent study and secret prayer. Sermons that are haphazardly prepared will have a blunt edge rather than be the sharp, two-edged sword of the Scripture. Sermons that are diligently prepared without secret prayer

---

[31] Davies, *Sermon Preached before the Reverend Presbytery of New-Castle*, 9.
[32] Andrew A. Bonar, *Memoir and Remains of Robert Murray McCheyne* (London: The Banner of Truth Trust, 1966), 158.

will be like Ezekiel prophesying to the valley of dry bones. Earnest prayer beseeches the ministry of the Holy Spirit as the only One who can make dry bones come alive. The secret of Davies' preaching was that he knew the human voice was incapable of reaching the hearts and consciences of sinners. Thus, he made frequent, heartfelt excursions to God while preparing his messages even as he exhorted the ministers of the Presbytery of New Castle to do likewise. Another reason ministers must be frequent in prayer is to receive insight into the passage they are studying. As Charles Spurgeon wrote in *Lectures to My Students*:

> Texts will often refuse to reveal their treasures till you open them with the key of prayer. . . The closet is the best study. The commentators are good instructors, but the Author himself is far better, and prayer makes a direct appeal to him, and enlists him in our cause. It is a great thing to pray one's self into the spirit and marrow of a text; working into it by sacred feeding thereon, even as the worm bores its way into the kernel of the nut.[33]

Davies' encouragement to his brethren in New Castle Presbytery was also his daily practice in his own study. The unique insight he gained into Scripture passages was not the result of diligent study alone, but especially the result of his secret prayer before the God of all grace.

Preaching Evangelical Doctrines

The third constituent element of gospel preaching, according to Davies, is that it must "insist on those subjects that are purely *evangelical*, or peculiar to the *Religion* of Jesus, as best adapted to the great ends of our Ministry."[34] And, what are those subjects that are purely evangelical? Davies elaborates:

> Let us lay open the present Degeneracy of human Nature in all its naked deformity; alarm the secure Conscience with the Glare of Conviction; awaken hardy Impenitents by the Terrors of the Lord; overturn, overturn, overturn their presumptuous Confidences, and sweep away their Refuge of Lies, and wound them, that they may give a welcome Reception to the Physician.

---

[33] C. H. Spurgeon, *Lectures to My Students* (Grand Rapids, Michigan: Associated Publishers and Authors, Inc, n.d.), 42.

[34] Davies, *Sermon Preached before the Reverend Presbytery of New-Castle*, 11.

> Let us then bring them into the glorious Light of the Gospel. Let us open up the Method of Salvation by free grace alone, thro' the Mediation of the great Redeemer. Let us exhibit the blessed Jesus to a guilty World in all its Glories, and in all the sufferings of his mediatorial Character; the infinite Dignity of His Divinity, and the Innocence of his Humanity, and the infinite Merit of his Obedience resulting from both these Sources. Let us exert all the Power of Language to represent the Agonies of Gethsemane, and the Tortures of Calvary, and the guilty Cause and benevolent design of all these sufferings. Let us point to him lifted up on the cross, as the great Expiation for Sin, and the resistless Magnet to draw all men to him. Let us lay open the Tenderness of his Heart, and his Willingness to entertain the vilest of Sinners upon their application to him. Let us principally dwell upon what is generally distinguished by the name of experimental religion, the nature and necessity of regeneration, of faith, repentance, and other Christian Graces. Let us adapt our discourses to the various cases of Saints and Sinners, to instruct, to wound, to comfort and support, according to their respective Exigencies.[35]

Davies commended to New Castle Presbytery preaching which proclaims ruin by the fall, righteousness through Christ, and regeneration by the Spirit. He believed carnal security and the impenitence of sinners had to be swept away before they would "give a welcome reception to the physician."[36] Once sensible of their native depravity, Davies then believed the minister is to "bring them into the glorious light of the Gospel"[37] and to dwell upon the nature of experimental religion.

The Personal Holiness of Preachers

Davies' fourth constituent element of gospel preaching was personal holiness. Later in this sermon to New Castle Presbytery he enforced this point:

> That *the Force of Example is greater than that of Precept*, is a trite and true Observation. A deviation from our own Instruction will disqualify us to declare the whole Counsel of God, as it will either confuse and dash us with conscious *Shame* or tempt us, in Mercy to ourselves, not to urge the *Strictness* of evangelical Holiness. An imitable Practice will *adorn the Doctrine of Godliness,* and prevent *the Name of God,* from being *blasphemed* in

---

[35] Ibid., 12-3.
[36] Ibid., 12.
[37] Ibid.

the World; and it will procure Veneration to the Ministerial Office, and so facilitate our Access to the Minds of Men, and promote our Success.[38]

The subject of holiness was one of Davies' favorites. He was especially interested in practical works on personal holiness and had begun to gather materials for a book which he hoped to write on the morality of holiness. He never wrote such a book, but his studies helped prepare him for a controversy in which he was embroiled a few years later.

Davies' personal holiness was evidenced in many ways, but especially in the manner in which he responded to unjust treatment by others. He put the best interpretation upon the actions of others and defended himself while showing respect for his opponents. His boyhood friend, John Rodgers, once said concerning him:

> I never saw him angry during several years of unbounded intimacy, though I have repeatedly known him to be ungenerously treated.[39]

Turning the other cheek was a constant practice of the New Light minister. Concerning the criticism he received from the Anglican pastors in Virginia, Davies remarked:

> Tho' the pulpits around me, I am told, ring with exclamatory harangues, accusations, railings, warnings, etc, etc., etc., against New-Lights, Methodists, Enthusiasts, Deceivers, Itinerants, Pretenders, etc., etc., etc., yet I never design to prostitute mine to such mean purpose.[40]

As Davies preached, so he lived. People flocked to hear him preach because they saw his life as a walking testimony of grace. He first preached to himself and then fed his flock. He took seriously the admonition of Paul to Timothy: "Pay close attention to yourself and to your teaching," (1 Timothy 4:16).

Davies' Influence on His Flock

John Holt Rice conversed with elderly Virginians nearly fifty years later who had heard Davies in their youth. They conveyed to Rice "that his

---

[38] Ibid., 18-9.
[39] Samuel Finley, "Sermon on the Death of the Rev. Samuel Davies," in Samuel Davies, *Sermons on Important Subjects*, I (New York: J & J Harper, 1828), 22. Footnote reference.
[40] Samuel Davies, *The Impartial Trial, Impartially Tried, and Convicted of Partiality* (Williamsburg: William Parks, 1748), 26–27.

[Davies'—DR] powers of persuasion seemed sufficient for the accomplishment of any purpose which a minister of the gospel would undertake."[41] As Rice expounded:

> Many, for instance, who had grown up in ignorance of religion, who were married and settled in life, and had children around them, were prevailed on to learn the elements of religious knowledge. A mother might often be seen rocking her infant in a cradle, sewing some garment for her husband, and learning her catechism at the same time. A girl employed in spinning would place her book of questions at the head of the wheel, and catching a glance at it as she ran up her yarn on the spindle, would thus prepare for public catechising; and boys, were often to be seen, while their horses were feeding at midday, learning the weekly task. Young and old were willing to be taught by their preacher; and when assembled for catechetical instruction, the elders of the church, and heads of families, were always examined first. This course of instruction however was not brief, and quickly finished as is the case now.[42]

The heads of each household in the Hanover congregation were provided with standard works on experimental theology which they were expected to read and teach to their families. Books such as Watson's *Body of Divinity*, Boston's *Fourfold State*, Luther on *Galatians*, Flavel's *Works*, Baxter's *Call to the Unconverted* and *Saints' Everlasting Rest*, Alleine's *Alarm to the Unconverted*, and others lined the mantles of almost every fireplace.[43] In this way, Davies turned his churches into schools where his people were trained in holiness. Assessing the situation in the early nineteenth century, Rice said, "The effect of this discipline remains to this day."[44]

Quotes from Davies' Sermons

There are few sermons dated from the first five years of Davies' ministry in Virginia. The earliest known sermon from this period was preached in October of 1748 from Song of Solomon 5:16, "Christ the Beloved and Friend." The title clearly indicates that he viewed Canticles, the Song of Solomon, as an allegory which points to the believer's relationship with

---

[41] John Holt Rice, "Memoir of the Rev. Samuel Davies," *Virginia Evangelical and Literary Magazine*, I (Richmond: William W. Gray, 1819), 202.
[42] Ibid.
[43] Ibid.
[44] Ibid.

Christ and not just a song about human love. A few months later, on January 19, 1749, Davies preached from Luke 14:27, "Whoever does not carry his own cross and come after Me cannot be My disciple." In explaining what it means to bear one's own cross, Davies applied his message as follows:

> Do you take up your cross in parting with your former sinful delights & gratifications? Have you abandoned those sins to which you have been enflamed? Have you changed your company for companions of the pious mould? Or don't you rather shun the conversations of the godly, & choose those of a looser turn, as more of your temper & spirit? Are you not frequently among the swearers, drinkers, rovers, & frolickers? Is this taking up your cross, & following Christ?[45]

Such pointed application was typical of all Davies' sermons. He first applied the message to his own heart and then asked piercing questions in the second person plural form. He was not conceited of his own blamelessness concerning these matters, but was convinced that using second person plural pronouns was the most forceful way to reach the consciences of his hearers.

Other sermons preached by Davies in these early years included several messages from 1 John in November and December of 1750; a sermon on "Self-Dedication" from Romans 6:13 on June 15, 1750; "The Law and the Gospel" from Galatians 3:9, 10 on August 19, 1750; "Separation from God the Most Intolerable Punishment" on January 13, 1751; and, "The Conflagration" from 2 Peter 3:11 on January 27, 1751. These messages were never printed but we know the titles because of poems that he wrote for each of them. What we see in them is the same thing we see in his printed sermons; that is, that the spiritual needs of his flock were never far from his view. As John Holt Rice commented:

> All persons who ever heard Mr. Davies preach agree in the opinion, that his sermons were the most impressive they ever heard. An old Presbyterian elder of much knowledge and experience, who lived west of the Blue Ridge, told the writer, that when a young man he heard him preach his sermon on the "The One Thing Needful," on the text, "Martha, Mar-

---

[45] Samuel Davies, MS sermon on Luke 14:27 and dated January 19, 1749. Samuel Davies Collection (C1042). Manuscripts Division, Department of Rare Books and Special Collections, Princeton University Library, Princeton, New Jersey.

tha,"etc., and that the solemnity of his manner in pronouncing the text produced a greater effect on his mind than any sermon he had ever heard.[46]

In that particular sermon, "The One Thing Needful," Davies delineated the essential difference between Christians and unbelievers:

> In that day it will be found, that the main difference between true Christians and the various classes of sinners is this: God, Christ, holiness, and the concerns of eternity, are habitually uppermost in the hearts of the former; but, to the latter, they are generally but things by the by; and the world engrosses the vigour of their souls, and is the principal concern of their lives.[47]

The Effect of Davies' Preaching and Ministry

The sermons of Davies produced spiritual benefit to many people who were not even Presbyterians.

> A few years after [his] departure, the Baptists spread over Virginia like a torrent, and their converts proceeded to give a public account of their religious awakening and experience, nothing was more common than for a person to begin by saying, "At such a time and place I heard the Rev. Mr. Davies preach, and had my mind deeply impressed."[48]

Some of those converted under Davies became Baptist ministers. In Goochland County, a young man named Reuben Ford "professed vital faith"[49] through the joint ministry of Whitefield and Davies, was baptized into the Baptist communion in 1769, and became a minister of that denomination.

Samuel Brame, the son of an elder at Hanover, grew up under the influence of Davies' voice. In adulthood, he became a Baptist preacher of the "most conspicuous talents."[50] Likewise, his mother joined the Baptist church at the Reeds[51] in her later life. In earlier years, "she frequently heard Mr. Whitefield in his travels through America, and sometimes had

---

[46] Charles, Hodge, ed., *The Biblical Repertory and Princeton Review*, IX (July 1837), 363
[47] Samuel Davies, *Sermons on Important Subjects*, I (New York: J & J Harper, 1828), 342.
[48] Hodge, *Biblical Repertory and Princeton Review*, 362.
[49] G. W. Beale, rev., Robert Baylor Semple, *A History of the Rise and Progress of the Baptists in Virginia* (Richmond: Pitt and Dickinson, 1894), 25.
[50] Ibid., 153.
[51] The Reeds is an area in Cumberland County, Virginia, that was originally named after the plantation owned by the Corbin family—one of the leading families of colonial Virginia.

him in her house."[52] One who interviewed her during this later period of her life commented:

> 'Tis pleasant to hear this mother in Israel tell the interesting anecdotes which she treasured respecting these great men of God. Mrs. Brame is truly one of the daughters of Sarah.[53]

Samuel Thompson often heard Davies in his youth before moving to Nottoway County. In 1768, Thompson was instrumental in a revival among the Baptists of Nottoway in the same manner that God used Samuel Morris in Hanover. "He was not a preacher, yet, willing to do what he had talents for, he read publicly to such as would come to hear Whitefield's and Davies's sermons. By this means some of his neighbors obtained a hope of eternal life."[54] The result was people sought the services of Baptist ministers who preached similar doctrines and "a great work broke out in those parts."[55]

Through Davies' numerous labors, it seemed that an entire colony was aroused by his voice or his example. Multitudes were delivered from darkness into everlasting light. The revival did not come through the established clergy, but resulted from the humble, gospel-centered ministry of the New Light Presbyterian minister in Hanover.

Conclusion

The ministry and sermons of Davies are a sobering tonic to the frothy, lighthearted preaching of our modern world. It is easy to see why he is considered by many to be one of the greatest preachers of all time. Yet, we should not be discouraged when we read his sermons. Davies certainly preached the Scriptures, but he did more than that. He preached with the purpose of casting the gospel net as widely as possible in order to win souls for Christ. His messages remind us that we are not just Bible teachers. We are to be fishers of men. In that respect, let us follow his example as he was following the Lord. Reading his sermons provides a better example than is often found with others. Davies would have agreed with the words of Charles Bridges on preaching:

---

[52] Ibid., 154.
[53] Ibid.
[54] Ibid., 263.
[55] Ibid.

The Scriptural rule for preaching is—"If any man speak, let him speak as the oracles of God;" forming all our discourses according to the sacred model, "as Moses was ordered to make all things according to the pattern showed him in the mount." This rule implies great care to give to every point in the system, its just weight and proportion. Every man takes his own view of the truth of God. The bias of individual constitution or of circumstances, unconsciously places him in imminent danger of preaching either a defective or a disproportioned Gospel. Our rule will however frame itself into the determination of the Apostle—"not to know anything among our people, save Jesus Christ and him crucified." This is the one mode of preaching that God has promised to bless.[56]

Few preachers in the history of the church have so consistently restricted themselves to proclaim only the oracles of God, especially the gospel in all its glory, as did Davies. What Davies proclaimed to New Castle Presbytery was his own practice and the grand reason the Lord so imminently blessed his ministry.

---

[56] Charles Bridges, *The Christian Ministry* (London: The Banner of Truth Trust, 1967), 240.

-10-

The College of New Jersey

"The nature and history of the Log College and its blooming into Princeton form a subject of much greater significance to the latter institution than at first appears or than has ever been considered. There are vital interests of Princeton at stake, and to which its friends will do well to give good heed. Its calling as well as its true interest is to follow in substantially the same course that was clearly pointed out by the providence of God in the founding of that institution from which it sprang."[1]

~*Thomas Murphy*~

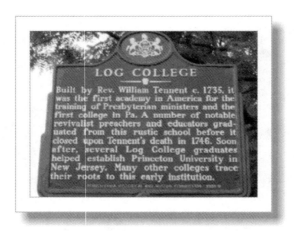

Location sign for William Tennent's "Log College"
in Bucks County, Pennsylvania

---

[1] Thomas Murphy, *The Presbytery of the Log College; or, The Cradle of the Presbyterian Church in America* (Philadelphia: Presbyterian Board of Publication, 1889), 129-130.

The College of New Jersey

William Tennent, Sr. died at home on May 6, 1746, aged 73, "a good old age, like a shock of corn fully ripe."[2] Declining health had forced him to resign his pastorate at Neshaminy, Pennsylvania, in 1742, while his Log College had been in a floundering condition for several years prior to his death. With Tennent's passing, Jonathan Dickinson[3] and Aaron Burr[4] spearheaded efforts by the New Light Presbyterians to establish a college equal to any in America. The New Light pastors were disaffected with Yale, the Alma Mater of several of them, because of the expulsion of David Brainerd,[5] Burr's brother-in-law, in 1741 for expressing in a private conversation that Professor Chauncey Whittlesley had "no more grace than a chair."[6] Brainerd's statement was overheard by another student who reported it to the university.[7] Burr later declared:

> If it had not been for the harsh treatment received by Mr. Brainerd at Yale, New Jersey College would never have been erected.[8]

John Hamilton, the acting Governor of New Jersey in 1746-7, assisted the New Lights in the fall of 1746 to draft a charter for the college which would be governed by seven trustees: Aaron Burr, Ebenezer Pemberton,[9] Jonathan Dickinson, Samuel Blair, Gilbert Tennent, William Tennent Jr., and Edward Shippen,[10] a Philadelphia merchant. Shippen was the only one of the original trustees who was not a minister. With this charter in hand, the College of New Jersey officially commenced in May of 1747 at

---

[2] Archibald Alexander, *The Log College* (London: The Banner of Truth Trust, 1968), 22.
[3] Jonathan Dickinson (1688–1747) was pastor at the First Presbyterian Church in Elizabethtown, New Jersey
[4] Aaron Burr (1716–1757) was married to Esther Edwards, the daughter of Jonathan Edwards, and was pastor at the Presbyterian Church in Newark, New Jersey. His son, Aaron Burr, was the third Vice President of the US.
[5] David Brainerd was another son-in-law of Jonathan Edwards and brother-in-law to Aaron Burr. He was the famous missionary to the Crossweeksung Indians.
[6] Alexander, *Log College*, 69.
[7] Ibid.
[8] Ibid., 70.
[9] Ebenezer Pemberton (1704–1777) was a graduate of Harvard College in 1721 and was pastor at First Presbyterian Church in New York City, New York from 1727 to 1753. He then returned to Boston to pastor the Middle Street Church.
[10] Edward Shippen (1703–1781) was an influential merchant in Philadelphia who formed a firm with Thomas Lawrence for the lucrative fur trade. He was elected Mayor of Philadelphia in 1744 and later served as a judge on the Court of Common Pleas.

Elizabethtown, New Jersey. Dickinson was elected the first President and taught the students in the parlor of his home. When Jonathan Belcher became Governor of New Jersey in the latter part of 1747, he issued a new charter that made two important changes to the governing board: (1) It allowed for equal representation of ministers and laymen among the trustees, and (2) It permitted members of various denominations to sit on the governing board. The Log College men, though, were uneasy with Gov. Belcher's changes because he placed himself and four members of the council on the Board of Trustees while removing some of the former trustees.

On October 14, 1748, Jonathan Edwards wrote Ebenezer Erskine of Scotland that the College of New Jersey was "in somewhat of an unsettled state"[11] as a result of these changes to the charter. Yet, he expressed satisfaction in Gov. Belcher's Christian character as one who desired to be approved by the Lord and who requested prayer for God's guidance on his administration.[12] Gov. Belcher subsequently wrote to Edwards the following May giving him an account of his faith and his assessment of the affairs of the College of New Jersey:

> As to our embryo college, it is a noble design, and, if God pleases, may prove an extensive blessing. I have adopted it for a daughter, and hope it may become an *alma mater* to this and the neighboring provinces... I will lay out and exert myself in every way to bring it to maturity, and thus to advance its future welfare and prosperity; for this, I believe, will be acceptable in the sight of God our Savior, a relish for true religion and piety being a great stranger to this part of America. The accounts I receive from time to time give me reason to believe that Arminianism, Arianism, and even Socinianism, in destruction of the doctrines of free grace are daily propagated in the New England colleges. How horribly and how wickedly are these poisonous notions rooting out those noble principles on which our ancestors founded those seminaries.[13]

Belcher realized the college needed a permanent home and adequate buildings. Writing to Gilbert Tennent on July 30, 1748, the Governor stated:

---

[11] Edward Hickman, rev., *The Works of Jonathan Edwards*, Volume One (Edinburgh, Scotland and Carlisle, Pennsylvania: The Banner of Truth Trust, 1974), ci.
[12] Alexander, Log College, 71.
[13] Ibid., 72.

And if, finally, money cannot be raised for *the House* and to support the necessary officers, the thing must be given up.[14]

Dickinson continued as president of the college until 1751 when his untimely death led to Burr being elected to the Presidency. The College was then moved from Elizabethtown to Burr's home in Newark, New Jersey. The Synod of New York erected a permanent structure the following year at Princeton, New Jersey, which was half way between Philadelphia and New York. Belcher had written to a Mr. Walley in 1747:

> There has been striving at what place the College should be *built*, and I have persuaded those concerned to fix at Princeton, and I think it as near the center of the province as any, and a fine situation.[15]

Davies and Gilbert Tennent Chosen as Emissaries for the College

Contributions from the colonies were insufficient to endow the College, which convinced the Synod of New York to send a representative to Great Britain to appeal for support. Ebenezer Pemberton of New York City was chosen by the committee of Synod in 1751 to undertake this mission, but he was unable to comply. The committee next turned to President Burr, who readily consented, but stipulated that his friend, Caleb Smith, become the acting president of the college in his absence. Smith declined this proposal and Burr was unable to leave his duties. Synod then unanimously elected "two of their members, viz. Messrs. Gilbert Tennent and Samuel Davies, to take a voyage to Europe on the important affairs of said college."[16]

When the offer came to Davies in 1751, he immediately declined it. The offer was renewed in 1752 and he again refused, expecting to hear nothing more from the trustees. The board surprisingly re-elected him unanimously for a third time at the winter meeting of 1752–53, which caused him anxiety:

> When I was informed of it by a letter from the worthy President Burr, it struck me into a consternation and perplexity unknown before. All the tender passions of the husband, the minister, the father and the son, (all which relations center upon me) formed an insurrection in my breast

---

[14] John MacLean, *History of the College of New Jersey* (New York: Arno Press, 1969), 147.
[15] Ibid., 148.
[16] Ibid.

against the proposal; and with these I have struggled ever since. My conjugal anxieties were increased by the languishing state of my tenderer and better part, which my absence for so long a time might perhaps increase. I was also afraid lest my dear congregation, whose hearts are so excessively set upon me, should suffer by my absence. The dangers of the seas likewise appeared terrible: and above all, my just consciousness of my want of qualifications for so important an embassy, sunk my spirits; and yet my remonstrances on this head would not be regarded by others.[17]

Davies overcame his initial objections and fixed on two things as conditions for his acceptance of this mission: the financial support of his family, and supply pastors for his congregation during his absence.[18] He was especially concerned that Jane's illness was a symptom of a consumptive disease. He therefore made it a condition of any acceptance of this mission that he could return home if his wife's health deteriorated. These two proposals were then sent to the Trustees in a letter both by mail and by a courier who could return with an answer from the Trustees.[19] With the messenger's return, he learned of the Trustees' hearty agreement with his requests, and that they fully expected him to undertake the mission.

Gilbert Tennent, bereaved of both his mother and his wife in May of 1753, seventeen days apart, was asked by the Trustees to undertake this journey with Davies. Davies esteemed Tennent as a partner who would overcome any unfitness he had to undertake this mission alone.[20] Davies' family and congregation either consented to the mission or submitted with a reluctant spirit to his duty in this matter which helped him make his decision to undertake the mission.[21] If any of these parties had resisted, he likely would have rejected the Trustees' invitation.

Davies believed this mission would provide him with several important opportunities in addition to the good that could be accomplished for the College of New Jersey. First, he could represent the cause of the Dissenters in Virginia before the appropriate officials in Great Britain.

---

[17] George W. Pilcher, ed., *The Reverend Samuel Davies Abroad: The Diary of a Journey to England and Scotland, 1753–1755* (Urbana, Chicago, London: University of Illinois Press, 1967), 6.
[18] Ibid.
[19] Ibid.
[20] Ibid.
[21] Ibid.

His congregation could not afford to send him on such a mission, and he was convinced both that it was the right time and he was the right person to lay this matter before the officials in Great Britain.[22] Second, he could raise contributions in Great Britain to support missionaries to the American Indians.[23] The Scottish Society for the Propagation of Christian Knowledge (SSPCK) had already given some money for this purpose. Davies desired to see the Indians become true disciples of Jesus for which alone this trip would be well worth it.[24] Finally, this mission would promote his personal improvement in areas where he was most deficient, especially his reclusive inclinations.

Despondency was Davies' frequent companion while preparing for this mission. He was particularly anxious about his dear wife. He expressed his concerns as follows:

> I think I could break [through] the strongest, complicated ties of the paternal and filial relation, and cast my helpless family upon the care of providence: But the [thought] that my wife should pine away in my absence, without the satisfaction my company would afford her; or that by the anxieties of separation, her constitution should be injured; this [thought] seems utterly insupportable, and alarms all my tender and anxious passions.[25]

He eventually determined to proceed with this mission with the stipulation he would return immediately to Virginia if he received word Jane was dangerously ill. He offered a prayer in view of these concerns:

> O! Thou God of our life, with all the importunity so languid a soul is capable of exerting, I implore thy gracious protection for her, that she may be supported in my absence, and that we may enjoy a happy interview again.[26]

He was additionally embarrassed with respect to his temporal affairs and concerned how his family would provide for themselves if he were removed from this world.

---

[22] Ibid.
[23] Ibid.
[24] Ibid.
[25] Ibid.
[26] Ibid.

John Wright Sent to Supply the Hanover Congregation

John Wright, Davies' former pupil and friend, arrived in Hanover on July 13, 1753, by order of New Brunswick Presbytery, to supply the Hanover congregation during his absence. Jane Davies was then recovering from her sickness, and their sons—Billy and Johnny—were also on the mend. Wright surprisingly informed Davies that he saw no need for him to assist Tennent on this mission; that he was unwilling to supply his pulpit for the entire time of the journey; and, that he was anxious to preach at vacant congregations in hopes of receiving a call. Davies overcame his perplexities with the realization the Trustees were in the best position to judge of his necessity for this mission. His close friend, John Todd, was absolutely convinced he should go.

Wright's preaching at Hanover over the next three weeks displeased some members of the congregation, but became more acceptable to them over time.[27] In his private conversations with Wright, Davies observed that some of the thoughts of his former student deserved to be remembered. For one thing, Wright had considered the notion that compassion is essentially selfish in nature because people at the extremes of misery are incapable of it.[28] Eventually, Wright rejected this notion, but his thoughts were passed along to Davies through Samuel Finley, who had also enjoyed close fellowship with Wright.

Davies Leaves Virginia for the Fund Raising Mission

On Monday, September 3, Davies parted with his wife, his parents, his children, and several of his closest friends. He had publicly parted with his congregation the day before. On this occasion, he was overwhelmed with deep emotion at the thought of this painful separation and offered a prayer for all of them. Samuel Morris and Melchizedek Brame—two of his elders at Hanover—rode with Davies and Todd as they set out for the annual meeting of the Synod of New York. Davies began to feel a more submissive spirit to the will of God along the way, but sudden anxieties still assaulted him.

They arrived at Samuel Finley's home in Nottingham, Pennsylvania, on Saturday, after five days of riding 250 miles by horseback. At Finley's

---

[27] Ibid., 9.
[28] Ibid., 9–10.

home, Davies found the time and solitude to reflect more deeply on his family back in Hanover and offered this prayer: "May the Lord bless all that are dear to me, and favour me with a happy return to them!"[29] The next day, he preached a sermon from Deuteronomy 10:13 which was well received by the Nottingham congregation. He had previously preached the same message at Hanover but he was displeased with his efforts on this occasion, and he lamented:

> Alas! I have lost that spirit with which it was delivered: and indeed I can but very rarely retain the spirit of preaching in the hurries of a journey.[30]

The solemnity of the congregation, he wrote, was also far short "of what I have seen in this place in the days of the right hand of the most High!"[31]

Davies and Finley engaged in a delightful conversation that evening in which the former communicated his thoughts "upon the great influence which the body has to deprave the Soul."[32] Davies believed Scripture uses the metaphor *flesh* for human depravity because the body and bodily habits have a special tendency to corrupt the soul. He reasoned that, otherwise, it would be just as proper to use spirit or soul to define sin,[33] which the Bible never does.

Homesickness overwhelmed Davies after his first week away. He was unable to find relief from his vexing thoughts of home in any relaxation or in his devotions.[34] He entertained himself partly with the reading of a pleasing book by an Anglican author, but it did not lessen his melancholy. This homesickness was a reminder of the depravity of his own heart, as he lamented:

> Alas! I have been perplexed this day with the vigorous insurrections of sin in my heart; but my resistance and humiliation has not been proportioned. Oh wretched man that I am, etc![35]

---

[29] Ibid., 9.
[30] Ibid.
[31] Ibid., Davies' first wife, Sarah Kirkpatrick, was the daughter of a ruling elder in this congregation, John Kirkpatrick.
[32] Ibid.
[33] Ibid.
[34] Ibid., 11.
[35] Ibid.

Rev. John Cuthbertson and the Reformed Presbyterians

Davies was occupied for the next few days of September with a committee of New Castle Presbytery composed of himself, John Roan[36], Robert Smith[37], and Samuel Finley. It was tasked with investigating and responding to the alleged errors of Rev. John Cuthbertson. This committee drafted a warning for the New Castle Presbytery against the alleged errors of Cuthbertson who was the first missionary of the Reformed Presbyterian Church to the Colonies. He arrived in America at New Castle, Pennsylvania (later Delaware), in August of 1751 and soon undertook the charge of three Associate Reformed Presbyterian congregations in Bart, Cumberland, and Martie, Pennsylvania. For two decades, Cuthbertson was the only minister of his denomination in America and he had to travel great distances to minister to all the Reformed Presbyterians who had immigrated to the colonies. The committee of New Castle Presbytery alleged he taught the following errors:

> That God has made over [Christ] and all his benefits to all that hear the Gospel, by a deed of gift (as he affects to speak) so that every sinner that hears the Gospel-offer, ought to put in a claim of right to him as his Saviour in particular—that saving faith consists in a persuasion that [Christ] is *mine* and that he died for *me* in *particular*—that redemption is universal as to purchase—that civil government both heathen and [Christian] is derived from [Christ] as mediator.[38]

Shortly after arriving in Pennsylvania, Cuthbertson attracted the attention of some of the New Light Presbyterians. On September 1, 1751, he conversed with Andrew Bay and Samuel Blair, both of whom were New Light ministers in Pennsylvania, concerning some of his sermons.[39]

---

[36] John Roan was a graduate of the Log College and had been sent as a missionary to Hanover, Virginia in 1744.

[37] Robert Smith was the father of Samuel Stanhope Smith (1751–1819) and John Blair Smith (1756–1799), both of whom were illustrious Presbyterian ministers. Samuel Stanhope Smith was the founding President of Hampden-Sydney College in Hampden-Sydney, Virginia and the seventh President of the College of New Jersey from 1795–1812. John Blair Smith was the second President of Hampden-Sydney College from 1779–1789 and also President of Union College in Schenectady, New York from 1795–1799. He died eight months after returning to the pastorate.

[38] Pilcher, ed., *Reverend Samuel Davies Abroad*, 11.

[39] *Diary of Rev. John Cuthbertson*. Accessed on June 29, 2016 at: http://www.bennett-twins.com/documents/Diaries/Cuthbertson/index.php?imageNumber=2.

Bay pastored a two church field in Adams and York counties in Pennsylvania. Cuthbertson was ministering in Lancaster County which was bordered by Chester County on the east and York County on the west. Bay and Blair, therefore, were probably the pastors most affected by Cuthbertson's new ministry. This meeting with Cuthbertson did not clear up all the concerns of the New Light ministers, and Blair subsequently began drafting a warning against his teaching which he was prevented from completing due to his death in 1752. On October 31, 1752, Cuthbertson wrote a letter to John Roan for what he said were "false representations told."[40] Cuthbertson's alleged errors were similar to statements taught by the Marrow men in Scotland which had been wrongly condemned by the General Assembly of the Church of Scotland in 1721. Certain of their statements had the appearance of teaching universal redemption though they strenuously denied that charge while affirming particular redemption. The Marrow men claimed that they were only teaching the same thing as Robert Rollock who wrote:

> We do affirm and defend the certainty of special grace. In the gospel, grace is procured and offered not only in general to all, but in special to every one; wherefore the certainty of special grace is required in every one. The Spirit of Christ, when any general promise or sentence touching Christ and His mercy is alleged, doth no less particularly apply the same to every man, by speaking inwards to the heart of every one, than of old Christ did by His holy voice apply these particular promises to certain persons, as to the woman at Simon's house, to Zaccheus, to the thief upon the cross.[41]

Rollock affirms in that quote both the accomplishment and the application of redemption; both the objective grace of Christ's atonement and the subjective grace of the Holy Spirit in uniting the recipient with Christ through saving faith. The particular way in which Cuthbertson and the Marrow men expressed the free offer of the gospel sounded novel, but the New Light Presbyterians were, in reality, in agreement with them on this point—even though they did not realize it. Davies freely offered the gospel to sinners in his sermons and wooed them with all of his persua-

---

[40] Pilcher, ed., *Reverend Samuel Davies Abroad*, 11.
[41] James Walker, *The Theology and Theologians of Scotland 1560–1750* (Edinburgh: Knox Press, 1982), 88.

sive powers to turn to Christ. Yet, Davies and the New Lights recognized that no sinner can come to Christ without the special working of the Holy Spirit. Their emphasis on this special grace of the Spirit "speaking inwards to the heart of every one" was one of the differences the New Lights had with the Old Light Presbyterians. It was, therefore, a misunderstanding of Cuthbertson's views that caused this committee of New Castle Presbytery to sound a warning against him. What James Walker, the nineteenth-century Scottish historical theologian, said concerning the views of the Marrow men should also be said about Cuthbertson's statements:

> What they aimed at is clear in their reply to the questions put by the General Assembly. First of all, a glorious object is presented to your view, offered to your acceptance, brought more and more home to you in His worth and suitableness, and grace and beauty; nearer He comes, and nearer; your soul closes with Him; and as, in the hand of the Holy Ghost, the heavenly call presses in on you with supernatural power,—in a faith divine, of living soul conviction, you take the offered One, take Him as yours; yours His blood, yours His righteousness, yours all the fulness of His salvation, all He has done and suffered for poor sinners; so that with Paul you say, "I live, yet not I; and the life which I now live, I live by the faith of the Son of God, which loved me and gave Himself for me." I do not see how one with anything of living faith, heart to heart with the divine reality, can be said, as in the Catechism, to embrace Christ, without having more or less strongly an experience like this.[42]

Davies' diary does not inform us what the final outcome of this warning against Cuthbertson was, but it surely resulted in a breach of fellowship which was never remedied by New Castle Presbytery. A small book was published in 1754 by New Castle Presbytery titled, *A Warning of the Presbytery of New Castle to the People under their Care Against Several Errors and Evil Practices of Mr. John Cuthbertson*. This little volume was no doubt the finished product of the committee's work on which Davies served and his hand surely wrote several parts of it. While Cuthbertson may have been guilty of certain errors, he was also in basic agreement with the New Light ministers on the essentials of the gospel. Cuthbertson often referred in his diary to the sermons of Ralph and Ebenezer Erskine

---

[42] Ibid., 89–90.

which he sometimes read to congregations when his travels prevented him from sermon preparation. It is to be regretted that the New Lights opposed one who should have been welcomed as a friend.

Davies' Travels in Pennsylvania and New Jersey

After completing this work for the committee of Presbytery on the Cuthbertson matter, Davies rode to Fagg's Manor on Thursday, September 13, in the company of Robert Smith,[43] for a visit with Samuel Blair's widow. Both Davies and Smith had been students at the Samuel Blair's Fagg's Manor classical school. Smith was now the pastor of the Presbyterian Church at Pequa in Lancaster County, Pennsylvania, where he started a classical school. Upon their arrival, the sight of Mrs. Blair and the house where he spent so many happy days flooded Davies' heart with a variety of wonderful thoughts. When he saw the meetinghouse where the great Blair had preached, he exclaimed:

> Oh! How dreadful is this place! This is no other than the house of God, and this is the gate of Heaven.[44]

Davies traveled to Philadelphia on Friday and Saturday, stopping at Chester overnight. He was warmly greeted in Philadelphia by Gilbert Tennent and other friends. He learned to his chagrin through Capt. William Grant that Dennys Deberdt[45] of London felt the Dissenters in England viewed the principles of the College of New Jersey as "antiquated and unfashionable."[46] Davies was disturbed that this bit of information would be a bad omen for their mission.[47] Tennent preached an excellent sermon the next morning on one of the petitions of the

---

[43] Robert Smith was the father of Samuel Stanhope Smith (1751–1819) and John Blair Smith (1756–1799), both of whom were illustrious Presbyterian ministers. Samuel Stanhope Smith was the founding President of Hampden-Sydney College in Hampden-Sydney, Virginia and the seventh President of the College of New Jersey from 1795–1812. John Blair Smith was the second President of Hampden-Sydney College from 1779–1789 and also President of Union College in Schenectady, New York from 1795–1799. He died eight months after returning to the pastorate in Philadelphia.
[44] Pilcher, ed., *Reverend Samuel Davies Abroad*, 11.
[45] Dennys DeBerdt was a London merchant of Dutch descent who was interested in American politics and a friend of many Dissenters in the colonies.
[46] Pilcher, ed., *Reverend Samuel Davies Abroad*, 13. It is also true that many of the Dissenters in England had succumbed to liberal views on theology.
[47] Ibid.

Lord's Prayer, "Deliver us from evil," "in which he exposed the wiles and devices of Satan in a very judicious manner."[48] Davies preached the afternoon and evening sermons to Tennent's congregation. The most pleasing part of the day, though, was the delightful conversation he had that evening with Tennent, whom he called, "my spiritual Father."[49]

Monday was spent calling on people who might be beneficial for their journey: particularly the governor of Pennsylvania, James Hamilton, and the secretary, Richard Peters. Peters was a member of the Church of England and a warm friend of George Whitefield. Neither Hamilton nor Peters was at home, so they visited with three Lutheran ministers and a German Reformed minister, Michael Schlatter, of whom Davies commented:

> How pleasing it is to see the Religion of Jesus appear undisguised in Foreigners! I am so charmed with it, that I forget all national and religious Differences; and my very Heart is intimately united to them.[50]

The next three days he traveled by horseback from Philadelphia to Newark, New Jersey. Davies stopped at Trenton on Tuesday evening for a visit with David Cowell,[51] but he was too exhausted for lively conversation. He lodged with Elihu Spencer,[52] the pastor at Elizabethtown, New Jersey, on Wednesday evening with whom he enjoyed a pleasing conversation. He traveled on Thursday to Newark where he was received by President Burr and had a pleasing conversation with the Governor of New Jersey, Jonathan Belcher.

Burr informed Davies that the College expected him to furnish his own wardrobe for this mission, which embarrassed and temporarily consternated him. He concluded on reflection: "Notwithstanding all the pliableness of my nature, I must insist upon their providing for me

---

[48] Ibid.
[49] Ibid. This phrase may be an indication that Davies was converted through Tennent's preaching.
[50] Ibid.
[51] Cowell was an Old Light Presbyterian minister and a Trustee of the college. He was not an opponent of the New Lights like some Old Light pastors were, particularly Robert Cross.
[52] Elihu Spencer (1721–1784) was a relative of David and John Brainerd and was the pastor at Elizabethtown, New Jersey where Jonathan Dickinson had pastored. He was an able minister who was praised by Jonathan Edwards.

in *this* respect, as one condition of my undertaking the voyage."[53] His small salary at Hanover rendered him incapable of procuring a new wardrobe.

The valedictory address given by President Burr to the graduating class of the College of New Jersey on Sunday, September 23, was very pleasing to Davies. Afterwards, they debated a proposition which had been formulating in Davies' mind for some time, viz., "That persons in this age may be said virtually to have crucified [Christ] because they have the same temper with the Jews, and because their conduct towards [Christ] is as like to that of the Jews as their circumstances will allow."[54] Burr did not completely agree with this proposition, though Davies, who always enjoyed a lively debate, labored to prove his point.

A sore leg that had afflicted Davies for several weeks was dangerously infected by this date. Davies had fallen out the door of his house before setting out on his journey, which caused a slight wound. Through neglect, constant traveling, and preaching, the injured leg was now inflamed and infected. Two days later Davies was forced to take medication for it, and he was afraid (or rather wished) it would prevent him from making this trip.[55]

On Wednesday, September 26, Davies delivered his thesis for the Master of Arts degree to the trustees of the College of New Jersey in which he defended the doctrine of the Trinity[56] against three opponents in a public dispute. Afterwards, he was conferred the Master's degree by the Board, and dined that evening with Gov. Belcher, President Burr, and the Trustees. The next morning Davies "received 80 pounds proc. from the treasurer to bear the expenses of the voyage."[57] This amount appeared to be generous, but proved inadequate to meet his expenses in Great Britain.

---

[53] Pilcher, ed., *Reverend Samuel Davies Abroad*, 14.
[54] Ibid., 15.
[55] He also hoped, in part, that his injury would allow him to return to his family without making the trip.
[56] The thesis was, "Personales Disctintiones in Trinitae sunt Aeternae," or "Personal Distinctions in the Eternal Trinity."
[57] Pilcher, ed., *Reverend Samuel Davies Abroad*, 16.

Synod of New York Meeting

By October 1, Davies began to retrace his steps from Newark in order to attend the Synod of New York meeting in Philadelphia on October 3–6 and the meeting of the Presbytery of New Castle at Fagg's Manor on October 9–12. He left Newark in the company of Aaron Richards (1718-1793), pastor of the First Presbyterian Church of Rahway, New Jersey. Davies described him as "a pious minister under the deepest melancholy and temptation, harassed with perpetual suggestions to cut his own throat."[58] Richards' melancholy reminded Davies of his own depression after the death of his first wife, and thus he gave Richards his best advice based on his own experiences. Davies spent that evening with John Brainerd, the brother of David Brainerd, at Cranbury, New Jersey, and visited the mission to the Crossweeksung Indians the next morning before riding on to Philadelphia.

At Synod, Davies was reunited with John Rodgers and many of his friends in the ministry. Synod succeeded in obtaining the services of Rodgers, John Brainerd, Hugh Henry, Andrew Bay, John Blair, and John Finley, in addition to John Wright, to supply the Hanover congregation. Davies also learned at Synod that Gilbert Tennent was apparently offended at his earlier "conduct as too forward and assuming; but it was soon removed by a free conversation."[59]

Davies was appointed at this meeting of Synod to be a member of a committee to redress certain grievances of the First Presbyterian Church of New York City against its pastor, Ebenezer Pemberton. Davies remained in Philadelphia after Synod concluded to worship at Gilbert Tennent's church, a privilege he seldom experienced, but often desired.[60] Several ministers from the Synod were still in Philadelphia, with the pulpit duties on the Lord's Day divided among Azariah Horton, Andrew Bay, and David Bostwick. Davies heard several of them and felt that Horton preached "an honest, judicious sermon";[61] Bay "was much daunted and confused";[62] and Bostwick had "the best style extempore, of any man I have ever

---

[58] Ibid., 17.
[59] Ibid., 18.
[60] Ibid., 19.
[61] Ibid., 18.
[62] Ibid.

heard."[63] Davies preached Monday morning at Tennent's congregation from Isaiah 66:1, 2 and was aware of God's blessing. As he said:

> What tended not a little to [increase] my affection was my observing the venerable Mr. G. Tennent weeping beside me in the pulpit. Spiritual poverty and humility appeared very amiable and charming to me.[64]

Several of his brethren then visited the Philadelphia Academy,[65] which was under the leadership of Provost William Smith, an Anglican, and Francis Alison, an Old Light Presbyterian minister who was the primary teacher of the school. Some of the students were delivering the orations of Brutus and Mark Antony, which evoked Davies' comment on modern oratory:

> They were extremely languid, and discovered Nothing of the Fire and Pathos of a Roman Soul. Indeed this is one great Defect of modern Oratory; a Defect few seem sensible of, or labour to correct.[66]

Meeting of New Castle Presbytery
He rode that evening to Chester, which was halfway to Fagg's Manor. He arrived early and "sat up late, and wrote letters to my Hanover fiends, particularly to my dear spouse, full of anxieties. How does she attract my heart!"[67]

New Castle Presbytery convened the next day and examined John Brown for ordination as the pastor of the Timber Ridge Presbyterian Church in Virginia. Davies was asked to preach Brown's ordination sermon, which he gladly delivered from Acts 20:28 after a few hours of preparation. He felt his discourse was filled with "a good deal of inaccuracy and confusion," but also "with some tender sense of the subject."[68] Presbytery adjourned on Friday and Davies "parted with [his] favorite friend Mr. Todd, not without tears,"[69] who then departed for Virginia.

---

[63] Ibid
[64] Ibid., 19.
[65] This school had formerly been the Old Light School at New London, Pennsylvania, before being moved to Philadelphia and being united under the joint supervision of an Anglican minister and Francis Alison.
[66] Pilcher, ed., *Reverend Samuel Davies Abroad*, 20.
[67] Ibid.
[68] Ibid.
[69] Ibid.

Visiting Friends from Philadelphia to the Welsh Tract

Davies rode with John Rodgers and Charles Tennent to White-Clay Creek, Pennsylvania at the adjournment of Presbytery. Rodgers continued to St. George's, Delaware, on Saturday, and Davies joined him there Sunday evening. Davies was indisposed at St. George's with colic and spent the next several days in retirement at Rodgers' home. On Wednesday, he preached for Rodgers and visited with some old friends, though he was still not over his cold. By Friday, he felt well enough to plan a journey with Rodgers to New York City to hear the complaints of the First Presbyterian Church concerning their pastor, Ebenezer Pemberton. Yet, Rodgers' wife became suddenly ill before they could leave and gave premature birth to their first child, a girl, which caused them to forego the trip.

Davies spent the next two weeks visiting several friends between Philadelphia and Delaware. On October 22, Davies records:

> Mrs. Rodgers unbosomed herself to me, and gave me an account of some affecting, over-whelming Views of the Wisdom of God in the Works of Redemption . . . that were truly astonishing.[70]

He also preached several times for Gilbert Tennent in Philadelphia during this period. Once, he rode with George Ross, an Episcopalian minister from Chester, Pennsylvania, to St. George's. Ross inquired about Davies' objections to ordination in the Episcopal Church. Davies calmly mentioned a few of his objections and Ross "fell into an unreasonable passion."[71]

On Sunday, November 11, he was back in the fellowship of Rodgers at St. George's, where he received the Lord's Supper. Rodgers preached the sacramental sermon in which he exposed the insensibility of most sinners to the sufferings of Christ, so unlike the general response to news about the agonies of mere mortals.

Davies walked through the Welsh Tract on Monday and visited with his relatives. His journal describes his solemnity on that occasion:

> [W]hen I past by the Places where I had formerly lived, or walked, it gave a solemn Turn to my Mind. Ah! How much I have sinned, wherever I

---

[70] Ibid., 22.
[71] Ibid., 23.

have been! And what solemn Transactions have been between God and my Soul in these my old Walks! Visited two Grave-Yards in my Way, to Solemnize my Mind among the Mansions of the Dead. O how solemn Eternity appeared! How frail and dying the Race of Mortals! And how near my own Dissolution![72]

Waiting on the *London* to Arrive

The next few days were spent waiting for the *London* to come to port at Reedy Island. The ship was somewhat delayed, but the time in waiting was not wasted. Davies and Rodgers unburdened themselves "with all the freedom of [Christian] friendship."[73] Davies, in particular, communicated to his friend his habits concerning his religious devotion. Then, Mrs. Elizabeth Dushane, a friend of Davies from St. George's, asked him to compose an epitaph for the tombstone of her sister. He hurriedly composed three and left them with some of her friends to choose what they considered to be the best of them.[74]

Davies was anxious about the ship's delay since his mission was not yet begun after ten weeks away from home. At this point, he wrote:

> I find the Enterprize to which Providence seems to call me more and more difficult.[75]

When Tennent arrived on November 16, Davies found his "spirit was revived with his facetious, and in the mean time spiritual conversation."[76] It was just the tonic Davies needed before he set out on the most important and dangerous journey of his life.

Conclusion

It is difficult for twenty-first century Christians to understand the trepidation and concern that someone in the eighteenth century would feel before embarking on a passenger ship for a six-week journey across the Atlantic. In Davies' situation, there were the added concerns of Jane's delicate health and the care for both his family and his congregation. There were many reasons to be concerned about the voyage itself. Food

---

[72] Ibid., 26.
[73] Ibid.
[74] Ibid.
[75] Ibid., 27.
[76] Ibid.

and water were often in short supply on such ships. Seasickness was a constant companion of many. Shipwrecks were a fact of life. Without the means of tracking oceanic storms, some ships sailed right into the eye of hurricanes. Then, there were pirates that patrolled the waterways and took command of ships whenever the opportunity presented itself. In the midst of one oceanic storm, John Wesley was constrained to ask himself, "'How is it that thou hast no faith?' being still unwilling to die."[77] Then, he described what happened on another occasion while they were having a worship service on board:

> In the midst of the psalm wherewith their (i.e., the Moravians—DR) service began, the sea broke over, split the mainsail in pieces, covered the ship, and poured in between the decks, as if the great deep had already swallowed us up. A terrible screaming began among the English. The Germans calmly sang on. I asked one of them afterward, "Were you not afraid?" He answered, "I thank God, no." I asked, "But were not your women and children afraid?" He replied, mildly, "No; our women and children are not afraid to die."[78]

Davies and Tennent, unlike Wesley, would not have the happy pleasure of sharing a voyage with such dedicated Christians as a large contingency of Moravians. Instead, they were more apt to hear vile oaths and cursing in the midst of storms than the singing of psalms. Yet, the dangers of the turbulent Atlantic would scarcely be any less violent in 1753 than it was for Wesley in 1736. The two Americans were not afraid to die if it was God's will, but they hoped to live and serve God.

---

[77] Percy Livingston Parker, ed., *The Journal of John Wesley* (Chicago: Moody Press, n.d.), 35.
[78] Ibid., 35–36.

A drawing of First Presbyterian Church in Philadelphia; Robert Cross was the pastor of this church and he sent letters to Great Britain to prejudice churches against the mission of Tennent and Davies.

The Tower of London which Davies records seeing from the ship

-11-

Fund Raising in London

"The College of New-Jersey, erected about 8 years ago with the most ample Privileges, is of great Importance to the Interests of Religion and Learning in 3 Colonies, New-York, the Jerseys and Pennsylvania, and to the Dissenters in Maryland, Virginia and both Carolinas. There is now about £3000 in the College Fund; but this will hardly be sufficient for the Erection of proper Buildings; and if it should be laid out for that End, there will be Nothing left for the Maintenance of the Professors and Tutors, to furnish a College Library, and to support pious Youth for the Ministry, who are unable to maintain themselves at Learning."[1]
~*Samuel Davies, July 2, 1753*~

Westminster Palace in London, England, as seen today

---

[1] George William Pilcher, ed., *The Reverend Samuel Davies Abroad: The Diary of a Journal to England and Scotland, 1753-55* (Urbana, Chicago, London: The University of Illinois Press, 1967), 1-2.

Davies and Tennent waited four days at New Castle, Delaware, for the passenger ship *London* to harbor at Reedy Island on the Delaware River. Finally the ship arrived and they boarded at midnight on November 18, 1753. Davies reflected on this voyage with the fear that he "may never set my Foot on Shore more, 'till I land in the eternal World."[2] He then offered a prayer that his and Tennent's conversation would be useful to the ship's company and that they would be sanctified by any sickness at sea.[3]

After a few hours of sleep, Davies was awakened at 5 a.m. when the *London* set sail under a fair wind. The noise on deck filled him "with a Kind of pleasing Horror,"[4] but he was "shocked with the Thought that I may never see my dear Friends, and particularly my other Self any more."[5] Yet, he was thankful for this opportunity and for Tennent's companionship.

Their first day at sea was a Sunday, but they were unable to preach to the crew because of seasickness and all the pressing needs of their journey. Davies spent part of the day in writing letters, particularly one to John Rodgers. The *London* made it into the Atlantic that afternoon and was out of the sight of land by the next day.

The winds and waves were violent for the next eleven days, which brought on severe bouts of seasickness for Davies.[6] He was extremely melancholy with little relish for conversation, but he still marveled at the wonders of the great deep:

> It is a most majestic Survey, to see how the Waves rise in Ridges of Mountains, pursue each other, and dash in angry Conflict: and it is most amazing how we can possibly live upon so turbulent an Element. To form and rule such an Ocean is a Work becoming a God.[7]

Davies occupied his time on ship by reading sermons, conversing with Tennent, praying, and revising sermon notes. Pensive thoughts of his family, his congregation, and Virginia often depressed him. A season

---

[2] Ibid., 28. Davies' travel journey is the basis for almost all the information in this chapter.
[3] Ibid.
[4] Ibid.
[5] Ibid.
[6] Ibid.
[7] Ibid., 30.

of intercessory prayer for them on December 8 caused him to exclaim:

> How my heart longs and pines after my dearest Creature and the little Pledges of our mutual Love! Oh! When shall I see them again![8]

The College of New Jersey and Lotteries

In addition to sending Tennent and Davies to Great Britain to *solicit* contributions, the Trustees the College of New Jersey availed themselves of the expedient scheme of a lottery to raise additional funds for a new building. The Trustees petitioned the General Court of Connecticut in the latter part of 1753 for the right to establish a lottery for the benefit of the College. They intended to sale 8,888 tickets with 3,088 of them being "fortunate" or attended with prizes. Such lotteries were used to support a number of enterprises in colonial days, including the erecting of churches in many colonies. This lottery for the College was advertised in the *New York Gazette or Weekly Post Boy* on November 26, 1753 and the *Pennsylvania Gazette* on August 8, 1754. In that notice the Trustees wrote:

> As publick seminaries of learning not only tend to promote the private welfare of the communities in which they are founded, but to advance the honour, the reputation, and the happiness of a country in general; it is hoped, that all those who would encourage the progress of the liberal sciences, and are well wishers to the propagation of christianity in these parts of the world, will cheerfully become adventurers here.[9]

Yet, the practice of lottery schemes was not without critics—even in colonial days—and this decision of the Trustees of the College was an open invitation for such second-guessing. An anonymous person, Pennsylvanicus, wrote a letter to the citizens of Pennsylvania that was published in *The Pennsylvania Journal* on February 8, 1759, in which he stated:

> Moved by a disinterested regard for your welfare and the good of the country, I have endeavor'd to show from some reason and experience, in two former pieces on lotteries their pernicious tendency and effects to the community. My design was to point out the deformity of the vice, which if not stop'd in its progress, will ruin the credit of the province.

---

[8] Ibid., 34.
[9] William Nelson, ed., *Documents Relating to the Colonial History of the State of New Jersey*, Volume XIX (Paterson, N.J.: The Press Printing and Publishing Co., 1897), 385.

The example drawn from the practice of *"New York, Connecticut* and the trustees of the College of *New Jersey,"* are no proof that *Lotteries are Justifiable*. . . Will *examples alone,* and especially examples against law, prove the virtue, legality or morality of any act? If so, theft, adultery, and even murder itself may be justified. . .[10]

On February 1, 1759, *The Pennsylvania Journal* carried a reply by an anonymous person to the earlier charges of Pennsylvanicus that lotteries are "the enemies of Religion and of the Poor, the abettors and patrons of the most contagious and dangerous vice."[11] The respondent argued that lots are not forbidden by God in Scripture and "were used by the apostles themselves."[12] That line of reasoning confuses lots with lotteries. When lots were drawn in Scripture, money was not involved whereas lotteries are totally dependent on money and are a form of legalized plunder. The views of Pennsylvanicus prevailed in that colony at least. In 1762, the Pennsylvania legislature passed an act against lotteries for the following reasons:

> Whereas many mischievous and unlawful games, called lotteries, have been set up in this province, which tend to the manifest ruin and impoverishment of many poor families; and whereas such pernicious practices may not only give opportunities to evil disposed persons to cheat and defraud the honest inhabitants of this province, but prove introductive of vice, idleness, and immorality, injurious to trade, commerce; and industry, and against the common good. . .[13]

While the needs of the College were great, this decision to engage in a lottery scheme was unwise and contradicted the spiritual foundations of that institution. Perhaps their faith was not as strong as it should have been that the Lord would move His people to generously support them. Their decision to send Tennent and Davies to Great Britain was the right one and proved beneficial beyond all expectations. Yet, the use of a lottery for fund raising was a misguided decision by the Trustees which resulted in being publicly shamed by an anonymous party.

---

[10] William Nelson, ed., *Documents Relating to the Colonial History of the State of New Jersey*, Volume XX (Paterson, N.J.: The Press Printing and Publishing Co., 1898), 325.
[11] Ibid., 320.
[12] Ibid., 321.
[13] Nathan Tankus, "Jackpot: For Colonial Slaves, Playing the Lottery was a Chance at Freedom," JSTOR Daily, February 2, 2016. Accessed on October 26, 2016 at: http://daily.jstor.org/jackpot-for-colonial-slaves-playing-the-lottery-was-a-chance-at-freedom/

Davies and Tennent Arrive in Great Britain

The *London* arrived along the coast of Great Britain on December 17, after four weeks at sea, and began the tedious journey to London via the English Channel and the Thames River. Six weeks earlier the *Britannia* had wrecked on a sandbar in the channel and thirteen people were killed, including the ship's captain. The southeastern coast of England provided them a magnificent view of the white cliffs of Dover and the Dover Castle, but the shocking sight of an executed pirate was seen as the ship passed Northfleet and Greys, two small villages on the coast. The landscape was a pleasing scene of green cornfields, forests, Gothic churches, villages, and a stately hospital at Greenwich. Davies was fascinated with English oysters because, unlike American oysters, they were almost round and flat.

The ship harbored at London on Christmas Day, and the two colonial ministers walked past the Tower of Big Ben as they got off the ship. The bells of a nearby church were ringing with "the most manly, strong and noble Music"[14] that Davies had ever heard. The steeple of St. Dunstan's Church, an Anglican church built in the twelfth century, was described by Davies as consisting of "such curious Architecture that when the Bells ring, it rocks, like a tree shaken with the Wind, tho' it consists of Stone."[15] Both men were invited to dine that afternoon with Richard Neate and William Neave, partners in a mercantile business and part owners in the *London* on which Davies and Tennent had their conveyance to Great Britain. Neate and Neave had many customers in America and were warm friends of the Dissenters.

In the evening, Davies and Tennent were escorted to the home of Dennys Deberdt, who had made most of the arrangements for their trip. Tennent "was extremely low-Spirited," which made Davies "afraid of conversing freely, lest [he] should seem to arrogate the Preference."[16]

Thomas Gibbons, pastor of the Independent congregation at Haberdasher's Hall, paid a visit to Davies and Tennent the following day. Gibbons informed them "of the general Apostasy of the Dissenters from the Principles of the Reformation."[17] Also, Richard Crutenden called on them

---

[14] Pilcher, ed., *Reverend Samuel Davies Abroad*, 43.
[15] Ibid.
[16] Ibid.
[17] Ibid.

and provided Davies with "10 pounds Sterling worth of Books to be distributed among the Poor in Virginia."[18] In the evening, Davies and Tennent visited George Whitefield, who invited them "to make his House [their] home during [their] Stay."[19] Since many Dissenters were disaffected with him, they determined "that a public Intercourse with him would be imprudent in our present Situation." Nonetheless, Whitefield "spoke in the most encouraging Manner as to the Success of our Mission, and in all his Conversation, discovered so much Zeal and Candour, that [Davies] could not but admire the Man."[20] After this visit, Tennent's "Heart was all on Fire" and they "prayed together 'till about 3 o'clock in the Morning."[21]

Whitefield's biographer, Arnold Dallimore, stated with some justification that Davies and Tennent were "not willing to bear [Whitefield's] reproach."[22] This decision of the two Americans forced them to solicit contributions from those who were not sympathetic to the doctrines of grace and caused them several embarrassing moments. Whitefield, though, acquiesced in their decision and informed William Grimshaw, "I shall help them all I can."[23] Yet, he was probably referring to their refusal of his offer when he stated later in this letter:

> At the great day all things will be laid open.[24]

Davies and Tennent had already spent more than 125 pounds by this date, which gave them a sense of urgency for their mission. Yet, they were perplexed where to begin because of the number of parties among the Dissenters. As Davies remarked:

> The Independents and Baptists are more generally Calvinists, than the Presbyterians; tho' I fear some of them are tainted with Antinomianism.[25]

---

[18] Ibid.
[19] Ibid., 44.
[20] Ibid.
[21] Ibid.
[22] Arnold A. Dallimore, *George Whitefield: The Life and Times of the Great-Eighteenth Century Revival*, Volume II (Westchester, Illinois and Edinburgh, Scotland: Cornerstone Books and The Banner of Truth Trust, 1979), 361.
[23] Ibid., 362.
[24] Ibid.
[25] Pilcher, ed., *Reverend Samuel Davies Abroad*, 46.

Davies spent his first days in London sightseeing. He walked to the top of the monument to "the dreadful Fire of 1666," from which he "could take a View of this vast overgrown City, and the People in the Streets seemed degenerated into Pygmies,[26]; strolled through St. James's Park, "a beautiful Place"; walked to the New Bridge at Westminster, "the most noble Piece of Workmanship of the Kind. . .in the World"; and visited Westminster Hall, where he was impressed that the building was "supported without one Pillar."[27] He was struck by the number of beggars who lined the streets, but the impostors made it "hard to distinguish real Objects of Charity."[28]

Davies preached his first sermon in England on Sunday morning, December 30, to the Independent congregation at Moorfields. His text was taken from Isaiah 66:1, 2, and he lamented that he was "dull and senseless" in the delivery. He dined with Samuel Morton Savage, assistant pastor at the Independent congregation in St. Mary Axe, whom he esteemed "a most valuable Christian."[29] The afternoon message was from Jeremiah 31:18, 20, and was delivered with "some freedom" to the Baptist congregation at Great Eastcheap, pastored by Samuel Dews. He was also grieved "to see how small the Congregations are in this vast City."[30]

Tennent went that same morning to hear Samuel Chandler, minister to an Independent congregation in the Old Jewry, which bordered on the Jewish ghetto area of London. Chandler was moderately Calvinistic with leanings towards Arianism. That theological combination is usually an indication of neonomian tendencies and a downplaying of experimental religion. Nonetheless, Chandler's support of their mission was considered to be important for their success in London. Davies spent that evening with a Mr. Edwards, a merchant, who was a member of the Committee for the affairs of the Dissenters. From Edwards, he learned that Joseph Stennet, a Baptist pastor at Little Wild Street, had "the most influence in Court, of any of the dissenting Ministers."[31]

---

[26] Ibid., 44.
[27] Ibid., 45–46.
[28] Ibid., 46.
[29] Ibid., 45
[30] Ibid.
[31] Ibid.

On New Year's Eve, Davies and Tennent sought an appointment with the Marquis of Lothian,[32] William Kerr, but they arrived too late for the meeting and found that he had already left. Two days later, they dined in the evening with both the Marquis and the Earl of Leven, Alexander Melville. The Marquis "kindly received them" and "gave all the Encouragement in his Power with regard to our Embassy."[33] Davies was impressed with "the unaffected Grandeur of the Nobleman, and the Simplicity and Humility of the [Christian]."[34]

Davies heard Chandler preach a New Year's Day sermon on "the Parable of the unjust Steward", but he "did not discern so much of Experimental Religion in his Discourse as [he] could wish."[35] Afterwards, he went to the Amsterdam Coffee-House, "where the Congregational and Baptist Ministers meet on Tuesdays."[36] He had a pleasing conversation at the coffee house with Samuel Price, a former colleague of Isaac Watts, who co-pastored the Independent congregation in Berry Street, St. Mary Axe. He went later that evening to hear a sermon by Whitefield at the Tabernacle on "the Parable of the Barren Fig Tree." "Tho' the Discourse was incoherent," Davies recorded, "yet it seemed to me better calculated to do good to Mankind than all the accurate, languid Discourses I have heard."[37] Following the sermon, Whitefield invited Davies to his house for fellowship and conversation, which was pleasing to them both.

On January 3, 1754, Davies sought advice from Thomas Gibbons, Richard Crutenden, and Dennys Deberdt about the best method of raising funds. There were many obstacles: The two colonists had too few letters of introduction to the Presbyterians, "the most numerous and rich" of the Dissenters; the Dissenter congregations, as a whole, were small enough "to damp one's Zeal in preaching to them[38]"; many of the Presbyterians had imbibed Arminian or Socinian principles and were "shy of

---

[32] The Lord High Commissioner of the General Assembly of Scotland.
[33] Pilcher, ed., *Reverend Samuel Davies Abroad*, 47.
[34] Ibid.
[35] Ibid., 46.
[36] Ibid.
[37] Ibid., 47.
[38] Ibid., 58.

us";[39] and certain key individuals would give their support to this mission only if the charter of the college were more catholic instead of Calvinistic.

On January 5, Davies and Tennent visited with the Mauduit brothers, Jasper and Israel. The brothers were wool merchants and hearty friends to the Dissenters in Virginia. Jasper was on the Committee that represented the civil affairs of the Dissenters before the king. After Jasper promised Davies that action should be taken in favor of the Virginia Dissenters before he returned home, the conversation turned to the mission for the College of New Jersey. When Tennent emphasized that Calvinists were "the principal Persons concerned in it," they discovered that the Mauduits "were both of latitudinarian[40], anticalvinistic Principles, and would not countenance the College, unless it were upon a catholic Plan."[41] Being shown the charter, though, they were satisfied with its catholicity.

The diverse theological views of the various groups of Dissenters in London provided Davies and Tennent with their chief impediment in soliciting support for the college. Whitefield thought they were not taking "the best Method in endeavoring to keep in with all Parties."[42] He urged them to "'come out boldly'. . .which would secure the Affections of the pious People from whom" they "might expect the most generous Contributions."[43] It is hard to argue with success, but the advice of Whitefield had a great deal of merit. Davies and Tennent were frequently in embarrassing situations by trying to win the support of those who were not warm friends of the Great Awakening.

By the middle of January, the two Americans had determined that Chandler's support was essential to their success. On January 17, they "stayed at Home preparing a petition in behalf of the College"[44] because of the rainy weather. They submitted this petition to Chandler

---

[39] Ibid., 54.
[40] Latitudinarianism was initially a pejorative term to describe the rejection of any strict standards or confessions. The latitudinarians were too tolerant of doctrinal deviations from evangelical theology. This tolerance led many of them to adopt Arminianism, Socinianism, Neonomianism, and Arianism.
[41] Pilcher, ed., *Reverend Samuel Davies Abroad*, 49
[42] Ibid., 55.
[43] Ibid.
[44] Ibid., 57.

for his correction the next day. He suggested they include some statement that the college would teach the children of German immigrants the English language. Though believing that the college was not designed for this purpose, Davies reluctantly submitted to the change when Tennent agreed to it. The irenic spirit of Tennent during this trip was sometimes an overcompensation for his Nottingham sermon thirteen years before. Tennent repented overmuch for the harshness he had exhibited in that controversy and sometimes tried to be agreeable when he should have been more decisive. This instance was one of those times.

Over the next three days, Davies and Tennent spent several hours in revising the petition. On January 22, they returned to Chandler's home to solicit his approval of the final draft. To their surprise, Michael Schlatter[45], whom Davies had briefly met in America, and William Smith, the Provost of the Philadelphia Academy, were also there. After some small talk, the conversation turned to the mission of the college. When Davies and Tennent commented that the College of New Jersey would unite the Calvinists among the German Reformed with the English Presbyterians, "Mr. Smith replied that an Union would not be desirable; for a Separation would keep up the Balance of Power."[46] Not realizing that a trap had been laid, Tennent urged "that Union in a good Thing is always desirable."[47] Davies' journal records what happened next:

> Upon which Mr. Chandler says, "I have seen a very extraordinary Sermon against Union," and he immediately reached to Mr. Tennent his Nottingham-Sermon. It threw us both into Confusion, and gave such a Damp to my Spirits as bro't me in Mind of my Mortifications in the General-Court in Virginia. Mr. Tennent went about to vindicate himself, and when I had recovered from my Consternation, I put in a Word. But all had no Effect. We found that Sermon and the Examination of Mr. Tennent's Answer to the Protest, had been put into Mr. Chandler's Hands; and he had formed his Judgment so precipitantly from a partial View of the Case, that he told us, "He would do nothing for us."[48]

---

[45] Michael Schlatter (1716–1790) was a German Reformed missionary who served congregations in and around Philadelphia.
[46] Pilcher, ed., *Reverend Samuel Davies Abroad*, 59.
[47] Ibid.
[48] Ibid.

Davies had conversed with William Smith at the St. Dunstan's Coffee-House three days before and commented afterwards that "he did not appear so great an Enemy to our Design, as we expected."[49] Yet, he was too charitable in his judgment of Smith. At Chandler's home, Smith "alleged that the College was a Party-Design"[50] and did not represent true catholicity. After he and Tennent returned to their rooms and prayed for direction, Davies recorded that he was "shocked to think of the inveterate Malignity of the Synod of Phila. who have sent their Accusations after Mr. Tennent so far."[51]

An anxious night of concern for their mission followed before Davies and Tennent met with Chandler again to allay his concerns and win his support. Davies records what happened next:

> Tennent made honest humble Concessions with regard to the Nottingham Sermon . . . that it was written in the Heat of his Spirit . . . that Some of the Sentiments were not agreeable to his present Opinion. . . that he had painted sundry Things in too strong Colours. . . that it was now 13 Years ago and that since he had used all his Influence to promote Union between the Synods; of which he produced his Irenicum[52]. . .that if the Sermon was faulty, it was but the Fault of one Man, and should not be charged upon the whole Body.[53]

Davies supplemented Tennent's plea with a passionate description of the hardships under which the New Light Presbyterians labored. At these words, Chandler appeared to soften, promised to contribute towards their mission, and invited Davies to preach for him on the evening of February 3.

Leaving Chandler's house, Davies and Tennent waited on Samuel Lawrence, a Presbyterian minister, who advised them to circulate two petitions as follows:

> One for the Presbyterians, and one for the Independents; for the Animosi-

---

[49] Ibid
[50] Ibid., 59.
[51] Ibid., 60.
[52] In 1749, Tennent produced his *Irenicum Ecclesiasticum, or A Humble Impartial Essay on the Peace of Jerusalem*. The purpose of this work was to heal the divisions in the Presbyterian Church and promote the reunion of the two sides. He was profusely apologetic for his role in the division and vindicated the Old Light ministers whom he had formerly castigated.
[53] Pilcher, ed., *Reverend Samuel Davies Abroad*, 60.

ties among some of them were so strong that the very Sight of the Names of one Party would hinder the other from Subscribing.[54]

Heeding Lawrence's advice, they went to work to gain signatures to their petitions. By February 16, they had obtained the signatures of sixty-seven men (including Chandler), had raised nearly £200, and had published 500 copies of their petition for distribution.

Their method of soliciting signatures was to visit ministers in their homes and meetinghouses or mingle with them at the various coffee houses in the city. The English Dissenters generally lacked the formal connections of the Church of England, and thus their ministers would meet together on Tuesdays in London's coffee houses. The Independents, Calvinistic Presbyterians, and Baptists frequented the Amsterdam Coffee-House. Other Presbyterians, generally of Arminian or Socinian sentiments, went to Hamlin's Coffee-House. Davies and Tennent would visit both places and, as a result, received numerous invitations to preach which they happily accepted.

On January 20, Davies recorded that he "heard Mr. Tennent P.M. preach an honest, plain Sermon; and while I was pleased with its Simplicity, I was uneasy lest its Bluntness might be offensive."[55] When Tennent preached for Gibbons, Davies commented that "a good Number of People are displeased with his using Notes."[56] Also, their mission had to overcome "the Prejudices raised in the Minds of some by Mr. Tennent's Nottingham Sermon, which is dispersed thro' the Town from Hand to Hand very officiously."[57] While there was no indication of friction between the Americans, Archibald Alexander rightly observed that "Davies carried off the palm as to popularity in London and other places."[58]

Davies' manners "were polished and calculated to please" while those of Tennent "were rough, blunt, and not at all courtly."[59] Gibbons was the first to offer to publish one of Davies' sermons, but, by February 4th, a number of people pressed him to publish his poems and his sermon before the Presbytery of New Castle. Davies nevertheless declined,

---

[54] Ibid., 61.
[55] Ibid., 58.
[56] Ibid., 55.
[57] Ibid., 75.
[58] Archibald Alexander, *The Log College* (London: Banner of Truth Trust, 1968), 50.
[59] Ibid

for he was "afraid of every Thing that might be looked upon as ostentatious in my present Circumstances."[60] One of the few criticisms Davies received on this trip was a remark by Samuel Savage that his message on Isaiah 45:22 "was not sufficiently evangelical,"[61] which is hard to imagine. Whether or not Tennent was jealous of Davies' growing popularity in London, he was certainly humbled by his own Nottingham sermon.

On January 13, Davies "spent the Evening in pleasing Conversation with dear Mr. Gibbons."[62] Two days later, he and Tennent enjoyed the fellowship of both Gibbons and Whitefield. Davies recorded that "Tennent's Heart was opened for free religious Conversation, and we spent a few Hours very profitably."[63] Both Americans visited Savage the evening of January 30 and found "the good man was cooled towards us."[64] Savage felt that the Americans were taking the wrong course by associating with "Persons of all Denominations promiscuously" and by not keeping "a more public Intercourse with Mr. Whitefield."[65] Earlier that day, their visit with John Gill, "the celebrated Baptist minister," revealed him to be "a serious, grave little Man."[66] Gill signed their petition but did not encourage them in their efforts.

On another occasion, Davies and Tennent dined with Thomas Bradbury, an Independent pastor at Carey Street in New Court. Bradbury read them some letters between Whitefield and himself from 1741 over the latter "singing a Song in a Tavern in a large Company in praise of old English Beef."[67] After Bradbury sang his song, Davies observed that it "would be offensive to the greatest Number of serious People" but he "knew 'twas his peculiar Whim, Nor took it ill—as come from him."[68]

When not preaching, Davies enjoyed listening to the sermons of others. Upon attending Salter's Hall, where the Presbyterian minister John Barker[69] was preaching, Davies noted that "his Sermon was very accu-

---

[60] Pilcher, ed., *Reverend Samuel Davies Abroad*, 69.
[61] Ibid., 71.
[62] Ibid., 54.
[63] Ibid., 55.
[64] Ibid., 65.
[65] Ibid.
[66] Ibid.
[67] Ibid., 62.
[68] Ibid.
[69] Barker (1682–1762) pastored a congregation at Mare Street, Hackney, and was 71 or 72 at

rate and judicious, and in the Calvinistic Strain."[70] It was Davies' opinion that "the greatest Number of learned and polite Preachers are among the Presbyterians,"[71] notwithstanding that many of them had adopted Arminian and Socinian views.

On February 17, Davies heard Dr. David Jennings[72] preach an eloquent sermon from Romans 8:7, 8 with much conviction.[73] Seventeen days later, he listened to a sermon by John Halford at Samuel Chandler's Meeting-House. The occasion for this message was to collect funds for the support of the widows and children of Dissenting ministers.[74] Halford was greatly overcome with fright and his delivery evidenced his nervousness.[75] Davies spoke to Halford before the sermon, and described the exchange:

> I met him at the Door, as he was coming into the Meeting-House, and asked him, how he did? He answered, 'I am in fear and much trembling'; and when I told him that I hoped the Lord would be with him, the good Man burst into Tears. This gave me occasion to reflect upon my own Presumption, who preached there with much less Diffidence.[76]

After attending a number of congregations, Davies surely agreed with John Patrick, who served a Scottish Presbyterian congregation at Lisle Street, that the Dissenters had undergone a "Declension of Religion in London," and "the Revivals of Religion which they had, were chiefly in the Church of Eng. by Means of Mr. Whitefield."[77] To his dismay, he found that the Great Awakening in Great Britain had left most of the Dissenting congregations untouched. This very fact made it difficult for Davies and Tennent to determine the best method for raising funds in England. It was not likely that they would have had much success among the Church of England congregations as Dissenters.

---

the time of this event.
[70] Pilcher, ed., *Reverend Samuel Davies Abroad*, 72.
[71] Ibid.
[72] Jennings conducted an academy in the home of Samuel Savage and regularly preached to a Presbyterian congregation at Little St. Helen's.
[73] Pilcher, ed., *Reverend Samuel Davies Abroad*, 75.
[74] Ibid., 80.
[75] Ibid.
[76] Ibid.
[77] Ibid., 66.

Davies was seldom pleased with his own preaching on this trip. He would typically comment after a sermon: "The Hearers were attentive, tho' neither they nor myself was very solemn,"[78] or, "I could see little Signs of Solemnity among them; and alas! I neither had, nor tho't it proper to indulge a passionate Solemnity."[79] When preaching for Chandler on February 3, he blundered in introducing his text and he "did not recover thro' the Whole Discourse."[80] Afterwards he "had no Heart for Conversation"[81] while drinking tea and "returned home exceedingly dejected."[82] A similar incident took place on February 27 when Davies preached "a charity sermon at Mr. King's Meeting-House"[83] with a large number of ministers present. Davies was unnerved when he was unable to find his sermon notes, which he normally kept in his pocket. Yet, he felt his message was with "as much Freedom and Tenderness as [he had] had in this City."[84] After a sermon on February 24, Davies commented:

> Alas! that Spirit of awful Solemnity, so commanding and impressing to an Audience which has frequently animated my Sermons, seems now to be departed from me: and when I speak on solemn Subjects with the Air of Unconcernedness, or mere natural Vivacity, I feel guilty and seem to myself to make a very ridiculous Appearance. Such preaching, alas! has but little Weight with an Auditory.[85]

Yet, Davies' sermons were admired by almost all who heard him. He had to acknowledge his greatest problem "under so much applause" was "to repress the workings of vanity."[86] He humbly thanked God for raising him "from a mean family and utter obscurity, into some importance in the world."[87]

While in London, Davies and Tennent resided at Winchester Street in the heart of the city, within walking distance of most of the churches

---

[78] Ibid., 83.
[79] Ibid., 85.
[80] Ibid., 67.
[81] Ibid.
[82] Ibid.
[83] Ibid., 78.
[84] Ibid.
[85] Ibid., 77.
[86] Ibid., 84.
[87] Ibid.

where they preached. Davies preached about fifty sermons to twenty-six congregations during this part of their mission. Nineteen sermons were delivered to Presbyterian congregations, twenty-one at Independent churches, and eight at Baptist meetinghouses.

If Davies' efforts did not come up to his own standards, it was his opinion that "the Hurries of our Business, the Variety of Company and Objects, and the want of Time for Tho'tfulness and Retirement have dissipated my Tho'ts, and deadened my Devotion."[88] He lamented not having sufficient time to complete his journal or to maintain correspondence with his family and friends. He was constantly tired from his labors and was able to cultivate "little rational solid Concern about my own immortal State."[89] As he explained on one occasion:

> Tho' I take but too superficial Notice of it, yet alas! I feel Sin still strong in me. . .When I seriously think how depraved I am, I hardly know what Conclusion to draw about myself. God pity me, the vilest of his Creatures.[90]

Homesickness contributed most of all to Davies' low spirits. These were "days of cruel Absence" which he longed to "be over."[91] Such despondency made it impossible for him to feel the unbounded freedom that he had previously experienced in preaching. After writing a few letters on February 13, 1754, he remarked about Hanover:

> That dear Place contains all that is dearest to me in the World, my congregation, my Friends, my Parents, my Children and especially my dearest Chara. Alas! my Heart breaks at the Tho't.[92]

By March 19, Davies still had not received a letter from his wife, which made him "extremely anxious" about her health. He remained convinced, though, that "did they know my Uneasiness, I am sure they would write to me."[93] On another occasion, he exclaimed: "Oh! that I knew how she is! I find neither Time nor distance can ease her Image

---

[88] Ibid., 74.
[89] Ibid., 87.
[90] Ibid., 75.
[91] Ibid., 48.
[92] Ibid, 73.
[93] Ibid., 85.

from my Heart."[94] When a letter from John Todd brought news about Jane on April 14, Davies recorded: "The very Sight of it, threw me into a passionate Ferment, that did not soon subside. O how kind is God to me and mine!"[95]

Davies also redeemed sufficient time in London to prosecute the needs of the Dissenters in Virginia. On February 27, he took a coach to Pinners-Hall to wait on the Committee composed of Benjamin Avery, Joseph Stennet, and Jasper Mauduit, which managed the affairs of the Dissenters. It was the judgment of the members that the only paragraph of the Act of Toleration that could properly apply to the Colony of Virginia was the part that indemnified "Dissenters from Penalty for Exempting themselves from the Established Church."[96] This position surprised Davies as he still considered that his "Reasons for [his] former Opinions are unanswerable."[97] Yet, the committee advised him to draft a petition, have it signed by "the Dissenters in the frontier Counties" of Virginia, and submit it to the King and Council. Davies was pleased with this advice and offered the prayer: "May the Providence of God smile on the Attempt."[98]

Five days later, Davies was dismayed to learn that "Peyton Randolph Esquire, my old Adversary, is now in London: and will no doubt oppose whatever is done in Favour of the Dissenters in Hanover."[99] Nevertheless, he went forth with the drafting of the petition, which was corrected by Dr. Avery on March 16 and sent to Virginia on April 7.

In addition to Randolph's presence, Davies felt there were other factors that would adversely affect the petition's success. First, the prime minister, Henry Pelham Esquire, suddenly died on March 6, "which has struck the Town into a Consternation."[100] Second, the Church of England's plan to send a bishop to America would not aid the Dissenters in Virginia. And third, there was "Confusion between the Governour and

---

[94] Ibid., 80.
[95] Ibid., 86.
[96] Ibid., 79.
[97] Ibid.
[98] Ibid.
[99] Ibid.
[100] Ibid., 80.

the General Assembly in Virginia"[101] over this matter. Thus, the committee did not feel the time was right to make applications for the Virginia Dissenters. Yet, Davies prevailed on Stennet to use all his influence in their favor.

By April 7, Davies and Tennent could praise God that they had already received £1200. At first, they did not expect to raise above £300 in all. Davies considered this to be "the most signal interposition of providence"[102] he had ever seen, and doubted that the friends of the college in America could receive the report of their success with the same surprise. Their success can be traced to their decision to continue the practice, begun on board the *London*, of praying together twice daily. In their times of prayer, they learned to "use the most unbounded Freedoms" with one another. After their earlier disappointment of February 23 at the promiscuous distribution of his Nottingham sermon, Tennent's spirits were so low that he considered returning to America. Yet, the next morning both of them praised God for "raising us up after a Dejection."[103] Tennent called that same day on William Belcher, Esquire, from whom they expected nothing. To their surprise and joy, Belcher gave £50 despite the fact that he appeared to "have no sense of Religion." That was a harbinger of their future success on this mission to which Davies exclaimed:

> Our friends in America cannot hear the news with the same surprize, as they do not know the difficulties we have had to encounter with; but to me it appears the most signal interposition of providence I ever saw.[104]

Davies and Tennent posted a letter to President Burr on April 30, 1754, about their success on this part of their journey. Burr wrote to one of the Trustees, David Cowell, pastor at First Presbyterian Church in Trenton, New Jersey on August 5, 1754 with the agreeable news:

> Yesterday I receive'd Letters from Messrs Tennent and Davies dated Apl 30 which brings agreeable News yt they have in Hand & Promise £1400 Ster.

---

[101] Ibid.
[102] Ibid., 85.
[103] Ibid., 76.
[104] Ibid.

Our good Friend Mr. Cross[105] has endeavored to prepare ye Way for them in Scotland. I think he is fair Way to lose the little Remains of Credit he has left. But I forbear my Censures till I am better informed what he has wrote.[106]

Conclusion

By the beginning of May, Davies and Tennent began their journey to Scotland for the session of the General Assembly of the Church of Scotland in May. The success of their mission thus far was far more than they could reasonably have expected, despite the numerous obstacles in their way. Yet, their decision to ignore Whitefield's advice to "come out boldly" caused them a number of difficulties in England. Many of the Dissenters in England were not warm friends of the Great Awakening and they often had to solicit contributions from those whose theology was diametrically opposed to their own views and to the views of the principal founders of the College of New Jersey. It was in that situation that Davies was better suited than Tennent. Davies was more dignified and prudent than Tennent—and he was able to find a point of connection with others without compromising the gospel better then the fiery-spirited Tennent.

---

[105] President Burr was referring to Robert Cross, the Old Light pastor of First Presbyterian Church in Philadelphia, who was a virulent opponent of the College of New Jersey.
[106] William L. Ledwith, "Six Letters of President Burr," *Journal of the Presbyterian Historical Society*, Vol. I, No. 5 (Sept. 1902), 322.

An 1801 picture of William Smith who was the Provost of the Philadelphia Academy in 1753. He was at Samuel Chandlers' home in London when Davies and Tennent visited Chandler.

Picture of George Whitefield (1714- 1770) preaching;
Davies and Tennent visited with Whitefield in London.

-12-

North to Scotland

"I met with more [Christian] friendship in Edinburgh than anywhere in Great-Britain. There is too general a Decay of experimental and practical Religion; and yet there is a considerable Number of pious People in the city."[1]
~*Samuel Davies, June 15, 1754*~

**Edinburgh Castle and Old Town Edinburgh
in the Eighteenth Century**

---

[1] George William Pilcher, ed., *The Reverend Samuel Davies Abroad: The Diary of a Journey to England and Scotland, 1753-1755* (Urbana, Chicago, London: University of Illinois Press, 1967), 99.

On Friday, May 3, Davies and Tennent commenced their six-day journey to Edinburgh, hoping to attend the General Assembly of the Church of Scotland which would convene on the twenty-third of the month. They traveled by post-chaise, a four-wheeled closed carriage, which was the fastest mode of transportation for long distances even though it necessitated a change of horses every ten to fifteen miles at designated posts.

There were two accidents between London and Newcastle upon Tyne, which they happily escaped without much harm. One of the horses became so unruly near Caxton, nine miles west of Cambridge, that he broke the shaft and harness to pieces and completely unnerved the two Americans. Two days later, the hostler accidentally pulled back on the chaise while Davies and Tennent were in it. Tennent's head was caught and forced backwards with such violence that blood spewed from his nose, but he quickly got the bleeding to stop.

When they arrived at New Castle on May 7, Davies and Tennent were able to meet with six Dissenting ministers in that town. Two of them, Richard Rogerson and Samuel Louthian, were colleagues at the Westgate Church and had adopted Arminian and Socinian sentiments. Nonetheless, they all promised to promote the mission of the college. By rejecting Whitefield's counsel, the two Americans were often constrained to solicit donations from those whose theological sentiments were far removed from their own orthodox views. Such was the case in this instance.

Edinburgh and the General Assembly of the Church of Scotland
The Americans arrived in Edinburgh on Thursday, May 9. The following day they learned that Robert Cross, the Old Light minister in Philadelphia, had sent a malignant, prejudicial letter to several of the ministers in the Church of Scotland against this mission of the College of New Jersey. Additionally, Davies and Tennent were informed that the Scottish General Assembly had recently approved three general collections and they were also expecting an application from Holland, which gave the two Americans doubts concerning the future success of their fund-raising efforts in Scotland.

Davies and Tennent spent a week in Scotland before they attended the Synod of Lothian and Tweeddale, which convened on May 16. At that meeting, Davies observed firsthand the ruinous effects of the Patronage Act[2] on the ministry of that denomination and commented:

> Alas! There appears but little of the Spirit of serious Christianity among the young Clergy. The Patronage-Act is like to be ruinous to the Church of Scotland; for of 980 Parishes in it, about 700 are in the Gift of the King, or of the prime Minister and therefore are used as Engines of ministerial Power, tempt the Clergy to cringe to the Court, and introduce Mercenaries into the Churches.[3]

The first package from home reached Davies a few days later, which brought him news about his wife and family. Jane had recently recovered from a severe illness, but he feared his friends were concealing the worst from him and that made him uneasy. Despite the letters from friends with news about Jane, he was overcome with anxious feelings which only a letter from her own hand could relieve.[4]

Davies preached the following day, Sunday, May 19, to a crowded congregation at the Tolbooth Church—one of the four congregations occupying St. Giles Church at the foot of the road leading up to Edinburgh Castle. His message on this occasion pleased many and edified most, but his use of notes was considered distasteful by a congregation which regularly feasted on extemporaneous preaching.[5] A week later, he commented:

> I think Scotland may boast a greater Number of good Speakers, than any Country I have been in; and I believe their accustoming themselves to speak extempore, has been of great Service to them in it.[6]

When Wednesday, May 23, arrived, the General Assembly was opened amid great pomp and ceremony with a procession of the nobility through Edinburgh's crowded streets lined with soldiers. Alexander Webster, minister of Edinburgh's Tolbooth Church, delivered a "master-

---

[2] The Patronage Act was a 1711 Act of the Parliament of Great Britain. It allowed nobles and other patrons to present ministers to vacant churches within their geographical districts which gave them control of those congregations within the Church of Scotland.
[3] Pilcher, ed., *Reverend Samuel Davies Abroad*, 91.
[4] Ibid., 92.
[5] Ibid.
[6] Ibid., 95.

ly, oratorial Discourse"[7] from Psalm 137:5, 6 and Robert Hamilton, Professor of Divinity at the University of Edinburgh, was elected as the Moderator. The Committee for Bills of the Assembly considered the petition from the Trustees of the College of New Jersey on Friday and decided to send it to the floor of the Assembly with their approval on the following Monday. This agreeable news seemed a precursor of God's blessings on their mission to Davies.

James Watson, minister at the Canon-Gate Church in Edinburgh, asked Davies to preach on Sunday morning, May 26, which he did from 1 John 3:2 with a large number of ministers present. That occasion gave him the opportunity to favorably impress the Scottish ministers and he felt "considerable Freedom and Solemnity"[8] in his preaching. In the evening, he dined with John Jardine, minister at the Tron Church in Glasgow:

> Supped with the Reverend Mr. Jardine, who intimated that he expected the Assembly would be divided in their Sentiments about our petition, according as they were Friends or Adversaries to Mr. Whitefield, which gave us very alarming Apprehensions because his Friends are the Minority.[9]

After this meal, Davies spent a sleepless night in anxious concerns over the success of their mission. On Monday morning, John Lumsden, Professor of Divinity at King's College in Aberdeen, rose to speak in favor of the Petition, giving the following reasons for his support:

> [T]he Importance of a learned Ministry—The Necessity of the College of New Jersey for that End—The Duty of the General Assembly to promote Institutions in general—and especially among Presbyterians in those Colonies, "who (says he) are a Part of ourselves, having adopted the same Standard of Doctrine, Worship and Government with this Church."[10]

This motion was passed by a voice vote to the great relief of the Americans and gave them the freedom to solicit support throughout the Church of Scotland. Later that same day, Davies received another package from home which included "a most tender, ingenious letter from my

---

[7] Ibid., 93.
[8] Ibid., 94.
[9] Ibid., 95.
[10] Ibid., 95–6.

dearest, which I could not but read over and over with the most passionate emotions. How God is good to me in preserving her life, so important to my happiness, notwithstanding of threatening sickness."[11]

Various speeches on an overture to the meeting of the General Assembly concerning the ordination of ministers informed Davies that John Owen and Philip Doddridge could not have held ministerial credentials in the Church of Scotland and probably would have been deposed if they had.[12] Naturally, Davies found that position to be extreme since both men agreed with the fundamentals of the faith as expressed in the Westminster Standards. Their differences with Presbyterianism concerned various matters of church government. Davies believed that some ministers in the Church of Scotland "carried church-power to an extravagant height, deny to individuals the right of judging for themselves, and insist upon absolute, universal obedience to all the determinations of the General Assembly."[13] True church power, according to Davies and the New Light Presbyterians, is ministerial and declarative only and does not carry with it the power of coercion or civil authority. Thus, the true exercise of church power should never be authoritarian, dictatorial, or hierarchical.

One young minister, Jonathan Witherspoon (whom Davies identified as "Weatherspoon"), wrote an ingenious piece against the Church of Scotland's view of church power which was described by Davies as follows:

> It is a Burlesque upon the High-flyers under the ironical Name of Moderate Men; and I think the Humour is Nothing inferior to Dean Swift.[14]

Davies could not have envisioned at this time that Witherspoon would one day succeed him as President of the College of New Jersey. Yet, both men were exactly right concerning the extravagant exercise of church power. Church history shows that when church power rises to an extravagant height the result is that moderatism or progressivism in theology is not far behind.

Numerous preaching opportunities in Scotland kept Davies busy

---

[11] Ibid., 97.
[12] Ibid.
[13] Ibid.
[14] Ibid., 99.

throughout May and June. By June 10, he could state that his popularity seemed to be growing among the Christians in Scotland.[15] He also found more Christian friendship in Edinburgh than anywhere else in Great Britain. About these friendships, he concluded that there was in general a serious declension of true spirituality among many professing Christians, but there were a good number of truly pious people in Edinburgh nonetheless.[16]

Tennent Leaves for Ireland; Davies Travels throughout Scotland
Following the General Assembly of the Church of Scotland, Davies and Tennent parted company on June 15 to expand their efforts. Davies remained in Scotland and Tennent set out for his native Ireland. They planned to reunite in London later in the year. Davies visited with Ralph Erskine at Culross and was impressed with his character, zeal, knowledge, and genius. He believed Erskine promised "much service to the Church of Scotland."[17]

Rev. John Adams of Falkirk escorted Davies to Glasgow, after his visit with Erskine, where Davies addressed Adams' large congregation who listened attentively to his preaching.[18] When it came time to part with Adams, Davies found his heart rebelling against this rupture from his new friend.[19] Adams later wrote to Joseph Bellamy about Davies' visit:

> He did me the favour—and, indeed, it was a most obliging one—to pass two or three days at my house, and to preach to my congregation. I think, in my life, I never met with a more agreeable person. How happy is America in ministers![20]

Davies remained in Glasgow for ten days and preached six sermons, including three times for John Gillies,[21] whom he considered to be a well-formed and mature Christian who was "uncommonly zealous and labo-

---

[15] Ibid., 98.
[16] Ibid., 99.
[17] Ibid.
[18] Ibid.
[19] Ibid., 100.
[20] Richard Webster, *A History of the Presbyterian Church: From Its Origin Until the Year 1760*, (Philadelphia: Joseph M. Wilson, 1757), 555.
[21] Gillies later compiled historical accounts of the Great Awakening, including materials from and about Davies.

rious in his ministry."[22] He was particularly impressed by the faithfulness of the Magistrates of Glasgow to attend Sunday and weekday services.

The obscure village of Cambuslang, southeast of Glasgow, was the scene of Davies' next visit. He spent an evening there with William McCulloch, who was so instrumental in the revival of 1742 in that area. On February 18, 1742, McCulloch preached a sermon from Jeremiah 23:6: "And this is the Name whereby he shall be called, The LORD our Righteousness." That sermon is lost to posterity, but its effects on several people are recorded. Many, no doubt, agreed with the report of one person who "thought that sermon was, as it were, a new Gospel to me."[23] About fifty people came under distress for their souls during McCulloch's sermon and they were described by John Willison (1680-1750), a serious and well-respected minister in Dundee, Scotland, a few months later as follows:

> Having resided in Mr. *M'Culloch's* House I had occasion to converse with many who had been awakened... some who had been very wicked and scandalous, but now wonderfully chang'd...very rude and boisterous before, they now had the mildness, and meekness of the Lamb about them...Tho' I conversed with a great Number both Man and Women, Old and Young, I could observe nothing *Visionary* or *Enthusiastick* about them... Upon the whole, I look on the Work at C——g, to be a most singular and marvellous Out-pouring of the *Holy Spirit*.[24]

Those days of revival were now all in the past at Cambuslang, but Davies was much pleased with the company of McCulloch, his wife, and their son, who all showed visible signs of deep piety. He described McCulloch as "a humble, holy minister of [Christ] not formed for popularity; which is a strong presumption that the late religious commotion there was not the effect of oratory, but of divine power."[25] Indeed, the absence of fanaticism at Cambuslang is a clear indication that McCulloch was a kindred spirit to Davies himself and was, undoubtedly, the reason the American felt such pleasure in his home.

---

[22] Pilcher, ed., *Reverend Samuel Davies Abroad*, 101.
[23] Arthur Fawcett, *The Cambuslang Revival: The Scottish Evangelical Revival of the Eighteenth Century* (London, The Banner of Truth Trust, 1971), 108.
[24] Ibid., 111.
[25] Pilcher, ed., *Reverend Samuel Davies Abroad*, 103.

While at Cambuslang, Davies learned to his agreeable surprise that Governor Dinwiddie of Virginia had written to his brother, Provost Laurence Dinwiddie, a Glasgow merchant with whom Davies corresponded; to his brother-in-law and Davies' host in Cambuslang, William McCulloch; and, to various friends in Scotland in behalf of the College of New Jersey. Thus, Davies was convinced that the Governor would support the Dissenters in Virginia "were it not so opposite to his interest."[26] McCulloch discussed with Davies the possibility of a very generous donation of £200 for the work of evangelizing the Indians. They also had an agreeable conversation on the cause of the Dissenters in Virginia which was most helpful to Davies.

There were continuous solicitations in Scotland for Davies to publish copies of his sermons. He determined to finish a collection of them for that purpose upon his return home, prophetically reasoning that his sermons in printed form "may be of service in places far remote from the sphere of my usual labours."[27]

Davies' Return Trip through England to London

Davies returned to Edinburgh on Monday, July 1, after two weeks near Glasgow, where he parted with his friends in that city under the strongest expressions of emotion and began his return journey to England. He rode to Haddington, twelve miles away, in company with James Robertson, Professor of Hebrew at the University of Edinburgh. Proceeding in a southeasterly direction, he passed through Berwick, Alnwick, and Morpeth before arriving at Newcastle in the late afternoon of Friday, July 5th.

A slightly erotic play, "The Careless Husband,"[28] by the English playwright, Colley Cibber, was being performed at the theater in Newcastle that evening and Davies was in the audience. He excused his attendance in the following way, "As I apprehended I should not be known, and consequently could give no offence, I went to gratifie my curiosity. But the entertainment was short of my expectation."[29] The play,

---

[26] Ibid.
[27] Ibid.
[28] Colly Cibber, *The Careless Husband: A Comedy* (London: J. and R. Tonson and S. Draper, 1750). Written by the English playwright, Colly Cibber (1671–1757).
[29] Pilcher, ed., *Reverend Samuel Davies Abroad*, 106.

esteemed to be Cibber's best, depicted the wisdom of a wife in wooing back her straying husband. Whatever motives led him to attend this play, he did not hide the fact from posterity. It is probably not surprising, though, that he was plagued the next day with convictions of his sinfulness about which he commented:

> I hardly know a Truth attested by such long, uninterrupted Experience as this, that no Change of Climate, no public Character, no Exercises, no Company, and in a Word, Nothing that I have ever tried, can extirpate the Principle, or suppress the Workings of Sin in this depraved Heart.[30]

Davies spent Sunday evening, July 7, at Newcastle in the company of Samuel Louthian whom he had met on his travels to Scotland. Davies and Louthian had a friendly debate on the doctrine of original sin. Louthian had imbibed the theology of John Taylor of Norwich, England, whose most well-known work, *The Scripture Doctrine of Original Sin*, was really an attempted refutation of the scriptural and Calvinistic doctrine of sin. Taylor's book was vigorously opposed by Jonathan Edwards who classed him among the "many late writers, who are enemies to the doctrine of original sin."[31] Louthian thus looked upon heart failures as innocent in themselves and evidence only that we are men, not angels. Davies asserted that heart failures are just as truly sinful as actions, which means that a person who has little heart for the worship of God is guilty of sin.

Joseph Bowes, Esquire, a Member of Parliament from the county of Durham, was Davies' host on Saturday, July 13. Bowes "took an ambitious pleasure like Hezekiah, to shew [Davies] all his glory"[32] and his large estate. Bowes possessed one plate valued at £17,000 Sterling, but he only gave five guineas to support the college. Davies was naturally unimpressed.

On the Sabbath, July 14, Davies preached three times, successively for Messrs. Atkin, Louthian, and Ogilvie. He also received a package from home that day which included a letter from his wife. His diary entry comments: "Her generous self-denial in not desiring me to hasten home

---

[30] Ibid.
[31] Edward Hickman, rev. and corr., *The Works of Jonathan Edwards*, Volume One (Edinburgh, Scotland and Carlisle, Pennsylvania: The Banner of Truth Trust, 1974), 143.
[32] Pilcher, ed., *Reverend Samuel Davies Abroad*, 108.

till I have finished my mission, gave me an agreeable [surprise], and made me reflect with shame upon my own impatience."[33] He learned in that same letter that John Rodgers was received with great acceptance at Hanover and John Wright was now laboring in Cumberland.

The seaside town of Scarborough was the scene of Davies' relaxation for the next few days. He then rode on July 19 to the town of Hull in the company of Thomas Ellis, a former pupil of Doddridge, and the minister at Cave. Ellis, like many of the Dissenting ministers in Great Britain, had adopted the latitudinarian principles of modern divinity. Davies observed about them, "They take greater liberties than I should [choose]. They make no scruples of gaming, attending on horse-races, mingling in promiscuous companies on the bowling-green, etc."[34] He further elaborated:

> It is a strong Presumption with me against these new Doctrines, that I have observed, wherever they prevail, there practical, serious Religion, and generally the dissenting Interest too, declines, and People become careless about it. Some of them go off into the Ch. of England, and others fall into Deism. And it is a Matter of Complaint, that the Deists generally, if not universally, are of the Whigg-Party, and join the low-Churchmen. Alas! How are the Principles of Liberty abused![35]

The latitudinarian principles against which Davies complained have often led those who began as evangelicals to veer towards Arminianism, Pelagianism, Socinianism, Arianism, or Deism. Initially, they first simply imbibe the neonomian doctrine that Christ has made a new law in the New Testament which is easier to keep than the Mosaic laws. Original sin, regeneration, justification by faith alone, the imputation of Christ's righteousness, assurance of salvation, and many other scriptural doctrines are then sacrificed for this "new law." Ceremonialism replaces vital piety and the Spirit's work in the believer's heart. The diminishing of Christ's redemption results in the denial of His divinity and leads to Arianism and/or Deism. It is as true today as it was in the eighteenth century. It was for that reason that Davies complained about the difficulty of trying to raise funds among such ministers and churches:

---

[33] Ibid.
[34] Ibid., 110.
[35] Ibid., 113.

> In conversation with the Gent. of the new Scheme, I am generally upon the Reserve about my own Principles, lest it should prejudice them against the Business of my Mission. But when I reflect upon it, I seem to despise myself as a Coward. My Conscience indeed does not generally accuse me of Guilt, in this Respect; but a Sense of Honour or Pride or I know not what to call it, makes me look mean and sneaking to myself.[36]

As mentioned previously, the decision by Davies and Tennent to ignore the advice of Whitefield to "come out boldly" in their fundraising efforts is what set the table for this predicament. They chose instead to indiscriminately solicit contributions from all Dissenters, some of whom had veered far from evangelicalism. In such a situation, it was difficult if not impossible to have the boldness to be faithful to the principles and doctrines of the gospel. This procedure did not cause as much difficulty in Scotland or Ireland as it did in England—where the few Presbyterians were mostly supporters of the new divinity and latitudinarianism. It is my opinion that the blame for this decision was probably owing more to Tennent than to Davies. Ever since his "Nottingham" sermon, which had caused such a furor throughout the colonies, Tennent had repented overmuch. No man in the history of the church has suffered more verbal abuse over one sermon delivered in the heat of passion than Tennent did for that sermon. Indeed, he is still being castigated for it almost three centuries later. Unlike Tennent, Davies knew how to dispassionately but boldly stand for the truth which is why he felt like a coward in this circumstance.

On Sunday, July 21, Davies preached at Hull for Mr. Witters and Mr. Wildboar, ministers at the Presbyterian and Independent churches respectively. Although he had some measure of freedom, he was disappointed in his labors. This caused him to lament, "Alas! That solemn, affectionate address which once I was capable of, I now seem to have lost; and I am some times afraid of returning to my own people, lest I should not recover it."[37] Two days later, Davies received a letter from Tennent informing him of the latter's success in Ireland. Collections were being raised in both the Synod of Ulster and the Presbytery of Antrim. Tennent

---

[36] Ibid., 113–4.
[37] Ibid.

was also soliciting private contributions in Dublin, and expected to complete them in August.

Mr. Root, a local minister, gave Davies a tour of the city of York. Davies was especially impressed with the wall that surrounded the city, the magnificent cathedral, and the jail, which he said was "the most stately building for that purpose that I have ever seen."[38] On Saturday, July 27, he proceeded to Wakefield, where he had the pleasure of entertaining some acquaintances from Virginia: Col. William Beverly and Thomas Smith, a divinity student who had studied under Davies and boarded with him at Hanover.

On Sunday, Davies preached for Mr. Whitaker in the morning and for Thomas Walker in the evening. Both men were infected with Arminian and Socinian sentiments, which made it difficult for Davies "to unite prudence and faithfulness in conversation with them."[39]

Passing through Sheffield, Chesterfield, and Derby, he reached Nottingham on August 2 where he found several people who warmly held to the doctrines of grace. They were probably members of the congregation served by James Sloss who retained the faith of the Apostles.[40] The other Dissenting minister in Nottingham was Dr. Samuel Eaton, who agreed with the new doctrines. Both ministers received Davies' mission very favorably, and he remained in Nottingham for another week. Members of the two churches contributed more than £60, the largest amount received up until that date.

Davies dined with John Dean, Esquire, during his time in Nottingham. Forty years earlier, Dean had experienced delivery from a terrible storm at sea, and his published account of that experience was both remarkable and extraordinary.[41] Additionally, Dean had served Peter the Great of Moscow for fifteen years before being banished "because he would not join in a war against the English."[42]

Mrs. Hallows, a member of Dr. Eaton's congregation, was Davies' breakfast guest one morning in Nottingham. She was a learned opponent of the Trinity and a vigorous discussion ensued, causing Davies to reflect

---

[38] Ibid., 112.
[39] Ibid., 113.
[40] Ibid., 115.
[41] Ibid., 117.
[42] Ibid., 116.

that he had "seldom been so closely attacked upon the proper Divinity of the Son of God; and it cast [him], afterwards, in to a pensive melancholy Study upon the Point."[43]

Davies proceeded to Northampton, where his departed friend and correspondent, Dr. Philip Doddridge, had served. He spent five days in the city, preaching in Doddridge's pulpit on the Lord's Day morning and evening, August 11, and collecting £16 for the College. He visited with Mrs. Doddridge on three occasions, finding great pleasure in her friendship and conversation. He was particularly struck with a remark she made about her deceased husband:

> "That she rejoiced that the dear Deceased was called to the Tribunal of his Master with a Heart full of such generous Schemes for the good of Mankind, which he had zeal to project, tho' not Life to execute." May this be my happy Case! There are such Charms in a public Spirit, that I cannot but wish I could imbibe more of it.[44]

In and Around London
The following morning, Davies continued traveling toward London, arriving there on August 14, after a brief stop in St. Albans. He was particularly impressed with the grain fields between St. Albans and London, but was "shocked with the Blasphemy and Profaness [sic] of the Inhabitants, especially of the Vulgar."[45]

Reunion with some friends he had made in London revived Davies' spirit, and he spent the next week in their company. Most of his acquaintances in London thought the mission had prospered as much as possible and there was no reason to continue his labors. He rejected that advice and solicited further contributions from the cities and towns near London over the course of the next few weeks.

Ipswich was the scene of some of the happiest days he spent in England. William Notcutt, pastor of an Independent congregation, reminded him of Simeon in the Gospel of Luke, being eighty-three at the time. Davies formed a close friendship with Notcutt's assistant, William Gordon, whom he considered to have "experimental Religion much at Heart."[46]

---

[43] Ibid., 117.
[44] Ibid., 119.
[45] Ibid., 120.
[46] Ibid., 121.

On August 25, Davies preached morning and afternoon for Notcutt from Jeremiah 31:33 and Isaiah 66:1, 2 "with some Freedom; and the good People seemed eagerly to drink in the Doctrine."[47] He preached that evening for the Presbyterian minister, Thomas Scott, whom some considered guilty of Arminianism and Arianism, but Davies asserted, "He loves and speaks well of many Calvinists and Trinitarians."[48] Notcutt's congregation gave £23 and 9 shillings for the College the following day.

Leaving Ipswich, Davies rode through Woodbridge, Wickham-Market, and Saxmundam on his way to Oxford. While traveling by horseback, he "formed a Resolution, to draw up a Hystory on my Return, of my present Mission, the state of the Dissenters in England, of the Church in Scotland, etc. as far as I had Opportunity of making Observations: and present the M.S. to the College of New Jersey."[49] Yet, he doubted the success of this project since "the most of my Schemes of this Kind are unexecuted."[50]

The next ten days were spent by Davies in Norwich—the third largest city in England—where he lodged with Thomas Paul, a pious young man who had been affiliated with the Methodists until the terrible immoralities of James Wheatley became publicly known. Wheatley left the Methodists in 1751, but he continued to preach at the Tabernacle in Norwich. Davies commented about him:

> This unhappy Man had preached a long Time here with great Warmth and Earnestness; endured with the most Lamblike Patience, the most cruel Treatment from the Mob, which even endangered his Life, and been instrumental to awaken Multitudes to a serious Sense of Religion. But at last has been found guilty of repeated criminal Commerce with sundry Women, [though] his own wife was then alive. With what a loud Voice does this Event cry to all the Professors of Religion; "Be not high-minded, but fear!" O that none that seek thy Face, O Lord may be ashamed on my Account![51]

At Norwich, Davies preached on Sunday evening, September 7, for Mr. Fozer from Isaiah 45:22. Afterwards, two members of the congrega-

---

[47] Ibid.
[48] Ibid., 122.
[49] Ibid.
[50] Ibid., 123. Davies never began this project and his fears proved true.
[51] Ibid., 124.

tion, John Scott and Mr. Lincoln, raised £47 for the College through private contributions from the leading members of the church. Davies dined with Scott, Lincoln, Paul, and other friends in the evening on Saturday, September 13 when a health issue caused him some concern. After supper, they were engaged in conversation while Davies was smoking a pipe. He suddenly felt sick and determined to part their company for his lodgings. Proceeding from the parlor, Davies instantaneously "fell down dead on the Floor, and continued. . .without any Appearance of Life for near 2 minutes."[52] The record in Davies' diary is as follows:

> Then I began to struggle, and draw my Breath with great Force and Difficulty, so as to agitate my Breast, and my whole Frame. In about 2 Minutes I suddenly came to myself; and was greatly [surprised] to find myself fallen on the Floor, and my Friends about me in such a Fright, rubbing my Hands and Temples: for I had lost all Consciousness, and did not in the least perceive my violent Fall. They immediately sent for a Surgeon; but before he came, I began to recover. I was able to walk home, with one supporting me. And tho' I was greatly enfeebled and exhausted, and my Heart heaved and struggled to throw off the Blood; I had a little refreshing Sleep.[53]

The next morning, Davies had a chest pain near his heart which he believed was "occasioned . . . by the Difficulty of the Circulation of Blood."[54] Nonetheless, he preached that day for Mr. Bourn in the morning and Mr. Fozer in the evening. To his surprise, an offering of £20 was raised at the door following the latter message.

The effects of his sickness, diagnosed by the attending surgeon as an apoplectic fit, continued with Davies for the next ten days. The fact that Davies had just started smoking his pipe before the symptoms would possibly indicate a connection between the two. In the eighteenth century, there was little knowledge of the connection of smoking with strokes and cardiovascular problems. On the Monday following this attack, he had blood drawn because it was thought that his problem was caused by the stagnation of blood. Yet, this experience made him realize once more

---

[52] Ibid., 126
[53] Ibid.
[54] Ibid.

"How thin the Partition [is] betwixt Time and Eternity."[55] Concerns for his family, especially his wife, flooded his thoughts:

> Nothing in this World affected me so much, as to foresee the Effect which the News of my sudden Death would have upon my dear Chara. Lord, prepare us both for the parting Stroke.[56]

He was especially thankful that he had not suffered this fall while riding a horse, which might have killed him. Interestingly enough, he did suffer a fall from a horse a few weeks later, on September 30, as he rode toward Chelmsford. While Davies was galloping along, the horse suddenly "fell down, and tumbled almost quite over."[57] Davies was feared to be in great danger but he escaped without any injuries. He looked upon both these experiences as remarkable evidences of God's providential deliverance of his life.

At Sudbury, Davies preached to the congregation of Mr. Hextal on September 22 and they raised £61 for the College in addition to the £5, 5 shillings contributed by Mrs. Rowe of Long Melford. Samuel Ruggles, a wealthy gentleman of Braintree, contributed £50 to the mission. The congregations at Braintree and Chelmsford gave £6 each to the college. Altogether, Davies raised an additional £250 in forty days after being discouraged in London from even making the effort. Thus, he could justly say, "I have taken all the means in my power to promote my important mission."[58]

On October 1, Davies returned to London, where letters from Tennent, John Rodgers, Captain Grant, and Mr. Allen awaited him and brought him good news. Tennent's letter related that he expected to return to London immediately and would embark for America shortly thereafter. Davies was anxious for the voyage home but was melancholy because he was still "a little intimidated at the Dangers of the Seas."[59] The letters from America informed him that all was well at home except for the continued oppression of the Dissenters by the Church of England.

---

[55] Ibid., 125.
[56] Ibid., 127.
[57] Ibid., 131.
[58] Ibid.
[59] Ibid.

On October 5, Tennent arrived in London with the news that he had collected "about 500 pounds in his tour."[60] Davies was revived by Tennent's return and was delighted in his success in Ireland. Two weeks later, they determined to sail for Philadelphia as soon as they could board a ship. Their expenses had far exceeded their budget, but their success in collecting funds was also far more than they originally envisioned.

Several congregations in and around London invited Davies to preach over the next month. He noted in his diary: "I observe a Set of Hearers that generally attend me wherever I Preach, particularly the young Students in the Academy."[61] On October 26, Tennent and Davies met with the Wesley brothers, John and Charles. This meeting caused Davies to observe:

> Notwithstanding all their wild Notions, they appear very benevolent, devout and zealous Men, that are laboring with all their Might to awaken the secure World to a Sense of Religion; and they are honoured with Success. But I am afraid their encouraging so many illiterate Men to preach the Gospel, will have bad Consequences. I heard one of them last Tuesd. Nt. . . . but he explained Nothing at all. His sermon was a meer Huddle of pathetic Confusion, and I was uneasy, as it might bring a Reproach upon experimental Religion. The despised Methodists, with all their Foibles, seem to me to have more of the Spirit of Religion than any Set of People in this Island.[62]

Davies discerned that the essential problem with the Wesleyan Methodists was their failure to combine true spirituality with doctrinal purity. They were fervent for experimental religion and the subjective grace of the Holy Spirit. Yet, they were often deficient in the objective truths of the gospel. True Christianity must be maintained by holding to a happy balance of both. Some, like the Old Light Presbyterians in America, were guilty of the opposite error of the Methodists and were unconcerned for maintaining the true spirit of Christianity. Others, like the Moravians and Methodists, fell into the error of de-emphasizing doctrinal purity. It was the great desire of Davies and other such New Light Presbyterians

---

[60] Ibid.
[61] Ibid., 132.
[62] Ibid., 133.

to hold to doctrinal purity, to the importance of experimental religion, and to fervent evangelism.

The Return Voyages to America
Tennent parted with Davies on November 13 to sail for Philadelphia under Captain Hargrove. Davies prepared to embark directly for Virginia, which would keep him from having to travel overland to his home. The men decided on separate journeys when they realized it would be unlikely that they could get all the trustees together for a meeting on their return.

Before leaving London, Davies received the signed petition from Virginia, for which he had been awaiting its return, concerning the cause of the Dissenters. He immediately presented this petition to Dr. Benjamin Avery, Jasper Mauduit, and the other members of the Committee for the Affairs of the Dissenters. He was concerned that since most of the members of the Committee were not sufficiently evangelical they would support this petition before the Court only as a cause of liberty—and not from principle. Thus, he particularly sought the help of Dr. Samuel Stennet, from whom he expected more than from the Committee. If the petition failed, Davies still expected that the alternative of being licensed by the Bishop's Court would be successful in relieving the distress of the Dissenters in Virginia.

On November 15, Davies left London and boarded the *Charming Anne*, commanded by Captain Richard Baker. For the next two weeks the ship sailed down the Thames River toward the English Channel. Yet, contrary winds kept them from setting out into the channel for several days. On December 1, the ship's crew attempted to set sail but had to return the next day to Plymouth, where they were forced to harbor until the 20th day of the same month. Finally, after five weeks, they were able to begin their passage to America.

There were thirty-two persons on board, but most were so foul and full of blasphemies that Davies was unable to find even one agreeable companion for serious conversation. His efforts to preach either met with little success or were interrupted by more pressing duties. Thus, he was uncertain what means to take for the reformation of the ship's passengers. His most solemn endeavors to convince them of their sin produced no good effects, especially with the captain, who otherwise had many noble qualities. Despite his words, they would soon forget themselves and pour forth imprecations in his hearing.

On January 31, 1755, a violent storm blew up about ten o'clock at night and lasted for thirty-six hours. Davies considered it to be the most violent storm he had ever witnessed. Four days later they were in the midst of another terrible storm, which lasted forty-eight hours. During these storms, Davies recorded:

> I often fell upon my Face, praying in a Kind of Agony, sometimes for myself, sometimes for the unhappy Ship's Company, and sometimes for my dear, destitute Family, whom the nearest Prospect of Death could not ease from my Heart. . . May God pity us, and deliver us from this dangerous Element, the Territory of Death.[63]

Twelve days later, February 12, the ship's crew spotted land and supposed that they were off the coast of North Carolina, about sixty miles south of Cape Henry. The next day the *Charming Anne* harbored at York, Virginia.

Davies Returns to Hanover

From York, Davies traveled to Williamsburg on February 14 where he met with the Governor and rode that evening to the home of his mother-in-law, Margaret Holt. The following morning he rode home where he was reunited with his family after eighteen months, and found all to be well. No doubt his reunion with his sickly wife and three boys was joyous for all parties.

Davies' return to Hanover on February 15, 1755 was a joyous homecoming and reunion with his family. There were numerous entries in his travel diary of the homesickness he felt while away and his concerns for the health of his dear wife. Having lost his first wife due to the complications of childbirth, he was more anxious than was normal in such a situation, especially when he received news of Jane's sicknesses. Davies' diary entry of that reunion is very brief:

> Arrived in York, Feb. 13, 1755. The next Day, called in Williamsburg, waited on the Governour, and rode to Mrs. Holt that Night. Came home the next Morning Feb, 15. and found all well. What shall I render to the Lord for all his Goodness![64]

---

[63] Ibid., 144–145.
[64] Ibid., 146.

After enduring a terrible storm in the middle of the Atlantic two weeks before, there is no doubt that Davies keenly felt what he wrote. He indeed considered it a manifestation of God's goodness that he was still alive. There can be no doubt that this reunion was filled with all the tenderness and joy that his loving heart could express. It was not long, therefore, before that reunion bore fruit. Jane, his "Chara," became pregnant with their fourth child within days of his return and their first daughter, Martha, was born on November 14, 1755. The happy parents now had four children six years old and under, despite his absence from home for eighteen months.

While Davies was on his voyage back to Virginia and to his family, all the Church of Scotland congregations in Edinburgh were involved in a general collection for a period of a week "for educating Students of Divinity at the College of New Jersey in America, in order to supply the many vacant and desolate Congregations in those Parts of his Majesty's Dominions, with Ministers of Piety and Learning."[65]

Davies and Tennent were slow to write to their many acquaintances in Great Britain after their return home. This negligence caused some concern on the part of many friends in the British Isles. William Hogg of Edinburgh, in particular, was concerned when he heard an alarming report that Davies had died on his voyage to Virginia but was relieved to learn later that the news was false. Nevertheless, Hogg complained to Aaron Burr of the College of New Jersey on August 28, 1755, that "it's very surprising neither Mr. Tennent nor Mr. Davies wrote one scrape to any person in this country on their arrival which we think they ought to have done."[66] This oversight of Davies and Tennent was due, no doubt, to the necessities of their congregations which had been without their labors for eighteen months—but it was still inexcusable.

---

[65] William Nelson, *Documents Relating to the Colonial History of the State of New Jersey*, Volume XIX (Paterson, N.J.: The Press Printing and Publishing Co., 1897), 490. This information was first printed in the *Pennsylvania Gazette* on May 1, 1755 through a communication from Scotland dated February 11, 1755.
[66] William Hogg to Aaron Burr, August 28, 1755, "Catalogue Colegii. Neo-Caesarensis. Princetonae," *The Biblical Repertory and Princeton Review*, XII (1840), 378.

Conclusion

The work of Davies and Tennent was a great success in raising funds for the college despite this criticism by Hogg. Hogg informed Burr in that same letter that £1,000 would be coming shortly from Scotland, with many of the smaller parishes not yet accounted for. Also, Hogg estimated that the collections in England and Ireland would total £4,000.[67] In addition to these amounts, Davies and Tennent raised £600 for the Synod of New York for a scholarship to train ministers and £200 for a work among the Indians. These figures totaled nearly £6,000, and more funds continued to be given to the college up until the American Revolution. By every consideration, this trip was a great success and a fitting conclusion to another important period of Davies' life.

---

[67] Ibid., 380.

-13-

Charity and Truth United

"If to live like the Multitude, will carry a Man to Heaven; if that Degree of Virtue & Holiness is Sufficient, which the most of Mankind content themselves with; then the Way of Life is certainly very broad & easy; & cannot be missed by fashionable Sinners. And what can be more acceptable than this to the numerous Friends of Sin, who cannot bear the Strictness of universal Holiness?"[1]
~*Samuel Davies, "Charity and Truth United"*~

William Parks' Print Shop in Williamsburg, Virginia

---

[1] Thomas Clinton Pears, Jr., ed., Samuel Davies, "Charity and Truth United, or The Way of the Multitude Exposed in Six Letters", *Journal of the Presbyterian Historical Society*, Vol. XIX (1941), 204.

George Whitefield's fifth visit to America coincided with Davies' eighteen-month absence from Virginia. Whitefield passed through Virginia in the winter of 1754-55 and preached at several places in the colony. Henry Patillo recorded in his diary for January 16, 1755 that "God has sent that flying Angel Mr. Whitefield among us."[2] On that date, Davies was aboard the *Charming Anne* somewhere in the Atlantic on his return voyage to America. It cannot be known for certain, but Whitefield's visit to Hanover was probably arranged through Davies' visit with the great evangelist. Whitefield preached "seven sermons and two lectures on the following subjects—*That Ye May Know the Love of Christ—That Christ may be all in all—Behold the Bridegroom Cometh—Wherefore he saith Awake Thou that Sleepest—A Refuge from the Storm—Whom Having Not seen Ye Love—The Gospel Supper—The Miracle of Loaves—Of Dives and Lazarus.*"[3] The crowds that heard him were described as "gazing multitudes."[4] Patillo exclaimed about him, "O what a burning and shining light he is."[5] Patillo hoped the impression of Whitefield's "amazing preaching would never leave him" and prayed "God would return him to us soon."[6]

John Todd's congregation, Providence Church in Louisa County, was also visited by Whitefield at this time. Todd informed Whitefield in a letter that "the impressions of the day [he] preached" for him would "never wear out of my mind."[7] Multitudes gathered at Todd's congregation on the day of Whitefield's visit to hear the news of salvation from his lips. This experience made Todd's parting with Whitefield "more distressing"[8] than any he had ever experienced. He described the scene of the great evangelist preaching to the gathered crowds:

> I still have the lively image of the people of God drowned in tears, multitudes of hardy gentlemen, that perhaps never wept for their poor souls

---

[2] Manuscript Journal in the Patillo Papers, Special Collections, William Smith Morton Library, Union Presbyterian Seminary, Richmond, VA.
[3] Ibid.
[4] Ibid.
[5] Ibid.
[6] Ibid.
[7] John Todd to George Whitefield, June 25, 1755, in John Gillies and Horatius Bonar, *Historical Collections Relating to Remarkable Periods of the Success of the Gospel* (Kelso, Scotland: John Rutherford, 1845), 505.
[8] Ibid.

before, standing aghast, all with signs of eagerness to attend to what they heard, and their significant tears, expressive of the sorrows of their hearts, that they had so long neglected their souls. I returned home like one that had sustained some amazing loss, and that I might contribute more than ever to the salvation of perishing multitudes amongst us, I resolved I would labor to obtain more of that sacred fire which the God of all grace had so abundantly bestowed on you for the good of mankind.[9]

Whitefield's visit was an unexpected blessing to Davies' congregation and to the other Presbyterian congregations in Virginia. New Castle Presbytery struggled to send supply ministers to supply Davies' flock, but was able to secure John Blair and John Rodgers for this purpose. Blair held a communion service, probably in 1754, at which "many souls got Refreshing."[10] Patillo described him as "a burning Light."[11] Rodgers returned to Virginia in the spring of 1754 for the first time since his application for a license was refused in 1748. There were threats of persecution against him but nothing of that nature happened. Rodgers was naturally apprehensive of the consequences of this visit, but he preached "with great assiduity and acceptance."[12]

First Presbyterian Church of New York City
Sometime while Davies was in Great Britain, an invitation, whether formally or informally, was extended for him to become the pastor of First Presbyterian Church in New York City. That congregation was eagerly searching for a new pastor after their minister, Ebenezer Pemberton, resigned due to an unresolved conflict concerning the government of the church. Pemberton was a New Light minister who was more sympathetic to the polity of Congregationalism than Presbyterianism. For that reason, the church had been governed by Trustees and Deacons, but not Ruling Elders, until 1753. With the death of Dr. John Nichols in 1753, a medical doctor who had managed the temporal affairs of the church during his lifetime and had sought contributions from Scotland in 1718 for the erecting of their first building, these differences erupted into an open

---

[9] Ibid.
[10] Patillo Papers.
[11] Ibid.
[12] Samuel Miller, *Memoir of the Rev. John Rodgers, D.D.* (New York: Whiting and Watson, 1813), 95.

fissure. It is likely that Nichols had maintained the appearance of peace among all the parties by the power of his presence while alive. With his passing, those differences were resolved only by Pemberton's resignation following twenty-six years of service to the church.

Pemberton had been the first minister in New York City to welcome George Whitefield into his pulpit when the great evangelist was visiting the city in 1739. At that time, First Presbyterian Church was a small congregation whose building was much larger than was needed for weekly services, but Whitefield's visit changed things. The congregation began to grow rapidly after his visit and in 1748 the building was enlarged at "considerable expense." The new building was erected of stone and contained 121 pews. Many of the new members were Scotch-Irish who wanted to sing psalms exclusively and others were from England or New England who preferred Watts' hymns to be sung. These differences grew stronger from 1750–1754 and the Presbytery was unable to help the congregation resolve them. Thus, a new pastor was needed and sought.

The search for a new pastor was primarily focused on Joseph Bellamy of Bethlehem, Connecticut, but he refused their invitation on several occasions and urged the officers to seek someone else as their pastor. Samuel Lowden then wrote Bellamy on October 7, 1754 with the following information: "We have been refused Mr. Davies."[13] It is likely Davies was not aware of this invitation to such an important pastorate due to his absence from the country. He makes no allusion to this matter in the journal of his trip to Great Britain. Thus, the refusal may have come from the elders of the Hanover congregation, New Castle Presbytery, or the Synod of New York on his behalf. Yet, Davies alluded to various offers from other churches in a sermon he preached at Hanover on July 20, 1755:

> If I consulted either my safety or my temporal interest, I should soon remove my family to Great Britain or the northern colonies, where I have had very inviting offers.[14]

---

[13] Samuel Lowden to Joseph Bellamy, October 7, 1754. MS letter in Joseph Bellamy Papers, Hartford Seminary Library, Hartford, Connecticut.

[14] *Sermons by the Rev. Samuel Davies*, Viol. 3 (Morgan, Pennsylvania: Soli Deo Gloria Publications, 1995), 321.

The pulpit of the First Presbyterian Church in New York City was filled in July of 1755 when David Bostwick, pastor at the First Presbyterian Church in Jamaica, Long Island. It is possible that Davies had personally turned down this pulpit after his return from Great Britain. It would have been a great opportunity for him and a great blessing to the cause of Christ. His gifts were certainly equal to the needs of such a prominent pulpit.

Charity and Truth United

A different type of challenge soon occupied Davies' time. It concerned the sermon that William Stith, President of William and Mary College in Williamsburg, VA, had delivered before the General Assembly of Virginia on November 11, 1753. Stith's sermon was a belated response to Davies' pamphlet, *The Impartial Trial, Impartially Tried, and Convicted of Impartiality*, which defended the cause of the New Lights. Peyton Randolph, the King's attorney and Davies' staunchest adversary, was among those present at Stith's sermon. Afterwards, the House of Burgesses arranged for it to be published and sold in Virginia under the title, "The Nature and Extent of Christ's Redemption."

Davies had spent that Lord's Day in 1753 at St. George's, Delaware, where his friend, John Rodgers, preached a communion message from 1 John 4:10. Unaware of this new attack on the New Light Presbyterians in Virginia, Davies likely did not see a copy of Stith's sermon until he returned to Virginia in 1755.[15]

Stith's opening remarks from the "Strait Gate" passage in Matthew 7:13, 14 referred to the concluding paragraph of Davies' work as follows:

> These words, at first view, seem to carry a terrible aspect, and to declare, that the greatest part of mankind will miss their way to eternal life, and perish everlastingly. And accordingly we find them so understood by some persons, and particularly a late author from our press says: "Is it not certain, that the most of mankind perish? And to hope the contrary, however natural it is to a generous soul, is blasphemously to hope, that God will be a liar."[16] This violent denunciation against the greatest part of mankind is founded, I presume, upon this, and some other parallel texts of Scripture. But however cautious I would be, of incurring the horrid

---

[15] In his travel diary, Davies nowhere mentions either hearing about this sermon or receiving a copy of it.
[16] Davies is the author to whom Stith refers and quotes.

crime of blasphemy, yet I must confess myself to be one of those generous souls, who not only hope, but firmly believe better things.[17]

Stith declared the atonement of Christ is the only basis for salvation, but those who have never heard the gospel can still be saved without a direct faith in Christ. As a specimen of his thought, he quoted from the Protestant divine, Philippus a' Limborch (1633-1712):

> If, by the light of nature they sincerely repent them of their sins, and humbly ask pardon for them, and fly to God's favour and mercy, that then God will apply to them the grace obtained by Christ, for his sake will impute righteousness to them, and grant them remission of sins.[18]

Limborch was a Dutch Remonstrant[19] theologian who embraced Arminianism and edited the antitrinitarian works of a Socinian[20] author, Samuel Przypkowski (1592–1670). In 1668, Limborch became the Professor of Theology in the Remonstrant Seminary in Amsterdam. While maintaining with Limborch that "the salvation of all mankind is founded in Christ's propitiary sacrifice,"[21] Stith also acknowledged that a direct faith in Christ *is* required of those who have heard the gospel. In conclusion, Stith feebly attempted to reconcile the obvious conflict between his text and his peculiar views with the following words:

> For had the Scriptures said, that many will be saved and few damned, it might have tended to make us remiss in our Christian warfare, and negligent in the way of God's commandments: or had God acted by these men's advice, and declared with the vehemence and passion, that the kingdom of heaven should be shut against all but a few choice saints, it would have been apt to hurry men into despair, and to have made them give over a pursuit, of so great difficulty, and so little chance of success.[22]

---

[17] William Stith, *The Nature and Extent of Christ's Redemption* (Williamsburg, VA: William Hunter, 1753), 9.
[18] Ibid., 28–29.
[19] The Remonstrants were followers of Jacobus Arminius (1560–1609), who under the leadership of Simon Episcopius (1583–1643), formulated the Five Articles of Remonstrance in 1610. One of them stated that the atonement was universal as to design. In response to them, the Synod of Dordrecht (1618–9) developed the Five Points of Calvinism.
[20] Faustus Socinus (1539–1604) was an Italian Protestant who denied the divinity of Christ; as do his followers, the Socinians.
[21] Stith, *Nature and Extent of Christ's Redemption*, 28–29.
[22] Ibid, 31.

Upon his return from Great Britain, Davies began drafting a response to Stith's sermon which had been unanswered for some fifteen months. He completed the rough draft by July 4, 1755 in the form of six letters which he titled, *Charity and Truth United*. Before going to press, he circulated these letters to his friends for their judicious comments and corrections. He also granted Stith[23] a private interview before the completion of this work. Five days later, the colony was shocked and alarmed with the news of General Braddock's defeat at Fort Duquesne which was the beginning of the French and Indian War. Davies thus resolved to hold off publication until he could be sure of gaining the attention of the general public. In the succeeding interval, Stith suddenly and unexpectedly died on September 19, 1755. Considering it injudicious to reply against a deceased opponent, Davies laid aside his treatise which destined it to become a posthumous work.[24]

Charity and Truth United is, in the estimation of Thomas Clinton Pears, Jr., "valuable for its theology and its learning, greatly raising our impressions of [Davies'] talents as a logician, and his attainments in the literature of theology."[25] One of the most impressive aspects of the work is the "very catalogue of names which he marshalls in support of his argument. . . Plato, Socrates, Hesiod, Aristotle, Cebes, Cleanthes, Epictetus, Porphyry, Virgil, Horace, Seneca, Juvenal, Cicero, Eusebius, Athanasius, Lactantius, Augustine, Hilarius, Theophylact, Guyse, Wolfus, Marloratus, Poole, Grotius, Locke, Sir George Littleton[26], Doddridge, Atterbury, Jenkins, Clarke, Cave, Watts, Oecolampadius, Brennius, Jacob Bohme, Sir Thomas More, Swift, Young, and Alexander Pope."[27]

---

[23] Stith was formerly rector of a parish in Henrico County where Davies also supplied a meeting house. They were, no doubt, familiar with one another. This interview took place at Davies' initiation.

[24] In 1760, the Rev. Charles Beatty was entrusted by Davies to carry the work to William McCulloch in Cambuslang, Scotland. Upon McCulloch's death in 1771, it remained with his family until the founding of Knox College in Toronto, Canada, when it was given to Dr. Burns. In 1853, William Sprague and Richard Webster began preparing it for publication by the Presbyterian Historical Society, but it was not printed until 1941—186 years after it was originally drafted.

[25] Pears, Jr., ed., "Charity and Truth United," 198.

[26] The spelling of the surname is different, but this is the same man to whom Stith dedicated his sermon.

[27] Pears, "Samuel Davies, Charity and Truth United," 199.

Stith's False Premise

In his first letter, Davies expressed his conviction that Stith's sermon would have the "tendency to prove itself false, by hindering the salvation of many, instead of proving that the most shall be saved."[28] He also disavowed the allegation that he himself was gratifying "a malignant temper" in endeavoring "to alarm mankind with a just sense of their danger" and in encouraging sinners "to pursue everlasting life with that vigor and earnestness without which they cannot obtain it."[29] Even Stith admitted that his doctrine could have the dangerous tendency "to make us remiss in our Christian warfare."[30] To which Davies replied:

> When such a declaration, even by God himself, would have a bad tendency, must it not have a bad tendency, when made by you? Or were you so modest as to think, that nobody would believe it upon your word, and consequently it could do no mischief; but that it might be believed, and consequently render men remiss in the concerns of religion, if established by Divine authority, in the Sacred Writings?[31]

Davies retorted that Stith "impeach[ed] the Doctrine of particular Redemption, as a Cause, why so few are saved."[32] He then declared that "Christ's Redemption is perfectly sufficient, for all who are willing to believe in him; & that none perish, because there was no Saviour for them, but because they would not accept of a Saviour."[33] Davies, likewise, repudiated Stith's view that sinners who never hear the gospel can be saved by Christ's redemption without a direct faith in Him.

An Ancient Proverb

Davies' second letter answered Stith's contention that Matthew 7:13-14 was to be restricted in its application to the Jews of Christ's day. Quoting from ancient poets and philosophers, Davies proved that thoughts similar to the words of this text had passed into the form of a proverb among the nations prior to the time of Christ. The moralist, Cebes, described the difficulty of attaining wisdom:

---

[28] Ibid., 208.
[29] Ibid.
[30] Stith, *Nature and Extent of Christ's Redemption*, 31.
[31] Pears, "Samuel Davies, Charity and Truth United," 209.
[32] Ibid., 217.
[33] Ibid.

It is seated on a certain eminence, where nobody dwells, but it seems a mere [desert]—it has a little gate; and a way leading to it, which is not much frequented, and but very few walk in it; because it seems difficult, rugged and stony—the eminence seems high, and the ascent is very narrow.[34]

The ancient philosophers and poets agreed concerning the difficulty of attaining to a truly virtuous life. Socrates, renowned for his works on ethics, stated: "I urge men to virtue, to which the ascent is steep, and unfrequented by most."[35] Apollo is credited by Eusebius with the following oracle concerning knowledge: "The way of the blessed is extremely rugged and of difficult ascent. The entrance is secured by brazen gates—and the roads to be passed through impossible to be described."[36] The Roman poet, Virgil, wrote concerning hell: "The path that leads down to hell is easy: and the gate of the infernal deity stands wide open night and day; but few enjoy the happy Elysian Fields."[37] Hesiod, a Greek poet thought to be a contemporary of Homer, wrote concerning virtue: "The gods have annex[ed] sweat to the pursuit of virtue; and the way to it is tedious and very rough at first."[38] Horace, the leading lyric poet during the reign of Caesar Augustus, also spoke of "the difficult way of virtue."[39] Lactantius, advisor to the Roman Emperor, Constantine I, and author of one of the first books on Christian theology, summarized the teachings of the poets and philosophers: "The way of virtue is, at first entrance, difficult and very rough; but that of vice, is at first, very pleasant, and much beaten down."[40] Thus, Davies proved that the words of Christ were a common proverb as much as 700 years before his birth and could not be restricted to the Jews of Christ's time in any sense.

Total Depravity
The third letter consisted primarily of a sermon preached by Davies in Caroline County on August 3, 1753 to a congregation of approximately one thousand hearers. In it, he defended the doctrine of total depravity

---

[34] Ibid., 220.
[35] Ibid.
[36] Ibid., 221.
[37] Ibid.
[38] Ibid.
[39] Ibid.
[40] Ibid.

and argued that the Jews contemporary with Christ were no more wicked than other nations. The colony of Virginia, he reasoned, was just as guilty of crucifying the Messiah through their refusal to comply with the terms of the gospel. As he elaborated:

> Forgive me if I insinuate that multitudes seem to love Christ [through] mistake. They form an idea of Him as a soft, easy being, all good nature and indulgence to them, notwithstanding that they forget Him, and provoke Him with their practices: and with such an image as this, they may not be a little delighted. But did they see how holy he is, how full of resentment against sin, and how justly severe in His reproofs of it: and did He appear to them under a cloud of obscurity, as he did to the Jews, the enmity of their carnal minds would rise against Him, and they would shun Him as intolerably precise.[41]

Though the ancient Jews pretended "a mighty veneration for the prophets which their fathers had put to death"[42], other nations are guilty of the same crime. Thus, according to Davies, the Jews were not more sinful than other nations:

> Was it the peculiar Sin of the Jews, to be careless about eternal Things, & insensible of their Guilt, their Depravity, & their spiritual Necessities? Was it peculiar to them to love Sin, & hate the Strictness of Piety? to struggle against Conviction, when Things discovered were contrary to their corrupt Inclinations & Prejudices? to be Impatient of plain Dealing, &c? Are not these Sins of all Ages, & of Multitudes among us? Nay, have we not all been guilty of them, in a greater or lesser Degree? Then we have all been Jews in our Hearts; & had it been our Fate to live among them, we would have joined with them in their Infidelity.[43]

Davies further contended that Christ would have received the same treatment from any other nation as He did from the Jews because "the malignant Darkness diffused over the whole Earth, would not comprehend the sacred Light from Heaven."[44] The prophets and apostles all suffered the same fate that Christ endured in their attempts to plant the true religion among the Gentile nations. Socrates, who boldly set himself

---

[41] Ibid., 237–8.
[42] Ibid., 244.
[43] Ibid., 243.
[44] Ibid., 248.

against polytheism, superstition and immorality, met the expected fate of death as a criminal. Thus, Davies quoted Plato:

> That whenever there arises a faithful reprover and zealous reformer of the world, he may expect to be treated like the vilest malefactor; and mankind will conspire to rid themselves of such a troublesome person.[45]

No Holiness, No Heaven
The fourth letter proved that men carry with them into eternity the same hearts, desires and habits which they have on earth. If there is to be any change in their affections, it must take place before their death. Addressing his readers in the hortatory style, Davies states:

> Are you not conscious that your hearts and affections are thus eagerly attached to things below; and that your principal love and delight are not fixed upon God; nor is His service the sweetest employment of your lives? And how can you expect to be happy in the employments and services of the heavenly world, where there is nothing but perfect holiness? Your depraved temper renders you incapable of happiness there; it would render you unhappy in the very region of happiness; miserable in Paradise itself. And will the all-wise God do so unfit a thing, as, to bring you thither, while such? No; such shall be turned into Hell; and there is as much propriety and justice in it, as in confining madmen in Bedlam, or the sick in their beds.[46]

The Prerequisites for Eternal Life
The fifth letter answered the question: "What are the prerequisites of eternal life?"[47] Davies described the characteristics of the moralist, the mere professor of Christianity, the reformed sinner, and the religious formalist. After painting them in their best light, he showed how deficient the character of such persons is when compared to the scriptural requirements for salvation.

The religious formalist may be faithful in religious duties—reading the Bible, attending public worship, and praying—and may appear to be very devoted and may even have the reputation of an eminent saint. Yet, all of these things do not qualify him to receive eternal life for the

---

[45] Ibid., 251.
[46] Ibid., 257.
[47] Ibid., 277.

reason which Davies states:

> Such, with all their [show] of religion may indulge themselves in some sin, so that their character is not uniform and consistent; or they may be lukewarm and heartless in all their religious performances; or they may have no regard to the inward temper of their minds, but only to the externals of devotion; or they may trust in these things to procure them acceptance with God, instead of the all-perfect righteousness of Jesus Christ; and any one of these defects is sufficient to ruin them.[48]

The ancient Pharisees had all the outward virtues of the religious formalist, but they were severely condemned by John the Baptist, Christ, and the Apostles as being destitute of saving grace. They were deficient in the one thing that is an essential mark of true salvation—personal holiness. For, "holiness is necessary, according to the very nature of things, to naturalize you. . . to the heavenly regions."[49] Each of the classes which Davies depicted was deficient in this fundamental area.

Though Davies recognized holiness will never be found without some blemishes, yet it is the prevailing character in those who have it. As he expounded:

> Holiness gives the soul a strong bent and propensity towards God, and every thing that is pleasing in his sight; & renders it averse to sin in its most alluring Forms. . . The Heart where holiness resides, is "a heart of flesh", tender & susceptive of impressions from divine things: . . it is contrite, & broken with ingenious penitential relentings for Sin:. . . it "trembles at the Word of the Lord": . . & feels a divine power in that Gospel, which others neglect as a trifle:. . . it is enflamed with the love of God;. . . & delights in him, more than in the whole creation.[50]

He concluded this fifth letter with the assertion that Stith either must prove that men can be saved without this universal holiness of heart and life or that the greater part of mankind in all ages has attained it.

The Alleged Injustice of God
In the sixth and final letter, Davies addressed two objections which might seem to mitigate the positions he took in *Charity and Truth United*.

---

[48] Ibid., 283.
[49] Ibid., 286.
[50] Ibid.

The first objection is that if attaining eternal life is so difficult then Christianity must be a very gloomy and melancholy religion. The second objection, stated by Stith in his sermon, is that such a view of Christianity is to "cast a stain of cruelty and injustice upon the Gospel" and to represent God as a tyrant. To the first objection, Davies retorted:

> If the difficulties of the Christian life were ten times more formidable, are they not more than compensated by deliverance from eternal misery, and the most perfect happiness through an endless duration? If we have no alternative, but either to cut off an offending right hand, or be cast entire into Hell, there is no room to hesitate: common sense may show us, what our interest is; and the principle of self-preservation may prompt us to submit to the painful operation, in order to avoid what is infinitely more terrible.[51]

Since the present life is a state of trial, Davies asserted that the Christian's life will be attended with numerous difficulties. Moreover, a state of trial can hardly be expected to be a state of perfect rest and tranquility. Nevertheless, he said:

> When your souls can say unto God, "Thou art my portion," is it not a thousandfold more than a compensation, in this life, for all the guilty pleasures you abstain from, and all the difficulties you groan under.[52]

Concerning the second objection, Davies stated that there is as much of a stain on the gospel through the damnation of one sinner as through the destruction of the greater part of the human race. The actual number of the damned does not alter the case. As he stated:

> But if impenitent offenders, however numerous, may justly be punished; if all that are not "made meet for the inheritance of the saints in light," however many, may be justly excluded; then the perfections of God are as effectually vindicated as if you supposed but a few will meet with that dreadful doom; nay, much more so, than if you supposed he will admit crowds of unholy sinners, while such, into his immediate presence, and eternal intimacy with Him.[53]

According to Davies, people are so biased by self-love that they are altogether unfit judges to determine what constitutes true justice on God's part. Yet, God's wisdom does not cater to their sinful ignorance.

---

[51] Ibid., 298.
[52] Ibid., 299.
[53] Ibid., 301.

As he wrote:

> Is it not the greatest absurdity, and subversive of all government, that men should judge in matters, which are not only above their comprehension, but in which they are so nearly interested, that criminals should be privileged to determine the demerits of their offence, and the degree of their punishment?[54]

And again, he wrote:

> Were this liberty allowed, very few of the most daring malefactors would fall by the hand of public justice. Everyone would take care to ascribe to his Judge as much mercy, as would be sufficient to acquit himself: and were he to fix the limits of justice, he would no doubt confine it from doing him any injury.[55]

In conclusion, Davies stated his opinion that the combination of holy angels and redeemed saints in heaven may actually exceed the number of demons and reprobate sinners in hell. About the former, he said:

> To John they appeared as "a great multitude, which no man could number, from all nations, kindreds, people, and tongue." (Rev. 7:9). And if you add all these to the number of the elect angels, I think it highly probable, they far exceed the miserable part both of the human and angelic nature.[56]

Conclusion

The six letters of *Charity and Truth United* together comprise a work of approximately 120 pages. In a theological sense, this treatise was Davies' *magnum opus*. Yet, there is no doubt that a more worthy work would have come forth from his pen if his life had been spared. For several years, he carefully collected materials in anticipation of writing a treatise on the morality of gospel holiness. This work came as close to accomplishing that task as anything that ever came from his pen. It is to be regretted it was never published in his lifetime because it spoke to the circumstances of colonial Virginia in a very singular way. If President Stith had lived, he would have been dismayed that his scholarship was no

---

[54] Ibid., 306.
[55] Ibid.
[56] Ibid., 312.

match for the penetrating insight of Davies. In *Charity and Truth United*, Davies shows that he was arguably the second-best theologian in Colonial America next to Jonathan Edwards. No one writes such a detailed, closely argued treatise within a few months' time without having a vast storehouse of accurate knowledge. His circumstances in Virginia allowed him little leisure to devote his energies to writing theological treatises. The needs of his extended flock required him to be a man of action—not a man of retirement. Yet, his sermons indicate clearly that he was a masterful theologian, as did *Charity and Truth United*.

Davies had no delight in polemics for arguments' sake. His heart's desire was to preach and write about subjects that build up God's people in the faith. It is to be much regretted, therefore, that he was never able to fulfill his desire to write a non-polemical work on the subject of holiness. Such a work, if it had been written, would have doubtlessly occupied a place beside J. C. Ryle's *Holiness* and Edwards' *The Religious Affections* on the shelves of spiritually minded Christians.

-14-

The French and Indian War

"Christians should be patriots. What is that religion good for that leaves men cowards upon the appearance of danger? And permit me to say, that I am particularly solicitous that you, my brethren of the dissenters, should act with honour and spirit in this juncture as it becomes loyal subjects, lovers of your country, and courageous Christians."[1]
~Samuel Davies in a sermon, "On the Defeat of General Braddock"~

Hanover Courthouse where Davies raised
Captain Samuel Overton's militia

---

[1] *Sermons by the Rev. Samuel Davies*, Vol. 3 (Morgan, Pennsylvania: Soli Deo Gloria Publications, 1995), 321.

The French and Indian War (1756-1763) pitted two superpowers of the eighteenth century—France and Great Britain—against one another for control of the North American Continent. Winston Churchill called the French and Indian War "the first world war."[2] Eclipsed today in the minds of most Americans by the Revolutionary War, the French and Indian War, nonetheless, rightly deserves to be considered the war that made America. The delicate balance of power between the French and British that had dominated both America and Europe was overturned by this war. George Washington, who was intimately involved in both the French and Indian War and the Revolutionary War, always considered the former to be the defining moment of his life. The Revolutionary War gained freedom from the British Empire for the Colonies, but the French and Indian War secured Protestant Christianity as the dominant religion for the fledgling nation.

Catholic France and Protestant Great Britain were natural enemies on two continents in the 1750's—Europe and North America. The French and Indian War in America involved the competing interests of the British and French—and, to a lesser degree, the Spanish—for domination of the colonies and the trading empires of North America, including the lucrative fur trade and the fishing rights of the great waterways. The French controlled eastern Canada and territories west of the mountains; the Spanish controlled Florida; and, the British had colonies east of the mountains and along the Atlantic Ocean. There had been numerous skirmishes between the French and British since at least 1744 as both nations attempted to expand their territorial rights. This war began in earnest in 1754 as a result of the execution of a plan devised by the Governor of Canada, Roland Michael Barrin, Marquis de La Galissoniere, to construct nine forts along important American waterways, including the Great Lakes; the Ohio River and its tributaries; and, the Mississippi River as far south as New Orleans.

The French Encroachment on Virginia

When the French moved south of their fort at Pesque Isle on Lake Erie, encroaching on territory claimed by Virginia, Governor Robert Dinwid-

---

[2] Fred Anderson, *The War that Made America: A Short History of the French and Indian War* (New York: Viking Penguin, 2005), v.

die hastily dispatched Major George Washington to Fort Le Boeuf in November of 1753 to warn the French that they were trespassing. Dinwiddie also wanted Washington to locate a suitable site for a fort to be erected where the French could be countered in their expansionist maneuvers. In 1754, Washington's forces erected a fort along the Alleghany River, near present-day Pittsburgh. The French succeeded, though, in pushing back Washington's men from this fort and causing him to return to Virginia. The French intended by these maneuvers to restrict the British colonists to the land east of the great mountain ridges and to control the expansion into the western part of North America. By 1755, the drumbeat of war was in the air and the British colonies anxiously awaited the issue which would determine their interests in America.

Davies had returned to Virginia from his trip to Great Britain only eighteen days before a day of fasting and prayer was observed throughout the colonies. On that occasion, March 5, 1755, he preached a sermon from Daniel 4:25, "God the Sovereign of All Kingdoms," in which he detailed several instances of God's providential intervention in behalf of Great Britain, including the defeat of the Spanish Armada in 1588. He also described what a French victory in this conflict would mean to the colonies:

> Let us take a view of the French government and of our wretched circumstances if we should fall under it. . . There you must conform to all the superstitions and idolatries of the church of Rome, or lose your life; or at best be obliged to flee your country, hungry and famishing, and leave all your estate behind you. . . And can you bear the thought, that you and your children should have such an iron yoke as this riveted about your neck? Would you not rather die in defence of your privileges? I am sure you would, if you had the spirit of men or Christians. Therefore, improve your religion, lest you lose it: make a good use of your liberty, lest you forfeit it; and cry mightily to God for deliverance.[3]

The primary concern of Davies was the cause of the gospel and religious freedom. A French victory would result in the loss of both with the Church of Rome enforcing her superstitions and idolatries. Davies knew that the basic principle of Rome is the spirit of domination. Towards the

---

[3] Samuel Davies, *Sermons on Important Subjects*, Volume IV (London: W. Baynes and Sons, 1824), 178–179.

close of the sermon Davies roused his hearers to action by reminding them that God governs the world through secondary causes which makes it necessary for us to do our duty:

> We have no ground for lazy confidence in divine Providence; nor should we content ourselves with idle, inactive prayers; but let us rouse ourselves, and be active. Let us cheerfully pay the taxes the government has laid upon us to support this expedition. Let us use our influence to diffuse a military spirit around us. I have no scruple thus openly to declare, that such of you whose circumstances allow it, may not only lawfully enlist and take up arms, but that your so doing is a Christian duty, and acting an honorable part, worthy of a man, a freeman, a Briton, and a Christian.[4]

There are many voices, past and present, that tell us that politics and religion should never be mixed. Davies, for one, certainly would not have agreed. The political condition of a nation affects the church in numerous ways. He saw clearly, as one who had struggled for religious toleration in Virginia for several years, that freedom of religion would be completely squelched if the French gained the dominant position in America. The separation of church and state only means that neither one dominates the other. The state cannot establish a religion or prohibit the free exercise thereof; and, the church does not exercise control over the state, as was the case with the Roman Catholic Church before the Protestant Reformation. Yet, such separation of church and state does not prevent the prophetic voice of the church—and its clergy—from addressing the state. It also does not prevent the clergy from preaching on subjects that concern all citizens. The Scripture addresses every area of life, either directly or by inference. Christians are exhorted to pray for rulers, to be in subjection to them, and to resist them when they require actions that are sinful. Davies had no difficulty in preaching the whole counsel of God which, in this instance, was a message addressing the Lordship of Christ over all other kingdoms.

Virginia's Governing Officials Welcome Dissenters Support

As a result of such sermons, the governing officials of Virginia, who had previously viewed the Dissenters as enemies, now saw them as true patriots and warm supporters of the British crown. These war sermons

---

[4] Ibid., 180.

probably did more to gain favor for Davies and the Dissenters than all their other efforts combined.

The Presbyterian settlements in western Virginia had particularly been welcomed by the Governor and his Council because they were a buffer of defense against the barbarous Indians and brutal French. John Craig, the Old Light Presbyterian minister in Augusta County, was a strong advocate of frontier defense and turned his meetinghouse into a well fortified structure. The other Dissenting ministers, whether Old Light or New Light, were of the same conviction. In the face of these dangers of war, the problem of religious toleration for the Dissenters became trivial by comparison.

The French were outnumbered by thirty or forty to one in America, but they were very enterprising and active while the British were generally indolent and secure. On April 25, 1755, Davies wrote to Joseph Stennet of London, for whom he had preached while visiting there, and informed him of the ominous situation of the British colonies with this assessment:

> I cannot but be alarmed Sir, at the present dangerous situation of the British colonies, particularly Virginia. . . This summer probably the decisive stroke will be given. May all-ruling Heaven decide it in favour of religion, liberty & prosperity. . . But really, sir, I cannot but fear for my country, even in my most serene & placid moments, when I consider the gross immoralities and irreligion that burden it, & loudly demand public exemplary punishment.[5]

General Braddock's Defeat

While the colonies were in an uproar over these dangers, Hugh McAden, a recent graduate of the College of New Jersey, set out from John Kirkpatrick's house in Lancaster County, Pennsylvania, on June 3, 1755. McAden had been appointed by New Castle Presbytery as a missionary to North Carolina. His southward journey placed him in Virginia from late June to July 23. It was during this period that the conflict between the French and the British became a war.

In late June of 1755, Col. Washington led 600 men from Fort Cumber-

---

[5] Samuel Davies to Joseph Stennett, April 25, 1755, MS Letter in Samuel Davies Collection (C1042). Manuscripts Division, Department of Rare Books and Special Collections, Princeton University Library, Princeton, New Jersey.

land to guide the 800 soldiers under the command of Major General Edward Braddock to Fort Duquesne, near Pittsburgh. On July 10, these two companies of solders were ambushed and soundly defeated by inferior French and Indian forces just south of Fort Duquesne along the Monongahela River. Braddock's stunning loss sent shock waves throughout the British colonies, causing alarm and panic for most Virginians.

McAden was unaware of Braddock's defeat when he preached to the Timber Ridge congregation for John Brown on the following day, Friday, July 11. Brown had called for a day of fasting and prayer due to the prospects of war and the savage murders of Virginians by the Indians. The congregation was fairly large and McAden "felt some life and earnestness in alarming the people of their dangers on account of sin, the procuring cause of all evils that [befall] us in this life."[6] The congregation was so attentive to McAden's message that when a sudden storm blew up they were no more distracted by it "than if the sun had been shining on them."[7]

It was Wednesday, July 16, before McAden received the news of the French victory at Fort Duquesne. By that date, he had traveled to the home of Joseph Lapsley in Augusta County, about two miles from the Forks. McAden describes the terror with which most inhabitants on the frontiers of Virginia received these reports and the daily murders of their fellow countrymen.

> A cold shuddering possessed every breast, and paleness covered almost every face. In short, the whole inhabitants were put into an universal confusion. Scarcely any man durst sleep in his own house—but all met in companies with their wives and children, and set about building little fortifications, to defend themselves from such barbarians and inhuman enemies, whom they concluded would be let loose upon them at pleasure.[8]

Rev. Alexander Craighead and numerous other residents of western Virginia—who were the closest to danger—hastily fled the area for the more peaceful country of North Carolina. McAden, likewise, was escorted out of the territory on the same day he learned of the solemn news.

---

[6] William Henry Foote, *Sketches of North Carolina: Historical and Biographical* (New York: Robert Carter, 1846), 163.
[7] Ibid.
[8] Ibid.

His guide was a young man from Robert Henry's congregation in Lunenberg who was visiting at Warm Springs. Together they traveled twenty-six miles to Luny's Ferry where they spent the night at a hastily constructed fort. The following day Major Smith dispatched a guard to guide them across the mountains and they continued on to Bedford Court House, thirty-two miles away, where they stayed with a Mr. Sable. On Friday, they reached Falling River, a journey of twenty-three miles, and were entertained at the home of Thomas Dickson. Robert Henry supplied a congregation at Falling River once a month and the people there prevailed on McAden to preach a sermon to them on Sunday.

Davies' Sermon on Braddock's Defeat

Davies heard the shocking news of Braddock's defeat on July 17 while preparing a message from Isaiah 22:12-14, so he was constrained to change the scope of his sermon from this passage. When Sunday, July 20, arrived, he preached at Hanover a sermon titled, "On the Defeat of General Braddock, Going to Forte-De-Quesne." His pathos is revealed in the following words:

> And oh, Virginia! oh my country! shall I not lament for thee? Thou art a valley of vision, favoured with the light of revelation from heaven, and the gospel of Jesus: thou hast long been the region of peace and tranquility; the land of ease, plenty, and liberty. But what do I now see? I see the brazened skies, thy parched soul, thy withering fields, thy hopeless springs, and thy scanty harvests. Methinks I also hear the sound of the trumpet, and see garments rolled in blood—thy frontiers ravaged by revengeful savages; thy territories invaded by French perfidy and violence. Methinks I see slaughtered families, the hairy scalps clotted with gore; the horrid acts of Indian and popish torture. And, alas! in the midst of all these alarms, I see thy inhabitants generally asleep, and careless of thy fate.[9]

Davies discouragingly observed those who were closest to the danger were too ready to flee and those who were not in imminent danger were overcome by a stupid security. For this cause, Davies was constrained to lament:

> And shall I not weep for thee, O my country! Yes; when I forget thee, O Virginia, "let my right hand forget her cunning, and my tongue cleave to

---

[9] Davies, *Sermons on Important Subjects*, IV, 136.

the roof of my mouth". . . . What can I do for thee, O my country? What but weep over thee, pray for thee, and warn thy careless children? To give this seasonable warning is my present design.[10]

Anticipating an uprising among the slaves, Davies counseled them to be loyal to their masters and to give no assistance to the French and Indians whom he described as "a cruel, barbarous people; and if you should disobey them, they would torment you, or put you to death in the most shocking manner."[11] Moreover, those slaves who had been converted were warned "that if you should fall into the hands of the French, you must either give up your religion, or be tied to a stake, and burnt to ashes for it."[12]

Virginia Raises a Militia for Its Defense
On August 5, 1755, the subdued members of the Virginia General Assembly met together with Gov. Dinwiddie in the Council Chamber in Williamsburg to hear a report of Braddock's shocking defeat. After listening to the Governor's passionate plea for the defense of "religion and civil liberty," the Assembly passed an act to raise £40,000 through a poll tax for the protection of the Virginia frontiers.

Yet, the frontiers were already being ravaged by Indians who raided settlements, destroyed the tobacco crops, killed the men, and stole away with the younger women to gratify their lusts. To counteract this danger, many counties set about to raise their own militias and to support them from their own pockets. The first county to respond was Hanover and Davies was asked by Captain Samuel Overton to address the citizens with a recruiting sermon. On August 17, 1755, Davies preached from 2 Samuel 10:12 on the subject, "Religion and Patriotism, the Constituents of a Good Soldier." In this message, he exhorted the people to exercise courage and defined a just war:

> We are engaged in a righteous cause; we are not urged on by an unbounded love of power or riches, to encroach upon the rights and properties of others, and disturb our quiet neighbors: we act entirely upon the defensive, repel unjust violence, and avenge national injuries: we are

---

[10] Ibid., 137.
[11] Ibid., 151.
[12] Ibid.

fighting "for our people and for the cities of our God." We are also engaged in a cause of the utmost importance. Shall we tamely submit to idolatry and religious tyranny? No, God forbid: "let us play the man", since we take up arms for our people, and the cities of our God.[13]

It was in this sermon Davies made his famous observation about George Washington:

> As a remarkable instance of this, I may point out to the public that heroic youth, Col. Washington, whom I cannot but hope Providence has hitherto preserved, in so signal a manner, for some important service to his country.[14]

Surprisingly, James Maury, the Anglican rector at Fredricksville Parish in Louisa County, complained in writing to Commissary Dawson about the assistance which Davies and John Todd had given to these independent militias. In that letter, dated October 6, 1755, Maury informed Dawson:

> It seems not improper to inform You that the [Reverend] [Messengers] Davies and Todd have lately been guilty of what I think Intrusions upon me, in having preached each of them a Sermon at a Tavern in my Parish... What was their real Motive to this conduct, I [don't] undertake to determine: but an apparent one was, the Request of Capt Overton to Davies, and of Capt Fox to Mr. Todd, to preach an occasional Sermon to their respective Companies, at the Time of their Departure to range upon our Frontiers.[15]

Spiritual leaders like Maury provided little assistance in awakening Virginians from the false security which Davies detected among them!

Great Britain Declares War; The Synod of New York Calls a Fast
Great Britain's official declaration of war against France was not made until May 17, 1756. Gov. Dinwiddie received this information sometime in July when he proceeded through the formalities of declaring war against France in behalf of Virginia on August 7, 1756.

The Synod of New York, therefore, called for a general fast for Octo-

---

[13] Ibid., 385–6.
[14] Ibid., 382.
[15] "Letters of Patrick Henry, Sr., Samuel Davies, James Maury, Edwin Conway and George Trask," in *William and Mary College Quarterly Historical Magazine* (1921), 277.

ber 28, 1756 to be observed by all her ministers and members. On that day, Davies preached from Jonah 3:9 on, "The Crisis; or, the Uncertain Doom of Kingdoms at Particular Times". The general lack of repentance was a special concern to him and he reminded his hearers the war could turn against them unless Virginia and the British colonies repented:

> We are engaged in a war with a powerful, exasperated enemy, and blood is streaming by sea and land. Some decisive blow will probably be struck ere long; but, on what party it will fall, and what will be the issue of this struggle and commotion among the nations, is an anxious uncertainty. It seems but too likely, though it strikes me with horror to admit the thought, that a provoked God intends to scourge us with the rod of France, and therefore gives surprising success to her arms.[16]

Davies reminded his hearers, in this same message, that there was even then a deadly distemper passing through his congregation which had taken whole families to their premature deaths. Despite the threats of a famine, the sounds of war, and the spread of a pestilence, most people carried on their business as though they lived in "a healthy neighbourhood, and a peaceful unmolested country."[17]

New Year's Day of 1757 was appointed by the Presbytery of Hanover as another day of fasting and prayer because of the war. When the day arrived, Davies preached in Henrico from James 4:1, "Serious Reflections on War." After summarizing the defeats and disappointments, the terror and the alarm, the desolation and slaughter of the previous year, Davies looked forward to a day of peace:

> Blessed be God, vice shall not always be triumphant in the world. The cause of truth and righteousness shall not always be kept under. Heathenism, Mahometism, and Popery, though now supported by the powers of the earth, and seemingly invincible, shall yet fall before this gospel, and rise no more. Jews and Gentiles, whites and blacks, shall all submit to Jesus, and own him as their saviour and Lord. Of this grand and happy revolution in the world of mankind we have abundant evidence. . . This happy period is represented as the reign of Christ for a thousand years, when Satan shall be bound, and no more tempt the nations. O blessed period! how long will thou delay, blessed Jesus! thy kingdom come! O pop-

---

[16] Davies, *Sermons on Important Subjects*, Volume III (London: W. Baynes and Sons, 1824) 408.
[17] Ibid., 419.

ish powers?. . . France and her allies are all papists; and Britain and her allies hasten it, that we may live no more in this turbulent ocean, but enjoy the blessings of perfect peace.[18]

Virginia's Expeditionary Force

In the meantime, the war with France was not going well for Virginia and the other British colonies. The Virginia Regiment, due to vacillating orders and leadership, refused to take the offensive on the Ohio River and seemed to be content with a defensive posture. The result was that the borders of the British colonies were continually being pushed back by the inferior French forces.

Due primarily to poor health, Gov. Dinwiddie left Virginia and America in 1758. John Blair, the nephew of the former Commissary James Blair, became the acting governor. With this change in the government of Virginia, the war with France turned for the better. A spirit of optimism swept through the British colonies and there was hope the French could be defeated. Major General James Abercrombie was appointed Commander-in-Chief of the King's army in America and quickly requested an expeditionary force of 2,000 men from Virginia to recapture Fort Duquesne. The General Assembly of Virginia agreed in early April of 1758 to raise a second regiment and to provide for their support.

Davies was asked once more to preach a recruiting sermon for the militia of Hanover County—this time for Captain Samuel Meredith. Choosing Jeremiah 48:10 as his text, he preached a sermon on May 8, 1758, titled "The Curse of Cowardice." He reasoned that God Himself was calling the colony to arms to defend themselves against the superstitions of Popery and the barbarities of the Indians. In asking for volunteers, he touched on all the motives of the human heart at such a time:

> May I not reasonably insist upon it, that the company be made up this day before we leave this place? Methinks your king, your country, nay, your interests command me: and therefore I must insist upon it.—Oh! for the all-prevailing force of Demosthene's oratory—but I recall my wish, that I may correct it—Oh! for the influence of the Lord of armies, the God of battles, the Author of true courage, and every heroic virtue, to fire you into patriots and soldiers this moment!. . . Ye that love your country, enlist; for honor will follow you in life or death in such a course. You that

---

[18] Davies, *Sermons on Important Subjects*, IV, 131.

love your religion, enlist; for your religion is in danger. Can Protestant Christianity expect quarters from heathen savages and French papists? Sure, in such an alliance, the powers of hell make a third party. Ye that love your friends and relations, enlist; lest ye see them enslaved or butchered before your eyes. Ye that would catch at money, here is a proper bait for you; ten pounds for a few months service, besides the usual pay of soldiers.[19]

The result of Davies' appeal was that a company was formed within minutes and more men volunteered than were authorized to serve under Captain Meredith. As Davies attempted to tether his horse, "the whole regiment followed him, and pressed around him, to catch every word that dropt from his lips. On observing their desire, he stood in the tavern porch, and again addressed them, until he was exhausted with speaking."[20] Only then was he able to mount his horse and ride home.

Though most Virginians were dejected about the war by May of 1758, Davies' message rekindled their optimism. As Enoch Pond, Davies' biographer, wrote:

> As the preacher poured forth the strains of eloquence, his own spirit was transformed into his hearers, the cheek that was blanched with fear reddened, and the drooping eye kindled with martial fires, and at the conclusion, every voice was prepared to say, 'Let us march against the enemy! Let us conquer or die!'[21]

Conclusion

The French and Indian War continued until February 10, 1763 when a peace treaty was signed in Paris between the British, French, and Spanish. In the Treaty of Paris, the French lost their claims to Canada and were compelled to give their possession of Louisiana to Spain. The Spanish, likewise, relinquished Florida to Great Britain. This treaty secured peace for the thirteen American colonies by removing their European adversaries from both their southern and northern borders. Virginia was not troubled by hostilities in Canada or Florida, but was harassed by marauding bands of French and Indian adversaries on its western bounda-

---

[19] Davies, *Sermons on Important Subjects*, III, 432–433.
[20] Enoch Pond, *Memoir of the Rev. Samuel Davies* (Boston: Massachusetts Sabbath School Society, 1834), 77.
[21] Ibid., 75.

The French and Indian War

ries from Pittsburgh to Georgia and South Carolina; and, in territory that is in modern day Tennessee. This war had a solemn effect on everything Davies did in Virginia for the rest of his ministry there. Militias had to be raised; churches in the mountains needed protection; slaves had to be warned not to desert their masters for the French; Indians had to be wooed to the British side; and, slumbering citizens had to be aroused concerning their danger. The vital concerns of religious freedom were more directly at stake in this contest than during any other conflict, before or since, on American soil. This war secured spiritual freedom for the colonies, whereas the American Revolution secured political freedom. The role that Davies played in rousing Virginians to be good soldiers of Christ in the midst of this conflict must not be minimized. If the French and Indian War was the first world war, then Davies was the champion of religious freedom by his stirring war sermons.

-15-

Hanover Presbytery

"Hanover Presbytery was the first Presbyterian judicatory in Virginia and the first in the South connected with the main body of Presbyterians. Many individual churches had already been established in the colony, but those congregations and the ministers who supplied them were usually connected with presbyteries north of the Potomac River."[1]
~*William M. E. Rachal, "Early Minutes of Hanover Presbytery"*~

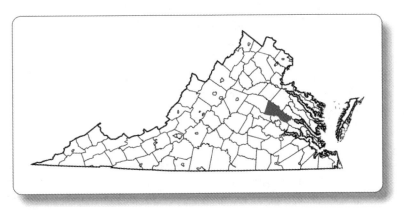

Map of Virginia with Hanover County highlighted

---

[1] William M. E. Rachal, "Early Minutes of Hanover Presbytery," *The Virginia Magazine of History and Biography*, Vol. 63, No. 1 (Jan. 1955), 53.

The flourishing of Presbyterianism in Virginia was apparent to all when the Synod of New York approved the erecting of Hanover Presbytery at its meeting on October 13, 1755. Samuel Davies, John Todd, Robert Henry, John Wright, John Brown and Alexander Craighead were commissioned to form this new Presbytery. All those ministers to the south and east of John Hoge's congregation along the Opequon Creek[2], near Winchester, Virginia, were given liberty to unite with them. The first meeting was set for December 3 of that year with Davies appointed to open it with a sermon. Davies, Todd, Brown, and Henry gathered at Hanover on the appointed day, but Craighead and Wright were inexplicably absent. Samuel Morris, Alexander Joice, and John Maccey represented their congregations as ruling elder commissioners.

Davies was elected the first moderator, but was unable to preach due to an illness. Instead, Todd delivered a sermon from Zechariah 4:7- "Who art thou, O great mountain? Before Zerubbabel thou shalt become a plain: and he shall bring forth the headstone thereof with shoutings, crying, Grace, Grace unto it." That passage spoke to the situation which had faced the New Light Presbyterians in Virginia. The strong arm of the law had been aligned against them, but the grace of God had leveled that mountain into a plain. Through many conflicts, the right of religious freedom had been won in that Anglican colony and the future portended greater blessings to come for the Dissenters.

These early ministers of Hanover Presbytery were all worthy and able men. Davies and Todd were the first New Light Presbyterians to reside in Virginia, but others soon followed.

John Brown

John Brown was born in Ireland in 1728 and immigrated to America as a young man. His family lived in Augusta County, Virginia, about halfway between Staunton and Rockfish Gap. He was converted under Davies' ministry and completed his education at Princeton. After graduation in 1749, he was ordained on October 11, 1753 at Fagg's Manor, Pennsylvania, with Davies preaching the ordination sermon from Acts

---

[2] The Opequon Creek is a 64 mile long tributary stream of the Potomac River which flows in a northeasterly direction, passing through both Winchester, Virginia and Martinsburg, West Virginia.

20:28. He then assumed the pastorates of the Timber Ridge and Providence congregations in Cumberland County which called him on July 22, 1753. He was esteemed by Davies "as a youth of piety, prudence and zeal."[3] The Rev. Dr. Benjamin McWhorter, as a youth, heard Brown preach from Psalm 7:12, "If the wicked turn not." McWhorter "was impressed and led to the Saviour"[4] through that sermon. Brown also started an academy which became Washington and Lee University. In his later years, he moved to Frankfort, Kentucky, where he became the patriarch of several leading families of the Commonwealth.

Robert Henry
Robert Henry graduated from the College of New Jersey in 1751 and was sent to Virginia by the Synod of New York sometime after September 29, 1752. He was installed as pastor at the Cub Creek and Briery churches in Lunenberg County on Wednesday, June 4, 1755. Davies and Todd were commissioned by New Castle Presbytery to install Henry with Todd tasked to preach the installation sermon. Todd and Davies remained with Henry for nearly two weeks and conducted a sacramental service on Sunday, June 8th. The daily services were attended with the evident blessing of the Lord in a large manner. According to Todd, "there was comfortable evidence of the power of God with us every day. Believers were more quickened, and sinners were much alarmed."[5] One man, in particular, reminded him of the conversion of the Philippian jailer: "One, I remember, came to me trembling and astonished, the nearest image I ever saw of the trembling jailor, crying out, 'What shall I do to get an interest in Christ?'"[6] After Todd returned home following the meetings, he "made an excursion to preach to a number of people who had never before heard a new light."[7] He hoped "the word of God was attended with Divine power to many of their hearts."[8]

---

[3] Richard Webster, *History of the Presbyterian Church in America, From Its Origin Until the Year 1760* (Philadelphia: Joseph M. Wilson, 1857), 656.
[4] Ibid.
[5] John Todd to George Whitefield, June 26, 1756 in John Gillies, *Historical Collections Relating to Remarkable Periods of the Success of the Gospel* (Kelso, Scotland: John Rutherford, 1845), 505.
[6] Ibid., 505–6
[7] Ibid., 506
[8] Ibid.

Davies wrote an account of those meetings to John Gillies in Scotland on July 14, 1756. He reported that he assisted Henry in administering the sacrament and "in thirteen days preached eleven or twelve sermons, with encouraging appearances of success."[9] Davies was impressed that Henry and Wright were both continuing to be blessed in their labors which the crowds at this sacramental service confirmed. There were "in that wilderness. . . about 2000 hearers, and about 200 communicants."[10] The use of communion tokens insured there were always more hearers than communicants, but those who attended gave serious attention to the preaching of the Word. Davies wrote Gillies that "a general seriousness and attention appeared among them" and "a considerable number of thoughtless creatures are solicitously inquiring after religion."[11]

Foote described Henry as "somewhat eccentric in manners,. . . ardently pious and devoted to his work as a gospel minister."[12] He was very animated in preaching, "sometimes approaching vociferation" and "his vein of humor often breaking out in his sermons, rendered him peculiarly acceptable to the African race, among whom he gathered many converts."[13] Short notes were all he generally used in the pulpit, but on one occasion he decided to make more careful preparation.

> Having written a sermon, he commenced reading from a small manuscript in his Bible. Of course he appeared to go on tamely. A gust of wind suddenly swept the paper from the Bible. He watched its progress as it sailed along to an old elder's seat. The old gentleman had been listening seriously, and as the paper fell at his side he deliberately put his foot upon it. Mr. Henry waited for him to bring it back to him. The old gentleman looked up as if nothing had happened; and Mr. Henry finished his sermon in the best way he could. It was the end of his written preparations to preach.[14]

Every other week, Henry preached at the Briery Church and spent Saturday night at Little Joe Morton's house. While riding on his horse to

---

[9] Ibid.
[10] Ibid.
[11] Ibid.
[12] William Henry Foote, *Sketches of Virginia: Historical and Biographical*, Second Series (Philadelphia: J. B. Lippincott & Co., 1856), 51
[13] Ibid.
[14] Ibid., 52.

his appointments, he would often become so absorbed in his devotions that he would become oblivious to everything else.

> As he rode on his solitary way, he dropped the bridle, and lifting up his heart and voice and hands in prayer, suffered the quiet, faithful beast to take his own time. Often his horse stopped at Mr. Morton's door, with his good master still engaged in worship, as if alone in the forest.[15]

Sometimes, Henry would mistake his own horse after preaching and start to mount the horse of someone else. He was absentminded and possessed strong natural passions, but he was a man of uncommon spirituality. Henry Patillo once informed a young minister about Robert Henry, "He required grace enough for two men, to keep him in order, and he had it."[16]

John Wright

John Wright, a native of Scotland, was reared in Virginia and was tutored by Davies before attending the College of New Jersey, from which he graduated in 1752. He became friends with Jonathan Edwards while a student and lived with him during the summer after graduation. Edwards once wrote to John Erskine of Scotland in behalf of Wright who wanted to correspond with a minister in his native country. Wright was highly esteemed by Aaron Burr and described by Edwards as "a person of very good character for his understanding, prudence, and piety."[17]

Wright was installed as the pastor at Cumberland, Virginia, on the last Sunday of June in 1755. Captain John Morton, Davies' former companion on his preaching tours, was one of the founders and leading elders of this congregation. Morton was "a man of warm, generous heart, ardent in his piety, and public-spirited in a high degree; so that his heart and his hands were ever ready to engage in any good work."[18]

There were many remarkable conversions in Wright's congregation beginning in the summer of 1756 and continuing for several months. Wright described these convictions as "more deep and pungent last year than formerly, and that more got clear views of salvation this summer,

---

[15] Webster, *History of the Presbyterian Church in America*, 652.
[16] Foote, *Sketches of Virginia*, Second Series, 51.
[17] Ibid., 53.
[18] Ibid.

than I have known since I came to Virginia."[19] Three sacramental services brought an increase of 210 to 230 communicants. One hundred were added in July of 1756, eighty to ninety in August, and another thirty to forty in November of that year. There were fewer new communicants in November, but Wright considered that communion service to be "a day of special outpouring of the spirit" and that "Christ triumphed among us."[20] There were only five or six young people who came to the Table in July, but the number increased to "between fifty or sixty"[21] in November. Wright wrote a correspondent in Scotland about the conversions among the youth:

> Do tell this to the young in Scotland, that the wild Virginians may shame them. Alas, when I lived there, I loved play more than the cross of Christ.[22]

There was also an awakening among little children and slaves in Wright's congregation. He felt five or six slaves had recently gained "a title to heaven."[23] Benjamin Fawcett of Kidderminster sent a present of Bibles to be given to the slaves who were encouraged to learn to read. The secret behind these awakenings was given by Wright when he mentioned that a "goodly number of ministers in this country entered into a concert of prayer on Saturday evening and Sabbath morning, not only for the church in general, but for one another in particular."[24] The Lord of the harvest first gives His people a desire to pray before He gives them the blessings of the gospel.

There were other remarkable conversions under Wright's ministry. One man who attended his ministry was under the influence of the Quakers and refused to join a church or be baptized. Some Quakers came to the Cumberland area in the summer of 1756 and this man was deeply affected. Wright considered him to be "irrecoverably confirmed in that awful heresy. . . but the Sabbath before the August sacrament, the

---

[19] Gillies, *Historical Collections*, 520.
[20] Ibid.
[21] Ibid.
[22] Ibid.
[23] Ibid.
[24] Ibid.

snare was broken and his eyes opened."[25] The man came to Wright the week before the sacrament and earnestly entreated him to be allowed to come to the Table which he now believed to be scriptural. Wright was satisfied with his religious experience and records his profession: "He told me he endeavored after the light within, till he found himself nothing but darkness, and everything horrible."[26] This former Quaker, once baptized and admitted to the Lord's Table, brought his six children to Wright for baptism also.

A young woman was awakened in the spring of 1756 under Wright's preaching, but she did not converse with him directly until that November. She married in September and her husband was vigorously opposed to her becoming a Presbyterian. She went to talk with Wright two weeks before the sacrament which shocked her husband. Wright believed he had "not seen any instance of deeper distress for many years."[27] About her Wright recorded:

> Forgetting God so long, slighting Christ when relations highly prized him, stifling convictions when she had them, seemed to her unpardonable sins. But her ignorance of God in consequence of that, and aversion to duty, she thought rendered her case quite helpless; and which added to her distress, she said her husband was averse to religion.[28]

Wright quickly discerned the woman's husband would be her biggest snare and counseled her to pray earnestly for his salvation. Her husband was in a rage when she returned home and demanded to know everything the preacher had said. The woman refused to answer him in that condition, but gave herself to prayer for him. Her conduct was such a testimony to his conscience that the Saturday and Sunday before the sacrament "he neither could eat nor sleep, telling her that she was holy and a lover of God, but he was a beast and infinitely worse."[29] When the Sabbath came for the sacrament, she was prepared to attend and expected him to accompany her. He at first refused on the grounds that he was a beast, but then consented. Wright "saw him leaning upon her shoulder,

---

[25] Ibid.
[26] Ibid.
[27] Ibid., 521.
[28] Ibid.
[29] Ibid.

pale as death, with the tears running in abundance"[30] after the evening service. Wright wrote him a letter a few days later and encouraged him to pray in his family. The man observed some slaves praying one morning soon afterwards. He was so overcome that he would not leave the house until both he and his wife had cried bitterly before the Lord. Their bitter tears were repentance unto life.

Another convert was the husband of one of Wright's new communicants in the summer of 1756. Initially, Wright described him as a "young rake." This man attended the services after his wife's conversion, but was displeased with the solemnity of the people. He asked his wife why all the people looked "as if they were afraid of thunder and lightning"[31] and was told if he ever got a true view of his sinfulness he would be the same way. The man's response was "that he must have some strange new light before he could possibly be so. But on Sunday he was so struck, that he was like to roar in the meetinghouse. Ever since," Wright recorded, "he is a constant hearer, and has set up prayer in his family."[32]

Wright succumbed to a sickness in 1757 which caused him to lay aside his ministry for a season. He later recovered, but it proved to be short-lived. Hanover Presbytery rebuked him on June 19, 1759 for "taking more spiritous Liquor at this Presbytery than his Constitution would bear."[33] Foote states he was under the delusion, then prevalent in some circles, that a sufficient quantity of liquor would permanently cure him of his drinking problem. Instead, the alcohol led to other problems. He was later charged by Alexander Miller and Samuel Black of sodomy, drunkenness, popery, and racing. Those charges were never proven, but Presbytery suspended him in 1763 from the ministry and he was never reinstated. Thus, Foote concluded:

> His morning of expectation went down in clouds, never to be brighter till Christ the Lord shall come. Then we hope it may appear that wandering he was not finally lost."[34]

---

[30] Ibid.
[31] Ibid.
[32] Ibid.
[33] Rachal, "Early Minutes of Hanover Presbytery", 174.
[34] Foote, *Sketches of Virginia*, Second Series, 55.

John Martin

John Martin was trained for the ministry by Davies. He was the first person both licensed and ordained by the Presbytery of Hanover. He was licensed on August 25, 1756, and ordained on June 9, 1757. The ordination sermon was preached by Davies at Hanover from 1 Timothy 3:1, "The Office of Bishop a Good Work." He described the minister's duties in the following quote from that message:

> To employ his hours at home, not in idleness or worldly pursuits, but in study and devotion, that his head and heart may be furnished for the discharge of his office—to preach the word, instant in season and out of season, with that vigorous exertion, and those agonies of zeal, which exhaust the spirits, and throw the whole frame into such a ferment as hardly any other labor can produce—to visit the sick and to teach his people from house to house, in the more social and familiar forms of private instruction—to do all this, not as a thing by the bye, or a matter of form, but with zeal, fidelity, and prudence, and incessant application, as the main business of life; deeply solicitous about the important consequences—to do all this with fortitude and perseverance, in spite of all the discouragements of unsuccessfulness, and the various forms of opposition that may arise from earth and hell—to abide steady and unshaken under the strong gales of popular applause and the storms of persecution—to bless, when reviled; to forbear, when persecuted; to entreat, when defamed; to be abased as the filth of the world, and the off-scouring of all things; to give no offence in any thing, that the ministry be not blamed; but in all things to approve himself as the minister of God; to preach Christianity out of the pulpit, by his example, as well as in it, by his discourses; and to make his life a constant sermon.—This, this, my brethren, is the work of a bishop, or a minister of the gospel. "And who is sufficient for these things?"[35]

Henry Patillo

Henry Patillo was Davies' first student theological student and the circumstances surrounding his settlement in Hanover were given in Chapter 8. He married Mary Anderson in 1755 with whom he had been engaged for a considerable time. Patillo wrote Davies while the latter was in Great Britain to get his advice about this marriage, but was disappointed with his mentor's advice. He received Davies' counsel as an

---

[35] Samuel Davies, *Sermons on Important Subjects*, IV (London: W. Baynes and Son, 1824), 369–70.

"Army of formidable weighty objections and determined a resignation thro' all the anxieties of a disappointed Love."[36] He laid Davies' letter before his fiancée and her parents, but his objections to this marriage gave them all a terrible shock. Patillo then drafted a response to Davies' objections.[37] Apparently, Davies planned on Patillo completing his education at Princeton and viewed this union as a hindrance to that scheme. Patillo retorted, in his diary, that he would willingly finish his course under Davies' hand; that he considered "it a greater evil to leave an innocent young Creature in Love than to marry her through several difficulties;"[38] that his true friends would not be offended by this arrangement since he intended to pursue his studies; and, that any money raised in England for him could be given to some other needy student. Patillo respected Davies' scholarship so highly he felt any student "finished by his hand would not come under contempt any more than many shining Lights now in the Church."[39]

A small house in Hanover of sixteen feet by twelve feet with a fireplace to provide heat was the first residence of Patillo and his new bride. He taught a few young scholars at his house and husbanded his income very carefully to support them while continuing his own studies. He observed a day of fasting and prayer on May 30, 1755, together with the other young men[40] then studying under Davies. His prayer on that occasion was for "quickening of vivacity in religion... His blessing on me as a student that I may pursue my studies assiduously. . . That he may give me extensive experience in Christian exercises. . . that I may know how to detect and expose counterfeits. . . that I may have a sufficient fund of useful knowledge. . . that I may have courage, prudence, zeal, diligence and success in the ministry."[41]

Patillo's small house was burned to the ground on June 13, 1757, when the roof was struck by lightning. He was in the home when the thunderous bolt set it ablaze. His wife, their daughter, his wife's sister,

---

[36] Diary of Henry Patillo in Patillo Papers, Folder 1/5, Special Collections, William Smith Morton Library, Union Presbyterian Seminary, 19.
[37] Our only hints at those objections are from Patillo's response.
[38] Diary, Patillo Papers, 19.
[39] Ibid., 19–20.
[40] John Martin, William Richardson and David Rice were certainly other students under Davies.
[41] Diary, Patillo Papers, 21.

six students, and a slave boy were also in the house with him—who were all amazingly protected from harm.[42] Observing the burned, charred remains of his former house afterwards, he "exclaimed to his wife, 'O my dear, are my books safe?' And on being assured that they were, he devoutly praised God."[43]

Patillo was ordained by Hanover Presbytery on July 13, 1758—one year and one month to the day after the loss of his home. Davies preached the ordination sermon from 1 Thess. 2:8, "The Love of Souls a Necessary Qualification for the Ministerial Office." This message was delivered in Cumberland County where John Brown labored. Part of that sermon states the importance of the love of souls for a minister:

> Hence it appears, that the most effectual method to convince our hearers we love them, is, to be under the strong influence of that benevolent passion which we profess. The sacred fire of love will blaze out in full evidence, and afford the strongest conviction they can receive, that their minister is their *friend*, and aims at their best interest, even when he denounces the terrors of the Lord against them, or assumes the unacceptable character of their reprover; and, when they are thus happily prepossessed in his favour, they will take almost anything well at his hands. . . That must be a base, ungenerous sinner indeed, that can look up to the pulpit, and there see an affectionate *friend* in the person of his minister, adorned with smiles of love, or melting into tears of tender pity, and yet resent the faithful freedoms, and hate him as his enemy for telling him the truth. Some ministers are not loved in a suitable degree by their people. But not to mention, at present, the criminal causes of this neglect on the side of the people, I am afraid one common cause is, that *they* do not sufficiently love *them*. Love is naturally productive of love; it scatters its heavenly sparks around, and these kindle the gentle flame where they fall. Oh! that each of us, who sustain the sacred character, may purchase the love of our people with the price of our own love! And may we distribute this to them with so liberal a hand, as always to leave them debtors to us in this precious article! That people should love their minster more than *he* loves *their* souls, is a shocking, unnatural disproportion![44]

Patillo's first call was to the churches of Willis Creek, Byrd, and Buck Island in Albemarle County, Virginia. He moved to the Harris Creek and

---

[42] Ibid, 28.
[43] James W. Alexander, *Life of Archibald Alexander*, (New York; Charles Scribner, 1854), 152.
[44] Davies, *Sermons on Important Subjects*, Volume IV, 326–7.

Deep Creek congregations in Cumberland County four years later. Some churches in North Carolina called him in 1765 where he labored for fifteen years. He then became the minister of the Nutbush and Grassy Creek congregations in North Carolina, "largely made up of converts under the ministry of Davies."[45] He was very attentive to the spiritual needs of the slaves and said about them, "of the religious negroes in my congregation, some are intrusted with a kind of eldership, so as to keep a watch over others: any thing wrong seldom happens."[46] The supply of books for slaves from Great Britain stopped after the Revolutionary War and Patillo "lamented... that he had none to give away to the servants."[47]

Patillo became an author later in life. One small volume contained a letter "On Predestination" written to Francis Asbury, the Methodist minister, on June 14, 1787. Some of his sermons were also printed, one of which was on the death of George Washington. A note attached to another of his sermons "broached the same doctrine concerning Christ's human nature, which. . .[was later] so offensively taught by Edward Irving."[48]

William Richardson

William Richardson was born in Egremont, England, near White Haven. In America, he lived in Davies' home and studied under his care. He was taken on trials by the Presbytery on June 9, 1757, and was licensed the next January. He was ordained with Patillo on July 13, 1758. More information will be given concerning Richardson in the chapter on the mission to the Cherokee Indians.

James Waddell

James Waddell was born in Ireland in 1739 and immigrated with his family to America as an infant. They settled in Pennsylvania near the Maryland line. As children, he and his brothers one day were chasing a rabbit into a tree. They attempted to cut the rabbit out and James was struck by an axe which severed his hand almost in two. He never regained feeling in his hand and fingers and, as a result, his parents provided him with a

---

[45] Webster, *History of the Presbyterian Church in America*, 677.
[46] Ibid.
[47] Ibid.
[48] Alexander, *Life of Archibald Alexander*, 152.

classical education. He also suffered from poor eyesight all his life due to the early onset of cataracts which eventually left him totally blind in adulthood.

Waddell set out for South Carolina at the age of nineteen where he hoped to teach school. He passed through Hanover and called on Davies. He quickly "felt the attractive influence of that good man"[49] during their conversation and was persuaded to make his home in Virginia. Davies arranged for Waddell to assist Todd at the classical school at Payne's Mill and begin preparations for the ministry. He was subsequently taken into the Presbytery as a candidate in April of 1760 and licensed on April 28, 1761. Ordination to the ministry followed in 1762 when he took the charges of the churches in the Northern Neck of Virginia. Waddell was known as the "Blind Preacher," in William Wirt's *British Spy*. His mind was very active and he was an eloquent preacher. He married Mary Gordon, the daughter of Col. and Mrs. James Gordon, of Lancaster County, in 1768.

James Hunt

James Hunt was the son of John Hunt, one of Davies' elders at Hanover, who was part of the revival in Virginia before Robinson's visit in 1743. Davies was influential in the spiritual development of the younger Hunt and encouraged him to study under Todd before attending Princeton. Hunt graduated from Princeton in 1759, was licensed by New Brunswick Presbytery in 1760, and ordained in 1761.

David Rice

David Rice was born on December 20, 1733. His father, David Rice, Sr., was a farmer and another one of the founders of the Presbyterian Church in Hanover County. Rice witnessed the scenes of the revival under Robinson and the famous "Morris reading room" during his youth. He joined the church at the age of twenty after a hopeful conversion through the preaching of Davies. He soon started attending the academy taught by Todd. He struggled to support himself by raising "a

---

[49] William Henry Foote, *Sketches of Virginia: Historical and Biographical*, First Series (Philadelphia: William S. Martien, 1850), 351.

hogshead of tobacco with his own hands"[50] and teaching at an English grammar school.

Rice entered the junior class of the College of New Jersey in 1759 and graduated in 1761. He immediately returned to Virginia where he was licensed by Hanover Presbytery in 1762. He assumed the pastorate of Davies' former congregation in Hanover the following year. A dispute between two of the leading elders of the congregation over the matter of slavery led to Rice's resignation in 1768. He served a congregation in Bedford County, Virginia, for thirteen years before moving to Kentucky in 1783. He achieved his greatest success in Kentucky and was affectionately known as "Father Rice." He is still esteemed as the greatest Presbyterian minister to ever serve in that state.

Rice married Mary Blair, the daughter of Samuel Blair, Davies' former teacher. This union produced eleven children. He spent his final days confined to his home, in poverty and poor health, from 1812 until his death to influenza on June 18, 1816 in Green County, Kentucky at the age of eighty-three.

The hand of Davies can be prominently seen in the lives of each of these early ministers of Hanover Presbytery. He was in a true sense the father of the Presbytery. There were notable qualities about each of them, as well as many who followed them at a later period, but none of them eclipsed the gifts or graces of Davies himself.

Seasons of Refreshing

In addition to his influence on younger ministers, Davies continued to be active in preaching throughout the colony. He held a communion service at Hanover in July of 1756 and was assisted by Todd. He felt a tender, "pastoral heart" in his "affectionate concern for [his] flock" on this occasion, but feared he did not have "a proportional liberty to vent it."[51] The sermon he preached on this occasion, July 11, 1756, was from Isaiah 53 and was titled, "The Sufferings of Christ and Their Consequent Joys and Blessings." Part of his tenderness in applying the message is given in the following lines:

---

[50] Foote, *Sketches of Virginal*, Second Series, 78.
[51] Ibid.

And, O! that the lost sheep would this day return, that their kind Shepherd may rejoice over them: he came from heaven in search of you, and will you keep out of his way, and fear falling into his hands? Let wandering prodigals return, that there may be joy in your Father's house, whose arms are stretched out to embrace you, and who is looking after you with eager eyes. O let the pleasure of the Lord prosper among us this day, and it will be a day gratefully to be remembered to all eternity![52]

He hoped this sacrament "was a refreshing time to some hungry souls"[53] as no doubt it was. There was also a remarkable work of God among the churches of Davies, Henry and Wright at this time. The revival affected a different class of people in each instance. The revival in Davies' congregation was principally among the slaves, in Henry's congregations it affected the youth, and among Wright's people it was of a general nature. The summer of 1756 was an extremely busy one for Davies. He "rode about five hundred miles, and preached about forty sermons"[54] during a period of two months.

The revival among Henry's young people flourished in the winter of 1756–7. "No less than seventeen of them were struck to the heart by one occasional evening lecture" and he informed Davies that he "has great hopes of the perseverance of sundry of them, and that hardly any of them appear discouraging."[55]

Davies' congregation in Hanover built a new meetinghouse called the Polegreen Church in 1757. It was a plain building of twenty-five feet by sixty feet with a balcony and was capable of seating several hundred people.[56] The back of the property sloped down to a spring where the worshipers could water their horses and get a drink for themselves before returning to their homes. The services were frequently held beneath a neighboring oak grove during warmer weather. The crowds on those occasions were estimated to be in the thousands, which made the Anglicans envious.

---

[52] Davies, *Sermons on Important Subjects*, Volume II (London: W. Baynes and Sons, 1824),163.
[53] Gillies, *Historical Collections*, 506
[54] John Holt Rice, "Memoir of the Rev. Samuel Davies," *Virginia Evangelical and Literary Magazine*, I (1819), 563.
[55] Gillies, *Historical Collections*, 521.
[56] This building was burned down in 1764 during the Civil War battle of Cold Harbor.

Domestic Life in the Davies' Home

There is very little information concerning the daily life of the Davies' family, but there is no doubt that Samuel was a conscientious husband and father. His journal entries during his trip to Great Britain reveal how affectionately he longed for his wife and children, and how concerned he was when he received reports of Jane's sicknesses. In a letter of May 18, 1757, Davies informed Samuel Hazard of his domestic circumstances: "God has given me the Blessing of another Daughter; & my Dear is recovered, in spite of my gloomy tears."[57] His parental responsibilities made a deep impression on Davies' tender conscience, according to a letter he wrote to Thomas Gibbons:

> There is nothing that can wound a parent's heart so deeply, as the thought that he should bring up children to dishonour his God here, and be miserable hereafter. I beg your prayers for mine, and you may expect a return in the same kind.[58]

The method of educating his children was given in another letter to Gibbons:

> We have now three sons and two daughters; whose young minds, as they open, I am endeavoring to cultivate with my own hand, unwilling to trust them to a stranger; and I find the business of education much more difficult than I expected. My dear little creatures sob and drop a tear now and then, under my instructions, but I am not so happy as to see them under deep and lasting impressions of religion; and this is the greatest grief they afford me. Grace cannot be communicated by natural descent; and, if it could, they would receive but little from me.[59]

The Revival at the College of New Jersey

While immersed in his numerous responsibilities in Virginia, Davies remained keenly interested in the reports of revivals in other places. He maintained a correspondence with many of the leading ministers of the day and prayed for an effusion of the Spirit on their labors. The reports of revival in other places caused him to rejoice in God's great goodness.

---

[57] Samuel Davies to Samuel Hazard, May 18, 1757, Library Company of Philadelphia, Historical Society of Pennsylvania, Philadelphia, Pennsylvania.
[58] Rice, "Memoir of Rev. Samuel Davies," 566.
[59] Ibid., 566–7.

Specimens of some of his correspondence from Great Britain were sent to Samuel Finley for his perusal. These letters gave an account of the "revival of religion in sundry parts of Great Britain, particularly among the clergy."[60] Finley wrote Davies on April 16, 1757, with news of a remarkable outpouring of God's Spirit at the College of New Jersey. Davies characterized it as "the best news that perhaps I ever heard in my life."[61] William Tennent, Jr., who was visiting the college, observed that the revival impacted all sixty students without exception and that "the whole house was a Bochim."[62] The convictions of sin were deep and pungent. They were followed by a sincere seeking for Jesus. This work began gradually, but "spread like the increasing light of the morning."[63] Tennent further exclaimed:

I felt as the apostles when it was told them the Lord had risen.[64]

Preaching was not the particular instrument which God used in this revival. It began, as Davies was informed by some of the students who had formerly been his pupils, with a young man from New York who became dangerously sick. In his sickness, this student was "awakened to a sense of his guilt."[65] His conversation affected a few of his friends who in turn spoke to still others. The revival became general before President Burr even knew of its existence. It no sooner flourished than it was opposed. First, there were misrepresentations of it which caused some fathers to withdraw their sons from the college. These students were sent back when the truth became manifest. Then, the wicked companions of other students enticed them into their former sins. Two or three of them returned to their former worldliness. The Lord, nonetheless, brought several of the students to a saving knowledge of Jesus Christ.

Davies wrote Joseph Forfitt on August 26, 1758 that he rejoiced "Heaven & Earth seem to conspire to assist me & my Fellow Labourers in this remote corner of the World."[66] He was unexpectedly interrupted

---

[60] Gillies, *Historical Collections*, 521.
[61] Ibid.
[62] Ibid. A "Bochim" is a place of weepers.
[63] Gillies, *Historical Collections*, 521.
[64] Ibid.
[65] Ibid.
[66] Letter of Samuel Davies to Joseph Forfitt, August 26, 1758. MS letter in the Beinecke Rare

in writing this letter by "a Young Man of good sense" who wanted "to know what he shall do to be saved."[67] He soon found the young man was reading Baxter's *Call to the Unconverted*. Davies felt this book "deserves to be adorned with the names of 100's of converts as trophies of victories on both sides of the Atlantic."[68] The young man appeared to be "a broken hearted humble Sinner seeking after Jesus."[69] Davies expressed his gratitude for the British friends, like Forfitt, who had abundantly supplied him with books for distribution and exclaimed:

> Blessed be God, there are some poor Sinners still pressing into the Kingdom of Heaven.[70]

Conclusion

There were some encouraging conversions in Virginia through the instrumentality of the newly ordained ministers in the latter part of the decade of the 1750s. The French and Indian War, the great Lisbon earthquake, the severe drought, and the season of sickness that spread across Virginia all contributed to this awakening. Despite the discouraging events of the time, Davies did not allow momentary events to prevent him from zealously pursuing his heavenly mission. As Ecclesiastes 11:4 teaches us: "He who watches the wind will not sow and he who looks at the clouds will not reap." There were storm clouds of danger all around Davies in the latter part of the 1750s. Yet, there had always been storm clouds from the beginning of his ministry. Instead of submitting to those howling winds, he surmounted them by faith. The Lord rewarded his faithful diligence with many new seals of his ministry and with an ever-increasing supply of co-laborers in the gospel.

Book and Manuscript Division, Yale University Library, Yale University, New Haven, Connecticut.
[67] Ibid.
[68] Ibid.
[69] Ibid.
[70] Ibid.

-16-

Evangelizing the African Slaves

"The divine right of kings to tyrannize over their subjects, and the unlawfulness of resistance to their authority on the part of the people, were formerly maintained by the very same kind of scriptural arguments which are now advanced in support of slavery. The arguments drawn from the Bible in favor of despotism, are, indeed, much more plausible than those in favor of slavery. We despised the former—how then should we disregard the latter?"[1]

~An Address by Rev. David Rice Against Slavery before the Synod of Kentucky in 1835~

African slaves working in a cotton field

---

[1] "An Address Against Slavery," in Robert L. Ferm, ed., *Issues in American Protestantism: A Documentary History from the Puritans to the Present* (Gloucester, Massachusetts: Peter Smith, 1976), 183.

Evangelizing the African Slaves

In 1740, George Whitefield wrote *A Letter to the Inhabitants of Maryland, Virginia, and North and South Carolina Concerning their Negroes* concerning the institution of slavery in the American Colonies. It was published in Philadelphia by his friend, Benjamin Franklin. This letter, addressed to the slave owners themselves, described the miseries the poor African slaves suffered which he observed while preaching throughout the Southern Colonies. Whitefield spoke out against an institution which frequently resulted in cruelty and misery for the slaves, but enriched the plantation owners. He said:

> As I lately passed through your provinces, I was touched with a fellow-feeling of the miseries of the poor negroes. . . I have no other way to discharge the concern that lies upon my heart, than by sending you this letter. How you will receive it I know not; but whatever be the event, I must inform you in the meekness and gentleness of Christ, that God has a quarrel with you for your cruelty to the poor negroes. Whether it be lawful for Christians to buy slaves, I shall not take it upon me to determine, but sure I am that it is sinful, when bought, to use them worse than brutes. And I fear the generality of you, who own negroes, are liable to such a charge, for your slaves, I believe, work as hard as the horses whereon you ride.
>
> These, after they have done their work, are fed and taken proper care of; but many negroes, when wearied with labour in your plantations, have been obliged to grind their own corn after they return home.
>
> Your dogs are caressed and fondled at your tables; but your slaves, who are frequently styled dogs or beasts, have not an equal privilege. They are scarce permitted to pick up the crumbs which fall from their master's tables. Nay, some, as I have been informed by an eye-witness, have been, upon the most trifling provocation, cut with knives, and have had forks thrown into their flesh: not to mention what numbers have been given up to the inhuman usage of cruel task-masters, who by their unrelenting scourges, have ploughed upon their backs, and made long furrows, and at length brought them even to death itself.[2]

Numerous newspapers throughout the Colonies republished Whitefield's letter and his sentiments quickly became known to multitudes in America. The institution of slavery was considered an essential part of

---

[2] Arnold A. Dallimore, *George Whitefield: The Life and Times of the Great Evangelist of the Eighteenth Century Revival*, Volume I (London: The Banner of Truth Trust, 1970), 495-6.

the fabric of Colonial society for economic reasons,[3] so Whitefield's rebuke was bitterly opposed by numerous slave owners throughout the south. Yet, Whitefield was neither the first nor the last minister who spoke out against slavery. The treatment of slaves in America by their owners was one problem, but the slave trade itself was another one.

The African Slave Trade
Slavery existed in ancient civilizations for centuries before Christ, but it came under its most severe attacks in the eighteenth and nineteenth centuries from anti-slavery voices in Great Britain and America. Regrettably, though, the Christian community did not always speak with a united voice against this social evil. Some Christians saw clearly the fundamental evil of the system of slavery, but other Christians either defended it or did not actively oppose it.

The African slave trade was one part of a triangular trade arrangement involving Great Britain (or some other European nation), Africa, and the Western Hemisphere. Ships would sail from Great Britain to the Atlantic coast of Africa with rum, tobacco, glass beads, iron bars, and red cloth[4] which were exchanged for slaves captured by African tribes for that purpose. The slaves were then transported to America and exchanged for rum, molasses, sugar and cocoa. Those goods were transported back to Great Britain and the molasses and sugar were used to make more rum.[5]

The living conditions of slaves on these ships were horrible in the extreme. Their food was inadequate, their quarters were unsanitary, and they were kept in chains below the deck. Many of them tried to jump overboard and nearly twenty percent of them did not survive the trip. There were also numerous insurrections on board these ships with nearly ten percent of the slaves disappearing during their passage.[6] Slaves always outnumbered the crew on slave ships and were sometimes able to break their chains and arm themselves. In such instances, they often

---

[3] Ibid., 497
[4] Joseph E. Holloway, "African Insurrections on Board Slave Ships." Accessed at: http://slaverebellion.org/index.php?page=african-insurrections on February 16, 2017.
[5] Ibid.
[6] Ibid. Out of 27,237 voyages from Africa, 2,788 disappeared. Some may have been lost due to shipwrecks, but most of them were insurrections.

overwhelmed and brutally killed the crew before taking the ship back to Africa where it was ditched.

The African Slaves in Virginia
Once slaves reached the New World, their lives did not generally improve. The cruel treatment of those slaves who survived the dangers of the sea resulted in a negative growth rate among them. In Virginia and other colonies, the killing of a slave that resisted arrest or capture by his master was not recognized as murder. Additionally, married slaves were often separated from one another and female slaves were too frequently subject to rape and sexual violation. Male slaves generally had a short life expectancy and the female slaves bore few children. For all these reasons, the slave trade continued unabated to replenish the labor force in the southern colonies.

The first shipload of slaves arrived in Virginia in 1619 aboard a Dutch vessel. By 1681, there were only 8,000 slaves in the colony, but that number increased rapidly to 59,000 by 1714 and nearly 250,000 when Davies arrived at Hanover in 1748. Many of them, no doubt, were treated inhumanely, which touched the sympathy of Davies with a desire to lead them to Christ and relieve their temporal circumstances. The evangelization of the African slaves in Virginia lagged behind even other parts of the south. In South Carolina, an Anglican minister, Rev. Edward Taylor (1642–1729), ministered in the St. Andrews community[7] with some success among the slaves. In 1713, he wrote his supporters a brief account of his work among them:

> I think it my indispensable and special duty to do all that in me lies to promote the conversion and salvation of the poor heathens here, and more especially of the Negro and Indian slaves in my own parish. . . If the masters were but good Christians themselves and would but concurr with the ministers, we should then have good hope of the conversion and salvation at least of some of their Negro and Indian slaves. . . But too many of them rather oppose than concurr with us and are angry with us, I am sure I may say with me for endeavoring as much as I doe the conversion of their slaves.[8]

---

[7] St. Andrews is a community a little to the northwest of Columbia, SC.
[8] C. E. Pierre, "The Work of the Society for the Propagation of the Gospel in Foreign Parts Among the Negroes in the Colonies," *The Journal of Negro History*, Vol. 1, No. 4 (1916), 351.

No doubt, too many of the slave owners in Virginia during the mid-eighteenth century were also opposed to efforts to evangelize the slaves and were angry with those who did so. There is no other explanation for why Virginia would be behind the rest of the southern colonies in this important work. Nonetheless, Davies trudged forward with what he knew to be the right thing to do after the example of other godly ministers. Davies baptized about forty slaves in the first three years of his ministry at Hanover, of whom he was satisfied the majority were sincerely pious. His practice was to catechize them for several months in the essential doctrines of the Christian faith and to examine them carefully for credible evidences of true faith and holiness before baptizing them. He baptized fifteen slaves in one day just prior to his trip to Great Britain in 1753. While in London, Davies had arranged a meeting with Robert Crutenden, Esq., a member of the Society for Promoting Religious Knowledge among the Poor, who gave him £10 Sterling worth of books to be distributed among the poor in Virginia—both whites and slaves.

Davies' Religious Education of the Slaves
A month after returning from Great Britain, Davies wrote to Crutenden with a request for an additional supply of books, which he desired in particular for the slaves. His reason is stated as follows:

> But the poor neglected Negroes, who are so far from having money to purchase books, that they themselves are the property of others; who were originally African savages, and never heard of Jesus and his gospel, till they arrived at the land of their slavery in America, whom their masters generally neglect, and whose souls none care for, as though immortality were not a privilege common to them with their masters: These poor unhappy Africans are objects of my compassion, and I think the most proper object of the society's charity.[9]

There were some three hundred slaves who regularly attended Davies' services in Hanover at this time and about one hundred of them were communing members of the church. Sometimes, in the midst of a sermon, he would glance to that part of the meetinghouse where they usually sat and would find them "eagerly attentive to every word" and

---

[9] John Gillies and Horatius Bonar, *Historical Collections of Accounts of Revival* (Edinburgh, Scotland and Carlisle, Pennsylvania: The Banner of Truth Trust, 1981), 502.

"frequently bathed in tears."[10] Most of these slaves had masters who were indifferent to religion, and few of them were fortunate to have their own Bibles. Since Davies had distributed all the Bibles and books that he had brought back from Great Britain, he was unable to supply all the "importunate petitioners for the same favours."[11] Rather, he was left to exclaim, "Alas, my stock is exhausted."[12]

Davies reported to Crutenden that there were "multitudes of them in different places who [were] willing and eagerly desirous to be instructed, and embrace[d] every opportunity of acquainting themselves with the doctrines of the gospel."[13] He further described their plight:

> Though they have generally very little help to learn to read, yet, to my agreeable surprise, many of them, by the dint of application, in their leisure hours, have made such a progress, that they can intelligibly read a plain author, and especially their Bibles, and pity it is that any of them should be without them.[14]

On Saturday evenings, which was the only time the slaves could spare, Davies gathered large numbers of them into his crowded house to teach them to read and to catechize them. These gatherings often erupted into heavenly music which prompted Davies to request the Society to supply him numerous copies of Isaac Watts' *Psalms* and *Hymns*. The reason for this request was given in Davies' words:

> I am the rather importunate for a good number of these, as I cannot but observe that the Negroes, above all the human species that I ever knew, have an ear for music, and a kind of ecstatic delight in psalmody; and there are no books they learn so soon, or take so much pleasure in, as those used in that heavenly part of divine worship.[15]

The Society did not give away copies of Watts' *Hymns* and *Psalms*, so Crutenden wrote to a friend in the English countryside requesting help in supplying these books. He outlined a plan which he had for some of these slaves. Part of that letter, dated September 19, 1755, read as follows:

---

[10] Ibid.
[11] Ibid.
[12] Ibid.
[13] Ibid.
[14] Ibid.
[15] Ibid.

The letter herewith sent you is the first of this kind I ever received, and as far as I know the first attempt of this nature that has ever been made with any considerable success. My soul triumphs in the thought of an African church formed and raised in the desert of America, nor can I wonder that my worthy friend esteems his congregation adorned with those outcasts of the earth, and flocking into Christ as doves to their windows... O how I love their black faces![16]

The Neglect of the Slaves by Their Masters

An unknown correspondent from Richmond, Virginia informed John Gillies, the Scottish pastor who wrote an account of various revivals, that the spiritual interests of the slaves in Virginia were neglected because their masters were engaged in "plays, races, cockfightings,"[17] etc. The slaves were, thus, frequently "working on Sabbath, or fishing,... or that they could not speak a word without swearing, and were ignorant almost as brutes of the evil consequences of such things."[18] This anonymous correspondent was himself engaged in the instruction of the negroes and ten or more of them would gather at his home every other Sabbath when they had no sermon from Davies. "Some persons..." objected "against their [slaves] learning, as if it made them worse,"[19] but this private citizen had not found it to be so. When he counseled "them not to learn when they should be working,"[20] they responded, "No... for that would be theft, to steal time from our masters."[21]

This unknown correspondent also gave an assessment of Davies' and Todd's work among the slaves to Gillies:

When I go among Mr. Davies's people, religion seems to flourish; it is like the suburbs of heaven. The poor negroes seem very thankful to any that instruct them. Mr. Tod informed me he preached a sermon to them and they thanked him, and seem desirous of farther knowledge. It is very agreeable to see the gentlemen in those parts at their morning and evening prayers with their slaves, devoutly joining with them.[22]

---

[16] Ibid., 503.
[17] Ibid.
[18] Ibid.
[19] Ibid.
[20] Ibid.
[21] Ibid.
[22] Ibid.

Davies wrote Crutenden nearly a year later on March 2, 1756 to thank him for the large supply of Bibles and books, numbering 400–500 volumes. Davies gave public notice of their arrival at the conclusion of one of his sermons in Hanover. He invited any of the slaves who could read and any of the whites too poor to supply themselves to come to his house for the books.[23] This was the occasion of one of Davies' sermon to masters and slaves,[24] "which proved a very popular topic of conviction, and made some impressions upon the minds of not a few."[25] There were about a thousand slaves who attended his services and Davies was unable "to give one of each sort to every particular person, but ordered them to borrow and lend among themselves."[26] He described the eagerness with which the slaves came to his house to receive these gifts:

> For some time after this, the poor slaves, whenever they could get an hour's leisure from their masters, would hurry away to my house, and receive the charity with all the genuine indications of passionate gratitude which unpolished nature could give, and which affectation and grimace would mimic in vain.[27]

The most popular books among the slaves, as Davies anticipated, were the *Psalms* and *Hymns* of Watts, which "enable[d] them to gratify their peculiar taste for psalmody."[28] He communicated to Crutenden that "sundry of them have lodged all night in my kitchen, and sometimes when I have waked about two or three o'clock in the morning, a torrent of sacred harmony poured into my chamber, and carried my mind away to heaven. In this seraphic exercise, some of them spend almost the whole night."[29] Davies was convinced if

---

[23] Ibid.
[24] The date given for the preaching of, "The Duty of Christians to Propagate Their Religion Among the Heathens, Earnestly recommended to the Masters of Negro Slaves in Virginia," is January 8, 1757 which was a Saturday. It appears that something is amiss concerning the date when the sermon was preached. It is certainly possible that Davies preached this sermon on some date in 1756 shortly after receiving the supply of books from the Society for Promoting Religious Knowledge since the dedication page is to that organization.
[25] Gillies and Bonar, *Historical Collections*, 504.
[26] Ibid., 505.
[27] Ibid., 504.
[28] Ibid.
[29] Ibid.

Crutenden could hear such music he would be more pleased than with "an oratorio or St. Cecilia's Day."[30]

Encouraging the Slaves

The gifts of the Society had the good effect of encouraging the slaves that there were some Christians who were vitally interested in their conversion. The slave masters were likewise "excited. . .to emulation, and. . .ashamed that strangers on the other side of the Atlantic should be at pains to teach their domestics Christianity, and they should be quite negligent themselves."[31] The illiterate slaves were encouraged by this charity to learn to read. Davies only gave books to those who were truly pious in the judgment of Christian charity,[32] which contributed to greater attention to the Christian faith on the part of all the slaves. He wrote:

> I am told that in almost every house in my congregation, and in sundry other places, they spend every leisure hour in trying to learn, since they expect books as soon as they are capable to use them. Some of them, I doubt not, are excited to it by a sincere desire to know the will of God, and what they shall do to be saved; others, I am afraid, are actuated by the meaner principle of curiosity, ambition, and vanity.[33]

The gift of these books and his other labors made Davies very popular among the slaves.[34] He wrote that "it gives me a very good opportunity of speaking seriously and with particular application to many who might not otherwise come in my way."[35] Surprisingly, even the slaves of those masters who opposed Davies were allowed to attend his congregations. Davies had the pleasure of seeing some forty slaves at the Lord's Table in the latter part February of 1755, "sundry of them with unusual evidence of sincerity."[36] The following week he "baptized seven or eight adults, who had been catechumens for some time."[37] One of

---

[30] Ibid.
[31] Ibid.
[32] Ibid.
[33] Ibid.
[34] Ibid.
[35] Ibid.
[36] Ibid.
[37] Ibid.

these catechumens conversed with Davies in private the evening before his baptism and expressed himself as follows:

> I am a poor slave, brought into a strange country, where I never expect to enjoy my liberty. While I lived in my own country, I knew nothing of that Jesus which I have heard you speak so much about. I lived quite careless of what will become of me when I die. But I now see that such a life will never do, and I come to you, sir, that you may tell me some good things concerning Jesus Christ, and my duty to God; for I am resolved not to live any more as I have done.[38]

Davies sent some of the books from the Society to John Wright in Cumberland County, Virginia, who labored to great advantage among the slaves. Wright "set up two or three schools among them, where they attend on Sundays, before and after sermon, for they have no other leisure time."[39] The slaves in that county received the books with the same degree of pleasure as those under Davies' care. By July 14, 1756, Davies could write:

> I had the pleasure of seeing the table of the Lord adorned with about forty-four black faces. Indeed, my principal encouragement of late has been among the poor negro slaves. A considerable number of them give good evidences of sincere conversion to Christianity; and in the land of their slavery, they have been brought into the glorious liberty of the sons of God. But alas! notwithstanding these promising appearances, an incorrigible stupidity generally prevails through this guilty land.[40]

A Plan for Indigenous African Missionaries

In addition to educating the African slaves through Christian literature, Crutenden envisioned the education of three or four of the choicest converts at the College of New Jersey to become missionaries to their own native country. Preferably, he hoped to find some slaves who were still young; eighteen to twenty years of age; who retained their native language; who had warm hearts; and, who were not afraid of the dangers. Inability to speak the language and a lack of familiarity with the customs, Crutenden believed, had prevented previous efforts to evangelize

---

[38] Ibid.
[39] Ibid., 505.
[40] Ibid., 506.

the dark continent[41] with the gospel. As such, Crutenden's plan was ahead of his time in one sense, but thoroughly scriptural. He envisioned Christianizing Africa through the education and training of indigenous pastors who would be steeped in the customs and culture of the people as well as fluent in their language. That is the biblical model of missions rather than the colonial model which has dominated most world mission efforts for the last two centuries. A scheme of this design was sent to Davies for his approval and communication to the other ministers in Virginia, but it is unknown what decision was made concerning it.

The missionary duties of Christians to heathens, especially African slaves, were the subject of Davies' sermon from Genesis 18:19, "The Duty of Christians to Propagate Their religion Among the Heathens, Earnestly recommended to the Masters of Negro Slaves in Virginia." He began this message with the assertion that the immortality of the soul is the great reason to evangelize every creature under heaven:

> A creature formed for *Immortality*, and that must be happy or miserable through an *everlasting* Duration is certainly a Being of vast Importance, however mean and insignificant he may be in other Respects. His Immortality gives him a kind of *infinite* Value. Let him be white or black, bond or free, a Native or a Foreigner, it is of no Moment in this View: he is to live *forever*! to be forever *happy* or forever *miserable*! Happy or Miserable in the *highest* degree! . . . In this View, the Crowds of neglected Negroe Slaves among us, have often appeared to me as Creatures of the utmost Importance. The *same* Immortality is entailed upon them, as upon us. They are Candidates for the *same* eternal State with us, and bound for the *same* Heaven or Hell.[42]

Later in this sermon, Davies held forth Abraham as an example of how every head of household is to care for those in his family, including slaves. He reasoned that Christianity is a universal religion and the Abrahamic covenant extends to Africans as well as Britons while making the following application to the masters of slaves:

> I am sure, such of you as are Lovers of Christ, begin already to feel the Force of this Argument. Did he live and die, to save poor Negroes? And

---

[41] Ibid.
[42] Samuel Davies, *The Duty of Christians to Propagate Their Religion Among the Heathens, Earnestly recommended to the Masters of Negro Slaves in Virginia* (London: J. Oliver, 1758), 7.

shall we not use all Means in our Power, to make them Partakers of this Salvation? Did he pour out the Blood of his Heart for them? And shall we begrudge a little Labour and Pains to instruct them? We are not called to agonize and die upon a Cross for them: but Jesus was; and He did not refuse. And shall we refuse those easier Endeavours for their Salvation, which are required on our part? If we are capable of such a Conduct, it is high Time for us to renounce all Pretensions of Regard to him, and his Example.[43]

Evangelization of the Slaves by Others in Virginia

Robert Henry, who served the congregations of Cub Creek and Briery, was also very successful in evangelizing the slaves. "He delighted in preaching to the negroes, and as the fruit of his labours, had nearly a hundred communicants at Cub Creek alone."[44] The effect of Henry's work was still evident when Archibald Alexander commenced his labors at Cub Creek some years later. More than seventy slaves sat under Alexander's ministry with twenty-five belonging to a Mrs. Coles on Staunton River.[45] Yet, Alexander stated that "their habit of indulging their feelings, by shouting, and their desire to have such feelings roused, presented an effectual bar to regular instruction."[46]

The conversions of slaves through Davies' ministry produced lasting results. Two brothers named "Will and Ned. . .who belonged to Col. Thomas Read of Charlotte. . .were eminent for piety."[47] Both men came to this country in their boyhood and were taught to read by Davies. "Will adhered to the Presbyterian Church. . .but Ned went over to the Baptists and became a preacher."[48] Another slave was Old Harry, owned by Ben Allen of Cumberland, who, in the words of Alexander, "was one of the most fervently devout men I ever met with."[49] Old Harry, who received a Bible from Davies in 1756, came to America as a grown man and spoke broken English, but "his soul appeared to be all on fire with love

---

[43] Ibid., 18.
[44] James Waddell Alexander, *The Life of Archibald Alexander, D.D.* (New York: Charles Scribner, 1854), 526.
[45] Ibid.
[46] Ibid.
[47] Ibid., 525.
[48] Ibid.
[49] Ibid.

to Jesus."[50] John Holt Rice gave the following account of other slaves who were converted:

> There is now a considerable congregation of their descendants at Polegreen, a church in Hanover, at present under the pastoral care of the Rev. John D. Blair. But many of the members of Davies' church belonged to the estate of Col. Byrd. These were sold, and several of them taken to the county of Charlotte. The writer has seen some of the survivors who could read well, and knew perfectly the Assembly's Catechism.[51]

Davies' letters to Crutenden passed through the hands of John Wesley who recorded parts of them in his journal. Wesley was in some measure responsible for the books which were sent to Virginia and Davies acknowledged this fact in a letter to him on January 28, 1757. He expressed his sincere love for the Wesleys in this same letter and the work which God prospered through them. He also gave Wesley a report of his labors among the slaves. Some of the blacks had evidenced, as he said, "the art to dissemble", but Davies had no doubt "the generality of them. . . [were] real Christians."[52]

Another supply of books and Bibles came from the Society in Glasgow, Scotland sometime in January of 1757. Davies wrote to Gillies and thanked him and the Society "for their liberal and well-chosen benefaction."[53] William Richardson, a ministerial student who was then living with Davies, assisted him in distributing this new supply of books to both the slaves and the poor whites.

Davies again wrote Crutenden on February 7, 1757, thanking him for his part in securing this latest gift of books which he said, "dissolved me into a flood of grateful tears, and has sent me more than once to return my thanks to Him who is the *Origin* of all that good, of which his creatures, in the height of their benevolence, are but *subordinate* instruments."[54] In the hope that the Society in London had some additional

---

[50] Ibid.
[51] John Holt Rice, "Memoir of the Rev. Samuel Davies," *The Virginia Evangelical and Literary Magazine*, Volume I (1819), 203.
[52] John Emory, editor, *The Works of the Rev. John Wesley, A. M.*, Volume III (New York: Carlton and Porter, 1856), 392.
[53] Gillies and Bonar, *Historical Collections*, 521.
[54] Samuel Davies, *Letters from the Rev. Samuel Davies, etc., Shewing the State of Religion in Virginia, Particularly Among the Negroes* (London: R. Pardon, 1757), 23.

funds for further gifts, he pointed out the former collections had been deficient in Watts' *Catechisms* and spelling books. Both of these books were especially useful in the instruction of the African slaves. In this same letter, Davies expressed hope that through a gift of spelling books many slaves and their posterity could be taught to read "with little trouble to their Masters."[55] Davies believed, "a taste for intellectual improvement would circulate among them; and they would unavoidably come to *know* something of Christianity, which is the first step towards *embracing* it."[56] Aware that most good plans are opposed in this world of sin, he was still confident that the four or five hundred slaves who were members of his congregation would be encouraged in this learning.

Davies also wrote to Joseph Forfitt of London with further news of the progress among the slaves on the same day he wrote Crutenden. About sixty slaves received their first communion at the last communion service and other slaves were catechumens for baptism. Yet, he feared the work had declined over the past few months because there were fewer converts coming to him than previously. Nevertheless, "multitudes [were] as *eager to learn* as before: Some, from a pious thirst after Christian knowledge; some, from curiosity; and, some from ambition."[57] What was most astonishing was the progress that multitudes of them made "with little leisure or assistance."[58]

An instance of the conversion of one of Davies' domestic slaves was given in this letter to Forfitt. The man in question was above forty years of age when he entered into service for Davies and had never learned to read. Davies described him as "a very *stupid, lubberly fellow* in appearance, and but very imperfectly acquainted with our language."[59] Davies despaired of his capacity to learn and intended to teach him the Christian faith in the best manner he could. The slave somehow was excited to study. He soon made so much progress that he could spell and was ready to learn to read before Davies was aware of it. Shortly afterwards, he could read English almost as well as he could speak it. His religion is given in the words of Davies:

---

[55] Ibid., 24.
[56] Ibid.
[57] Ibid., 28.
[58] Ibid.
[59] Ibid.

He can give but a very broken account of his Religion in *Words*, but when I look to his *Life*, there I can see the Christian. He is a faithful servant, and generally inoffensive to all. He has been sometimes overheard in *Secret Prayer*, perhaps for half an hour, or more, when it has been past midnight, and he supposed the rest of the family were in their beds.[60]

The difficulty of properly judging the spiritual experiences of these slaves was one of the hardest tasks Davies performed. Some slaves had the notion that merely being baptized would make them true Christians in an instant. Others were ignorantly seeking after some experience which they did not understand. Still others sought baptism as a fashionable duty. The wisdom of Davies in this matter is given as follows:

> Many such converse with me, whom I am obliged to exclude from that Ordinance. In general, I make their temper and conduct, rather than their speculative notions, the standard of my judgment concerning them; and when I can discover the Feeling, and Practice of a *Christian*, I think them proper members of a *Christian Church*, although they should be very ignorant of many of its important doctrines.[61]

Davies was confident many of the slaves were true sons of Abraham. As he wrote:

> Some of them are, indeed, astonishing monuments of divine Grace. There are ten of them in one quarter (so we call the little houses where the Negroes dwell) who, I have reason to hope, are all, or at least, nine in ten, sincerely and zealously engaged in the doctrines and duties of our holy Religion. This, indeed, is an instance, which, I am afraid, can hardly be paralleled, among either white or black, in these Parts.[62]

Sometime in 1757, Davies wrote Joseph Bellamy with the following information:

> What little success I have had, has been chiefly among the extremes of gentlemen and negroes. Indeed; God has been remarkably working among the latter. I have baptized about one hundred and fifty adults; and at the last sacramental solemnity, I had the pleasure of seeing the table

---

[60] Gillies and Bonar, *Historical Collections*, 529.
[61] Davies, *Letters from the Rev. Samuel Davies, etc., Shewing the State of Religion in Virginia, Particularly Among the Negroes*, 31.
[62] Ibid.

graced with about sixty black faces. They generally behave well, as far as I can hear, though there are some instances of apostacy among them[63]

Therefore, Davies warned the slaves not to confuse the ceremony of baptism with the reality of grace or to use church membership as an attempt to gain social equality with the whites:

> You will say perhaps, "other negroes are baptized; and why not I?" But, consider, some other negroes have been in great trouble about their souls; their hearts have been broken for sin; they have accepted Christ as their only saviour; and are Christians indeed: and when you are such, it will be time enough for you to be baptized.[64]

Davies, like Whitefield, was himself a slaveholder throughout his ministry in Hanover and never printed anything encouraging their emancipation. He, like most ministers of his day, held that Christianity did not abolish the system of slavery. "There never was a good Christian yet, who was a bad Servant,"[65] declared Davies. And again, he said, "A Christian may be happy, even in a State of Slavery."[66] Yet, Davies did have an unresolved dispute with two of his elders over slavery, and it must be assumed that he opposed the system which prevailed in the Colonies.

Some of those who were intimately associated with Davies were in later years outspoken critics of the institution of slavery. David Rice, whose father was one of Davies' elders at Hanover, delivered a speech to the Kentucky Convention in 1792, "Slavery Inconsistent with Justice and Good Policy," in which he stated that no legislature on earth had the right to enslave any human. That Convention was called to adopt the Constitution for Kentucky, and Rice spoke in favor of a motion on the floor to prohibit slavery throughout that commonwealth. Rice enforced his support of the motion with the following words:

> As creatures of God we are, with respect to liberty, all equal. If one has a right to live among his fellow creatures, and enjoy his freedom, so has another; if one has a right to enjoy that property he acquires by an honest

---

[63] Charles C. Jones, "Review of 'The Religious Instruction of the Negroes in the United States,'" *The Biblical Repertory and Princeton Review*, Volume XV (1843), 28.
[64] Samuel Davies, *Sermons on Important Subjects*, III (London: W. Baynes and Son, 1824), 418.
[65] Samuel Davies, *Duty of Christians to Propagate Their Religion Among the Heathens*, 28.
[66] Ibid., 20.

industry, so has another. If I, by force, take that from another, which he has a just right to, according to the law of nature, (which is a divine law) which he has never relinquished his claim, I am certainly guilty of injustice and robbery; and when the thing taken is the man's liberty, when it is himself, it is the greatest injustice.[67]

There are parts of Rice's speech that are reminiscent of Davies' sermon on the duty of Christians to propagate the Christian religion among the heathen. Rice would have been in his early twenties when he heard that message which, undoubtedly, helped shape his own ideas on the subject. Likewise, Davies would have been proud of the way his former church member and theological student acquitted himself in that most important speech.

Henry Patillo acknowledged several years after Davies' death that slavery was so entrenched in America that only God could uproot it. As he said, "The subject of manumission will greatly injure our interest as a church. I once touched upon it with caution: it offended some, & pleased none; tho' I mentioned it as a very distant object."[68] With prophetic insight, he declared: "This is an event, that all the wisdom of America seems at present unequal to: but which divine providence will accomplish in due time."[69] It is very likely that Rice and Patillo were influenced in their thinking by Davies.

Conclusion

The evangelization of the African slaves by Davies and others was an important first step towards their eventual manumission. Slavery made slave-owners insensible to the immortality of their slaves. They treated them as lower than animals, according to Whitefield's observation. For that reason, Davies first emphasized that slaves are creatures of God also and they have souls that will never die.

The evangelization of the African slaves had another good effect. Many of them were introduced into the enjoyment of a freedom which no power on earth could either grant them or deny them—the freedom

---

[67] David Rice, *Slavery Inconsistent with Justice and Good Policy* (New York: Samuel Wood, 1812), 6.
[68] Henry Patillo to William Williamson, December 4, 1799, MS in Sahne Collection, Presbyterian Historical Society, Philadelphia, PA.
[69] Henry Patillo, *The Plain Planter's Family Assistant* (Washington, NC: James Adams, 1787), 23.

of being children of the living God. That fact is not an excuse for slavery or a justification of the evils associated with that institution, but it is an important observation to make about the various missions to the slaves—especially the work of Davies among them.

-17-

Virginia's Danger and Remedy

"That if these unusual commotions and appearances are *intended* by divine Providence to be *premonitions* and *signs* of some grand and interesting revolutions among mankind, they would *miss* their end entirely upon us, unless we should regard them in that view; and we should be guilty of hardening ourselves against warnings kindly given us from heaven."[1]
~Samuel Davies in "Signs of the Times"~

Lisbon, Portugal in ruins from 1755 earthquake

---

[1] *Sermons by the Rev. Samuel Davies*, Vol. 3 (Morgan, Pennsylvania: Soli Deo Gloria Publications, 1995), 169-70.

Virginia's Danger and Remedy

On Saturday, November 1, 1755, there was a terrible earthquake in Lisbon, Portugal, which deeply affected Davies when he learned of it and impacted his preaching for much of 1756. Many citizens of Lisbon were gathering for worship on All Saints Day, when a devastating earthquake, with an estimated magnitude of 8.5 to 9.0, rocked their city. The first shock from this quake hit at 9:40a.m., with tremors being felt throughout Europe and Northern Africa. Chandeliers in Hamburg, Germany, began swinging back and forth; bodies of water from the Italian lakes to Scandinavia and Scotland, heaved and roared; tsunamis rocked all the ports along the coast of Portugal and Spain; seiches[2] were set off in the Atlantic Ocean as far as 1,500 miles from Lisbon; and, the effects of this turbulence reached to Martinique and Barbados in the West Indies. The death toll has been estimated from 60,000–90,000.

Rev. Charles Davy, a Church of England minister, was writing a letter in his Lisbon apartment when the quake struck. According to his eyewitness account:

> There never was a finer morning than the 1st of November; the sun shone out in its full luster; the whole face of the sky was perfectly serene and clear.[3]

Then, Davy's writing table suddenly began to gently shake until the whole building rattled from its foundations. Davy hesitated momentarily, not knowing if it was better to remain inside or to hurry out to the streets where the danger seemed just as great. The upper stories of his building began to fall which forced Davy to run out of his first story apartment as fast as he could. Large stones and rafter beams were falling all around him; the formerly serene sky was now ominously gloomy; great clouds of dust and lime rose up from the crashing buildings and nearly choked him as he ran away. Multitudes fell to their knees in the streets and began to pray as they feared for their lives. A general outcry began, "The sea is coming in; we shall be all lost." Davy saw a large body of water rising up as a mountain from the mouth of the Tagus River and crashing on the city. People began frantically running for their lives.

---

[2] A sudden fluctuation of water levels in a lake or inland sea.
[3] Eva March Tappan, ed., *The World's Story: A History of the World in Story, Song and Art*, 14 Volumes, Volume V: Italy, France, Spain, and Portugal (Boston: Houghton Mifflin, 1914), 618–628.

One large marble building fell on all those who had retreated there for safety, killing them all. Others were swept out into the ocean to their deaths. The "once flourishing, opulent, and populous city" was now "a scene of the utmost horror and desolation."[4]

Earthquake Tremors in North America

The Lisbon earthquake was followed seventeen days later by a tremor in North America at Cape Ann, north of Boston, estimated to have been 6.0 in magnitude. The effects of this earthquake were felt from Halifax, Nova Scotia, to Lake Champlain and as far south as South Carolina. The first tremor began at 4:30a.m. and lasted only a few minutes. It was followed by another tremor at 5:45a.m. Contemporary accounts estimated that 1,500 chimneys in Boston alone were either cracked or destroyed by the quake. The damage was far less than what Lisbon endured, but pastors in Boston soon conducted prayer services and fast days were proclaimed.

Jeremiah Newland (1731–?) of Massachusetts wrote a poem about the Cape Ann earthquake in which he opined, "Thy terrible hand is on the land, by bloody war and death; it is because we broke Thy laws, that Thou didst shake the earth."[5] Newland's view was shared by pastors and Christians throughout America. Thomas Prince, co-pastor at the Old South Church in Boston, preached several sermons which attributed the earthquake to the providential hand of God. Eliphalet Williams preached a sermon, "The Duty of People under Dark Providences," to his East Hartford, Connecticut congregation just ten days after the earthquake. The premise of Williams' sermon was that such dark providences were a warning to God's people to prepare to meet their God. Even Charles Chauncy (1705–1787), no friend of the revival or revivalists, attributed the cause of the late earthquakes to the anger of God. Chauncy was pastor at the First Church (Congregational) in Boston and was considered in those days to be a moderate or liberal in his theology. His opposition to the emotionalism of revival preachers such as George Whitefield[6] came very close to denying subjective grace and the need for regeneration by the Holy Spirit.

---

[4] Ibid.
[5] Jeremiah Newland, *Verses Occasioned by the Earthquakes in November, 1755* (Boston: 1755).
[6] Chauncy wrote *Seasonable Thoughts on the State of Religion in New England* in 1743 to counter the Great Awakening. He was one of the foremost opponents of that marvelous revival.

Yet, there was another voice, the voice of the famous French deist, Francois-Marie Arouet (1694–1778), known commonly as Voltaire, who expressed his views about this earthquake in a poem:

> Will you say, "This is the result of eternal laws
> Directing the acts of a free and good God!"
> Did Lisbon, which is no more, have more vices
> Than London and Paris immersed in her pleasures?
> Lisbon is destroyed, and they dance in Paris![7]

Voltaire denied that God was involved in such matters as earthquakes and, especially, denied that they are evidences of His wrath against sin. Immanuel Kant (1724–1804), the German philosopher, also sought to explain the Lisbon earthquake by natural causes. In many ways, that deistic approach to earthquakes and other acts of nature has prevailed in the modern world so that there is a practical atheism in denying God's providential governance of this world. It was such practical atheism that Davies saw as Virginia's greatest danger in 1756. Indeed, he preached a sermon on April 4, 1756, from Zephaniah 1:12 at Hanover, "Practical Atheism, in Denying the Agency of Divine Providence, Exposed," in which he stated:

> Whoever takes a review of the state of our country, for about two years past, or observes its present posture, must be sensible, that matters have gone very ill with us, and that they still bear a threatening aspect. If our country be entirely under the management of blind chance, according to the uncomfortable doctrines of Atheists and Epicureans, alas! we have reason to be alarmed; for the wheel of fortune has begun to turn against us. If all our affairs be entirely dependent upon natural causes, and wholly subject to the power and pleasure of mortals, it is time for us to tremble; for the arm of flesh has been against us. But if our land be a little province of Jehovah's empire; if all natural causes be actuated, directed, and overruled by his superintending providence; if all our affairs be under his sovereign management, and all our calamities, private and public, be the chastisements of his hand—if, I say, this be the case in fact, as every man believes and wishes, then it is high time for us to acknowledge it.[8]

---

[7] http://www.christianity.com/church/church-history/timeline/1701-1800/sermons-from-the-lisbon-earthquake-11630263.html, accessed on July 17, 2016.
[8] Samuel Davies, *Sermons on Important Subjects*, Volume IV (London: W. Baynes and Son, 1824), 204–5.

This practical atheism in denying that God is in control of even the elements of nature (except in the general sense of instituting the laws of nature) leaves people without any hope when bad circumstances descend on them. The only comfort we can have in the midst of trials is that God is able to deliver us out of them.

Davies probably became aware of the Lisbon earthquake through the *Virginia Gazette* sometime in early 1756.[9] His first known reference to this earthquake was on June 19, 1756, in a sermon from Isaiah 24:18-20, "The Religious Improvement of the Late Earthquakes," which was preached at one of the meetinghouses in Hanover County. He connected the two earthquakes in Lisbon and Cape Ann in the following way:

> Nay, the tremor has reached our continent, and has been very sensibly felt in Boston, and other parts of New England. Though much mischief has not been done in those parts, yet a loud warning has been given; and, oh! That it may not be given in vain. It would certainly be an instance of inexcusable stupidity for us to take notice of so dreadful a dispensation. Such devastations are at once *judgments* upon the places where they happen, and *warnings* to others.[10]

Davies described Portugal in another part of this sermon as "overrun with all the idolatry and ignorance, vice and barbarity of heathenism. . . They are either superstitious heathens or deluded Mahometans, and the knowledge of God is not to be found among them."[11] The impenitence of that part of the Old World was no consolation to Virginians, in Davies' opinion, because:

> Many parts of our country are languishing under the effects of a severe drought; and the French and Indians are invading our territories, and murdering our fellow-subjects: but what has God to do in all this? We will fight it out with them ourselves, flesh with flesh; and let him look on as an idle spectator. Horrid language, indeed! And, perhaps, the most au-

---

[9] The earliest account of this earthquake in the Pennsylvania Gazette was January 8, 1756. The news probably reached Virginia shortly thereafter with full accounts being printed in later editions of the newspaper.
[10] Davies, *Sermons on Important Subjects*, IV, 92. It is possible that Davies made some passing reference to the Lisbon earthquake in a sermon that has not been printed, but this sermon gives such a full picture of the quake that it was likely his first occasion to mention it.
[11] Ibid., 98–99.

dacious sinner among us would not venture to express it with his lips. But, what say the inward temper—what says the practice of our countrymen?[12]

The drought to which Davies alludes had started before 1756, but by that year it was general throughout the colony with the ruin of the main cash crop, tobacco, by the dreaded tobacco fly—a voracious enemy that can lay utter waste to tobacco fields. Droughts, wars, sicknesses, and earthquakes on the American continent were a loud call to repentance. The convergence of all these events made 1756 a year in which Davies was anxious for a revival like the one he had witnessed in his youth.

Davies believed Christians in the colonies were without excuse for their practical atheism in denying God's hand in the acts of nature. His melancholy observation was that such calamities alone could never produce revivals or conversions. "The Religious Improvement of the Late Earthquakes" was just one of several sermons he preached throughout 1756 in which he endeavored to arouse the colony to repentance and reformation:

> My brethren, I must speak to you without reserve: the general impenitence of our inhabitants, under all the providences of God to bring them to repentance, is by far the most discouraging symptom to me; much more so than our divided counsels, our routed armies, and our blasted schemes; indeed, I look upon it as the cause of all these. May I then hope to be heard, at least in the little circle of my own congregation, when, as an advocate for your country, I call you to repentance? O sirs, you have carried the matter far enough; you have trifled with your God, and delayed your reformation long enough; therefore from this moment commence humble penitents, and let your country and your souls suffer no more by your wilful wickedness. Whenever you recollect our past calamities, or whenever you meet with the like in time to come, immediately prostrate yourselves before the Lord; plead guilty, guilty: bewail your own sins: and bewail and mourn over the sins of the land. If even all this congregation should be enabled, by divine grace, to take this method, they might, in the sight of God, obtain the glorious character of *deliverers of their country*.[13]

---

[12] Ibid., 211.
[13] Ibid., 225.

Calls to Faith and Repentance

This practical impenitence compelled Davies to issue forth calls for repentance from the pulpit. In administering the Lord's Supper to his congregation in Hanover on July 11, 1756, he stressed the importance of repentance and faith. His sermon on that occasion was from Isaiah 53:10,11, "The Sufferings of Christ and Their Consequent Joys and Blessings." He expressed his hope that just as this passage from Isaiah was the means of the conversion of the Ethiopian eunuch and the penitent Earl of Rochester, so Christ would witness the conversion of many of the residents of Hanover. He used this sacramental sermon to call Hanover and Virginia to repentance unto life that they so greatly needed at this time, with such words as these:

> You cannot rebel against the crucified Jesus with impunity, for he is not now dying on the cross, or lying senseless in the grave. He lives! he lives to avenge the affront. He lives forever, to punish you for ever. He shall prolong his days to prolong your torment. Therefore, you have no alternative, but to submit to him or perish.[14]

Later in the summer, Davies preached the funeral sermons of two members of his congregation within a period of about eleven days. They were probably the first church members to die from the unusual sickness which suddenly swept through Virginia that year. The first funeral sermon, "Saints Saved with Difficulty, and the Certain Perdition of Sinners," was preached on August 21, 1756. The message was from 1 Peter 4:18, at the request of the deceased, Mr. James Hooper, whom Davies stated "knew so much from the trials he made in life, that if he should be saved, it would be with great difficulty, and if he should escape destruction at all, it would be a very narrow escape."[15] The other sermon, "Life and Immortality Revealed in the Gospel" was preached eleven days later on September 1 at the funeral of a young man, William Yuille, who died in the prime of life. After escaping dangers by sea and land, Yuille did not appear to be a candidate for a premature death. Davies used this fact as an instance to call other young people to repentance:

---

[14] Samuel Davies, *Sermons on Important Subjects*, Volume II (London: W. Baynes and Son, 1824), 150.
[15] Ibid., 57.

> Come to his grave, ye young and gay, ye lively and strong, ye men of business and hurry, come and learn what now may, and shortly must, be your doom. Thus shall your purpose be broken off, your schemes vanish like smoke, and all your hopes from this world perish. Death perpetually lurks in ambush for you, ready every moment to spring upon his prey.[16]

A Season of Unusual Sickness

An unexpected and unusual sickness shortly thereafter swept through Virginia with more than twenty of Davies' church members perishing in the span of a few days. Some whole families were swept away by this sickness. Davies himself was close to death at one point during the month of September. Thus, Thursday, October 21, 1756, was set aside by the elders for a congregational fast in Hanover on account of this raging sickness which was then at its height. Henry Patillo recorded that same day that he had "heard of the death of 7 or 8 persons within a few miles, and others expected to follow every hour, while some are just infected."[17] Some citizens of Hanover ignored the gravity of the circumstances, but Patillo observed that there was a fear "too deeply painted in most Faces not to be easily discerned."[18]

When Davies recovered from his own sickness, he immediately preached a sermon on October 2, 1756, from John 3:16, "The Method of Salvation through Jesus Christ" which he introduced with the following remarks:

> I have been solicitously thinking in what way my life, redeemed from the grave, may be of most service to my dear people. And I would collect all the feeble remains of my strength into one vigorous effort this day to promote this benevolent end. If I knew what subject has the most direct tendency to save your souls, that is the subject to which my heart would cling with peculiar endearment, and which I would make the matter of the present discourse. And when I consider I am speaking to an assembly of sinners, guilty, depraved, helpless creatures, and that if ever you are saved it will be only through Jesus Christ, in that way which the gospel reveals; when I consider that your everlasting life turns on this hinge, viz., the reception you give to this Saviour, and this way of salvation; when I

---

[16] Ibid., 179.
[17] Manuscript Journal in the Patillo Papers, Special Collections, William Smith Morton Library, Union Presbyterian Seminary, Richmond, VA.
[18] Ibid.

consider these things, I can think of no subject more suitable for recommending the Lord Jesus to your acceptance, and to explain and inculcate the method of salvation through his mediation.[19]

Davies' first point, "Without Christ, all are in a perishing condition," was a poignant reminder of this dangerous sickness which recently ravaged Hanover. He directed his hearers to consider the desperate sickness of their souls by nature and their hopeless condition without the gospel. The sermon was a model for strength and simplicity in presenting the truths of the method of salvation. Davies informed his congregation on November 14, 1756[20] about the effects of this sickness on his own family in another sermon, "A Time of Unusual Sickness and Mortality Improved," from Jeremiah 5:3:

> I would speak with more seriousness than, alas! is usual to me, to you mortals, about the great concerns of immortality! If I would do anything to save myself and them that hear me, I see I must do it quickly. I have for some time been languishing and indisposed myself, and the contagious disease made its entrance into my family; but, through the amazing and distinguishing kindness of God, which I desire publicly to celebrate, and, I hope, in answer to prayer, its progress has been stopped. And what better return can I make to my gracious Deliverer, than to devote that life, which he has spared, to his glory, and the service of your souls, with increasing zeal and industry. . . I am more sensible than usual that I must work while the day of life lasts: for, oh! it is short and uncertain; and the night of death is coming, when I cannot work.[21]

The Urgency to Save Souls

Portions of three letters Davies wrote to Thomas Gibbons of London are evidently from this same time period in 1756 when he was under this unusual sickness.[22] They all express the sense of urgency he felt to labor for the good of souls while there was time and opportunity. In the first letter, Davies stated:

---

[19] Samuel Davies, *Sermons on Important Subjects*, Vol. I (New York: J & J Harper, 1828), 75–6.
[20] Samuel Davies, *Sermons on Important Subjects*, Vol. IV (London: W. Baynes and Son, 1824), 61–2.
[21] Ibid.
[22] The extracts of these letters are undated, but their similarity in spirit with the above quote is reason for quoting them at this place.

I desire earnestly to devote to God and my dear country, all the labours of my head, my heart, my hand, and my pen; and if he pleases to bless any of them, I hope I shall be thankful, and wonder at his condescending grace.—Oh! my dear brother, could we spend and be spent all our lives in painful, disinterested, indefatigable service for God and the world, how serene and bright would it render the swift approaching eve of life! I am labouring to do a little to save my country, and which is of much more consequence, to save souls—from death—from that tremendous kind of death, which a *soul* can die. I have but little success of late, but blessed be God, it surpasses my expectation, and much more my desert. Some of my brethren labour to better purpose. The pleasure of the Lord prospers in their hands.[23]

An extract from a different letter to Gibbons revealed Davies' struggles with personal holiness and the difficulties he felt of preaching "in the sight of God":

As for myself, I am just striving not to live in vain. I entered the ministry with such a sense of my unfitness for it, that I had no sanguine expectations of success. And a condescending God (O how condescending!) has made me much more serviceable than I could hope. But, alas! My advancements in holiness are extremely small; I feel what I confess, and am sure it is true, and not the rant of excessive or affected humility. It is an easy thing to make a noise in the world, to flourish and harangue, *to dazzle the crowd, and set them all agape,* but deeply to imbibe the spirit of Christianity, to maintain a secret walk with God, to be holy as he is holy, this is the labor, this is the work. I beg the assistance of your prayers in so grand and important an enterprise. — The difficulty of the ministerial work seems to grow upon my hands. Perhaps once in three or four months I preach in some measure as I could wish; that is, I preach as in the sight of God, and as if I were to step from the pulpit to the supreme tribunal. I *feel* my subject. I melt into tears, or I shudder with horror, when I denounce the terrors of the Lord. I glow, I soar in sacred ecstasies, when the love of Jesus is my theme, and, as Mr. Baxter was wont to express it, in lines more striking to me than all the fine poetry in the world, "I preach as if I ne'er should preach again; And as a dying man to dying men." But, alas! My spirits soon flag, my devotions languish, and my zeal cools. It is really an afflictive thought, that I serve so good a Master with so

---

[23] Thomas Gibbons, "Divine Conduct Vindicated," in Davies, *Sermons on Important Subjects*, I, 35.

much inconstancy; but so it is, and my soul mourns upon that account.[24]

Davies again lamented his deficiency of holiness in the third letter to Gibbons:

> I am labouring to do a little good in the world. But, alas! I find I am of little use or importance. I have many defects, but none gives me so much pain and mortification as my slow progress in personal holiness. This is the grand qualification of the office we sustain, as well as for that heaven we hope for, and I am shocked at myself when I see how little I have of it.[25]

Davies undoubtedly truly felt he was deficient in personal holiness which sense was probably heightened as a result of his late sickness. His laments in these letters to Gibbons were not the result of excessive or feigned humility. Rather, his consciousness of sin contributed to his renowned holiness. Others who observed him saw someone that panted for God like the deer pants for the stream. He saw the enormous blemishes of his character. This vision compelled him to diligently pursue after holiness "without which no man can see the Lord" (Hebrews 12:14). His expressions of failure reveal the eminence of his holy character. His recent sickness compelled him to renew his vows and labor more sincerely for the conversion of sinners. He was frequently permitted to feel his subject, to deliver it with soaring pathos, and to melt into tears. Yet, he mourned the sinfulness which prohibited him from regularly experiencing such unction of the Spirit. Both his failures and his successes drove him to humble himself before God and to depend more and more on Christ. The words of J. C. Ryle about the relationship of a consciousness of sin and holiness shed light on this matter:

> He that wishes to attain right views about Christian holiness, must begin by examining the vast and solemn subject of sin. He must dig down low if he would build high.[26]

Davies, like all eminently holy ministers, was keenly aware of his deep depravity because he was digging down deep in order to build

---

[24] Ibid.
[25] Ibid.
[26] J. C. Ryle, *Holiness: Its Nature, Hindrances, Difficulties, and Roots* (Cambridge and London: James Clarke & Co., LTD.,1956), 1.

high. The same expressions of sinfulness have been made by such great saints as Robert Murray McCheyne, George Whitefield, Charles Spurgeon, Jonathan Edwards, and others. Davies lived in the presence of a lofty and exalted God and that vision, like Isaiah's in the sixth chapter of his prophecy, revealed him to be a man of unclean lips.

A Season of Spiritual Darkness over America

During his own sickness, Davies received letters from four ministers who lived in various parts of America and Great Britain. Each of them informed him of the general declension of Christianity in their regions. He shared these parts of those letters with his congregation in one of the sermons[27] he preached after this plague of sickness in Virginia. One of those correspondents was Joseph Bellamy of Connecticut who reported the sanguine news to him of the spiritual condition of New England:

> A dark cloud seems to be gathering over a sinful land. We have had a day of great grace—that is past and gone, and a day of great wrath seems to be at hand! Our northern army is sickly and likely to do nothing—our treasury is exhausted—people's spirits low—great *murmurings*, but no *reformation*. For all these things we feel and fear we do not return to the Lord.[28]

Bellamy's mention of the "northern army" which was "likely to do nothing" was a reference to the conflict with the French and Indians which was then troubling the colonies. Wars, exhausted treasuries, and a general depression among the people were still not enough to excite the colonists to repentance.

Another correspondent, John Blair, who had preached in Virginia in the 1740s prior to Davies' arrival, wrote him to the same effect as Bellamy:

> Alas! I have not enjoyed the sweet supports of success in my ministry! Under all this heavy scene of judgment, our people are manifestly more and more hardened; and that, notwithstanding a gracious God has stooped to assist me remarkably in preaching, frequently this summer. A dreadful omen this![29]

---

[27] Davies, *Sermons on Important Subjects*, IV, 68.
[28] Ibid.
[29] Ibid.

One of the Erskines of Scotland wrote to Davies about the slumbering spirit of that nation as follows:

> I hear of no such thing as a revival of religion in Scotland: a spirit of deep slumber seems to have seized us.[30]

Another correspondent, Rev. John Adams of Falkirk, Scotland, whom Davies esteemed to be a "most judicious, pious Minister," wrote further concerning Scotland's insensitivity to the Lord's judgments on the land:

> What is wanting to encourage our hopes is a spirit of repentance and reformation, in this age of distinguished inattention to the works, the word, and the ways of God. Is it not the general case, "Lord, when thy hand is lifted up, they will not see!" How loud are the alarms of which awful providence is sounding in our dull and heavy ears! The Lord's judgments are visibly in the earth; but where does it appear that the inhabitants are learning righteousness. In this country infidelity and immorality of all kinds make the most provoking progress. The cup of our iniquity appears to be brimful, and the cup of God's wrath now ready to be poured out upon the despisers of the riches of his goodness and long-suffering.[31]

These quotes indicate the effects of the Great Awakening were now in declension on both sides of the Atlantic. Davies believed the greatest danger facing his infant country was the practical denial of the agency of God in all her trials. Such practical atheism resulted in indifference towards revival and the salvation of sinners. The plague of sickness was only the most recent manifestation of the Divine displeasure with the impenitence of the Colonies. Therefore, he roused his congregation to labor for a general reformation in order to avert the impending judgment of God.

Wars and Rumors of War

Wars and rumors of wars were another manifestation of God's displeasure with the Colonies in Davies' estimation. Governor Dinwiddie addressed the General Assembly on September 20, 1756, warning that the crisis between the French and the British would soon evidence whether

---

[30] Ibid.
[31] Ibid.

Virginia's Danger and Remedy

or not the colonies would remain under the government of Great Britain. This crisis indicated that Virginia had, in Davies' opinion, "now come to a very dark time—a day of trouble, and rebuke, and blasphemy, and every day seems to grow darker and darker."[32]

Sometime after the Governor's speech[33], Davies preached on "The Signs of the Times."[34] He described the devastation which the Lisbon earthquake had caused and set forth his view that such phenomena are *"intended* by Divine Providence to be *premonitions* and signs of some grand and interesting revolutions among mankind."[35] This view, he contended, even if wrong, would be a profitable mistake because it calls to repentance.

In that message, Davies reminded his hearers that the earthquake was but one in a succession of strange phenomena which seemed to predict some shaking of earthly powers. Others were the modern phenomenon of the Aurora Borealis, the irregular tides at Rhone, France, and Charleston, South Carolina, the severe drought of the past season in Virginia, the strange winter hailstorms in England, and the prediction by Dr. Halley that a comet would appear in 1758. Halley's Comet was calculated by Sir Isaac Newton to be two thousand times hotter than red-hot iron.

The concurrence of several strange phenomena, according to Davies, frequently announced the shaking of earthly kingdoms. He appealed to both sacred and profane history for examples to prove his view, which included the destruction of Jerusalem in A.D. 70, the death of Christ, the captivity of the ten tribes of Israel by Assyria, the fall of the Medo-Persian, Grecian, and Roman empires, the death of Julius Caesar, and the breaking up of the Roman Empire. He reasoned from such examples it was unclear whether America could expect a judgment or a reformation by grace. If the latter, Davies expressed his convictions:

> But, on the other hand, what if the great God be now about to take him his great power and reign? What if the kingdoms of the earth are now

---

[32] Ibid., p. 27.
[33] The date of this sermon cannot be fixed with certainty, but it was sometime in late 1756 because Davies refers to the prediction that Halley's comet would appear in 1758 as being two years away.
[34] His text was Luke 21:10,11, 25, 26.
[35] Davies, *Sermons* on Important Subjects, IV, 2.

about to become the kingdoms of our Lord and of his Christ, and the long-expected period of the conversion of the Jews, and the fulness of the Gentiles, be just come? This would be a grand revolution indeed; and we cannot expect it will be brought about without much blood and desolation. Many thrones must totter and fall; many kingdoms must be overturned, which are now the support of Popery, Mahometanism, and heathenism. In this sense, the gentle Saviour came not to send peace upon earth, but a sword.[36]

Congregational Prayer Societies

Davies organized his congregation into prayer societies during these trials to petition God's mercy and grace. He encouraged each one, individually and corporately, to be prepared for all occurrences. The great need, as he saw matters, was for the pouring out of the Holy Spirit. He was convinced without a revival of practical, spiritually-minded Christianity, things would never be well with the colonies.

One other reference to the Lisbon earthquake was in Davies' sermon on "The Universal Judgment"[37] preached to the Polegreen Church in Hanover in 1756 or 1757. The crowd which gathered beneath the shade of the oak trees outside the church building was estimated at five thousand people. "The opponents of the Dissenters were exasperated at the sight of such crowds listening to the gospel in the deep shades of the forest,"[38] on this and other occasions. In that message, Davies declared that an earthquake is a fit symbol of the cataclysmic events which will introduce the Last Judgment. He described in detail the scenes of that Day with the separation of the sheep and the goats. Referring to those on the left hand of Christ, he said:

> See the astonished thunder-struck multitude on the left hand, with sullen horror, and grief, and despair in their looks, writhing with agony, crying, and wringing their hands, and glancing a wishful eye towards that heaven which they lost; dragged away by devils to the place of execution! See hell expands her voracious jaws, swallows them up! and now an eternal farewell to the earth and all its enjoyments! Farewell to the cheerful light

---

[36] Ibid., 30.
[37] His text was Acts 17:30, 31 and the sermon was probably preached sometime in 1756 or 1757.
[38] William Henry Foote, *Sketches of Virginia: Historical and Biographical*, First Series (Philadelphia: William S. Martien, 1850), 172.

of heaven! Farewell to hope, that sweet relief of affliction.[39]

He then described in equally vivid language the joys of the righteous on the Day of Judgment:

> With what shouts of joy and triumph do they ascend! with what sublime hallelujahs do they crown their Deliverer! with what wonder and joy, with what pleasing horror, like one that has narrowly escaped some tremendous precipice, do they look back upon what they once were! once mean, guilty, depraved, condemned sinners! afterward imperfect, broken-hearted, sighing, weeping saints! but now innocent, holy, happy, glorious immortals![40]

The vivid pictures that Davies drew in this sermon about the Day of Judgment had a great effect on the crowd which gathered in the open air. At the conclusion of his message, an awful solemnity fell over the congregation. Strong men saddled their horses or set out on foot without speaking a word to one another. Women returned to their carriages without engaging in polite conversation. Everyone was absorbed with the message and found no words to express the thoughts of their hearts. Eternity had entered their hearts, either to their conversion or to their condemnation.

Conclusion

The greatest danger for Virginia, in Davies' view, was that they would remain impenitent under the most severe of God's temporal judgments and, thereby, refuse the Lord's offers of free grace. Their remedy was to be ready for every circumstance—earthquakes, droughts, wars, sicknesses, spiritual apathy—and to turn to the Lord afresh in faith. The Scripture teaches in many places that the elements of nature fulfill God's word. For instance, Psalm 148:8 says, "Fire and hail, snow and clouds; stormy wind, fulfilling His word." Jesus said, "Are not two sparrows sold for a cent? And yet not one of them will fall to the ground apart from your Father" (Matthew 10:29). If a sparrow cannot fall to the ground apart from God's will, then the citizens of Lisbon or Boston or Hanover cannot do so either. Yet, if earthquakes, wind, and fire are

---

[39] Davies, *Sermons on Important Subjects*, II, 28.
[40] Ibid.

simply the result of natural causes outside God's special providence, then the Psalmist and Jesus and other Scripture authors are wrong. The sun and rain are dispensed by God on the just and unjust alike, but the Lord often uses the elements of nature to accomplish His purposes and to execute temporal judgments on the world. As Westminster Confession of Faith 5.1 says:

> God, the great Creator of all things, doth uphold, direct, dispose, and govern all creatures, actions, and things, from the greatest even to the least, by his most wise and holy providence, according to his infallible foreknowledge, and the free and immutable counsel of his own will, to the praise of the glory of his wisdom, power, justice, goodness, and mercy.

Thus, we find our only comfort in life and death in the sure knowledge of Christ or Savior. That message was enforced by Davies in his sermons throughout 1756.

-18-

Mission to the Overhill Cherokees

"The Commissioners for Indian Affairs will be glad of this opportunity for the Propagation of the Religion of Jesus among the poor Savages, and it is likely we shall succeed in raising Contributions for that end. And oh! How transporting the Tho't, that these Barbarians may be cultivated by divine Grace in the use of proper Means, and polished into genuine Disciples of the Blessed Jesus!"[1]
~Samuel Davies~

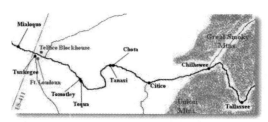

Location of the Cherokee town of Chota
near Fort Loudon, Tennessee

---

[1] George William Pilcher, ed., *The Reverend Samuel Davies Abroad: The Diary of a Journey to England and Scotland, 1753-55* (Urbana, Chicago, London: University of Illinois Press, 1967), 6.

Edward Winslow, who immigrated to America in 1620 aboard the *Mayflower* at the age of twenty-five and later became the third Governor of Plymouth Colony, expressed the sentiments of many of the first settlers to the New World concerning the American Indians:

> [T]he spiritual condition of the savage is itself an argument for Immigration. Every Christian has a duty. . . to spread true religion among the Infidels, and to win many thousands of wandering sheep unto Christ's fold.[2]

For more than a century before Davies was born, there had been great interest in the conversion of the heathen on the part of the Puritan immigrants to America, particularly John Eliot (1604–1690), "the Apostle to the Indians," who labored among the Algonquin tribes in Massachusetts. With the help of his translator, Cockenoe, Eliot translated the Scriptures into the Algonquin language which became the first complete Bible printed in America in 1663. Yet, such missions to these North American 'savages' were very difficult with little success because of their religious ideas as described by Neville Cryer:

> Along with "pow wow" magic and demon sorcery the colonists marvelled at the fanciful myths of the red man, and were left in no doubt that the entire background and philosophy of the Christian religion differed fundamentally from the native beliefs of the Indians. These aboriginal people had little thought of the hereafter and did not base their ethics upon their religion. Moral principles were not sharply defined. Dreams and visions, induced by fasting or drugs, wherein they regularly saw and spoke with individuals known to be dead, were proof enough to the Indians of the existence of a soul and an afterlife.[3]

Nonetheless, the conversion of the heathen in America to Christianity remained a prominent concern of the immigrants from Great Britain and Europe. In the 1740s and 1750s, the labors of David Brainerd, Jonathan Edwards, and Eleazar Wheelock among the Indians motivated Davies to establish a mission to the Overhill Cherokees of North Carolina. Brainerd's great success, in particular, was an inspiration to Davies. Before his death in 1747 at the age of twenty-nine from tuberculosis, the seraphic Brainerd gave vivid accounts in his *Journals* of the conversions among

---

[2] Neville B. Cryer, "John Eliot," in *Five Pioneer Missionaries* (London: The Banner of Truth Trust, 1965), 185.
[3] Ibid., 184.

the Crossweeksung Indians in New Jersey through his ministry. One day, August 8, 1745, stood out more than all others. That was a day of unusual power among them as the presence of the Lord seemed to fall on all age groups. Brainerd recorded for that day:

> Old men and women who had been drunken wretches for many years, and some little children not more than six or seven years of age, appeared in distress for their souls, as well as persons of middle age.[4]

Brainerd's father-in-law, Jonathan Edwards, labored among the Housatonic Indians (a branch of the Mohican tribe) at Stockbridge, Massachusetts, from 1751 to 1757 with little apparent success. Another missionary to the Indians was Eleazar Wheelock (1711–1779), pastor of the Congregational Church at Lebanon, Connecticut. Wheelock began teaching a Latin school in the 1730s but became increasingly convicted of the need to do something for the education of Indian youth. His plan was to take two or three of them from each tribe to be trained as Christian missionaries to take the gospel back to their respective tribes. His Latin school then became Moor's Indian Charity School which was instrumental in the education of a young Mohican, Samson Occum.[5] Occum had become a Christian during the beginning of the Great Awakening at the age of sixteen or seventeen. His description of his conversion is as follows:

> When I was 16 Years of age, we heard a Strange Rumor among the English, that there Were Extraordinary Ministers Preaching from Place to Place and a Strange Concern among the White People. . . But We Saw nothing of these things, till Some Time in the Summer, when Some Ministers began to visit us and Preach the Word of God. . . which it pleased the Lord, as I humbly hope, to Bless and accompany with Divine Influences to the Conviction and Saving Conversion of a Number among us; Amongst Whom, I Was one that was Impresst With the things We had heard.[6]

That awakening among the Mohican Indians would have taken place in 1739 or 1740, since Occum was born in 1723. Prior to this "Strange

---

[4] Ibid., John Thornbury, "David Brainerd," in *Five Pioneer Missionaries*, 47.
[5] His name is also spelled as Occom in various communications about him.
[6] Dick Hoefnagel and Virginia L. Close, "Eleazar's Two Schools," Accessed at: http://www.dartmouth.edu/~library/Library_Bulletin/Nov1999/Hoefnagel_Close.html?mswitch-redir=classic on January 23, 2017.

Rumor," the Mohicans,[7] like other Indians, had exhibited the greatest indifference to the Christian faith, as Occum stated:

> [T]hey Strictly maintained and followed their Heathenish Ways, Customs, & Religion, though there Was some Preaching among them. Once a Fortnight in ye Summer Season, a Minister from New London used to Come up, and the Indians, to attend; not that they regarded the Christian Religion, but they had Blankets given to them every Fall of the Year and for these things, they Would attend. . . and all this Time there Was not one amongst us, that made a Profession of Christianity.[8]

Occum clearly saw that a Divine influence was necessary for the conversion of the lost or else they would remain in their heathenish ways. The Great Awakening was a time when the Spirit of God was poured out on America with great power which resulted in the conversion of all classes of people. Yet, the mission which Davies was undertaking with the Overhill Cherokees was not being initiated in such a favorable time. That fact must be remembered.

The Missionary Society of Hanover Presbytery

In the latter part of the 1750s, Davies persuaded Hanover Presbytery to establish a missionary society for the purpose of evangelizing the American Indians. This society was one of the first founded in the southern colonies and "was the first one 'actually to deploy missionaries among the Indians.'"[9] The need for this mission had been carefully considered by Davies for several years before the society was begun. One of his reasons for undertaking the trip to Great Britain in 1753 was to plead the cause of the Indians before the appropriate missionary agencies in that country. Davies hoped that through a Christian minister the Indians could "be cultivated by divine grace in the use of proper Means, and polished into genuine Disciples of the Blessed Jesus!"[10]

In Great Britain, Davies had solicited contributions "for the Propaga-

---

[7] Mohican is also spelled as Mohegan.
[8] Hoefnagel and Close, "Eleazar's Two Schools," Accessed at: http://www.dartmouth.edu/~library/Library_Bulletin/Nov1999/Hoefnagel_Close.html?mswitch-redir=classic on January 23, 2017.
[9] A. Mark Conard, "The Cherokee Mission of Virginia Presbyterians," *Journal of Presbyterian History*, Vol. 58 (1980), 35.
[10] Pilcher, ed., *Reverend Samuel Davies Abroad*, 6.

tion of the Religion of Jesus among the poor Savages."[11] Davies and Tennent met with the Society in Scotland for Propagating Christian Knowledge (S.S.P.C.K.), "and at their Request, gave them our best Advice about the best Method of conducting the Mission among the Indians."[12] This meeting laid the groundwork for the support that the mission to the Indians in Virginia would receive from this society a few years later.

Rev. William McCulloch of Cambuslang, Scotland had entertained Davies in his home on July 5, 1754 and had promised to make "a Donation of £200 for propagating the Gospel among the Indians."[13] An anonymous donation of that same amount was given to the Synod of New York in 1755 to support the preaching of the gospel to the Indians which, no doubt, was the gift McCulloch had promised. Davies also had numerous contacts while in England with Jasper Mauduit, the treasurer for the New England Company since 1748, and formed a close friendship with him. The New England Company was a mission organization founded by John Eliot in 1649 for the propagation of the gospel in New England.

Encouraged by both McCulloch and Mauduit, Davies returned to the colonies in February of 1755 with the hope that a missionary work would soon be begun among the Indians. However, the French and Indian War erupted that summer which dashed his immediate plans. This providence convinced him of the additional need to evangelize the Indians in order to prevent their complicity with the enemies of the British colonies. Yet, it would be a few years before that dream could be realized.

The original idea was to send both a missionary and a schoolteacher to the Catawba Indians under the auspices of the New England Company. Officials of the New England Company were favorable to the proposal and requested Davies to supply them with all necessary information about such a mission for their consideration. Information about this proposed mission reached George Whitefield, and he wrote to Eleazar Wheelock on November 5, 1756 as follows:

---

[11] Conard, "Cherokee Mission," 37.
[12] Ibid.
[13] Pilcher, ed., *Reverend Samuel Davies Abroad*, 103.

Mr. Davies of Virginia prepares a mission among the Catawba Indians. Perhaps the Redeemer intends something by this stirring up of his Servants—Oh these Heathens! How Scandalously have they been neglected![14]

The missionary society was formed by November of 1757 and was "known variously as the Society in Virginia for Managing the Missions and Schools among the Indians, the Society for Promoting Christianity among the Indians, and the Society for Managing the Indian Mission in Virginia."[15] It was virtually identical with the membership of Hanover Presbytery, although there is nothing in the minutes of that Presbytery about its formation.

Virginia's Treaty with the Catawba and Cherokee Nations
The mission of Hanover Presbytery to the Catawba and Cherokee tribes was parallel, in some respects, to the efforts of Governor Robert Dinwiddie and the colony of Virginia to secure their support in the French and Indian War. A treaty was negotiated with those tribes on March 17, 1756. The negotiations had begun in December of 1755 when Governor Dinwiddie sent Peter Randolph and William Byrd to meet with all the sachems[16] and chiefs of those Nations. The Emperor of the Cherokee Nation was a chief named Old Hop, and King Heigler was the primary Chief of the Catawba Nation. There were also several subordinate chiefs of tribes in each of those Nations. The Catawba Nation practiced brotherly love and peace towards the settlers as did the Cherokees, for the most part. Yet, one of the Cherokee chiefs, Culloughculla, expressed his disappointment with certain aspects of their relationships with the Virginia government. Culloughculla had visited England and was entertained by the "Great King" who, he said, acknowledged the Cherokees to be his children as well as the English. The Cherokees had two requests of the Virginians before they entered into a treaty with them. First, they wanted their wives and children to be housed in a safe place during the conflicts. Second, they wanted some assurance that the Virginians would engage in more robust trade

---

[14] George Whitefield to Eleazar Wheelock, November 5, 1756. MS letter in Eleazar Wheelock MSS, Rauner Special Collections Library, Dartmouth College, Hanover, New Hampshire.
[15] Conard, "Cherokee Mission," 38.
[16] A sachem was a paramount chief.

with the Indians. As Culloughculla stated concerning the matter of trade:

> It gives us concern to find, that for so many Years our Brethren of Virginia, have declined a Trade with us. The King our Father, when I was in England, assured me that we should constantly be supplied with Goods; but we have hitherto found it otherwise. We tell you this, in hopes that when your Governor knows it, he will give proper Encouragement to some of his People to Trade with us. You perceive the nakedness of our People, and are very sensible, that we are unable to make any Thing but Bows and Arrows for our Defence; they are but bad Weapons, compared with Guns which kill at a great distance. The French supply their Indians with the best of Fire-Arms and in that they have the advantage of us; and therefore we again repeat our Request to you, to begin a Trade with us, which we hope will be to our mutual Advantage. —To enforce our request we present you with these Skins.[17]

The commissioners, Byrd and Randolph, had earlier informed the Cherokees and Catawabas that they would be amply "supplied with Arms, Ammunition and every Thing necessary for War."[18] Yet, the tribal chiefs needed greater assurances for the well-being of their people. Cullougculla promised to supply the colony of Virginia with at least 400 warriors as soon as a fort was constructed in Cherokee territory. The treaty had ten stipulations which were mostly to the benefit of the Ancient Dominion and required the warriors of the Nation to forbid by all means necessary the French from building a fort in that territory.

Two officers of the Virginia militia, Major Andrew Lewis and Captain Samuel Overton, were tasked by Virginia with the obligation of erecting the fort requested by the Cherokees. Overton was from Hanover County and his company was composed of Hanover volunteers. Davies had preached a sermon to the volunteers at the muster of this company on August 17, 1755 outside the Hanover courthouse. It was, therefore, probably through Overton that an arrangement was made by the Virginia government to support Davies' missionary efforts to the Indians. This treaty with the Cherokees and Catawbas, though, was counterproductive to the mission of teaching them about the gospel way of salvation. Arm-

---

[17] "A Treaty: Between Virginia and the Catawbas and Cherokees," *The Virginia Magazine of History and Biography*, Vol. 13, No. 3 (Jan. 1906), 253–4.
[18] Ibid., 240.

ing the tribes for war and evangelizing them were very opposite goals. Davies actively promoted patriotism and, in this instance, his own patriotism beguiled him into thinking that a mission to the Indians could be successful with two very opposite goals—one political and the other religious.

Mission to the Overhill Cherokees

After careful consideration of both the Cherokee and Catawba tribes, Davies decided to pursue a mission among the Overhill Cherokees, "a nation of much more importance, both in a political and religious view; and . . . there was some encouragement that they would embrace the same proposal with the Catawbas."[19] The Catawbas were still on his heart, but he considered a mission to the Overhill Cherokees to be more politically strategic for the interests of the colony. He estimated £240 annually would support two missionaries and two schoolteachers. The New England Company was unable to bear this whole expense and appointed a committee in October of 1756 to confer with the S.S.P.C.K. about assisting with their efforts. The two societies agreed together to support one missionary and one schoolteacher with each contributing £60 annually. The New England Company advised Davies to be as frugal as possible with the use of these funds.[20] Davies suggested members of the Byrd and Randolph families of Virginia as possible managers of this mission,[21] which was further blending the political and religious together. It is hard to understand exactly why Davies made this recommendation, but it certainly made the mission appear to be just another effort of the colony of Virginia to gain the support of the two tribes. Meanwhile, he "remained hopeful that work might eventually be started among the Catawba Indians as well."[22]

The Overhill Cherokees were one of the larger communities of the Cherokee nation, numbering approximately 12,000[23] at this date. The Virginia government considered their allegiance to be a great priority for Virginia, the Carolinas, and Georgia. Colonel George Washington, still in

---

[19] Conard, "Cherokee Mission," 37.
[20] Register House, S. S. P. C. K., Minutes, IV, 596; MS 7952.
[21] Conard, "Cherokee Mission," 38.
[22] Ibid.
[23] Ibid., 35.

his twenties, keenly assessed their importance to Virginia and the colonies in 1759 in the midst of the French and Indian War:

> They (the Cherokees) are more serviceable than twice their number of white men. Their cunning and craft cannot be equaled. . . their assistance is very necessary. One false step might not only lose us that, but even turn them against us.[24]

The Overhill Cherokees were strategically located "south of the Cumberland Mountains along the lower Little Tennessee river. . . . The nearest English settlement was Fort Loudon, situated at the juncture of the Tellico and Little Tennessee rivers near the principal Overhill Cherokee town of Chota."[25] Fort Loudon was the British fort erected in 1756 about twenty miles south of modern day Knoxville, Tennessee, (which was then part of the colony of North Carolina). Joe Guy describes the Cherokee town of Chota:

> Chota was a relatively large Indian town, having a few streets around the central square and townhouse. Part of the reason for Chota's larger population was that it was a town of refuge; a person in fear of his life, due to some blood feud or death sentence, might find sanctuary in its streets and houses.[26]

Davies sent a letter dated May 18, 1757, to Samuel Hazard (1713–?), a merchant and bookseller in Philadelphia, by way of his Hanover neighbor, Nicholas Sherrar. In that letter, Davies pointed out the strategic importance of evangelizing the Indians, particularly the Cherokees:

> We have, I think, about 300 Indians in the Colony. But they are not likely, I am afraid, to do us much service. Indeed the Chirokees behave suspiciously.[27]

Davies' letter also gave Hazard, an elder in the Second Presbyterian Church and an original Trustee of the College of New Jersey, valuable information concerning the progress of the French and Indian War and

---

[24] Joe D. Guy, *Indian Summer: The Siege and Fall of Fort Loudon* (Johnson City, Tennessee: Overmountain Press, 2001), 1.
[25] Conard, "Cherokee Mission," 36.
[26] Guy, *Indian Summer*, 34.
[27] Samuel Davies to Samuel Hazard, May 18, 1757. MS letter in the Ebenezer Hazard MSS, The Library Company of Philadelphia—Historical Society of Pennsylvania, Philadelphia, PA.

the proceedings of the Virginia General Assembly in response to these gloomy prospects. On November 3, 1757, Davies gave Hazard "free & candid Tho'ts at large, concerning the Ohio Scheme"[28]—a daring plan to aid the British cause in the French and Indian War. Davies also informed Hazard about the Cherokee mission thusly:

> Mr. Atkins, Superintendent of Indian Affairs, has been lately in Wmsburg, & reports, that the Chirokees are now unanimous in their attachment to the British Interest. May our good Management long keep them so![29]

Davies informed Hazard that the mission to the Cherokees was looking for the proper person and could afford £70 to £80 per year for a missionary and £25 to £30 per year for a schoolteacher. The advice of Hazard was readily sought on this important matter.[30]

John Martin Becomes the First Missionary to the Cherokees

The first missionary was John Martin (1730–1774), a native Virginian, who had studied for the ministry under Davies. He was the first Presbyterian minister to be ordained in the colony on June 8, 1757. Immediately, he was petitioned by congregations at Albemarle in North Carolina and the joint charge at Amelia, Prince Edward, and Lunenberg counties in Virginia before receiving this call to be a missionary to the Cherokees. After careful consideration, he refused both those calls sometime in 1757 to undertake the Cherokee mission. Hanover Presbytery was informed of this decision through Davies on January 25, 1758. Martin's prime consideration was that "he had already had some firsthand experience with Cherokees friendly to the colony of Virginia,"[31] and he hoped to build on this contact.

The formal approval for this mission was given by the colonial officials on December 14, 1757, and Governor Dinwiddie promised to write to Governor William Henry Lyttleton of South Carolina on behalf of Martin. Both Governor Dinwiddie and the Council of Virginia enter-

---

[28] Samuel Davies to Samuel Hazard, November 3, 1757. MS letter in Ebenezer Hazard MSS, The Library Company of Philadelphia—Historical Society of Pennsylvania.
[29] Ibid.
[30] Ibid.
[31] Conard, "Cherokee Mission," 38.

tained the notion that the mission "if duly managed, cannot fail of being productive of the greatest Good."[32] This new attitude indicated the tide had turned in favor of the Presbyterians in Virginia. Martin began his work among the Overhill Cherokees in the late spring of 1758 with the encouragement of Virginia's governing officials. He was "the first British missionary to work among the Indians in the southern trans-Appalachian region" and "the first Protestant minister to preach the Gospel in Tennessee."[33]

The news of this mission reached the ears of Ebenezer Pemberton in New York who wrote to his friend, Eleazar Wheelock, in Lebanon, Connecticut:

> I rejoice that a mission is set on foot among the Cheroquees, & that so suitable a person as Mr Davies is at the head of it—Nothing can be more Agreeable to our Christian Character tha[n] t[o] send the Gospel to the benighted Pagans; Nothing mor[e] Conducive to our Civil interests than to bring them to a Subjection to the Religion of Jesus.[34]

Pemberton stated that £200 in supporting zealous missionaries would do more good in securing their support than many thousands spent on trinkets. He lamented the guilty neglect of their temporal and spiritual interests by the colonists.

The New England Company and the Society in Scotland for Promoting Christian Knowledge were pleased with the first reports of the progress of Martin's work in this mission and entertained the hope they would soon need the additional missionary and schoolteacher that Davies envisioned. The Virginia Society presented a petition to the Synod of New York in 1758 "requesting that the Interest of the Money under the direction of this Synod for propagating the Gospel among the Indians, may be allowed them for one year."[35] This request was for the annual interest on the anonymous £200 gift to the Synod of New York. As Davies

---

[32] Ibid, 39.
[33] John Richard Alden, *John Stuart and the Southern Colonial Frontier: A Study of Indian Relations, War, Trade, and Land Problems in the Southern Wilderness, 1754–1775* (Ann Arbor: University of Michigan Press, 1944), 351–2; and, Ernest Trice Thompson, *Presbyterians in the South*, Volume 1 (Richmond: John Knox Press, 1963), 189f.
[34] Ebenezer Pemberton to Eleazar Wheelock, November 18, 1758, MS letter in Eleazar Wheelock MSS, Rauner Special Collections Library, Dartmouth College, Hanover, New Hampshire.
[35] Conard, "Cherokee Mission," 39.

was instrumental in securing this gift, the Virginia Society thought it reasonable the interest would go for the support of their mission. Yet, the Synod had already designated this interest for another year elsewhere. On October 1, 1755, Gilbert Tennent reported to the Synod of New York that he had a received a bill for £200 sterling for the propagation of the gospel among the Indians. The Synod of New York then appointed a committee consisting of Davies, Tennent, Samuel Finley, Elihu Spencer, and Jacob Green to propose a plan for the distribution of the funds. The committee corresponded with the anonymous donor of this money who directed it to be placed under the supervision of the Trustees of the College of New Jersey for the following purposes:

> Either towards the support of a pious and well qualified missionary in preaching the gospel among the Indians in North America, or supporting a pious and well qualified schoolmaster in teaching the Indians the English language, and the principles of natural and revealed religion; or for maintaining a pious and well qualified Indian youth at the college of New Jersey. . . or for maintaining a pious and well qualified youth of English or Scotch extract, at that college, during his preparatory studies for teaching or preaching the gospel among the Indians.[36]

The donor also directed that the Synod of New York determine every year which of the above uses should receive the annual interest on the funds. In 1756, the money was distributed to John Brainerd who had taken over the mission to the Crossweeksung Indians at the death of his brother, David, in 1745. In 1757, it was apparently given to support some pious youth in their studies at the College of New Jersey. And, in 1758, £20 was given to Rev. William Tennent, Jr. for the support of a schoolmaster at an Indian school under his care. Thus, the Synod regretfully denied the request from the Virginia Society.

Despite this disappointment, the early reports of Martin's labors among the Overhill Cherokees indicated hopefulness about this mission. In a letter to Davies, "Martin noted that the Indians were treating him with honor and affection, and they had consented to let him have a fair

---

[36] *Minutes of the Synod of New York, From A. D. 1745 to 1758* in *Records of the Presbyterian Church in the United States of America* (Philadelphia: Presbyterian Board of Publications, 1841), 269.

hearing."[37] Some of the Cherokees expressed a desire to be instructed in the Christian faith,[38] and Martin wrote that "there was sufficient Encouragement to employ another Missionary there."[39] William Richardson, who was already preparing for this mission, was thereafter sent to assist Martin in 1758.

Meanwhile, Davies continued to look for additional suitable missionaries for this venture. First, he pursued Gideon Hawley, who "had worked with Jonathan Edwards at Stockbridge and then served among the Iroquois until forced to leave them in May 1756."[40] He wrote Joseph Bellamy on February 23, 1757, to inquire whether Hawley "upon proper encouragement . . . would be willing to engage in this apostolic work among those southwestern Indians."[41] Yet, Hawley respectfully declined this invitation in order to renew his labors among the Iroquois.

Davies next sought the assistance of Samson Occum in the fall of 1758. Occum was teaching school among the Montauk Indians on Long Island at the time. Davies wrote to Samuel Buell, a Presbyterian minister who lived near Occum, and urged "in the most pressing manner . . . that Mr. Occum would by December be present with him as engaging in a Mission among the Cherokees."[42] Occum was not yet ordained, but he replied that he would be willing to go to the Cherokees in the spring of 1759. Occum was ordained by Long Island Presbytery on August 30, 1759, but never undertook this mission to the Cherokee Indians.

William Richardson Becomes the Second Missionary to the Cherokees

In February of 1757, "Davies noted that Richardson had his heart set on being a 'missionary among the *Indian Savages,*'"[43] and the New England Company expected him to be a candidate for the other missionary position even as Martin was beginning his work.[44] Richardson was ordained

---

[37] Based on letter of Samuel Buell to Eleazar Wheelock, October 17, 1758. MS letter in Eleazar Wheelock MSS, Rauner Special Collections Library, Dartmouth College, Hanover, NH.
[38] Ibid., 40.
[39] Samuel Davies, *Letters from the Rev. Samuel Davies, and Others; Shewing, the State of Religion in Virginia, South Carolina, &c. Particularly Among the Negroes,* (London, 1761).
[40] Conard, "Cherokee Mission," 41.
[41] Ibid.
[42] Ibid.
[43] Ibid, 40. Also, Davies, *Letters* (1757), 39.
[44] Ibid.

on July 13, 1758, and Davies petitioned the presbytery on September 13, 1758, on behalf of the Virginia Society, "that Mr. Richardson should be permitted to go as a Missionary among the Indians, as soon as his Health will permit."[45] The presbytery heartily agreed with this request, and the way was opened for his dispatch in October of that year to assist Martin. Richardson, Davies, and George Webb, a member of the Virginia Society, met with the new Governor of Virginia, Francis Fauquier, and the Council in Williamsburg in October.[46] Governor Fauquier gave Richardson letters of commendation to the governor of South Carolina and to "the Commanding Officers of the Forts in the Cherokee Towns."[47]

Richardson was just beginning his missionary labors, but Martin was unexpectedly retiring from his service to the Cherokees. Lieutenant Henry Timberlake of Hanover, who served in an army garrison among the Overhill Cherokees in 1761–62, gave the following information about Martin's lack of success among them:

> As to religion, every one is at liberty to think for himself; whence flows a diversity of opinions amongst those that do think, but the major part do not give themselves that trouble. They generally concur, however, in the belief of one superior Being, who made them, and governs all things, and are therefore never discontent at any misfortune, because they say, the Man above would have it so. They believe in a reward and punishment, as may be evinced by their answer to Mr. Martin, who, having preached scripture till both his audience and he were heartily tired, was told at last, that they knew very well, that, if they were good, they should go up; if bad, down; that he could tell no more; that he had long plagued them with what they no ways understood, and that they desired him to depart the country.[48]

This request by the Cherokees for his departure was certainly a great disappointment to Martin after he had declined two other calls in order to work among them. Yet, the religious ideas of the Cherokees were simply the same as the natural man believes. Despite this disappoint-

---

[45] William M. E. Rachal, ed., "Early Minutes of Hanover Presbytery," *Virginia Magazine of History and Biography*, LXIII (1955), 164.
[46] Conard, "Cherokee Mission," 40.
[47] Ibid.; also, *Executive Journals of the Council of Colonial Virginia*, Volume 6 (1754–1775), 110.
[48] Samuel C. Williams, "An Account of the Presbyterian Mission to the Cherokees, 1757–1759," *Tennessee Historical Magazine*, Series II, Volume I (1930–31), 126.

ment, Richardson continued his journey by horseback through the Piedmont area of central North Carolina to the town of Salisbury, on the south side of the Yadkin River. He learned that the Indians in this area entertained "hostile intentions towards the settlers nearest to their towns, some of whom had already been killed, others plundered and their homes put to the torch."[49] Richardson grew concerned about Martin's whereabouts and remained in Salisbury for a few days. He continued toward South Carolina, traveling as far as present-day Mecklenburg County in North Carolina, where he stopped at the home of Rev. Alexander Craighead. Richardson had been ordered by Hanover Presbytery to officiate in the installation of Craighead to his new pastorate, which was accomplished on November 6, 1758.

A few days later Martin and Richardson met up on the banks of the Enoree River in South Carolina. Martin had recently recovered from a bout of flux[50], which had made him very weak. He gave a good report to Richardson concerning the willingness of the Overhill Cherokees to hear the gospel, which Richardson says "disipated my Fears of the Indians & Encouraged me to proceed."[51] Martin also informed Richardson that the Overhill Cherokees were on their seasonal hunting trip and that he need not hurry to arrive there. Richardson waited until November 25 for the translator from Charles Town[52] before setting out alone for the final part of his journey to the Cherokee territory. He finally reached Fort Loudon on December 15. He was now 470 miles from Davies' home in Hanover. On December 18, he was then taken to meet Old Hop, the principal chief of the Overhill Cherokees until his death in 1761. Old Hop was also known as Kanagatoga or Standing Turkey. He had the ability of getting all the factions of the Cherokees to work together by avoiding making the decisions himself and remaining levelheaded. His nickname, Old Hop, was because he was lame in one foot. Yet, Old Hop often seemed cunning and scheming to the soldiers and the missionaries.

Richardson gave Old Hop a letter from Martin, and he seemed pleased Richardson would be taking Martin's place. He expressed inter-

---

[49] Ibid., 127

[50] A bloody inflammatory disorder of the intestines or colon which was called "bloody flux" or just "flux" in the eighteenth century.

[51] Williams, "An Account of the Presbyterian Mission to the Cherokees, 1757–1759," 128.

[52] An archaic spelling of Charleston.

est in learning more about the "Great Man above," as the Cherokees referred to God. He also promised to invite Richardson to their council once the warriors returned from their hunt. A hard frost that night and a snow the next day allowed Richardson to observe the method the Cherokees used to keep warm:

> He [Old Hop] was in his Hot-house [which] is built like a cone; this they heat as do ovens & then cover up the ashes & in this way they live in winter [which] keeps [them] warm.[53]

Richardson's interpreter did not arrive until January 3, 1759, because of the snow in that area, but Richardson visited the Cherokees at Chota on December 29. He "had some Discourse with Hop concerning God, the creation, etc; he seemed very thoughtful & afterwards said he was thinking on these Things he had heard."[54] At the Town-house, the Indians were dancing around a cane fire, dressed in leather, and working up a sweat. After an hour of dancing in this way, they ran outside into the cold air, and some of them jumped into the river to cool off. This practice frequently occasioned "great Colds" among them, as Richardson stated.

When the interpreter, Mr. Bunyan, arrived, Richardson hoped he would be able to start preaching to the Cherokees. He had previously been restricted to preaching to the soldiers at Fort Loudon, visiting the Cherokee settlements, and trying in vain to interject religious conversation. Unfortunately, the Cherokee warriors informed Old Hop that they were "engaged in other Matters"[55] and did not have time to listen to him. Their indifference was partly because of the treatment they received in Virginia, where some of their warriors were killed. The result was that "they are quite changed to what they were tho never much inclined, yet now they shew the greatest Indifference."[56]

The Cherokees informed Richardson he could live among them and speak in private to anyone who was interested, but could not speak publicly until they gave him permission. He moved to Chota on January 10, 1759, paying 100 shillings to rent a house for four months. He invited the Indians to eat with him in his new quarters, smoked the ceremonial pipe,

---

[53] Williams, "An Account of the Presbyterian Mission to the Cherokees, 1757–1759," 132.
[54] Ibid.
[55] Ibid., 134.
[56] Ibid.

and asked for permission to talk to them in public. He was once again rebuffed and told to wait longer. He provided presents out of his own salary for Cherokees who visited him, but found no encouragement from those efforts.

The difficulties between the Indians and the English continued to be a problem for Richardson. He was thankful he lived at Chota, "a beloved Town, a City of Refuge & no blood to be shed in it nor any to be put to Death."[57] The habit of the Cherokees was to kill the first white man they found when attempting to avenge one of their own. Their principle was man for man, even if the one they killed was not guilty. Richardson reflected on this habit and prayed:

> O Lord remove every Impediment out of the way of their Conversion for Jesus sake.[58]

The only encouragement Richardson received was in showing the Indians some pictures of prominent biblical events. The Indians were fascinated with these pictures, and Richardson believed they would soon learn what is contained in the Scriptures if they were communicated in picture form. Yet, Richardson never saw more results in this way than in any other method he used.

By February 1, Richardson was "out of all Patience"[59] with the Overhill Cherokees and felt he could stay no longer. He informed Old Hop he would have to leave unless he was allowed to speak to the Indians, but the ruler manifested great indifference toward him. The societies' expenses appeared to Richardson to have been all for no purpose. He was convinced by February 6 that he had no further appearance of usefulness. He left Chota for his journey to Fort Prince George, located near the villages of the Lower Cherokees. Here, Richardson hoped that he would be able to continue as a missionary to the Indians.

Richardson met with similar difficulties among the Indians at Fort Prince George, and resigned as a missionary on March 2. He sent an account of his labors to Davies on March 17, 1759. The New England Company still entertained thoughts of reviving the work among the Cherokees at a later time and made additional efforts until 1763 without any

---

[57] Ibid., 135.
[58] Ibid.
[59] Ibid., 137.

fruit being borne. On November 12, 1759, Davies received a letter from Eleazar Wheelock which communicated the following information:

> I much long for an opportunity to converse with you, particularly of our Indian affair. It seems Divine Providence is now by the success of our Northern Forces marvellously opening a door for the grand Design in view, and inviting all far & near who love our Lord Jesus Christ to put to a helping hand, to further a Design which the Heart of our great Redeemer is infinitely set upon. But when I may have, or whether ever, such an opportunity is all uncertain.[60]

The New England Company hoped Davies would help rekindle the work among the Cherokees at a later time. Yet, this never came to pass, and the mission died for several reasons: it was underfinanced; it was begun at a time when the Indians were suspicious of the English; the schoolteachers were never sent to the mission; both the missionaries were newly ordained with no pastoral experience; the interpreter was not always available when needed; and, Davies was to leave the colony in 1759. It was not surprising, therefore, that this work ended abruptly without accomplishing the hoped-for success. Yet, it was also a blessing that this mission did not continue because Fort Loudon fell to an uprising by the Cherokees against them in 1761. Those were turbulent times which did not portend much promise of success for the gospel to Indian tribes that were, at best, indifferent to that message.

Conclusion

The success of David Brainerd among the Crossweeksung Indians was during the period when the Great Awakening was at its height and his success cannot be the standard for missions during the ordinary days of the church. The Holy Spirit was moving mightily among Americans of all ethnic backgrounds and social standing at that time. The God of all grace, who once proclaimed "All souls are Mine," is as interested in the conversion of heathens as He is in the salvation of nominal Christians. The same power of God that began a work of conviction and repentance in the hearts of Virginians before they ever received a living voice to

---

[60] Eleazar Wheelock to Samuel Davies, November 12, 1759. MS letter in Eleazar Wheelock MSS, Rauner Special Collections Library, Dartmouth College. Hanover, New Hampshire.

preach the gospel to them was also at work in the Crossweeksung Indians to bow them like bulrushes before His sovereign grace.

It was neither the holiness of Brainerd alone nor the nobility of the Crossweeksung Indians more than others that caused the awakening among them. Nor was it the lack of holiness by Martin or Richardson that made the Overhill Cherokees harden their hearts against the gospel. Only the Spirit of God can open blinded eyes. From the response that the Overhill Cherokees gave to Martin, it is obvious that they did not understand the gospel. Even when faithful ministers preach the three R's of Christianity—ruin by the fall, regeneration by the Spirit, and redemption in Christ—blinded eyes will still twist the message to a scheme of salvation by works. Thus, we must realize that this mission failed because the Spirit of God was not moving among the Overhill Cherokees as He had once moved among the Crossweeksung Indians. The result was that they were left in their sins despite the efforts to convert them to Christ.

The French and Indian War was also a hindrance to missionary work in the latter part of the 1750s. Virginians were necessarily distracted by the encroaching sounds of war. The French used the Indians for their advantage and the horrendous thought of being scalped caused many Virginians to be filled with terror. It was difficult to carry on a peaceful mission among the Indians at a time when every church and school house was being turned into a fort of defense for protection against the French and their Indians. Indeed, the Great Awakening ended about the same time as the French and Indian War began. Wars and rumors of war will certainly prevail until the end of time, but they are almost never productive of any lasting good.

-19-

The Call to Nassau Hall

"At last he accepted the call to his important office of presiding in the college; and tells me, in a letter dated June 6, 1759, 'That the evidence of his duty was so plain, that even his skeptical mind was satisfied; and that his people saw the hand of Providence in it, and dared not to oppose it.'"[1]
~*Thomas Gibbons (1720-1785), pastor at an Independent Church at Haberdashers-Hall in London, England*~

Nassau Hall, the first building of the College of New Jersey

---

[1] Thomas Gibbons, "Divine Conduct Vindicated," in Samuel Davies, *Sermons on Important Subjects*, Vol. 1 (New York: J. & J. Harper, 1828), 33.

On March 22, 1758, earthquake tremors were felt all along the eastern seaboard of the American colonies. Landon Carter, a wealthy planter in Richmond County, Virginia, recorded in his diary for that day that he was awakened "with the rocking and trembling of my bed. Being confused by my sleep I thought the noise attending it was like the passing of many coaches under my window but a second rocking and trembling came that instant with a roaring in the heavens, not a rumbling."[2] The Maryland Gazette recorded in the next day's paper that the roaring, rocking, and trembling was actually an earthquake. It hit at 10:02 the previous evening and lasted for half a minute.

March 22, 1758, was also an epoch day in the history of the College of New Jersey. Jonathan Edwards, President of the College, suddenly died that same day from an adverse reaction to a smallpox inoculation after only four months in office. When Davies heard of Edwards' death, he considered it a sign that a righteous God was angry with America. The earthquake which hit that same day was confirmation to Davies of God's displeasure with the Colonies. As he told his congregation in a sermon:

> An earthquake spread a tremor through a great part of our solid continent on the melancholy day in which he died; but how much more did Nassau Hall tremble when this pillar fell![3]

Davies' First Election as President of the College of New Jersey

Edwards' predecessor and son-in-law, Aaron Burr, had died in office the previous September (1757) and the Trustees were now forced to search for their second new President within a seven-month period. The Board met in April of 1758 and elected the Reverend James Lockwood[4] of Wethersfield, Connecticut, to the post. Lockwood unexpectedly declined their invitation, though, and the Trustees reassembled in August to resume their search. Samuel Finley was considered at this meeting, but a majority the Board preferred Davies for his preaching gifts.[5] The Board

---

[2] Jack P. Greene, ed., *The Diary of Colonel Landon Carter of Sabine Hall, 1752–1778*, Volume I (Richmond, VA: Virginia Historical Society, 1987), 124.
[3] Samuel Davies, *Sermons on Important Subjects*, Vol. IV (London: W. Baynes & Son, 1824), 457.
[4] Lockwood was a Congregational minister who also turned down the College in 1766 at the death of Samuel Finley. He was well-qualified, but consistently unwilling to take this post.
[5] Thomas Jefferson Wertenbaker, *Princeton: 1746–1896* (Princeton: Princeton University Press, 1946), 44.

immediately dispatched two messengers, Caleb Smith and James Caldwell, to the colony of Virginia to inform Davies of his election as Edward's successor, which both surprised and confused him.

Davies was reluctant to decide on a matter of such importance, so he turned to Hanover Presbytery for advice. As Moderator, Davies called a meeting of Presbytery for September 13, 1758 to be held at his home. The two messengers from Princeton were invited to attend as guests of the court. When Presbytery convened, the Hanover congregation presented a petition, signed by all twelve of the congregation's elders, which expressed their "overwhelming grief" at the prospect of losing Davies who had relieved them "from numberless distresses as our spiritual father and guide to eternal life; defended us from the formidable confederacy of our numerous enemies, and has been mighty through God, to conquer all who oppose us, and to defend the cause of the Redeemer in this degenerate land. . ."[6] His value to the congregation and the colony of Virginia was such that "the eyes of almost all are directed to him as a leader."[7] This petition represented accurately the importance of Davies to the Hanover congregation and to the state of the Dissenters in Virginia, but that importance was only one side of the issue before Hanover Presbytery.

Many of the congregation's enemies had already begun to say about Davies, "Ah, he will go, no doubt, when he has a good bait laid to catch him."[8] His elders, though, were convinced he was "animated by nobler motives"[9] than to leave them for monetary gain. Yet, his loss, the elders asserted, would mean "this congregation will fall to ruins, when the band that now holds it is broken; and we shall never be gathered together, we fear, and united in another minister."[10] Presbytery deliberated on the matter and, while acknowledging Davies' competency for such a great position, denied the call because of his necessity for the work in Virginia. Their decision was expressed as follows:

> The Presbytery own and are deeply sensible of the vast Importance of the College of New Jersey; its present unsettled State, and the Need of a Skil-

---

[6] George Pilcher, *Samuel Davies: Apostle of Dissent in Colonial Virginia* (Knoxville, TN: University of Tennessee Press, 1971), 193–194
[7] Ibid., 194.
[8] Ibid.
[9] Ibid.
[10] Ibid.

ful healing Hand at the Head of it: They are also sensible of Mr. Davies' Influence, Popularity, Moderation, and in many Respects his Literary Accomplishments for so great a Trust. But the Presbytery being best acquainted with the State of Religion in Virginia, and best knowing Mr. Davies' Importance here, can by no means agree to his Removal, as they foresee Consequences very dangerous to the important Interests of Religion among us; and thereby cannot deliberately agree so sensibly to weaken our Hands, and so deeply wound that Cause we desire above all things to promote.[11]

Davies' Uneasy Acquiescence in the Decision of Presbytery

Immediately following this meeting of Hanover Presbytery, Davies sent a letter through Smith and Caldwell to the Board of Trustees rejecting their invitation. He acquiesced in Presbytery's decision for less than a day, though. The next day he wrote David Cowell expressing his anxious concerns not to injure the college by this refusal. He learned also that "presbytery could not positively determine it was my duty to leave Virginia and accept the invitation, yet they were sceptical about it, and wished I could have determined the matter for myself..."[12] Thus, Davies was "convinced, that if [he] had been able to form any previous judgment of [his] own, it would have turned the scale, and theirs would have coincided with [his]."[13] In part of that letter to Cowell, he stated:

> The very suspicion that I may have done it an Injury, by not accepting the honor the Trustees were pleased to confer upon me, causes me to appear almost an unpardonable Criminal to myself.[14]

The Trustees were urged to elect Finley as President, but Davies stated his willingness to consider a renewed invitation to the most important position "an ecclesiastic can sustain in America"[15] which he would look upon as an evidence of God's will. As he said:

---

[11] William M. E. Rachal, ed., "Early Minutes of Hanover Presbytery," *Virginia Magazine of History and Biography*, LXIII (1955), 164.
[12] Ibid.
[13] "New Jersey College and President Davies," *The Biblical Repertory and Princeton Review*, XII (1840), 384.
[14] Samuel Davies to David Cowell, September 14, 1758, MS Letter in Samuel Davies MSS, Presbyterian Historical Society, Philadelphia, PA.
[15] Rachal, ed. "Early Minutes of Hanover Presbytery," 164.

> My life, Sir, I should look upon as secured to God and the Public: and the Service of God and Mankind is not a *local* Thing in my View: Wherever it appears to me I may perform it to the greatest Advantage, There, I hope, I should [choose] to fix my Residence, whether in Hanover, Princeton, or even Lapland or Japan.[16]

Cowell and the other Trustees were encouraged by this letter that Davies would accept their renewed offer and could be inaugurated as President sometime during the winter of 1758–59. One of the tutors of the college, Mr. Halsey, was hastily sent to Virginia to renew their invitation to Davies.

David Bostwick informed Joseph Bellamy that Presbytery advised Davies to remain at Hanover "with much diffidence and hesitation,"[17] but expressed his confidence that he would accept this second invitation: "I make no doubt but he will come."[18] Halsey, though, betrayed his responsibility to the Trustees and informed Davies that certain members of the Board preferred Finley for his scholarship and teaching experience. Thus, Davies wrote to Cowell on October 18 that he had come to "view the matter in a different light"[19] and recommended Finley "as the best qualified person. . . in America"[20] to be President of the College. As for himself, Davies stated:

> Like an inflamed meteor, I might cast a glaring light, and attract the gaze of mankind for a little while, but the flash would soon be over and leave me in my native obscurity.[21]

The Board next asked Davies to become president pro tempore until they could appeal the decision of Hanover Presbytery to Synod, but he flatly refused this proposal, expecting to hear no more from them. The Board met again on November 22, 1758 to determine if Davies' answer should be considered as final and to elect the Reverend Jacob Green of Morris County, New Jersey, as the president pro tempore. Cowell then

---

[16] Davies to Cowell, MS letter September 14, 1758. MS Letter in Samuel Davies MSS, Presbyterian Historical Society, Philadelphia, PA.
[17] David Bostwick to Joseph Bellamy, October 10, 1758. MS letter in Joseph Bellamy Papers, Hartford Seminary Library, Hartford, Connecticut.
[18] "New Jersey College and President Davies," 384
[19] Ibid., 386.
[20] Ibid.
[21] Ibid.

wrote Davies on Christmas day to clear up any misunderstandings and to inform him that Halsey had "told a friend that he did not expect Mr. Davies would come, but his journey would have this good effect, that he should bring a final refusal from Mr. Davies."[22] Cowell also assured Davies he would be reelected at the next Board meeting in May and, if not, Finley would not be elected. He then appealed to Davies:

> I am sensible that your leaving Virginia is attended with very great difficulties, but I cannot think your affairs are of equal importance with the college of New Jersey.[23]

Meanwhile, Davies assured the Hanover congregation on November 12, 1758, that he intended to live and die among them. He related his decision to them as follows:

> Had interest been my motive, I should undoubtedly have preferred two hundred a year, before a scant hundred. Had honour been my motive, I should have [chosen] to have sat in the president's chair in Nassau Hall, rather than continued a despised and calumniated new-light parson in Virginia. Or had ease been my motive, I should have preferred a college life, before that of a fatigued itinerant. . .[24]

While warning them not to idolize him, he said, "I have indeed been shocked at the high character I have heard of myself on this occasion."[25] What he desired was the bonds of true Christian love to be knit ever tighter between them.

Continued Opposition and Persecution

While considering the Presidency of Princeton, Davies continued to labor faithfully for the expansion of vital Christianity throughout Virginia. He never made the mistake of letting his consideration of a new call affect his labors at his present call. In 1757, he had begun making missionary journeys to the Northern Neck counties of Lancaster and Northumberland which bordered the Chesapeake Bay. Despite the opposition of several Anglican ministers in the Northern Neck, Davies conducted his af-

---

[22] Ibid., p. 388.
[23] Ibid., p. 389.
[24] Ibid.
[25] Ibid.

fairs according to the laws of Virginia. In May of 1757, he applied to the Courthouses in Lancaster and Northumberland counties for the right to build a meetinghouse in each county. This application was granted as well as the privilege to preach within their bounds. He then preached in an orchard on the last Sunday and Monday of June in 1757 to a considerable crowd of anxious hearers in Northumberland County. He also preached on two successive days in July of that year to a large congregation in Lancaster County from a desk erected for him in the woods. He reversed the order of his tour in November, preaching in each place for three days.

The rise of Presbyterianism in the Northern Neck is primarily owing to the leadership of Colonel James Gordon (1714–1768), a wealthy and influential merchant in Lancaster County who immigrated to America from Ireland in early life. He was, no doubt, instrumental in the applications that came to Hanover Presbytery in July of 1757 for supply pastors to be sent to the Northern Neck. Presbytery appointed Davies to preach three Sabbaths in Lancaster and Northumberland counties before the spring meeting of 1758.[26] Henry Patillo and John Todd were also appointed by Presbytery to supply those counties. Todd fulfilled his duties by spending three days in each county in April of 1758.

One of Davies' persecutors in the Northern Neck was Adam Menzies, Rector of St. Stephens Parish in Northumberland County from 1758–1767. Menzies was joined by fellow Anglican ministers, David Currie and John Leland, who "wrote severe letters to Mr. Davies on his visits there" with the result "that many were for a time prevented from attending the Presbyterian meeting from the ridicule thrown upon them by influential men."[27] Currie was the rector at Christ's Church Parish in Lancaster County, Virginia, from 1741 until his death in the winter of 1791–2. He also taught Richard Henry Lee and Francis Lightfoot Lee, both signers of the Declaration of Independence and ancestors of Robert Edward Lee, the Commanding General of the Confederacy during the Civil War. John Leland was rector of the Wicomico Parish in Northumberland County, Virginia. On April 12, 1758, they wrote Commissary Dawson to

---

[26] William Henry Foote, *Sketches of Virginia, Historical and Biographical*, First Series, (Philadelphia: William S. Martien, 1850), 360.
[27] Ibid., 371.

complain of Davies' preaching tours in Lancaster and Northumberland counties in 1757–58.[28]

Despite the opposition he faced, Davies' labors were abundantly blessed in the Northern Neck and the church "grew to be large and flourishing under the pastoral labors of James Waddell, D.D. By means of his [i.e., Davies'—DR] preaching in this place, several persons of the first class of society were converted. The enemy raised up opposition, and some person composed a kind of play intended to ridicule him and his coadjutor, the Rev. John Todd."[29]

One of those leading citizens initially disaffected to Davies was Col. Gordon's wife, Mary Harrison Gordon. She was "of the High Church of England, and very bigotted,—so much that she refused to hear Mr. Davies preach, although he was a favorite with her husband."[30] Mrs. Gordon was overcome by a protracted sickness about this time which caused great concern to her husband. Davies was invited to preach in the Gordon's home and the door to her bedroom was left open so she could hear the sermon. As Davies preached, Mrs. Gordon was brought under conviction of her sins. She became an exemplary Christian who taught the Scriptures to her children and later died full of faith.

On those occasions when there were no ministers to supply the mission churches in the Northern Neck, Col. Gordon would go with his wife to White Chapel Church which was a chapel of ease supplied by David Currie, rector at Christ Church Parish in Lancaster County. Gordon recorded his view of one of those occasions as follows:

> Went with my wife to White Chapel Church, where we heard Mr. Currie—a very indifferent discourse—nothing scarce but external modes; much against Presbyterians—so that I was much disappointed, for it was misspending the Lord's Day. How I lament the want of a good minister for our own church, that we may see the things that belong to our peace, before it be too late![31]

---

[28] David Currie and John Leland to Commissary Thomas Dawson, MS letter in the William and Thomas Dawson Papers, Library of Congress, Washington, DC. Much of the material in the next few paragraphs is based on this letter.
[29] *The Biblical Repertory and Princeton Review*, IX (July 1837), 364.
[30] Foote, *Sketches of Virginia*, First Series, 387–8.
[31] James Gordon, "Journal of Col. James Gordon, of Lancaster County, Va.," *The William and Mary Quarterly*, Vol. 11. no. 2 (Oct. 1902), 109.

Currie, according to Gordon's diary entry, was evidently one of those Anglican ministers who emphasized the externals of religion — particularly the outward observance of the sacraments and various ceremonies — and neglected the glory of the cross. A few days later, Gordon visited Currie at the vestry to register a complaint against him for his remarks about Presbyterians. Currie was speechless, but Gordon's directness had the apparent good effect of silencing his attacks against Presbyterians from the pulpit.

There were several others who supported Currie in his attacks on the Presbyterians. Colonel Edwin Conway[32] (1681–1763) of Lancaster County was an outspoken opponent of the Presbyterians in the Northern Neck. On March 3, 1758, Conway wrote to Commissary Thomas Dawson as follows:

> I expect the Gentlemen of the Clergy, from these Parts, will let your Hon. know the Evil Consequences of a Dissenter's Preaching among us.[33]

Gordon and Conway had previously been close friends, but this matter put a strain on their friendship. Conway's letter to Thomas Dawson did not have the desired effect and by January 9 he had received a letter from Benjamin Waller, clerk of the General Court of Virginia, "that dissenters have the power to build houses and enjoy their religion by Act of Toleration."[34] That opinion represented quite a turnaround in the position of the Virginia Court since the arrival of Davies in the Colony.

Despite the opposition of the Anglicans, a meeting place for Presbyterians was erected in Lancaster County which measured sixty feet by thirty feet which both Currie and Leland considered much larger than was necessary. They said there were only about twenty Dissenters in both counties combined and most of them attended the Anglican services prior to Davies' preaching tours. They underestimated the number of communing Presbyterians in those counties and did not consider the large number of people who attended the services whenever a Presbyter-

---

[32] Conway was a relative of several important families in Virginia. His wife, Anne Bell Conway (1686–1763) was a half sister to Mary Ball Washington, the mother of President George Washington. Edwin was also a great-uncle of President James Madison.

[33] "Letters of Patrick Henry, Sr., Samuel Davies, James Maury, Edwin Conway and George Trask," *The William and Mary Quarterly*, Vol. 1, No. 4 (Oct. 1921), 279.

[34] Foote, *Sketches of Virginia*, First Series, 361.

ian minister supplied them. Leland, Currie, and Menzies agreed with Westmoreland County (just northwest of Northumberland County along the Maryland border) which refused a license for a meetinghouse to Davies on the grounds the Act of Toleration did not extend to Virginia. Their arguments against the Dissenters were the same ones which had already been proven to be false and, therefore, would prove ineffective in the Northern Neck to stop the progress of the New Light Presbyterians.

Davies' last trip into the Northern Neck was in the early spring of 1759. Colonel Gordon met Davies and several leaders from Hanover, including Samuel Morris and John Todd, on March 21, 1759. Davies spent four or five days in the Northern Neck counties and held communion on Sunday, March 26, for forty-four people with 800–900 people present at the service.[35] Menzies, who lived near the Gordons, was probably upset at the loss of influential members of society from the communion of his parish. In his rashness, he cast several aspersions on the character of Davies which prompted an exchange of letters between the parties. On April 9, 1759, Col. Gordon delivered a letter from Davies to Mr. Menzies which "seemed to give him much uneasiness, and I am persuaded he will not enter into a dispute with Mr. Davies if he can avoid it."[36] Nonetheless, Menzies replied with a letter to Mr. Davies three weeks later, via Col. Gordon, which Gordon described as "very stupid and foolish."[37] Menzies wanted to resolve this matter through a private interview with Davies in his own home which was refused on the grounds that Menzies had made public assertions against Davies. Davies felt Menzies must be willing either to prove those matters in a public debate to which all would be allowed to attend or to publicly repent of his false statements. Davies implied in his last letter that Menzies was a hypocrite with the following words: "To insult the Insolent, & Scorn the Scorner, is Natural, and thus naturally would I treat you, were it not that the Benevolence of that Religion, which you profess, & I practice, rather inclines me to overcome Evil with Good."[38]

---

[35] James Gordon, "The Diary of Col. James Gordon," *The William and Mary Quarterly*, Vol. 11, No. 2 (Oct. 1902), 102.
[36] Foote, *Sketches of Virginia*, First Series, 362.
[37] Ibid.
[38] Ibid.

Davies advised him to "no longer fret & Vex yourself in feeble ineffectual opposition" to one he considered to be "the Troubler of Israel"[39] since he would soon be leaving the colony.

Davies Accepts the Call to Nassau Hall

As a result of his earlier communications with Davies, David Bostwick wrote Bellamy on January 1, 1759, to inform him of Davies' "absolute refusal"[40] of the Board's second invitation and of the determination of a majority of the Trustees, alarmed by Halsey's communications to him, to make one more effort to obtain him for the College. Acknowledging that party spirit among the Trustees ran high, Bostwick exclaimed to Bellamy: "I fear the Consequence."[41]

A month later, William Kirkpatrick[42] informed Bellamy that the Trustees had sent another messenger[43] to Hanover with an invitation for Davies "to the Presidentship of our College."[44] After the two previous denials, Kirkpatrick succinctly stated the anxious attitude of the Trustees: "We wait the event."[45] This third invitation, which was also presented in an undated letter from Cowell, grew out of an informal meeting of at least a portion of the Board members.[46]

Davies replied to Cowell's letter on March 12, 1759, by expressing his wish that he had received it a few days earlier when he could have sent a reply by W. P. Smith.[47] Matters had "taken such an unexpected, unaccountable turn"[48] that he determined to leave things entirely in the hands

---

[39] Ibid.
[40] David Bostwick to Joseph Bellamy, January 1, 1759. MS letter in Joseph Bellamy Papers, Hartford Seminary Library, Hartford, Connecticut.
[41] Ibid.
[42] Kirkpatrick was the brother of Davies first wife, Sarah Kirkpatrick, and a Presbyterian minister.
[43] Evidently this messenger was W. B. Smith who was in Hanover during part of March, if not also part of February.
[44] William Kirkpatrick to Joseph Bellamy, February 12, 1759. MS letter in Joseph Bellamy Papers, Hartford Seminary Library, Hartford, Connecticut.
[45] Ibid.
[46] Cowell himself, in a postscript to this letter, expressed his opinion that he understood it coming from the majority.
[47] Smith was obviously one of the two messengers sent by the Board to convince Davies to come to Princeton.
[48] "New Jersey College and President Davies," 389.

of the Trustees and the Synod. If the Trustees chose to reelect him to the presidency and the Synod confirmed the matter, then he would "immediately prepare to remove"[49] and assume his newly elected office. When the Board met on May 9, 1759, both Davies and Samuel Finley were proposed as candidates. Davies was again the choice of the Board. Caleb Smith, John Brainerd, and Elihu Spencer were ordered to be emissaries in presenting this matter before the reunited Synods of Philadelphia and New York.

The Synod of New York considered this matter at their annual meeting on May 16, 1759. Davies chose not to attend this meeting of Synod, but waited to receive word from John Todd concerning the decision of the body. The college submitted "an application. . . for the liberation of Mr. Davies from his pastoral charge"[50] and the Hanover congregation presented the same petition which they had submitted to Presbytery. The Synod first engaged in humble prayer for guidance and then determined:

> That the arguments in favor of said liberation, do preponderate, and agree, that Mr. Davies' pastoral relation to his congregation be dissolved, in order to his removal to the college, and do accordingly hereby dissolve it.[51]

Davies acquiesced with this decision and immediately began preparations to part from his congregation. He allowed his elders to review all the letters which had passed between him and the Trustees in order to satisfy their concerns. His final sermon at Hanover, "The Apostolic Valediction Considered and Applied," was preached from 2 Corinthians 13:11, "Finally, brethren, farewell. Be perfect, be of good comfort; be of one mind; live in peace; and the God of love and peace shall be with you." He told them with sincere emotion:

> Alas! and must we part? My heart fails at the thought. The most endeared friendship I have for you; the affectionate gratitude I feel for you as my benefactors; the anxieties that rush upon my honest heart, lest when you are, as it were, disbanded, and left, as it were, as sheep without a shepherd, you should wander, and the little religion among you should die

---

[49] Ibid.
[50] Pilcher, *Samuel Davies: Apostle of Dissent in Colonial Virginia*, 175.
[51] "New Jersey College and President Davies," 392.

away... these and a thousand other things, render this a very painful and melancholy parting to me. Yet part we must; therefore, "Finally, my brethren, farewell."[52]

Several people in the congregation took his departure with heavy hearts. Some of them felt that Davies had the power to refuse the College of New Jersey and to remain in Hanover. In answer to these objections by some members of his flock, Davies stated:

> It is, therefore, impertinent to object, that "I might stay after all, if I would." It is true, it is in my power to refuse to comply with my duty, even when it appears: it is in my power to violate my solemn vows, and incur the guilt of perjury by disobedience to my brethren in that judicature to which they belong: that is, it is in my power, as a free agent to sin. But this is a preposterous power, which I hope God will enable me never willingly to exercise.[53]

If Davies had flatly refused the Trustees from the outset, as Lockwood did, the matter would have ended there. Instead, he submitted to the collective wisdom of his brethren. As he stated:

> My difficulty was not to find out my own inclination, which was pre-engaged to Hanover, but the path of duty; and the fear of mistaking it, in so important a turn of life, kept me uneasy night and day.[54]

David Bostwick believed concerning Davies that:

> The unusual lustre with which [Davies] shone could not long be confined to that remote corner of the world, but soon attracted the notice and pleasing admiration of men of genius, or piety, far and near... Distressing as it was, both to him and his people, united in the strongest bonds of mutual affection, to think of a separation; yet a conviction of absolute duty, resulting from the importance of the station, from various concurring providences; and lastly, from the unanimous advice of his reverend brethren convened in synod, determined him to accept the proposal.[55]

News of Davies' parting quickly spread throughout Virginia causing many anxious hearts. Col. Gordon sent Davies a letter on June 22, 1759,

---

[52] Davies, *Sermons on Important Subjects*, IV, 460–61.
[53] Ibid., 459
[54] Ibid., 457.
[55] Ibid., 460–61.

by his son-in-law, Richard Chichester, in which he expressed appreciation for all his labors. Gordon also commented in his diary:

> His going away gives us here and in Hanover county, the greatest uneasiness. But I trust God will direct us in the way to heaven.[56]

Conclusion

In accepting the call to Hanover in 1748, Davies had submitted to the will of God and followed the "path of duty." At that time, he put his life in God's hands and acquiesced to take a call far from his native home. Now his "path of duty" led him in a different direction for the greater cause of the Church.

Davies was not one who could easily make a decision about a matter of such importance. Nor did he trust his own heart to make that decision without consideration of the judgment of others. Though the general call to the ministry and the special call to a specific field of service are distinct from one another, there are obvious similarities in both calls. In both, a man must listen to "the voice and power of the Holy Spirit, directing the will and the judgment, and conveying personal qualifications."[57] This leading of the Spirit is not the result of some audible voice or enthusiasm, but is manifested by a subservient spirit to the will of God. It will include both the desire to do the work of the ministry and a competent measure of gifts to perform the same.

The great question for Davies was whether or not he was suitably gifted to be the President of such a worthy institution as the College of New Jersey. All those who knew him were convinced that his gifts were equal to almost any task of the ministry. For his part, Davies was uncertain that his intellectual gifts and attainments were worthy to be ranked with the scholarship of his predecessors at Princeton, particularly Jonathan Edwards and Aaron Burr. For that reason, he was hesitant to accept this call as his new "path of duty" until he was certain that the Trustees of the College were convinced of his abilities to perform all the obligations of his new station. In that respect, he was very much like Robert Murray McCheyne, who wrote a century later when he was being enticed to take the St. Martin Parish in Perth, Scotland:

---

[56] Foote, *Sketches of Virginia*, First Series, 363.
[57] Charles Bridges, *The Christian Ministry* (London: The Banner of Truth Trust, 1967), 91.

My Master has placed me here with His own hand; and I never will, either directly or indirectly, seek to be removed.[58]

McCheyne's words should not be taken to mean that a minister should never leave the station where God first placed him. The fact is that McCheyne considered the matter carefully before rejecting the call. A fuller explanation of his sentiments is given by his friend and biographer, Andrew Bonar:

> Few godly pastors can be willing to change the scene of their labors, unless it be plain that the Cloudy Pillar is pointing them away. It is perilous for men to choose for themselves; and too often it has happened that the minister who, on slight grounds, moved away from his former watchtower, has had reason to mourn over the disappointment of his hopes in his larger and wider sphere.[59]

In that respect, Davies and McCheyne were exactly the same. They both were determined not to leave the place where the Lord of the Harvest had placed them unless the fire and the cloudy pillar moved ahead of them. Davies' deliberations in this matter are an example to other ministers of the gospel.

---

[58] Andrew A. Bonar, *Memoir and Remains of Robert Murray McCheyne* (London: The Banner of Truth Trust, 1966), 68.
[59] Ibid.

-20-

President of the College of New Jersey

"I am laboring to do a little good in the world. But, alas! I find I am of little use or importance. I have many defects, but none gives me so much pain and mortification as my slow progress in personal holiness. This is the grand qualification of the office we sustain, as well as that heaven we hope for, and I am shocked at myself when I see how little I have of it."[1]
~*Samuel Davies to Thomas Gibbons*~

Close-up of Nassau Hall front entrance

---

[1] Thomas Gibbons, "Divine Conduct Vindicated," in Samuel Davies, *Sermons on Important Subjects*, Vol. I (New York: J. & J. Harper, 1828), 35.

Princeton, New Jersey, sits on an elevation between the alluvial plains of the southern part of the state and the hill country of the north. It is almost equidistant from Philadelphia and New York City on the main colonial road—commonly known as the King's highway. In colonial days, Princeton was a borough, not a township, having received that name circa 1724. Kingston, Queenstown, and Princessville were nearby towns on the southwesterly road from New Brunswick to Trenton which explains the derivation of the name of this village. Its location in the colony of New Jersey gave it some of the most salubrious weather in all America with neither the scorching summers of the southern states nor the bitter winters of New England. Archibald Alexander, who spent over forty years as a professor in Princeton, once described that town to a friend as having "one of the finest climates in the solar system."[2] It was for that reason that a later President of the College of New Jersey, Jonathan Witherspoon, referred to Princeton as "the Montpelier of America"[3] after the Mediterranean coastal city in southeastern France. Jacob Frelinghuysen Hageman elaborates on the climate of Princeton as follows:

> Its winters are cold enough to produce a desirable supply of snow and ice. . . But such intense cold is exceptionable and of very short duration. Its summers are adapted to the growth and perfection of the crops and fruits of the season. When the mercury rises above ninety degrees, it is exceptionable and only of a few days' continuance. The autumn with its Italian sunsets, and its gorgeous foliage of brilliant hues, combines with an unsurpassed beauty, a most genial and uniform temperature.[4]

Princeton and the College of New Jersey were succinctly depicted in the travel journal of Francois Jean Marquis de Chastellux, Major General of the French Expeditionary Forces in the Revolutionary War and the principal liaison officer between General George Washington and General Comte de Rochembeau of France. Fluent in English, a man of letters, and a member of the French Academy, the Marquis de Chastellux commented on Princeton in a book of his travels in America following the War:

---

[2] Jacob Frelinghuysen Hageman, *History of Princeton and Its Institutions*, Volume I (Philadelphia: J. P. Lippincott & Co, 1870), 14.
[3] Ibid., 13.
[4] Ibid., 14.

> Beyond Kingston, the country begins to open, and continues so to Prince-Town. This town is situated on a sort of plateau not much elevated, but which commands on all sides: it has only one street formed by the high road; there are about sixty or eighty houses, all tolerably well built, but little attention is paid them, for that is immediately attracted by an immense building, which is at a considerable distance. It is a college built by the state of Jersey. . . on the left of the road going to Philadelphia, that is situated towards the middle of the town, on a distinct spot of ground, and. . . the entrance to it is by a large square court surrounded with lofty palisades.[5]

It was to that commanding town, with its healthy climate and attractive college, that Samuel Davies moved in 1759, having accepted the call to the Presidency of the College of New Jersey. The "immense building" which Marquis de Chastellux described was Nassau Hall, completed in 1756 through the funds raised by Davies and Gilbert Tennent in Great Britain. Setting back from the road a couple of hundred feet, it was shaded by several large trees and fronted on the right side by the President's house. It housed the President's office, the lecture halls, the library, and forty-nine small dormitory rooms for about 150 students. The first floor also had an elegant meeting hall, adorned on opposite sides by the portraits of King George I and Governor Belcher, with an organ and a stage which was used for the public orations of the students. From 1756 to 1766, this meeting room was also used by the First Presbyterian Church of Princeton, with the services conducted by the President of the College, until they could construct their first church building. A dining hall, a kitchen, and the steward's apartments were also on the first floor of Nassau Hall which was "esteemed to be the most conveniently planned for the purpose of a college, of any in North America."[6]

The Davies Family Moves to Princeton

Davies and his family, including both of his parents, arrived in Princeton on July 26, 1759. He had preached his farewell sermon to a mournful congregation at Hanover on July 1, 1759 and was dismissed from the

---

[5] Marquis de Francis Jean Chastellux, *Travels in North America in the Years 1780–82*, Translated from the French, 2 vols., Vol. I (London: G. G. J and J. Robinson, 1787), 138–9.
[6] George R Wallace, *Princeton Sketches, The Story of Nassau Hall* (New York: G. P. Putnam's Sons, 1894), 13.

Presbytery of Hanover eighteen days later. With his dismissal, the most fruitful ministry of any preacher in the history of Virginia came to a sudden end. Davies' family settled into the President's house upon their arrival and he immediately assumed the duties of the Presidency of the College. Tragedy quickly struck his family, though, before he could even be acclimated to his new post. His father passed away only sixteen days after this difficult move to New Jersey which Davies noted in his family Bible: "Lost my Father, aged 79, August 11, 1759."[7] The rigors of a weeklong journey in the oppressive heat of summer coupled with old age, no doubt, contributed to David Davies' death.

A few days later, Davies wrote to Peter Van Brugh Livingston, a Trustee of the College from New York City, who was primarily engaged in shipping furs and also, regrettably, the deplorable trading of slaves. The slave trade was so deeply intertwined in Colonial America that it was commonly accepted or overlooked even by those, like Davies, who had the spiritual interests of the slaves at heart. While Davies did not mention his father's passing to Livingston, this letter did reveal the humility with which he assumed his office:

> About three weeks ago I arrived here, and soon entered upon my new office. A Tremour still seizes me at the Tho't of my situation; and sometimes I can hardly believe it is a reality, but only a frightful portentious Dream. Indeed since I have presided I have had the Pleasure to find myself at the Head of a peaceable manageable Society; but I know myself and human nature too well, to flatter myself with the Expectation of its uninterrupted Continuance. . . I hope to have the Pleasure of seeing you at the Commencement; tho' that will be the terrible Day of my Mortification.[8]

Commencement Exercises at Princeton in 1759

In those days, Commencement exercises at Princeton were held at the beginning of the fall session with classes conducted throughout the summer. There were two six-week periods of recess between the two semesters of college. The spring recess was from the middle of May to the first of July and the fall recess was from the first of October to mid-

---

[7] Samuel Davies' MS Bible. Samuel Davies MSS, Virginia Historical Society, Richmond, Virginia.
[8] Samuel Davies to P.V. B. Livingston, *Proceedings of the New Jersey Historical Society*, Series I, Vol. I (Newark, New Jersey: Office of the Daily Advertiser, 1845), 77.

November.⁹ The fall session, therefore, was six months long and the summer session was only three months. This plan allowed young men to help their families during both planting and harvest.

At the Commencement in 1759, Davies was installed as President of the College of New Jersey on September 26 "by taking the several oaths as the charter directs."[10] He then delivered a Latin oration and an ode which were applauded by all present, including Governor Francis Bernard. His ode, "Perth Amboy,"[11] set to music by one of the students, James Lyon, regaled the peacefulness of life at Nassau Hall through all the consternations of war with France, and referred to King George II[12] of Great Britain as "the Friend of Man."

The Trustees held their annual Board meeting at these Commencement exercises and unanimously voted to pay Davies £200 per annum. His remuneration was to begin with the previous May and cover the whole period of the summer semester. Thereafter, he was to be paid in semi-annual payments at the end of each six months of service. They also voted to recompense Davies £60, 17 pence, and 5 shillings "to defray the expenses of removing his family from Hanover to Princeton."[13] The grammar school at Princeton was relinquished "into the hands of President Davies, to be wholly his property, as it was formerly the property of the late President Burr."[14] It was also decided that Davies' sons could be educated at the College "free from the charge of tuition money."[15]

---

[9] Benjamin B. Warfield, "How Princeton Seminary Got to Work," Journal of the Presbyterian Historical Society, Vol. 9, No. 6 (June 1918), 256. What Warfield writes about Princeton Theological Seminary was also the model for the school year of the College of New Jersey when Davies was President there.
[10] Ashbel Green, *Discourses Delivered in the College of New Jersey* (Philadelphia, New York and Trenton: 1822), 334.
[11] Perth Amboy was the Capitol of New Jersey from 1686 to 1776.
[12] King George II was born in Hanover, Germany. He was the son of George Louis, Prince of Brunswick-Luneburg and later King George I of Great Britain. Despite George II's immoral relations with several mistresses, he did accomplish several good things for the British Empire.
[13] Green, *Discourses Delivered in the College of New Jersey*, 334.
[14] Ibid.
[15] Ibid.

The College Library

At the behest of the Trustees, Davies began an examination of the college library shortly after his inauguration. This task was completed expeditiously and *A Catalogue of Books in the Library of the College of New Jersey* was published on January 29, 1760. The purpose of this catalogue was to acquaint generous friends and benefactors with the library's needs which held a paltry 1,281 volumes, nearly half of which had been donated by former Governor Belcher. A review of this catalogue reveals that the library's holdings were more complete in ancient authors than modern authors on most branches of knowledge. This deficiency was especially felt in the study of "Mathematics, and the Newtonian philosophy."[16] In comparison, the Yale library contained 2,600 volumes in 1741 when a similar catalogue was compiled by President Thomas Clap and the Harvard library, which was destroyed by fire on February 2, 1764, had contained approximately 5,000 volumes. Thus, the advantages of a well-endowed library were set forth by Davies in this pamphlet as follows:

> If they have Books always at hand to consult upon every Subject that may occur to them, as demanding a more thoro' Discussion, in their public Disputes, in the Course of their Studies, in Conversation, or their own fortuitous Tho'ts; it will enable them to investigate Truth through its intricate Recesses; and to guard against the Stratagems and assaults of Error. It will teach them Modesty and Self-Diffidence, when they perceive the free and different Sentiments of Men equally great and good.[17]

Davies' Improvements to the College

When Davies assumed the Presidency of the College of New Jersey in 1759, the school was in an unhappy situation "partly owing to the length of that melancholy period between the death of President Burr and his accession, and partly to the evil dispositions and practices of a few members of the society."[18] The prudent measures and personal example of Davies "soon surmounted these disadvantages; so that in a few

---

[16] Samuel Davies, *A Catalogue of Books in the Library of the College of New Jersey* (Woodbridge, New Jersey: James Parker, 1760), iv.
[17] John MacLean, *History of the College of New Jersey, 1746–1854* (New York: Arno Press, 1969), 207.
[18] "An Appendix" in Samuel Davies, *Sermons on Important Subjects*, I (New York: J & J Harper, 1828), 28.

months a spirit of emulation in learning and morality, as had been usual, evidently characterized the students of Nassau-Hall."[19]

It was the practice of Davies to improve the existing plans of the college rather than alter them. He was asked to "draw up a system of regulations concerning admission into the college, with the necessary qualifications for degrees."[20] He therefore instituted a system which included oral examinations and eliminated the automatic advancement of students from one class to another. Ashbel Green, a later President at Princeton, was of the opinion that "nothing has more contributed to render education in this institution efficient, than the strictness of examinations."[21]

Another of Davies' innovations was the practice of requiring members of the senior class to deliver monthly orations to the public in Nassau Hall on any subject. Davies reviewed their discourses before they were delivered and critiqued them afterwards. A gentleman who lived in Princeton during Davies' term as President has left the following information:

> About six of the young gentlemen delivered their orations in the afternoon of the first Wednesday in every month, to crowded audiences; and it is hard to say, whether the entertainment of the hearers, or the improvement of the students, was greater.[22]

Davies was anxious for the intellectual improvements of the students, but even more keenly interested in their spiritual progress. He was also sympathetic towards the disadvantaged. Thus, David Bostwick left the following statement concerning him:

> He knew that religion was the brightest ornament of the human, and the fairest image of the divine nature, that all true benevolence to men must have its foundation laid in a supreme love to God, and that undissembled piety in the heart was the best security for usefulness in every character of life. It was therefore his constant endeavour to promote the eternal as well as the temporal good of the youth intrusted to his tuition, not only by his fervent preaching and exemplary life, but by inculcating at the proper

---

[19] Ibid.
[20] Green, *Discourses Delivered in the College of New Jersey*, 334.
[21] Ibid.
[22] "An Appendix" in Davies, *Sermons on Important Subjects*, I, 29.

seasons the worth of their souls, and the vast, the inexpressible importance of their everlasting interests.[23]

Slight changes were made to the morning and evening devotions. One of the students was appointed by Davies to read a portion of the Scriptures out of the original languages at morning prayers. The singing of a Psalm was substituted for the reading of Scripture at evening prayers.

In governing the college, Davies had "the art of mingling authority and levity in such a due proportion, as seldom or never failed of the desired success."[24] He corrected their "youthful irregularities with the gentlest methods possible; nor did he ever inflict punishment, without reluctance and pain."[25] As a result, he "was revered and loved by every member of that collected family over which he presided."[26] Students cheerfully doffed their hats when passing President Davies and respectfully stood when he entered the room.[27]

Davies echoed the sentiments of both students and faculty when he wrote to Livingston on December 6, 1759 that "Affairs at College go on Smooth and easy; and we seem at least to have so much Goodness as to love one another."[28] He informed the new Governor of New Jersey, Thomas Boone, on July 8, 1760, that the College of New Jersey "shall continue with the utmost assiduity to instill into young minds such principles as thro' the blessing of Heaven form the Scholar, the Patriot, and the Christian."[29]

Davies' Personal Study as President

After eleven years of incessant activity in Virginia, Davies was keenly aware of his deficiencies as a scholar — whether real or merely perceived. Thus, he customarily studied until midnight and rose by five o'clock

---

[23] David Bostwick, "Character of the Author," in Samuel Davies, *Sermons on Important Subjects*, I (New York: J & J Harper, 1828), 50.
[24] Ibid., 51.
[25] Enoch Pond, *Memoir of the Rev. Samuel Davies* (Boston: Massachusetts Sabbath School Society, 1832), 118.
[26] Bostwick, in Davies, *Sermons on Important Subjects*, I, 51.
[27] Wallace, *Princeton Sketches*, 10–13.
[28] Davies to Livingston, *Proceedings of the New Jersey Historical Society*, Series I, Vol. I, 77.
[29] John MacLean, *History of the College of New Jersey, 1746–1854* (New York: Arno Press, 1969), 215.

when the morning horn sounded for the students. The high academic standards set by Dickinson, Burr, and Edwards made him "determined not to degrade his office, but to be in reality what his station supposed him."[30] In a letter to Livingston on January 18, 1760, he alluded to a fear of disappointing his friends:

> You do me great Honour, Sir, in presuming such favourable Things of my Administration in my present Station. If my future Management Should be so happy as to deserve the continuance of your Charity, I shall esteem it the greatest Blessing I can enjoy in Life. But should I disappoint my Friends and bring my own Fears upon me, I should hardly be able to survive it, but would pine away and die, like an useless or noxious Plant, blasted from Heaven. All my Encouragement proceeds from my anxious Industry night and Day, except what I derive from above.[31]

The short walks from his house to Nassau Hall were his only regular exercise during this time which was insufficient for one suffering from an advanced stage of a pulmonary disease. He surely found by experience what the Preacher in Ecclesiastes warned against: "[T]he writing of many books is endless, and excessive devotion to books is wearying to the body" (Ecclesiastes 12:12). If he did not always have time for diligent study in Hanover amidst all his other duties, he allowed the pendulum to swing too far in the opposite direction at Princeton. His delicate health depended on regular exercise to overcome his bodily afflictions, but he made no time in his schedule at Princeton for such.

Student Life at Princeton

College life during the mid-eighteenth century was more formal than in these modern times and this model of formality was especially observed on dining occasions at Nassau Hall. "It must have been a goodly sight to see the President, tutors, and students, all seated together in the wide dining hall, clad in the scholastic gown, and arranged according to rank and seniority."[32] Yet, the students were amply fed at Princeton as their diet consisted of "almost all the varieties of fish and flesh the country af-

---

[30] "An Appendix" in Davies, *Sermons on Important Subjects*, I, 28.
[31] Davies to Livingston, *Proceedings of the New Jersey Historical Society*, Series I, Vol. I, 78.
[32] George R. Wallace, *Princeton Sketches: The Story of Nassau Hall* (New York and London: G. P. Putnam's Sons, 1893), 17.

fords, and sometimes pyes."³³ New Jersey was especially prolific in the production of garden vegetables so those also would have adorned the tables at Nassau Hall. Their drink routinely consisted of beer or cider at dinner and milk or hot chocolate for supper.

Student life at Princeton was closely regimented with only a few hours of the day when they could leave their rooms without permission. Various laws governing student conduct are recorded as follows:

> None of the students shall play cards, or dice, or any other unlawful game, upon the penalty of a fine not exceeding five shillings for the first offense; for the second, public admonition; for the third, expulsion. No jumping, hollering, or boisterous noise shall be suffered at the college at any time, or walking in the gallery in the time of study. No member of the college shall wear his hat in the college at any time, or in the hall at any public meeting, or knowingly in the presence of the superiority of the college, without an upper garment, and having shoes and stockings tight.³⁴

Such laws were, no doubt, necessary to maintain discipline and develop an esprit de corps among the students, but were incapable of producing true spirituality inasmuch as the law can only be a schoolmaster to lead us to Christ. Only the Holy Spirit can awaken sinners from the dead and true obedience is "from the heart to that form of teaching to which you were committed" (Romans 6:17) even as a movement of the Spirit had produced a revival among the students at Princeton in 1757.

As with all colleges, dormitory life evoked peculiar temptations for the young men at the College of New Jersey. One of the students, Benjamin Rush, recorded his own assessment of the habit of housing young men in such close proximity to one another:

> Vices of the same species attract each other with the most force. Hence the bad consequences of crowding young men (whose propensities are generally the same) under one roof, in our modern plans of education.³⁵

---

[33] Ibid., 17–18.
[34] Ibid., 18, 21.
[35] David Freeman Hawke, *Benjamin Rush: Revolutionary Gadfly* (Indianapolis, Indiana and New York, New York: The Bobbs Merrill Company, Inc., 1971), 18.

Dr. Scudder Inoculates the Students

One of the first crises of Davies' administration happened in February of 1760 when a number of students at Princeton became sick and had to be inoculated by Dr. Nathaniel Scudder, a 1756 graduate of the college. Davies feared that an epidemic was about to break out and took precautions to protect the students and college. "In those days the preventive was at times as dangerous as the disease. The use of vaccines was in its experimental stage."[36] The Puritan minister, Cotton Mather, had introduced inoculations to the New World during a smallpox epidemic in Boston during 1721–22 which affected over half of the city's population of 11,000. Mather's actions were a milestone in the history of inoculations and led to the eradication of smallpox by the end of the eighteenth century through Edward Jenner's introduction of a smallpox vaccination.[37] Yet, other infectious diseases were not as easily eradicated and presented a dangerous threat to the mortality rates of every society. Such an infectious disease was now ravaging Nassau Hall.

One student of the college was infected with pleurisy[38] which caused Davies to fear for his life. Writing to the Trenton pastor, David Cowell, on February 15, 1760, Davies requested his assistance since he was knowledgeable of medicine. "Davies asked him to come to Princeton at once, for the young man's life was in danger and 'my Dear Mrs. Davies is so affected in the Mouth, etc., with the mercurial and antimonial Preparations, that she has been in exquisite Agony, and stands in great need of immediate Relief.'"[39] Trenton was only seventeen miles south of Princeton and there is every probability that Cowell answered this request as soon as he received the letter, but nothing further is known about this period of sickness.

---

[36] George H. Bost, "Samuel Davies as President of Princeton," *Journal of the Presbyterian Historical Society*, Vol. 26, No. 3 (September 1948), 174.

[37] "The Fight Over Inoculation During the 1721 Boston Smallpox Epidemic," December 31, 2014. Accessed on February 6, 2017 at: http://sitn.hms.harvard.edu/flash/special-edition-on-infectious-disease/2014/the-fight-over-inoculation-during-the-1721-boston-smallpox-epidemic/

[38] Pleurisy has many causes and symptoms. It could be the result of heart failure, pneumonia, influenza, rheumatoid arthritis, or even lung cancer near the pleural surface. In this case, it was probably the result of the flu or pneumonia.

[39] Bost, "Samuel Davies as President of Princeton," *Journal of the Presbyterian Historical Society*, 175.

Davies Travels to New England for the College

A couple of months later, during the spring recess of 1760, Davies took a trip into New England for the purpose of widening his and the college's circle of friends. He intended to proceed from New Haven in Connecticut to Bethlehem for a meeting with Joseph Bellamy whom he had "so long honored & loved."[40] Regrettably, he was detained in New York for more than a week and informed Bellamy, "I painfully feel myself unable to make an excursion to you."[41]

Davies did not mention the reason for his being detained in New York City for more than a week, but it was evidently with respect to the troubles in the First Presbyterian Church of that city. There had been a division in the congregation for several years between the Scotch-Irish members and the English members over the matter of exclusive Psalm singing. The majority of the congregation had introduced the hymnody of Isaac Watts. Neither Presbytery nor Synod was successful in their efforts to reconcile the parties, with the result that a split took place in 1761. It was surely with respect to this matter that Davies was detained. David Bostwick was the pastor of First Presbyterian Church from 1756 to 1763 and was a close friend of Davies as well as being a Trustee of the College of New Jersey.

Bellamy and Davies never had the occasion to meet in person, but their hearts were joined together in the things of the gospel.

Benjamin Rush

Benjamin Rush, Samuel Finley's nephew, was one of the outstanding students at Princeton during Davies' Presidency. Rush was enrolled in the junior class in the spring of 1759 as a junior and graduated in 1760. Several years later, he wrote that Davies "was truly dignified, but at the same time affable and even familiar in his intercourse with his pupils."[42] While a student at Princeton, Rush "discovered some talents for poetry, composition and public speaking, to each of which he [Davies—DR] was

---

[40] Samuel Davies to Joseph Bellamy, April 18, 1760. MS letter in Joseph Bellamy Papers, Hartford Seminary Library, Hartford, Connecticut.
[41] Ibid.
[42] James MacLachlan, *Princetonians, 1748–1768* (Princeton: Princeton University Press, 1976), 319.

very partial."[43] At his own Commencement in September of 1760, the *Pennsylvania Gazette* records that Rush "arose, and in a very sprightly and entertaining Manner, delivered an ingenious *English* Harangue in Praise of Oratory."[44]

In many ways, Rush became a true disciple of Davies on most of his main emphases. "During the next fifteen years, it would be difficult to distinguish where his thoughts began and Davies' ended when he wrote about slavery, religion, education, or patriotism."[45] Yet, Davies' absorption with metaphysics was particularly disgusting to Rush, and thirty years later he could recall with regret the wasted hours of listening to his mentor talk about such things as:

> [P]ossible existences, the infinity of space, the ubiquity of spirit, and many other such subtleties of the learning of the thirteenth and fourteenth centuries.[46]

Metaphysics is a system of philosophy which tries to answer the fundamental questions concerning the nature of being and the world. Primary topics of discussion include such matters as existence, space, time, objects, etc. Metaphysics was one of the primary works of Aristotle who developed his theory of change and causality under four causes: material, formal, efficient, and final. The late medieval Scholastic theologians of the twelfth through fifteenth centuries contributed to an age of learning in no small part due to their study of the ancient philosophers. Thomas Aquinas approached many subjects in his *Summa Theologica* by defining them according to Aristotle's theory of change in his effort to synthesize Christian theology with Aristotelian philosophy. One of the effects of this approach is that it allowed Aquinas and the Scholastics to both affirm and deny a matter at the same time. In other words, one thing would be the formal cause while another would be the efficient cause and another still would be the final cause.

One of the weaknesses of a classical education, which Davies had received and favored as an educator, was that it focused a lot of attention on the Scholastic theologians and the ancient philosophers of Greece and

---

[43] Ibid.
[44] *Pennsylvania Gazette*, October 9, 1760.
[45] Hawke, *Benjamin Rush*, 21.
[46] Ibid., 20–21.

Rome. There were certainly advantages in studying both in the development of various methods of thinking, but there were inherent dangers as well. Neither the Scholastics nor the ancient philosophers held to a correct understanding of salvation. As the great Scottish theologian, William Cunningham, wrote concerning the Scholastics, or Schoolmen as they were called:

> The schoolmen certainly did nothing to introduce a sounder method of theological investigation, by appealing to Scripture, and labouring to ascertain the true meaning of its statements; on the contrary, they may be said to have still further corrupted it, by introducing, in combination with tradition and mere authority, something resembling the rationalistic element of the supremacy of human reason,—not, indeed, that they formally and avowedly laid down this principle, but that their neglect of Scripture, and their unbounded indulgence in unwarranted and presumptuous speculations upon points in regard to which there could manifestly be no standard of appeal but just their own reasonings, had a tendency to encourage it.
>
> This leads us to notice the other great defect of the scholastic theology, and that is, its consisting, to a large extent, of the discussion of useless questions, which cannot be determined, and which would have no practical value if they could.[47]

No doubt, it was those useless, unwarranted, and impractical questions of the Schoolmen which caused Rush to be so bored when Davies turned his attention to the study of metaphysical discussions. Since such metaphysical questions were largely discussions of things that are outside the revelation of Scripture, it resulted in deciding such questions based on opinions rather than truth. In another place, Cunningham further comments on the relative value of the Schoolmen:

> As the schoolmen did not adopt a right rule or standard for deciding theological questions,—as they did not employ a right method of investigation—and indulged in presumptuous speculations upon many useless questions, which admit of no clear or certain solution—it is plain that they possess little of what constitutes the highest and most direct value of theological works—viz., establishing scriptural truths upon a firm foundation, and exposing anti-scriptural errors by satisfactory arguments. . .

---

[47] William Cunningham, *Historical Theology*, Volume 1 (London: The Banner of Truth Trust, 1969), 415.

> The writings of the Reformers not unfrequently exposed the errors and defects of the theology of the schoolmen, which they regarded as one of the bulwarks of the Popish system; and this fact of itself renders it desirable to possess some knowledge of their works.[48]

The danger of too close a study of the classics is brought out by Philip Schaff in the seventh volume of his *History of the Christian Church* concerning the German Reformation:

> Every true progress in church history is conditioned by a new and deeper study of the Scriptures, which has "first, second, third, infinite draughts." While the Humanists went back to the ancient classics and revived the spirit of Greek and Roman paganism, the Reformers went back to the sacred Scriptures and revived the spirit of apostolic Christianity. They were fired by an enthusiasm for the gospel, such as had never been known since the days of Paul.[49]

The classics lead back to paganism and represent a danger which has to be guarded against by the wary student. The unsuspecting can be deluded by the false knowledge of the ancient philosophers and, thereby, completely miss the mark of true Christianity. Yet, even Rush would have admitted that the study of the classics aided his intellectual development in other ways. Davies recommended that his students keep "a commonplace book, or 'Liber Selectorum' as he called it, in which to record passages from the classics that struck them forcibly."[50] To which Rush later wrote:

> By recording these passages, I was led afterwards to record facts and opinions. To this I owe perhaps in part the frequent use I made of pen and ink.[51]

Rush intended to study law after graduation, but his mind was changed by a visit with his uncle, Samuel Finley, who had taught and advised him from the age of six. Rush described what took place next:

---

[48] Ibid., 417–8.
[49] Philip Schaff, *History of the Christian Church*, Volume VII, The German Reformation (Grand Rapids, Michigan: Wm. B. Eerdmans Publishing Company, 1980), 17.
[50] Hawke, *Benjamin Rush*, 20.
[51] Ibid.

Just before I took leave of him on my return home he called me to the end of the piazza before his door, and asked me whether I had chosen a profession. I told him I had, and that I expected to begin the study of the law as soon as I returned to Philadelphia. He said the practice of the law was full of temptations and advised me of no means to think of it, but to study physic. "But before you determine on anything (said he), set apart a day for fasting and prayer, and ask God to direct you in your choice of a profession."[52]

Rush failed to set aside a day for prayer and fasting, but he did choose to be a physician. Davies shortly thereafter wrote a letter of recommendation for Rush to Dr. John Redman, a former student at the Log College, who took in Rush as a medical student. Rush studied under Redman for six years before completing his medical studies in Scotland. He became one of the most famous graduates of the College of New Jersey. He was elected to the first Continental Congress; he was the first Surgeon General; he was a professor in the Medical Department of the University of Pennsylvania; he was a signer of the Declaration of Independence; and he was Treasurer of the United States mint from 1797 to his death in 1813. At his death, he was arguably revered as highly as George Washington and Benjamin Franklin.

Religion and the Public Spirit
At the Commencement exercises in 1760, Davies delivered a valedictory address, "Religion and the Public Spirit," which set forth his views on the motives which the graduates should have in their service to God and country:

> Whatever, I say, be your Place. . . imbibe and cherish a public spirit. Serve your generation. Live not for yourselves but the public. Be the servants of the Church; the servants of all. Esteem yourselves by so much the more happy, honourable and important, by how much the more useful you are. Let your own ease, your own pleasure, your own private interests, yield to the common good.[53]

Later in this message, he reminded the graduates that "a college education does only lay the foundation; on which to build must be the busi-

---

[52] MacLachlan, *Princetonians*, 319
[53] Varnum Lansing Collins, *Princeton* (New York: Oxford University Press, 1914), 58

ness of your future life."[54] Davies counseled them in the choice of a career to "fix upon that which is most agreeable to your natural Turn, which in some measure is equal to your Abilities, and may be more conducive to the service of your generation."[55] He exhorted them to go into "publick life with a new heart and a new spirit. . . the new birth is the beginning of all genuine religion and virtue."[56]

Noteworthy Students at Princeton

In addition to Benjamin Rush, several of the students took Davies' words to heart and rose to distinction in their chosen professions. Among them were Samuel Blair, Jr., David Rice, John Rosbrugh, Jonathan Bayard Smith, and John Archer.

Samuel Blair, Jr.[57] (1741–1818) was the son of Davies' teacher at Fagg's Manor, the Rev. Samuel Blair. Blair graduated from Princeton in 1760 and was licensed to preach in 1764. He was offered the Presidency of the College of New Jersey[58] in 1767 at the age of twenty-six, but declined the appointment so that Jonathan Witherspoon could be elected to that position. He pastored the Old South Church of Boston from 1766 to 1769 when he resigned due to his poor health. He then moved to Germantown, Pennsylvania, and continued to study theology. In 1790, he received the Doctor of Divinity degree from the University of Pennsylvania. In December of 1790, Blair was appointed to be the second chaplain of Congress and served in that position for two years.

David Rice (1733–1816) of Hanover was the son of David and Susannah Rice who were plain farmers in that county. Rice's parents never owned slaves because his father considered it unprofitable and his mother thought it was morally wrong.[59] Both of them were Episcopalians by background until Davies came to the colony in 1748. Davies was the instrument of Rice's conversion and took him to Princeton with him when he was elected President. Rice had previously studied under both

---

[54] Ibid.
[55] Ibid.
[56] MacLachlan, *Princetonians, 1748–1768*, 319
[57] The son of Davies' former teacher at Fagg's Manor.
[58] The College of New Jersey is the institution referred to in this quote.
[59] William B. Sprague, *Annals of the American Pulpit: Presbyterian*, Vol. I (Birmingham, AL: Solid Ground Christian Books), 246.

Davies and Todd in Virginia before his enrollment in the junior class of the College of New Jersey in 1759. When he was soon overcome with financial difficulties, Davies arranged for his support through one of the Trustees, Richard Stockton. This aid allowed him to replace clothing which was so worn that he contemplated leaving Princeton. At his graduation, Rice delivered an oration on benevolence which expressed his gratitude.

After graduation in 1761, Rice returned to Hanover where he studied theology under John Todd and was licensed to preach by Hanover Presbytery in 1762. After serving as an evangelist along the Virginia and North Carolina border, Rice took a trip to Pennsylvania where he married Mary Blair, the daughter of Rev. Samuel Blair (then deceased) of Fagg's Manor On his return to Virginia, he stopped in Hanover and received a call to the Polegreen Church where Davies had previously preached. He remained there for five years before an old dispute erupted between two of Davies' elders over the issue of slavery. Eventually he settled in Kentucky where he affectionately became known as *Father Rice*.

John Rosbrugh, who graduated in 1761 at the age of thirty-seven, was another one of the students who depended on financial aid in order to complete his studies. The fund established through the efforts of Davies and Tennent to assist Calvinistic candidates for the ministry enabled students like Rosbrugh to continue their education. After graduation, he was licensed to preach in 1763 and served churches in New Jersey and Pennsylvania before becoming a chaplain in the Revolutionary War. He was the first American chaplain to ever be killed in war when he was surrounded by Hessians on January 2, 1777, outside the tavern where he had been dining; he tried to surrender but, instead, was bayoneted to death on the spot after being recognized as a Presbyterian minister.[60] Like his Master, he prayed for the forgiveness of his murderers and was brutally killed as soon as the prayer left his lips. The soldier who committed this evil deed ran into the nearby city of Trenton and bragged to the owner of a hotel that he had killed a minister. His body was so mangled that his dear wife could hardly identify him. A member of

---

[60] As a retired Army Reserve chaplain and former instructor at the US Army Chaplain Center and School, Rosbrugh's death in combat is especially meaningful to me.

Rosbrugh's congregation, John Hayes, took oversight of his body and arranged for his burial the next day.

Jonathan Bayard Smith (1742–1812) was the son of a merchant in Philadelphia, Samuel Smith, and graduated from Princeton in 1760. After graduation, he worked with his father before being elected to the Continental Congress in 1777–1778[61] where he signed the Articles of Confederation which established the United States of America. He later served as a Trustee for both Princeton College and the University of Pennsylvania. His body is interred in the cemetery of the Second Presbyterian Church of Philadelphia.

John Archer (1741–1810) was born in Churchville, Maryland, and attended Samuel Finley's West Nottingham Academy before matriculating at Princeton. After graduation in 1760, Archer first studied theology in preparation to be a minister, but a throat problem caused him to abandon that idea. He then studied medicine at the College of Philadelphia where he graduated in 1768 as a physician. From 1801 to 1807, Archer served in the U. S. House of Representatives for the Sixth District of Maryland.

Davies Supplies the First Presbyterian Church

Like his predecessors, Davies supplied the local Presbyterian congregation which met for worship in the main hall of the college. Such was the general delight with Davies' messages that when he invited a visiting minister to preach "it was scarcely possible to prevent the manifestation of the disappointment and regret which were universally felt."[62] His efforts on special occasions were universally acclaimed as Bostwick states:

> His performances at public anniversary commencements, as they never failed to do honour to the institution, so they always surprised his friends themselves by exceeding, far exceeding their most sanguine expectations. His poetical compositions, and his elegant taste for cultivating the Muses, gave additional embellishments to those performances, and greatly heightened the pleasure of his crowded auditors.[63]

---

[61] MacLean *History of the College of New Jersey*, 218.
[62] Green, *Discourses Delivered in the College of New Jersey*, 351.
[63] "An Appendix" in Davies, *Sermons on Important Subjects*, I, 51.

Bostwick's remark in a letter to Joseph Bellamy summarized the pleasure which everyone felt in President Davies: "I believe there never was a College happier in its President, or in a more flourishing state."[64] With Davies at the helm, the many friends of the College of New Jersey envisioned great things for the future of their beloved institution.

Conclusion

Davies' decision to improve the existing plans of the college rather than make wholesale changes to them was very wise. It enabled him to gain the trust and support of students, faculty, Trustees, and friends alike. His example, in this respect, is worthy of emulation by all ministers of the gospel. Unless a practice is contrary to the teaching of Scripture, it is best for those who are called to a new charge not to make wholesale changes to existing plans of that organization. Davies, therefore, put into practice Paul's principle in 1 Corinthians 9: 22, 23: "I have become all things to all men, so that I may by all means save some. I do all things for the sake of the gospel, so that I may become a fellow partaker of it." He started where the school was, won their confidence, and improved on the existing policies before considering any changes to them.

---

[64] David Bostwick to Joseph Bellamy, March 17, 1761. MS Letter in Joseph Bellamy Papers, Hartford Seminary Library, Hartford, Connecticut.

-21-

The Pamphlet War among Presbyterians

"Blessed are you when people insult you and persecute you, and falsely say all kinds of evil against you because of Me. Rejoice and be glad, for your reward in heaven is great; for in the same way they persecuted the prophets who were before you."
~Matthew 5:11-12~

Sketch of Christ Episcopal Church
in Philadelphia, Pennsylvania

The Pamphlet War with Episcopalians

In May of 1760, Samuel Davies and seventeen other Presbyterian ministers were involved in a circumstance which partially revived the animosities between the Old Light–New Light Presbyterians. The two sides had reunited in 1758, primarily due to the leadership of Gilbert Tennent, but it would be far amiss to state that all former differences had been amicably resolved. From the very beginning of the split, the New Lights had made numerous efforts to heal the breach, but those efforts were unreciprocated by the Old Lights. Tennent himself had published an apology for his actions soon after the 1741 meeting of the denomination and continued to appeal to both sides for reunion until such came to pass. Tennent also made a motion to the Synod of New York in 1749 to initiate inquiries with the Synod of Philadelphia concerning the prospects for such a reunion. Several members of the Synod of New York had previously expressed their desire for such a reunion and at least one unnamed member of the Synod of Philadelphia had done the same. Tennent's *Irenicum Ecclesiasticum*, published in 1749, set forth the beauty and excellence of the unity of the visible church.

> THE *Design* of the *Parable* is to shew that the visible Church or Kingdom of CHRIST, which is joined together by an external *Bond* of *Union,* is compos'd of good and bad, and will remain mixed till the End of Time; and that we ought to let it remain so, ought to let them grow together, because we are not capable to make a judicial actual *Distinction* between Saints and Hypocrites without doing Injury to the former. The Thing in view is the unlawfulness of breaking the *Churches* outward *Union,* because of our Judgment about *internals;*. . . As *Church fellowship* is a valuable Priviledge, so of consequence to be deprived of it, without just Cause, is unjust, as really as to be unjustly deprived of Life, tho' not in so great a Degree; and therefore all Attempts that are like to involve us in either of these Evils, should be carefully avoided.[1]

The tenor and sentiment of Tennent's *Irenicum Ecclesiasticum* is in sharp contrast with his fiery statements in the Nottingham sermon nine years before. Tennent did not change his agreement with the revival and still owned it as a work of God. What he changed was his own spirit to-

---

[1] Gilbert Tennent, *Irenicum Ecclesiasticum, Or a Humble Impartial Essay on the Peace of Jerusalem* (Philadelphia: W. Bradford, 1749), 23.

wards those within the visible church who cannot be charitably judged to be either saints or hypocrites.

A meeting between the Synods of Philadelphia and New York took place at Trenton, New Jersey, on October 5, 1749 but failed of its purpose in the short run. Over the next nine years, there were various communications and conferences between the two Synods which resulted in their reunion on May 29, 1758 in Philadelphia.

The two sticking points for the Synod of New York (New Light) had been: first, their desire to have the protest of 1741 (which resulted in their illegal exclusion from the General Assembly) made null and void; and, second, for both Synods to acknowledge the revival as a great work of God's Spirit. The Synod of Philadelphia countered that they could not annul an action which had never been officially adopted by their body. Technically, that was true, but they could have made a motion to the effect that the protest was illegal and unwarranted. Yet, the Synod of Philadelphia often hid behind procedure to the detriment of the substance of the issue.

Controversy Concerning William MacClenachan

The union of the two branches of the Presbyterian Church was soon tested by a new controversy centered on the ministry of the Reverend William MacClenachan and his service to the Christ (Episcopal) Church of Philadelphia. This controversy also aggravated the differences between the Presbyterians and Episcopalians.

MacClenachan had immigrated to the colony of Maine with a settlement of Presbyterians from Ulster, Ireland, in 1734. For the next ten years, he served as pastor of the churches at Brunswick and Georgetown in Maine, during which time he was strongly influenced by the spreading flames of the Great Awakening. After a short ministry at Blandford, Massachusetts, he became a colleague of the aged Rev. Thomas Cheevers in December of 1748 at Chelsea, Massachusetts, near Boston. Following Cheevers' death in 1749, MacClenachan took over the pastorate of the Old Suffolk Meetinghouse for the next five years. On Christmas Day in 1754, he abruptly decided to seek ordination as an Anglican priest and soon sailed to London to receive Holy Orders. The Anglican Church appointed him as an itinerant missionary to the Massachusetts Bay Colony in the spring of 1755. He preached in various places in New England before journeying to Virginia in December of 1758. There he was appointed to a vacant parish and was received with acceptance.

The Pamphlet War with Episcopalians

MacClenachan then traveled back to Boston to move his family to his new parish in Virginia in the early part of 1759. He stopped in Philadelphia to wait on the Reverend Dr. Robert Jenney, rector of Christ Church, who suffered from a paralytic and asthmatic condition that rendered him unable to perform the duties of the ministry. Dr. Jenney invited MacClenachan to preach the morning and evening services for the next Lord's Day, to which MacClenachan readily consented. He expected to leave Philadelphia by the next Tuesday, but was persuaded by Jenney to remain another week. When the following Lord's Day came, MacClenachan filled Jenney's pulpit once more. His preaching was received so favorably by the congregation that some members proposed he spend a probationary period among them as an assistant to Jenney.

Over the next several months, MacClenachan preached to large crowds at Christ Church while acting as Dr. Jenney's assistant and awaiting a license from the Bishop of London. He did much apparent good during this probationary period but also aroused much opposition. Most of this opposition was due to the New Light or evangelical views he expressed in his sermons.

One observer of MacClenachan's preaching was Provost William Smith, D.D., the first President of the College and Academy of Philadelphia. He described those sermons in a letter to the Archbishop of Canterbury, Thomas Secker, as follows:

> With a huge statue, and voice more than *Stentorian*, up he started before his Sermon, and, instead of modestly using any of the excellent forms provided in our Liturgy, or a form in the nature and substance of that enjoined by the 55th Canon, he addressed the Majesty of heaven with a long Catalogue of epithets, such as "Sin pardoning, all-seeing, heart-searching, rein-trying God" — "We thank thee that we are all here to-day and not in hell" — Such an unusual manner in our Church sufficiently fixed my attention, which was exercised by a strange extempore rhapsody of more than 20 minutes, and afterwards a Sermon of about 68 Minutes more; which I think could hardly be religion; for I am sure it was not Common Sense. I have heard him again and again, and still we have the same wild incoherent rhapsodies, of which I can give no account, other than that they consist of a continual ringing the Changes upon the words Regeneration, instantaneous Conversion, imputed Righteousness, the New Birth, etc — But I find no practical use made of these terms, nor does

he offer anything to explain them, or to tell us what he would be at. In short, My Lord, it would make the Ears of a Sober Christian tingle to sit and hear such Preachments.[2]

Smith's remarks made it clear he believed in a religion of "common sense" and was offended by preaching which insisted on the new birth. Such preaching he considered impractical because it did not encourage men to hope for their salvation through their own moral efforts. Smith was typical of those in the Church of England who opposed the ministries of Whitefield, Davies, the Tennents, and other New Light preachers. MacClenachan also had detractors within Christ Church due to the influence of their aged and palsied pastor, Dr. Jenney. He could not hope to escape criticism within the Anglican Church while many of her ministers opposed the doctrines of the gospel.

A further complication of matters was due to the feelings of jealousy and suspicion which Dr. Jenney had towards MacClenachan. Jenney began to view MacClenachan as a rival and was fearful of losing his position as rector of Christ Church. He and the vestry thus began political maneuvering to influence the Bishop of London not to grant MacClenachan a license as an assistant at Christ Church. MacClenachan had little realistic chance to gain the approval of the Bishop of London while the rector of Christ Church was opposed to him. Yet, a sizable number of the members of that church wanted MacClenachan to continue his efforts to become an assistant to Dr. Jenney and prevailed upon him to do so.

Seventeen Presbyterians Write the Bishop of London

The Presbyterians entered the picture at this point. MacClenachan received word in early 1760 that the Bishop of London was probably going to deny him the license he desired. He immediately sought the aid of his ministerial friends among the New Light Presbyterians, especially Gilbert Tennent, with whom he shared a close friendship. A letter of commendation for MacClenachan was sent to the Archbishop of Canterbury bearing the signatures of Samuel Davies, Gilbert Tennent, William Tennent, Charles Tennent, John Rodgers, John Blair, and James Finley,

---

[2] Horace Wemyss Smith, *Life and Correspondence of the Rev. William Smith, D.D.* Volume I (Philadelphia: S. A. George & Co.,1880), 225.

along with ten others. The Archbishop of Canterbury was President of the Society for the Propagation of the Gospel and the immediate superior of the Bishop of London. Most likely, Gilbert Tennent or Samuel Davies or Samuel Finley was the drafter of the letter—or some combination thereof.

The letter praised MacClenachan for the "public Specimens of his zeal for the Doctrines of Christianity, as contain'd in the Articles of the Church of England."[3] In the view of these Presbyterians, "so remarkable a Blessing [had] attended his Ministry in some striking Instances of unquestionable Reformation from Vice and Infidelity"[4] that they heartily recommended him to the Archbishop for licensure. The signers acknowledged they were intermeddling in the affairs of another denomination, but they pled they were motivated by "self-evident Disinterestedness and Impartiality."[5] In fairness, they were primarily supporting an Anglican priest who proclaimed the same doctrines of the gospel which they held. It quickly became apparent the sending of this letter was not the better part of wisdom—even if it was the act of true friends.

The immediate effect of the New Light[6] letter was that it provoked the wrath of many Anglicans in Philadelphia who demanded an explanation from the Synod of Philadelphia. A deputation of Anglicans was forthwith sent to a Synod meeting with a protest against the interference of the New Light ministers. The Anglicans also requested to see the letter and the signatures. The Synod was embarrassed and explained the letter was not an official act of that body. This explanation was unsatisfactory to the Anglicans who insisted on seeing the letter. Davies, who was Moderator of this meeting of Synod, provided them with a copy of the letter but refused to reveal the signatures. The Archbishop of Canterbury returned the original to Provost Smith months later and the identity of the seventeen signers became public.

---

[3] John W. Christie, "Presbyterians and Episcopalians in 1761," *Proceedings of the Ohio Presbyterian Historical Society*, II (1940), 19.
[4] Ibid.
[5] Ibid., 20.
[6] The reunion of the Presbyterian Church in 1758 did not change the fact there were fundamental differences between certain of the parties over the nature of the Gospel.

The Bishop of London Refuses to License MacClenachan

The Bishop of London then refused a license to MacClenachan and Christ Church closed its pulpit against him. Multitudes still clamored for his preaching and his voice was not cut off in Philadelphia. The Society of Friends (Quakers) provided him the use of the State House (Independence Hall) and one of them donated some land for the erection of a church building. Additionally, there were two lotteries[7] established which soon provided ample funds for the new building.

MacClenachan described his circumstances to the Archbishop of Canterbury:

> One door has been shut against me, God has opened another. I was dismissed by the Doctor and Vestry, in manner aforesaid, on Wednesday; the Bishop's Letter arrived the Saturday following; and I read Prayers and preached at the State-House on Sunday, to above, perhaps, Five Thousand Hearers. The Benefit of assembling, in this spacious Building, for the public Worship of God, we shall enjoy, till the Church be built, which will be with all possible Expedition.[8]

This new church, St. Paul's, became an independent congregation, and MacClenachan served them for the next four years which have been described as "turbulent."[9] Afterwards, MacClenachan served in rural Maryland at St. Martin's Parish which was his last charge before he died.

The Pamphlet War

It was at this point that several pamphlets were written by both parties to this dispute. The first of the pamphlets was a lampoon of the New Lights and was titled, "A True Copy of a Genuine Letter Sent to the Archbishop of Canterbury by Eighteen Presbyterian Ministers in America. With Some Remarks Thereon: in another letter to the Congregations of the Said Ministers." The pamphlet claimed to be written by "An Old Covenanting and True Presbyterian Layman." The identity of the author is unknown but it may have been penned by Provost Smith, by one of the Old Light ministers, or by a member of the Reformed Presbyteri-

---

[7] In colonial days, lotteries were used to support many religious projects and church leaders saw no harm in them.
[8] Smith, *Life and Correspondence of the Rev. William Smith*, 240.
[9] Christie, "Presbyterians and Episcopalians in 1761," 29.

ans—who were known as Covenanters.[10] Regardless, the author of this pamphlet evidenced such an in-depth knowledge of the New Light men that he was surely aided by a member of the Old Light party.

This pamphlet charged the New Lights had been unsuccessful[11] in the ministry "this many years past, whilst they were deluding their followers."[12] They were accused of:

> Craming down the Throats of the Vulgar the grosest Rhapsodies, abusing the characters of their fellow Teachers, dissolving the Solemn Tie of Peoples to their own Pastors, from the Imaginations, Conceit, Opinion, or Guess of the People,—representing the Clergy of this Generation, as "Varlets, the Seed of the Old serpent, Men whom the Devil drives into the Ministry, blind and dead Men, Men possessed with the Devil, Rebels and Enemies to God, Children of Satan, dead Drones, Dupes, Dunces. etc., etc." may readily be granted—But that this should affect Presbyterianism in general is an absolute Slander.[13]

This caricature of the New Lights, though patently false, revived the controversy concerning an unconverted ministry which had led to the split of 1741. William Tennent, Jr. and Samuel Finley both wrote pamphlets in defense of the actions of the New Light ministers.

Another of the pamphlets was titled, "The Mechanick's Address to the Farmer,"[14] and defended the New Light ministers and missionaries from the accusations against their personal lives. This pamphlet opened the way for a second pamphlet from the pen of the person described as "An Old Covenanting and True Presbyterian Layman." He pitied the laymen who sat under the ministries of the New Lights:

> I am sure if any people under the Sun have a just claim to pity and the prayers of true Christians it is you who are the New-Light laity. You have been taught that a sanctified appearance, a whining cant, strong lungs, and

---

[10] There is no documentary proof of who wrote this pamphlet or that Tennent drafted the letter to the Archbishop of Canterbury. Both are only suppositions.

[11] The New Lights had been much more successful than the Old Lights during the period of the division. This charge is completely unfounded.

[12] Christie, "Presbyterians and Episcopalians in 1761," 21.

[13] Ibid.

[14] This pamphlet was written by someone who claimed to be from Chester county, Pennsylvania. Judging by its contents, it was probably written by Samuel Finley with, perhaps, help from Samuel Davies. There is one reference early in the pamphlet to the "Path of Duty," a statement that was often used by Davies.

a holy twang of the nose were more principal requisites in a compleat preacher. But, thanks be to God, you have so far got the better of this strong delusion—that you do not now pin your faith to the sleeves of any particular set of men, and have opportunities of hearing those who have far higher accomplishments than the above, and have all along been uniform in their conduct. Beware therefore of a relapse into your former error.[15]

The author of this pamphlet represents the New Lights as ignorant and uncultured men who appear before the Archbishop of Canterbury at Lambeth Palace for the purpose of receiving ordination as an Anglican priest. In the ensuing mock interview, John Blair, Charles Tennent, John Roan, and John Todd, among others,[16] are represented as making fools of themselves through their lack of credentials for the ministry. The Archbishop concludes: "My advice to you is that you would pursue your respective trades and occupations, and quit all thoughts of preaching in any society of Christians—So I bid you farewell."[17]

The New Lights always contended the true minister must have both a divine call and a holy life in addition to proper educational training. Their opponents, the Old Lights, placed more stress on the necessity of proper credentials and an education at one of the classical colleges. The caricature of the New Lights as uncultured and uneducated is unjust. Davies, in particular, was a model of learning, piety and culture. He encouraged a form of preaching which was neither dry nor uncultured, but full of genuine pathos.

These attacks on the New Light ministers by the pamphleteers are reminiscent of Cardinal James Sadolet's letter to the citizens of Geneva, Switzerland, during the period that Calvin was exiled from the city. In that letter, Sadolet accused the Reformers of being jealous of the ecclesiastical advances of others within the Church while they themselves labored in unprofitable circumstances; of assailing the character of Catholic priests and leading many people to desert them; of preaching justification by faith alone as a cover for their lustful desires; and, of being guilty of sedition and schism.[18]

---

[15] Christie, "Presbyterians and Episcopalians in 1761," 24–25.

[16] It is interesting that Gilbert Tennent, Samuel Davies, and Samuel Finley are not represented in this interview by name.

[17] Christie, "Presbyterians and Episcopalians in 1761," 28.

[18] John Calvin, *Tracts and Letters*, Volume I: Tracts, Part I (Edinburgh, Scotland and Carlisle,

These pamphlets reopened the wounds within the Presbyterian Church. As a result, the Synod of Philadelphia adopted an apology on May 21, 1761, which expressed their hope that "the same good understanding which has hitherto happily subsisted between us and the Reverend Gentlemen of the Church of England may still continue."[19] This controversy reopened wounds which had not completely healed between the Old Lights and the New Lights, but did not result in a further breach of the external unity between these two sides.

Conclusion

George Pilcher, Davies' biographer, suggested this "represented one of the few times Davies acted foolishly and in a manner harmful to the interests of his Church."[20] A few facts must be considered before drawing such a conclusion. First, Davies always defended the New Light cause[21] throughout his ministry. Second, the signers of this letter to the Archbishop of Canterbury never referred to any former differences among the Presbyterians or to themselves as New Lights. Third, the letter was intended simply to be an endorsement for MacClenachan, but was used by unidentified parties to stir up former differences among the Presbyterians. Fourth, the embarrassment for the New Lights was due to the use of this letter as a source of division by the Episcopalians. We may fault Davies and the other signers of this letter for not realizing that it would provoke the malice of those Episcopalians at Christ Church opposed to MacClenachan, but it is hard to call their actions "foolish" or "harmful to the interests" of the Church. Their support for MacClenachan was similar to the support they would have given Whitefield under similar circumstances. Thus, the real controversy concerned the true gospel and the

---

Pennsylvania: The Banner of Truth Trust, 2009), 17–18.
[19] *Minutes of the Synod of New York and Philadelphia, From A. D 1758 to 1788* in *Records of the Presbyterian Church in the United States of America* (Philadelphia: Presbyterian Board of Publication. 1841), 306.
[20] George Pilcher, *Samuel Davies: Apostle of Dissent in Colonial Virginia* (Knoxville, TN: University of Tennessee Press, 1971), 184.
[21] A defense of the New Light Synod was in his work "The Impartial Trial, Impartially Tried and Convicted of Partiality." This controversy, in the opinion of this writer, questions the wisdom of the reunion with the Old Light Presbyterians in 1758. The Old Lights never conceded any point of their former opposition to the Great Awakening.

nature of conversion. If it is foolish to support a faithful minister who preaches the gospel, then we should all be such "fools for Christ's sake" (1 Corinthians 4:10).

-22-

Davies' Last Sickness and Death

"You know the tenderness and condescension with which he treated you; the paternal care with which he watched over you; the reluctance with which he at any time inflicted the prescribed punishment on a delinquent; and how pleased he was to succeed in reforming any abuse by private and easy methods. You felt yourselves voluntarily confined by the restraints of love, and obliged to subjection, not from slavish fear, but from principle and inclination. You have yet fresh in memory his instructive lectures, and can tell with what ease he communicated sentiments, and impressed ideas on your minds, and the enetretaining manner in which he would represent even a common thought."[1]
~*Samuel Finley to the College of New Jersey at Davies' death*~

Portrait of King George II (1683-1760)

---

[1] Samuel Finley, "Sermon on the Death of the Rev. Samuel Davies," in Samuel Davies, *Sermons on Important Subjects*, Vol. I (New York: J. & J. Harper, 1828), 25.

Davies' Last Sickness and Death

Following the commencement exercises of 1760, Davies visited Hanover in the fall for the first time since his removal to Princeton. The news of his visit reached Col. William Gordon, in the Northern Neck of Virginia, on October 10 through Richard Criswell, who was engaged to Gordon's daughter, Ann. The following day, Gordon was entertaining Criswell, James Hunt of Hanover, and a young man named Maring in his home when he learned to his chagrin that Davies did not intend to return to Princeton via Lancaster County.[2] Eight days later, Gordon dispatched Hunt to Hanover in the hope of persuading Davies to return to New Jersey through the Northern Neck of Virginia. Yet, Davies was unable to accommodate this request and, hastening back to Princeton, bypassed Gordon and Lancaster County.

After returning to New Jersey, Davies was ill for the final two months of 1760. His delicate health suffered from his taxing schedule and lack of exercise. Nonetheless, he continued to preach regularly in the college chapel and kept up all his normal duties of the Presidency.

Funeral Service for David Cowell

David Cowell, one of the Trustees of the College of New Jersey who had been intimately involved in the negotiations of calling Davies to the College, had developed a very close friendship with Davies over the past year and a half. During that time, Cowell's health had been steadily declining until his death on December 1, 1760. Davies was asked to preach the funeral service which he did, choosing Hebrews 4:11 as his text, "Let us labor, therefore, to enter into that rest." In concluding his remarks, Davies said:

> This church has lost a judicious minister of the Gospel, and, as we hope, a sincere Christian; the world has lost an inoffensive useful member of society; this town an agreeable, peaceable, benevolent inhabitant; the College of New Jersey, a father; and I have lost a friend, and I doubt not but public and private sorrow and lamentation will be in some measure correspondent, and express the greatness of the loss.[3]

---

[2] William Henry Foote, *Sketches of Virginia: Biographical and Historical*, First Series, (Philadelphia: William S. Martien, 1850), 364.
[3] John Hall, *History of the Presbyterian Church in Trenton, N. J.* (New York: Anson D. F. Randolph, 1859), 143–4.

Cowell's body was laid to rest in the cemetery on the church grounds near to the western wall of the church building. He had been the pastor of First Presbyterian Church in Trenton, New Jersey for twenty-four years before his death at the age of fifty-seven.

Davies' New Year's Day Sermon for 1761

In late December of 1760, while he was still nursing his sickness, one of Davies' intimate friends reminded him that the students and the local townsmen would be expecting a special sermon from him on New Year's Day. In this conversation, Davies' friend also related to him that:

> President Burr on the first day of the year wherein he died, preached a sermon on Jer. xxviii.16, "Thus saith the Lord, This year thou shalt die," and after his death, the people took occasion to say that it was premonitory.[4]

When Davies heard this anecdote, he commented that "although it ought not to be viewed in that light, yet it was very remarkable."[5] To the surprise and bewilderment of the audience, Davies took the same text from which President Burr had preached when the New Year arrived. In his sermon, Davies reminded the congregation:

> Thus it appears very possible, that one or other of us may die this year. Nay, it is very probable, as well as possible, if we consider that it is a very uncommon, and almost unprecedented thing, that not one should die in a whole year out of such an assembly as this. More than one have died the year past, who made a part of our assembly last New-year's-day. Therefore, let each of us (for we know not on whom the lot may fall) realize this possibility, this alarming probability, "This year I may die."[6]

How strange it must have seemed to an audience which thought President Burr preached his own funeral sermon to now hear Davies conclude this section of his sermon with the words: "This year I may die."

Thirteen days later, Davies preached a message from 2 Samuel 1:19, "On the Death of His late Majesty King, George II," who had died on Oc-

---

[4] Thomas Gibbons, "The Divine Conduct Vindicated," in Davies, *Sermons on Important Subjects*, Vol. I), 30.
[5] Ibid.
[6] Samuel Davies, *Sermons on Important Subjects*, Volume II (London: W. Baynes and Son, 1824), 320.

tober 25 from an aortic aneurysm which collapsed his right ventricle. The high esteem in which Davies held the late monarch, George II, is revealed in the opening words of that message:

> George is no more! George, the mighty, the just, the gentle, and the wise; George, the father of Britain and her Colonies, the guardian of laws and liberty, the protector of the oppressed, the arbiter of Europe, the terror of tyrants and France; George the friend of man, the benefactor of millions, is no more—millions tremble at the alarm. Britain expresses her sorrows in national groans. Europe re-echoes to the melancholy sound. The melancholy sound circulates far and wide. This remote American continent shares in the loyal sympathy.[7]

Nassau Hall was moved by Davies' eloquence for the second time in a fortnight as he spoke on the mortality of man—a notable subject in light of his own poor health:

> A thousand dangers lie in ambush for us. Nay, the principles of mortality lurk in our own constitutions; and sickness, the herald of the last enemy, often warns us to prepare. Yet how few realize the thought that they must die! How few familiarize to their minds that all-important hour, pregnant with consequences of great, of incomparable, of infinite moment! How many forget they must die till they feel it; and stand fearless, inapprehensive, and insolent, upon the slippery brink of eternity, till they unexpectedly fall and are engulphed for ever in the boundless ocean.[8]

Davies, of course, was not alone in preaching a sermon on George II's death. In Boston, Thomas Lowell and Thomas Foxcroft (minister of the Old Church) printed sermons on his death.

Davies Contracts a Cold

Davies contracted a severe cold four days later and was bled by leeches, most likely under the care of Dr. Nathaniel Scudder, a 1751 graduate of the College of New Jersey. Bloodletting was a common medical practice in the eighteenth century through the mistaken idea that any procedure to cure an illness was better than none. Though practiced by numerous civilizations for more than 3,000 years, modern medicine has generally

---

[7] Ibid., 355.
[8] Samuel Davies, *Sermons on Important Subjects*, Volume III (London: W. Baynes and Son, 1824), 357.

discredited bloodletting. The primary reason that bloodletting often worked, though unknown to colonial physicians, was because pathogens thrive on iron and this process deprived them of such. Yet, colonial physicians often took too much blood from their patients while simultaneously limiting their water intake. Thus, patients who were dehydrated became too weak to effectively fight the infection. One of the most enthusiastic supporters of bloodletting in the colonies was a 1759 graduate of the College of New Jersey, Benjamin Rush, who wrote:

> By the proximate cause of fever I have attempted to prove that the inflammatory state of fever depends upon morbid and excessive action in the blood-vessels. It is connected, of course, with the preternatural sensibility in their muscular fibers. The blood is one of the most powerful stimuli which acts upon them. By attracting a part of it, we lessen the principal cause of fever. The effect of bloodletting is immediate and natural in removing fever, as the abstraction of a particle of sand is the cure of an inflammation in the eye, when it arises from that cause.[9]

After his bloodletting, Davies seemed to quickly recover and resumed his normal schedule. He edited his sermon on the death of King George II over the next few days and wrote John Holt the following instructions for its publication:

> As to the terms, I almost leave them to yourself. . . But I would by no means have you run any risque; and therefore perhaps it might be best for you to print about 1000 copies; and, reserving 200 for me, to dispose of the rest in the best manner you can: and if it should be your misfortune to lose by it, I shall cheerfully indemnify you. But if you should gain anything, I shall claim no share in it.[10]

He dictated this letter because his arm was still sore from the blood letting, but he included a postscript, in his own hand, suggesting his brother-in-law send Mrs. Holt and "Miss Betsy" for a visit. He then remarked, "Mrs. Davies would visit you if she had not a house full of children."[11]

---

[9] Mario J. Azevedo, ed., *The State of Health and Healthcare in Mississippi* (Jackson, Mississippi: University Press of Mississippi, 2015), 42.
[10] Samuel Davies to John Holt, January 21, 1761. MS letter in Benjamin Rush MSS, Library Company of Philadelphia—Historical Society of Pennsylvania, Philadelphia, PA.
[11] Ibid.

Davies' Last Sickness and Death

The congregation which met at Nassau Hall heard Davies preach twice on January 22. He was seized with chills the next morning while sitting at the breakfast table and these were followed by an inflammatory fever and a violent relapse of his cold. He was soon cast into a delirium which "deprived him of the regular exercise of his reason the greater part of the time of his sickness."[12] He reflected on his New Year's Day sermon when alert and "mentioned it as remarkable that he had been undesignedly led to preach, as it were, his own funeral sermon."[13] Fearing his days were few, he called for Samuel Finley and suggested he preach his funeral sermon from Romans 14:7, 8. His heart for the Church was revealed despite the violence of this sickness. As Finley stated:

> Even in his delirium his mind discovered the favorite objects of his concern, the prosperity of Christ's church, and the good of mankind. His bewildered brain was continually imagining, and his flattering tongue expressing some expedient for these important purposes.[14]

Yet, Davies' end came suddenly and unexpectedly. His passing was like the flaming out of a shooting star shortly after being first noticed. No sooner had he attracted the attention of the Christian world than he was abruptly taken from view. For years he had labored in the backwoods of Virginia far from the gazing world. Then providence elevated him to a position of great eminence for which he was abundantly qualified. He seemed to have every gift required by the office to fulfill his duties as President of the College of New Jersey. His performances in that station were awe-inspiring and enkindled confidence in students, faculty members, Trustees, and fellow ministers alike. Moreover, he seemed to have youth on his side, despite his many years of battling a consumptive illness. His predecessor, Jonathan Edwards, was Davies' senior by twenty years when he rose to the same office. On the other hand, Davies should have been in the fulness of his manly strength when he labored at Princeton, but the secret appointments of God are known to no one. Ecclesiastes 3:1, 2a says, "There is an appointed time for everything. And there is a time for every event under heaven—A time to give birth and a time to die." Davies had an appointment awaiting him of which only the Lord of the universe was aware.

---

[12] Gibbons, "The Divine Conduct Vindicated" in Davies, *Sermons on Important Subjects*, I, 30.
[13] Ibid.
[14] Ibid.

An illness of only thirteen days resulted in Davies' death on Wednesday, February 4, 1761 at 2p.m. His sun went down in the prime of his life, three months into the thirty-eighth year of his life. He left behind a mournful wife, five young children who grieved at his passing, along with a widowed mother. The circle of his friends on both continents received the news of his departure as a shattering blow and an overwhelming sadness. A correspondent of the Rev. Dr. Thomas Gibbons of London described the College of New Jersey, thusly:

> Nassau Hall in tears, disconsolate, and refusing to be comforted.[15]

The news of Davies' death did not reach Virginia until a month later. Col. Gordon on receiving this report said:

> Yesterday heard the disagreeable news of the death of Rev. Mr. Samuel Davies. Never was a man in America, I imagine, more lamented. The Christian, the gentleman, and the scholar appeared conspicuous in him. Virginia and even Lancaster, I hope has great reason to bless God for such a minister of the gospel amongst us. But he that sent him can send another, and his labour be attended with as much success. But I am afraid our country is too wicked for such comfort.[16]

Three sermons preached on the occasion of Davies' death reveal how the shocking news was received by the Christian world. Samuel Finley preached Davies' funeral sermon on May 28, 1761, from the text supplied by Davies. His message, "The Disinterested and Devoted Christian," was preached at Nassau Hall to a tearful and mourning audience. In conclusion, Finley stated:

> Now one more shining orb is set on our world. Davies is departed, and with him all that love, zeal, activity, benevolence, for which he was remarkable. This the church, and this the bereaved college mourns. For this we hang our cheerful harps, and indulge the plaintive strains. Yet we are not to lament as those who are hopeless, but rather, with humble confidence to "pray the Lord of the Harvest," with whom is "the residue of the spirit," that he would send forth another Davies to assist our labour, and forward his work.[17]

---

[15] Ibid., 35.
[16] "Col. Gordon's Diary," in Foote, *Sketches of Virginia*, First Series, 365.
[17] Samuel Finley, "Sermon on the Death of the Rev. Samuel Davies," in Samuel Davies, *Sermons on Important Subjects*, I, (New York: J & J Harper, 1828), 26.

Thomas Gibbons, with whom Davies shared an intimate correspondence for several years, preached a discourse on March 29, 1761, at Haberdasher-Hall in London, "The Divine Conduct Vindicated." Gibbons placed Davies among the greatest ministers of that day in the following quote:

> A greater loss, all things considered, could not perhaps befall the church of God in the death of a single person. The God of nature had endowed Mr. Davies with extraordinary talents. Perhaps in sublimity and strength of genius there were very few, if any, who surpassed him.[18]

David Bostwick eulogized Davies with these words:

> But, alas! all his ample furniture of gifts and graces, all the amiable qualities of the mind, with the advantages of the happiest constitution of body, could not secure him from the fate of mortals. He is gone; he has quitted this inferior world amidst the unfeigned sorrows of his family, his friends, the college and our country: he has taken his flight to his native skies, and joined with kindred spirits in the regions of a glorious immortality, while his remains are gathered to those of his predecessors, in the dark and dreary repository of the grave. . . O the unutterable and extensive loss to a distressed family, to a bereaved college, to the ministry, to the church, to the community, to the republic of letters, and in short to all the valuable interests of mankind.[19]

Davies' Family after His Death

Davies left little estate behind to provide for his family. His salary at Hanover had been sufficient for the necessities of his family, but there was little left to store up for their future. Thus, the citizens of Philadelphia "collected £95 per annum for five years to support his three sons at College"[20] who were then twelve, ten, and eight years old respectively.

Jane Davies returned to Virginia with her two young daughters, Martha and Margaret, where she lived with her younger sister and her mother. John Todd described them to Gibbons in a letter:

---

[18] Ibid., 31.
[19] David Bostwick, "Character of the Author," in Davies, *Sermons on Important Subjects*, I, 26.
[20] David Bostwick to Joseph Bellamy, March 17, 1761. MS letter in Hartford Seminary Library, Hartford, Connecticut.

These three females, with Mrs. Davies's two little daughters, make up an amiable little family, who live together on the little fortune of the old lady, which keeps them from distress with proper frugality, retired from the noise of the world, and much taken up with the things of religion.[21]

Jane Davies' support was supplemented by a collection of four or five hundred pounds made by the citizens of Philadelphia and New York through the sale of lottery tickets, a common practice even among Christians in colonial times. Colonial lotteries were instrumental in the funding of major projects such as the building of churches, the founding of colleges (Princeton, Columbia, and the University of Pennsylvania all made use of lotteries for that purpose), roads and bridges, libraries, and various public works—which was a very generous sum of money for that time.[22] Though this collection handsomely provided for her material needs, she was overwhelmed by the loss of her husband in the prime of his life. "Great despondency and melancholy" often overtook her and she frequently could not compose herself to speak of her deceased husband "without a sensible commotion and tears."[23] She never remarried but lived out her days in a tender walk before her God.

Samuel's mother, Martha Davies, went to live with John Rodgers at St. George's, Delaware, with the passing of her son—near where she had lived most of her life. When Rodgers accepted the call from First Presbyterian Church of New York City, she moved with his family to that city. She died in New York City after 1765, but the exact date is unknown.

William Davies, the eldest son, was blessed with superior talents and powers of intellect. In the Revolutionary War, he rose to the rank of Colonel in the Army. After the war, he returned to Virginia, living in Norfolk, and continued to work for the government. Throughout his life, he maintained a friendship with Col. William Craighead of Hanover. While never joining a church, he thought Presbyterianism was not very well adapted to attract the masses, and that Romanism was at a decided advantage in this respect.

---

[21] John Todd to Thomas Gibbons, footnote in Samuel Davies, *Sermons on the Most Useful and Important Subjects, Adapted to the Family and Closet*, in Five Volumes, Volume I (London: J. Buckland and J. Payne, 1766), cxvi. Gibbons' edited this volume and included a poem, "An Elegiac Poem on the Death of Mr. Davies," which is not in later editions.
[22] Bostwick to Bellamy, March 17, 1761. MS letter in Hartford Seminary Library.
[23] Davies, *Sermons on Important Subjects*, I (1766), cxvi.

Samuel Davies, Jr. was a mercantiler in Petersburg, Virginia, who bore a striking resemblance to his father. He was an amiable but indolent man who never made a profession of faith. One of his sons, though, Samuel Davies, III, did become a respectable member of the Presbyterian Church.

John Rodgers Davies, the youngest son, chose the legal profession and maintained his practice in Amelia, Dinwiddie, Prince George, and the surrounding counties in Virginia. Though successful in his profession, he was never popular with the public. He was a skeptic in his religious views and never attended public worship. An elderly couple living in Amelia County, Col. Brooking and his wife, had often heard Mr. Davies preach when they were younger. John Rodgers was a frequent guest in their home and, on one occasion, Mrs. Brooking asked him to do her a special favor. When he immediately consented, Mrs. Brooking requested that he read the poem his father had written at his birth. John Rodgers replied, "Madam, you have imposed on me hard service"; adding that he had never read any of his father's writings and would not do so.[24]

Some years later, Archibald Alexander was traveling through the counties of James River as an itinerant evangelist. At Sussex, Alexander stayed with a Methodist named Chapel who informed him that there was a Presbyterian in the area who never attended church anywhere. To Alexander's surprise, this Presbyterian was John Rodgers Davies. Alexander relates what took place next:

> Mr. Chapel urged me to preach in the evening; and went himself to inform Mr. Davies of the service. But he could not by all of his arguments prevail on him to come. And finally, to get clear of his importunity, he said, "If the Apostle Paul were to preach at your house to-night, I would not go; nay, if my own father was to preach there I would not go."[25]

Thus, Davies' worst fears were realized in his third son. Instead of being an embryo-angel, John Rodgers to all appearances lived his life as an infant fiend who, by this time, had forgotten both his father and his God. We can only hope he did not die in such unbelief.

Martha Davies married Joseph Alexander, a graduate of the College

---

[24] James Waddell Alexander, *The Life of Archibald Alexander* (New York: Charles Scribner, 1854), 141–142.
[25] Ibid.

of New Jersey in 1763, who was ordained to the Presbyterian ministry in 1768. Together they had ten children and named one of them, Samuel Davies Alexander, who also became a minister. Little is known about the other daughter, Margaret, but she apparently never married.

Various Views of Davies' Death

In a letter to Joseph Bellamy on March 17, 1761, David Bostwick expressed the thoughts of many:

> Mr. Davies's Death has struck us into astonishment—and spread a gloom all over the Country—the loss cannot be expressed. . . . you can hardly conceive what prodigious uncommon gifts the God of Heaven had bestowed upon that Man, to render him useful to the World.—but he is gone,—O! what might he have been!—What might he have done, had he lived!—But methinks I hear the admonition,—be still & know that I am God.[26]

Samuel Davies completed a difficult but fruitful course in a brief period of time. When he first set out as a minister, he expected to live only a few years and hoped to prepare the way for a more useful servant of Christ. His life seemed like a candle snuffed out in full blaze, but it is hard to imagine how he could have accomplished more than he did. The eager crowds who flocked to hear him preach; the attentive slaves converted through his labors; the thick forests through which he rode from one preaching post to another; the governing officials who opposed him in court; the young ministers who were inspired by his example; the aspiring students who matriculated under his care; and countless others, all testify to his singular and faithful pursuit of his calling as a minister of the gospel.

The grave of Davies lies in that part of the Princeton cemetery where the presidents and professors are buried. The vaulted tomb of Davies is flanked on one side by that of Jonathan Edwards and on the other side by that of Samuel Finley. Close by are the graves of Charles Hodge, A. A. Hodge, Archibald Alexander, B. B. Warfield, and numerous others. What a glorious sight that will be when the hour comes that "all who are in the tombs will hear His voice, and will come forth; those who did the good deeds to a resurrection of life" (John 5:28, 29).

---

[26] Bostwick to Bellamy, March 17, 1761. MS Letter in Hartford Seminary Library.

Finley gave it as his opinion that the audience gathered for Davies' funeral should consider that he, though dead, was yet speaking those words to them. Towards the conclusion, he observed:

> But his persuasive voice you will hear no more. He is removed far from mortals, has taken his *aerial flight*, and left us to lament, that "a great man has fallen in Israel!" He lived much in a little time; "he finished his course," performed sooner than many others his assigned task, and, in that view, might be said to have died mature. He shone like a light set in a high place that burns out and expires.[27]

Finley expressed the more appropriate view of Davies' death. His life was not prematurely snuffed out before his time. Rather, he ran his course so quickly that his race was over sooner than others. As he lived for the Lord, so he died unto the Lord—and in the Lord's time. Perhaps, the best insight into Davies' death was expressed by his mother, as recorded by Foote:

> When the corpse of her son was laid in the coffin, she stood over it, gazed at it intently for some minutes, and exclaimed!—"There is the son of my prayers and my hopes,—my only son,—my only earthly supporter. But there is the will of God,—and I am satisfied."[28]

Conclusion

Someone once described Davies as first-rate among second-rate men. Such a view of his life is, in my opinion, uncharitable and wrong. He certainly was second in some respects. He was the second-best evangelist of his day, but the best was George Whitefield—who also happens to be the best evangelist in the history of the church. It is no shame for any minister to be the second-best evangelist to Whitefield. Davies was also arguably the second-best theologian in America during his lifetime, second to Jonathan Edwards—who was also one of the best theologians in the history of the church and perhaps the greatest American theologian of all time. The greatness of Davies' sermons is owing in no small part to his exact and detailed understanding of theology. His circumstances did not allow him the leisure to write the learned tomes that would have con-

---

[27] Finley, "Sermon on the Death of the Rev. Samuel Davies," in Davies, *Sermons on Important Subjects*, I (1828), 25.
[28] Foote, *Sketches of Virginia*, First Series, 304.

firmed his theological genius for all posterity, but he was more than capable of doing so. If he had lived longer at Princeton, I have no doubt that magnificent volumes on theology would have come forth from his pen in due course. Bostwick was correct when he stated:

> [Y]ou can hardly conceive what prodigious uncommon gifts the God of Heaven had bestowed upon that Man, to render him useful to the World.[29]

We know in part and we saw in part something of what those uncommon gifts were, but, for reasons known only to God, he was called to his heavenly home before all his gifts were manifested to the world. Yet, here is where Davies was perhaps best—he was arguably the best combination of evangelist, preacher, and theologian in the whole history of the church. With his passing, the American church lost her greatest preacher ever and one of the most astounding all-around ministers to ever grace an American pulpit.

---

[29] Bostwick to Bellamy, March 17, 1761. MS letter.

Samuel Davies' vaulted grave in the Princeton Cemetery
(between the graves of Jonathan Edwards
and Samuel Finley)

Select Bibliographies

Primary Bibliography

Alexander, Archibald. *The Log College: Biographical Sketches of William Tennent & his students together with an account of the revivals under their ministries.* London: The Banner of Truth Trust, 1968.

Alexander, Archibald, comp., *Sermons of the Log College.* Ligonier, PA: Soli Deo Gloria Publications, 1993.

Alexander, James Waddell. *Life of Archibald Alexander, D.D.* New York: Scribner, 1854.

An anonymous letter to the Bishop of London, February 1, 1754. MSS letter in the *Fulham Papers*, Lambeth Palace Library, Colonial Williamsburg Foundation Library, Williamsburg, VA.

"A Recovered Tract of President Davies: Now First Published." *The Biblical Repertory and Princeton Review*, IX, (1837).

"A Treaty: Between Virginia and the Catawbas and Cherokees." *The Virginia Magazine of History and Biography*, Vol. 13, No. 3. (Jan., 1906).

Barnes, Albert. "The Life and Times of the Author." Samuel Davies. *Sermons on Important Subjects*, Volume I. New York: Dayton and Saxton, 1841.

Blair, James. *Our Saviour's Divine Sermon on the Mount* in Four Volumes, Volume III. London: J. Brotherton and J. Oswald, 1740.

Blair, Samuel. *A Sermon Preach'd at George's-Town, in Newcastle County at the Funeral Service of the Reverend Mr. William Robinson, late Minister of the Gospel there, who departed this Life, August 3, 1746.* Philadelphia, Pennsylvania: William Bradford, n.d.

Blair, Samuel. "A Short and Faithful Narrative of a Remarkable Revival of Religion in the Congregation of New Londonderry," prefixed to *The Doctrine of Predestination Truly and Fairly Stated.* Baltimore: R. J. Matchettt, 1836.

Bost, George H. "Samuel Davies, Preacher of the Great Awakening," *Journal of the Presbyterian Historical Society*, Vol. XXVI, No. 2 (June, 1948).

Bost, George H. "Samuel Davies as President of Princeton." *Journal of the Presbyterian Historical Society.* (1943-1961), Vol. 26, No. 3 (September, 1948).

Bostwick, David. "Character of the Author." Davies, Samuel. *Sermons on Important Subjects*, I. New York: J & J Harper, 1828.

Bibliographies

Bostwick, David. David Bostwick to Joseph Bellamy, October 10, 1758. MS letter in Joseph Bellamy Papers, Hartford Seminary Library, Hartford, Connecticut.

Bostwick, David. David Bostwick to Joseph Bellamy, January 1, 1759. MS letter in Joseph Bellamy Papers, Hartford Seminary Library, Hartford, Connecticut.

Bostwick, David. David Bostwick to Joseph Bellamy, March 17, 1761. MS letter in Joseph Bellamy Papers, Hartford Seminary Library, Hartford, Connecticut.

Bridges, Charles. *The Christian Ministry With An Inquiry Into The Causes Of Its Inefficiency.* London: The Banner of Truth Trust, 1967.

Buell, Samuel to Eleazar Wheelock, October 17, 1758. MS Letter in Wheelock MSS. in Dartmouth College Library.

Caldwell, John. *An Impartial Trial of the Spirit Operating in this Part of the World: By Comparing the Nature, Effects, and Evidences of the Present Supposed Conversion, with the Word of God.* Williamsburg, VA: William Parks, 1747.

Christie, John W. "Presbyterians and Episcopalians in 1761." *Proceedings of the Ohio Presbyterian Historical Society*, II (1940).

Conard, A. Mark. "The Cherokee Mission of Virginia Presbyterians." *Journal of Presbyterian History*, Vol. 58. (1980).

Davies, Samuel, comp. *A Catalogue of Books in the Library of the College of New Jersey.* Woodbridge, New Jersey: James Parker, 1760.

Davies, Samuel. *A Sermon on Man's Primitive State; And the First Covenant.* Philadelphia: William Bradford, 1748.

Davies, Samuel. *A Sermon Preached before the Reverend Presbytery of New-Castle,* October 11, 1752. Philadelphia: Franklin and Hall, 1753.

Davies, Samuel. *An Appendix Proving the Right of the Synod of New York to the Religious Liberties and Immunities Allowed to Protestant Dissenters by the Act of Toleration.* Williamsburg, Virginia: William Parks, 1748. (This was appended to *The Impartial Trial, Impartially Tried, and Convicted of Partiality*).

Davies, Samuel. *Letters from the Rev. Samuel Davies, etc., Shewing the State of Religion in Virginia, Particularly Among the Negroes. Likewise an Extract From a Gentleman in London to his Friend in the Country, Containing Some Observations on the Same.* London: R. Pardon, 1757.

Davies, Samuel. *Letters from the Rev. Samuel Davies, and Others; Shewing, the State of Religion in Virginia, South Carolina, &c. Particularly Among the Negroes.* London, 1761. (This is a different set of letters from the item above).

Davies, Samuel. MS page from Davies' Bible in the Virginia Historical Society, Richmond, Virginia

Davies, Samuel. MS sermon on 1 Thessalonians 2:19, 20. Samuel Davies Collection (C1042). Manuscripts Division, Department of Rare Books and Special Collections, Princeton University Library, Princeton, New Jersey.

Davies, Samuel. MS sermon on Luke 14:27 and dated January 19, 1749. Samuel Davies Collection (C1042). Manuscripts Division, Department of Rare Books and Special Collections, Princeton University Library, Princeton, New Jersey.

Davies, Samuel. *Sermons*, 3 Volumes. Morgan, Pennsylvania: Soli Deo Gloria Publications, 1995.

Davies, Samuel. *Sermons on the Most Useful and Important Subjects, Adapted to the Family and Closet*. London: J. Buckland and J. Payne, 1766.

Davies, Samuel. *Sermons on Important Subjects*, in 3 Volumes. New York: Dayton and Saxton, 1841.

Davies, Samuel. *Sermons on Important Subjects*, in Three Volumes, Volume I. New York: J & J Harper, 1828.

Davies, Samuel. *Sermons on Important Subjects*, in Four Volumes, Volumes II, III, IV. London: W. Baynes and Son, 1824.

Davies, Samuel. *The Duties, Difficulties and Rewards of the Faithful Minister*. Glasgow: William Duncan, Jr., 1754.

Davies, Samuel. *The Duty of Christians to Propagate Their religion Among the Heathens, Earnestly recommended to the Masters of Negro Slaves in Virginia*. London: J. Oliver, 1758.

Davies, Samuel. *The Impartial Trial, Impartially Tried, and Convicted of Partiality*. Williamsburg, Virginia: William Parks, 1748.

Davies, Samuel. "The State of Religion Among the Dissenters in Virginia." *The Biblical Repertory and Princeton Review*, Vol. XI. Philadelphia: John T. Robinson, 1840.

Davies, Samuel. *The State of Religion among the Protestant Dissenters in Virginia; in a letter to the Rev. Mr. Joseph Bellamy, of Bethlem, in New England*. Boston: S. Kneeland, 1751.

Davies, Samuel to David Cowell, Five MSS letters in Samuel Davies MSS. Presbyterian Historical Society, Philadelphia, Pennsylvania.

Davies, Samuel to John Holt. Seventeen MSS letters in Benjamin Rush MSS. The Library Company of Philadelphia, Historical Society of Pennsylvania, Philadelphia, Pennsylvania.

Davies, Samuel to Joseph Bellamy, April 18, 1760. MS letter in Joseph Bellamy Papers. Hartford Seminary Library, Hartford, Connecticut.

Davies, Samuel to Joseph Forfitt, August 26, 1758. MS letter in the Beinecke Rare Book and Manuscript Library, Yale University Library, New Haven, Connecticut.

Davies, Samuel to Joseph Pomroy, May 18, 1749. MS letter in Beinecke Rare Book & Manuscript Division, Yale University Library, New Haven, Connecticut.

Davies, Samuel to Joseph Stennet, April 25. 1755. MS Letter in Samuel Davies Collection (C1042). Manuscripts Division, Department of Rare Books and Special Collections, Princeton University Library, Princeton, New Jersey.

Davies, Samuel to P.V. B. Livingston, *Proceedings of the New Jersey Historical Society*, Series I, Vol. I. Newark, New Jersey: Office of the Daily Advertiser, 1845.

Davies, Samuel to Samuel Hazard, May 18, 1757. MS letter in the Ebenezer Hazard MSS, Library Company of Philadelphia, Historical Society of Pennsylvania, Philadelphia, Pennsylvania.

Davies, Samuel to Samuel Hazard, November 3, 1757. MS letter in the Ebenezer Hazard MSS, Library Company of Philadelphia, Historical Society of Pennsylvania, Philadelphia, Pennsylvania.

Davis, Richard Beale, ed. *Collected Poems of Samuel Davies, 1723-1761*. Gainesville, FL: Scholar Facsimiles and Reprints, 1968.

Davis, Richard Beale. *Intellectual Life in the*

Bibliographies

Colonial South, 1585-1763, Vol. II Knoxville: University of Tennessee Press, 1978.

Edwards, B. E. *American Quarterly Register*, Vol IX, No. 4, May, 1837. Boston: Perkins and Marvin, 1837.

Fawcett, Arthur. *The Cambuslang Revival: The Scottish Evangelical Revival of the Eighteenth Century*. London, The Banner of Truth Trust, 1971.

Finley, Samuel. "A Funeral Sermon on the Death of the Rev. Samuel Davies." Samuel Davies. *Sermons on Important Subjects*, Volume I. New York: J. & J. Harper, 1828.

Finley, Samuel. *Faithful Ministers the Fathers of the Church: A Sermon Preached at Fogs-Manor. On Occasion of the Death of the Rev. Mr. Samuel Blair*. Philadelphia: W. Bradford, 1752.

Foote, William Henry. *Sketches of North Carolina: Historical and Biographical*. New York: Robert Carter, 1846.

Foote, William Henry. *Sketches of Virginia: Historical and Biographical*, First Series. Philadelphia: William S. Martien, 1850.

Foote, William Henry. *Sketches of Virginia: Historical and Biographical*, Second Series. Philadelphia: J, B. Lippincott & Co., 1856.

www.geni.com/people/David-Holt/6000000009023834558, accessed on February 13, 2016.

www.geni.com/people/John-Kirkpatrick/6000000003613958254, accessed on August 4, 2016.

Gewehr, Wesley Marsh. *The Great Awakening in Virginia: 1740-1790*. Durham, NC: Duke University Press, 1930.

Gibbons, Thomas. "Divine Conduct Vindicated." Samuel Davies. *Sermons on Important Subjects*, I, 1828

Gilborn, Craig. "Samuel Davies' Sacred Muse." *Journal of Presbyterian History*, Vol 41, No. 2. (June, 1963).

Gilborn, Craig A. "The Literary Work of the Reverend Samuel Davies." Unpublished Master's Thesis. University of Delaware, 1961.

Gillies, John. *Historical Collections Relating to the Remarkable Periods of the Success of the Gospel*, 2 vols. in One. Kelso, Scotland: John Rutherford, 1845.

Gillies, John and Bonar, Horatius. *Historical Collections of Accounts of Revival*, 2 Volumes in One. Edinburgh, Scotland and Carlisle, Pennsylvania: The Banner of Truth Trust, 1981.

Gordon, James. "Journal of Col. James Gordon, of Lancaster County, Va." *The William and Mary Quarterly*, Vol. 11. no. 2. (Oct., 1902).

Green, Ashbel. *Discourses Delivered in the College of New Jersey*. Philadelphia, New York and Trenton: 1822.

Hall, John. *History of the Presbyterian Church in Trenton, N. J.: From the First Settlement of the Town*. New York: Anson D. F. Randolph, 1859

Hodge, Charles. *The Constitutional History of the Presbyterian Church in the United States of America*, Part I, 1705-1741. Philadelphia: William S. Martien, 1839.

Hodge, Charles. *The Constitutional History of the Presbyterian Church in the United States of America*, Parts I and II. Philadelphia: Presbyterian Board of Publication, 1851.

Hodge, Charles, ed., *The Biblical Repertory and Princeton Review*, July 1837, IX. Princeton: 1837.

Bibliographies

Hodge, Charles. "The Theological Opinions of President Davies." *The Biblical Repertory and Princeton Review*. Philadelphia: John T. Robinson, 1842.

Hogg, William to Aaron Burr, August 28, 1755. "Catalogue Colegii. Neo-Caesarensis. Princetonae." *The Biblical Repertory and Princeton Review*, XII (1840).

Ingram, George H. "Biographies of the Alumni of the Log College: William Robinson," *Journal of the Presbyterian Historical Society (1901-1930)*, Vol. 13. No. 6 (June, 1929).

Ingram, George H. "History of the Presbytery of New Brunswick, Part III, Minutes of the Years 1740 and 1741, Inclusive." *Journal of the Presbyterian Historical Society* (1901-1930), Vol. 7, No. 3 (September, 1913).

Kirkpatrick, William to Joseph Bellamy, February 12, 1759. MS letter in Joseph Bellamy Papers, Hartford Seminary, Hartford, Connecticut.

"Letters of Patrick Henry, Sr., Samuel Davies, James Maury, Edwin Conway and George Task." Dawson Manuscripts, Library of Congress, *William and Mary Quarterly*, Second Series, I (October 1921).

Lowden, Samuel to Joseph Bellamy, October 7, 1754. MSS. letter in Joseph Bellamy Papers, Hartford Seminary Library, Hartford, Connecticut.

MacLachlan, James. *Princetonians, 1748-1768*. Princeton: Princeton University Press, 1976.

MacLean, John. *History of the College of New Jersey*. New York: Arno Press, 1969.

Miller, Samuel. *Memoir of the Rev. John Rodgers, D. D.* Philadelphia: Presbyterian Board of Publication, 1813.

Murphy, Thomas. *The Presbytery of the Log College; or, The Cradle of the Presbyterian Church in America* Philadelphia: Presbyterian Board of Publication, 1889.

"New Jersey College and President Davies." *The Biblical Repertory and Princeton Review*, XII (1840).

Patillo, Henry. *Diary of Henry Patillo*. MS in the Patillo Papers. Special Collections, William Smith Morton Library, Union Presbyterian Seminary, Richmond, Virginia.

Patillo, Henry to William Williamson, December 4, 1799. MS in Sahne Collection, Presbyterian Historical Society, Philadelphia, PA.

Patillo, Henry. *The Plain Planter's Family Assistant*. Washington, NC: James Adams, 1787.

Patillo Papers. Special Collections, William Smith Library, Union Presbyterian Seminary, Richmond, VA.

Pears, Thomas Clinton, Jr., ed. "Samuel Davies, Charity and Truth United," *Journal of the Presbyterian Historical Society*, Vol. XIX (Philadelphia, 1941).

Pemberton, Ebenezer to Eleazar Wheelock, November 18, 1758, MS letter in Dartmouth College Library

Pilcher, George William. *Samuel Davies: Apostle of Dissent in Colonial Virginia*. Knoxville, Tennessee: The University of Tennessee Press, 1971.

Pilcher, George William, ed. *The Reverend Samuel Davies Abroad: The Diary of a Journey to England and Scotland, 1753-55*. Urbana, Chicago, London: University of Illinois Press, 1967.

Pond, Enoch. *Memoir of the Rev. Samuel*

Bibliographies

Davies. Boston: Massachusetts Sabbath School Society, 1832.

Rachal, William M. E. "Early Minutes of Hanover Presbytery," *Virginia Magazine of History and Biography*, LXIII (1955).

"Records of the Old Londonderry Congregation, Now Faggs Manor, Chester Co., PA." *Journal of the Presbyterian Historical Society*, Vol. 8, No. 8 (December, 1916).

Records of the Presbyterian Church in the United States of America: Embracing the Minutes of the Presbytery of Philadelphia, From A.D. 1708 to 1716; Minutes of the Synod of Philadelphia, From A. D. 1717 to 1758; Minutes of the Synod of New York, From A.D. 1745 to 1758; Minutes of the Synod of Philadelphia and New York, From A. D. 1758 to 1788. Philadelphia: Presbyterian Board of Publication, 1841.

"Records of the Welsh Tract Baptist Meeting, Pencader Hundred, New Castle County, Delaware, 1701-1828," *Papers of the Historical Society of Delaware*, V, no. xlii, pt. 1. Wilmington, Delaware,1904.

Register House, S. S. P. C. K., Minutes, IV, 596; MS 7952.

Rice, John Holt. "The Origin of Presbyterianism in Virginia." *The Virginia Evangelical and Literary Magazine*, II. Richmond, VA: William W. Gray, 1819.

Rice, John Holt. "Memoir of the Rev. Samuel Davies." *Virginia Evangelical and Literary Magazine*, I. Richmond: William W. Gray, 1819.

Rice, John Holt, ed. *The Virginia Evangelical and Literary Magazine*, Vol. IX. Richmond, VA (1826).

Sprague, William B. *Annals of the American Presbyterian Pulpit*: Volume One. Birmingham, Alabama: Solid Ground Christian Books, 2005.

Stith, William. *The Nature and Extent of Christ's Redemption*. Williamsburg, VA: William Hunter, 1753.

Tennent, Gilbert. *Irenicum Ecclesiasticum, Or a Humble Impartial Essay on the Peace of Jerusalem*. Philadelphia: W. Bradford, 1749.

Vallandigham, J. L., Cooch, Mrs. J. Wilkins, Skinner, W. T., and Blake, George A. *History of the Pencader Presbyterian Church*, Glasgow, Delaware: The Woman's Missionary Society, 1899.

Webster, Richard. *History of the Presbyterian Church in America: From Its Origin Until the Year 1760*. Philadelphia: Joseph M. Wilson, 1857.

Wertenbaker, Thomas Jefferson. *Princeton: 1746-1896*. Princeton: Princeton University Press, 1974.

Wheelock, Eleazar to Samuel Davies, November 12, 1759. MS letter in Eleazar Wheelock MSS, Rauner Special Collections Library, Dartmouth College, Hanover, New Hampshire.

Whitefield, George to Eleazar Wheelock, November 5, 1756. MS letter in Dartmouth College Library. MS letter in Eleazar Wheelock MSS, Rauner Special Collections Library, Dartmouth College, Hanover, New Hampshire.

York, Edwin G. *The Pennington Area Presbyterians, 1709-1984*. Pennington, New Jersey: Pennington Presbyterian Church, 1985.

Secondary Bibliography

"A Short Genealogy of Edward Foulke (1651-1741)", *Bulletin of Friends' Historical Society of Philadelphia*, Vol. 6, No. 1 (Eleventh Month (November) 1914), p. 7, Published by: Friends Historical Publishers.

Anderson, Fred. *The War that Made America: A Short History of the French and Indian War*. New York: Viking Penguin, 2005.

Azevedo, Mario J., ed. *The State of Health and Healthcare in Mississippi*. Jackson, Mississippi: University Press of Mississippi, 2015.

Bailey Thomas Andrew, ed., *The American Spirit: United States History As Seen By Contemporaries*, Volume 1. Boston: D. C. Heath and Company, 1963.

http://baptisthistoryhomepage.com/morgan.abel.tbe.bio.html, accessed on January 30, 2015.

Beale, G. W., rev. Semple, Robert Baylor. *A History of the Rise and Progress of the Baptists in Virginia*. Richmond, Virginia: Pitt and Dickinson, 1894.

Benson, Louis F. "President Davies as a Hymn Writer." *Journal of the Presbyterian Historical Society*, Vol. II, No. 6 (September, 1904).

Benson, Louis F. "The Hymns of President Davies." *Journal of the Presbyterian Historical Society*, Vol. II, no. 7. (December, 1904).

Boles, John. "The Beginning of the Southern Bible-Belt," in Kenneth Kaulman, ed., *Critical Moments in Religious History*. Macon, Georgia: Mercer University Press, 1993.

Bonar, Andrew A. *Memoir and Remains of Robert Murray McCheyne*. London: The Banner of Truth Trust, 1968.

Bridges, Charles. *The Christian Ministry*. London: The Banner of Truth Trust, 1967.

Brydon, George MacLaren. *Virginia's Mother Church and the Political Conditions Under which it Grew, 1727-1784*, II, Richmond, VA: Virginia Historical Society, 1952

Brynestad, Lawrence E. "The Great Awakening in the New England and Middle Colonies." *Journal of the Presbyterian Historical Society*, Vol. XIV (1930-1)

Calvin, John. *Tracts and Letters*, Volume I: Tracts, Part I. Edinburgh, Scotland and Carlisle, Pennsylvania: The Banner of Truth Trust, 2009.

Campbell, Norine Dickson, *Patrick Henry: Patriot and Statesman*, New York: Devin-Adair, 1969.

Chastellux, Marquis de Francis Jean. *Travels in North America in the Years 1780-82*, Translated from the French, 2 vols. London: G. G. J and J. Robinson, 1787.

http://www.christianity.com/church/church-history/timeline/1701-1800/sermons-from-the-lisbon-earthquake-11630263.html, accessed on July 17, 2016

Cibber, Colly. *The Careless Husband: A Comedy*. London: J. and R. Tonson and S. Draper, 1750.

Collins, Varnum Lansing. *Princeton*, (New York: Oxford University Press, 1914.

Cormer, George W, ed. *The Autobiography of Benjamin Rush: His "Travels Through Life" Together with His Commonplace Book for 1789–1813*. Westport, Connecticut: Greenwood Press, 1970.

Bibliographies

Cremin, Lawrence A. *American Education: The Colonial Experience, 1607-1783*. New York: Harper and Row, 1970.

Cryer, Neville B. "John Eliot." *Five Pioneer Missionaries*. London: The Banner of Truth Trust, 1965.

Cunningham, William Cunningham. *Historical Theology*, Volume 1. London: The Banner of Truth Trust, 1969.

Dallimore, Arnold A. *George Whitefield: The Life and Times of the Great Evangelist of the Eighteenth Century Revival*, Volume 1. London: Banner of Truth Trust, 1970.

Dallimore, Arnold A. *George Whitefield: The Life and Times of the Great-Eighteenth Century Revival*, Volume II. Westchester, Illinois and Edinburgh, Scotland: Cornerstone Books and The Banner of Truth Trust, 1979.

Davenport, James to Joseph Bellamy, May 29, 1753. MSS letter in Joseph Bellamy Papers, Hartford Seminary Library, Hartford, Connecticut.

Davidson, Robert, *A History of the Presbyterian Church in Kentucky*, New York: Robert Carter, 1847.

Diary of Rev. John Cuthbertson. Accessed on June 29, 2016 at: http://www.bennett-twins.com/documents/Diaries/Cuthbertson/index.php?imageNumber=2.

Dwight, Sereno E. "Memoirs of Jonathan Edwards." *The Works of Jonathan Edwards*, Volume One. Edinburgh, Scotland and Carlisle, Pennsylvania: The Banner of Truth Trust, 1974.

Edwards, Morgan, "History of the Baptists in Delaware", *The Pennsylvania Magazine of History and Biography*, Vol. IX, Philadelphia: The Historical Society of Pennsylvania, 1885.

Elshout, Bartel, trans. Wilhelmus a' Brakel.

The Christian's Reasonable Service, Vol 1. Ligonier, Pennsylvania: Soli Deo Gloria Publications, 1992.

Emory, John, ed. *The Works of the Rev. John Wesley, A. M.*, Volume III. New York: Carlton and Porter, 1856.

Executive Journals of the Council of Colonial Virginia, 6:110.

Gayley, Samuel A. *An Historical Sketch of the Lower West Nottingham Presbyterian Church*. Philadelphia: Alfred Martien, 1865.

Gillespie, George. *A Letter to the Rev. Brethren of the Presbytery of New York*. Philadelphia: B. Franklin, 1740.

Gillespie, George. *Remarks Upon Mr. George Whitefield, Proving Him a Man Under Delusion*. Philadelphia: B. Franklin, 1744.

Glenn, Thomas Allen, *Merion in the Welsh Tract: With Sketches of the Townships of Haverford and Radnor*, Norristown, Pennsylvania: 1896.

Goold, William H., ed. *The Works of John Owen*, Volume XIII. London: The Banner of Truth Trust, 1967.

Greene, Jack P., ed., *The Diary of Colonel Landon Carter of Sabine Hall, 1752-1778*, Volume I. Richmond, VA: Virginia Historical Society, 1987.

Guy, Joe D. *Indian Summer: The Siege and Fall of Fort Loudon*. Johnson City, Tennessee: Overmountain Press, 2001.

Hageman, Jacob Frelinghuysen. *History of Princeton and Its Institutions*, Volume I. Philadelphia: J. P. Lippincott & Co, 1870.

Handy, Robert T. "John Rodgers, 1727-1811: 'A Life of Usefulness on Earth,'" *Journal of the Presbyterian Historical Society*, Vol. XXXIV, No. 2, (June, 1956).

Bibliographies

Hawke, David Freeman. *Benjamin Rush: Revolutionary Gadfly*. Indianapolis, Indiana and New York, New York: The Bobbs Merrill Company, Inc., 1971.

Hickman, Edward, rev. *The Works of Jonathan Edwards*, Volume One. Edinburgh, Scotland and Carlisle, Pennsylvania: The Banner of Truth Trust, 1974.

Hoefnagel, Dick and Close, Virginia L. "Eleazar's Two Schools", Accessed at: http://www.dartmouth.edu/~library/Library_Bulletin/Nov1999/Hoefnagel_Close.html?m switch-redir=classic on January 23, 2017.

Holloway, Joseph E. "African Insurrections on Board Slave Ships." Accessed at: http://slaverebellion.org/index.php?page=african-insurrections on February 16, 2017.

Holmes, David L. *A Brief History of the Episcopal Church: with a chapter on the Anglican Reformation and an appendix on the annulment of Henry VIII*. Valley Forge, Pennsylvania: Trinity Press International, 1993.

Isaacs, Rhyss. *The Transformation of Virginia, 1740-1790*. Chapel Hill, NC: The University of North Carolina Press, 1982.

James, John Angell. *An Earnest Ministry the want of the Times*. New York: M. W. Dodd, 1850.

Jones, Charles C. "Review of 'The Religious Instruction of the Negroes in the United States.'" *The Biblical Repertory and Princeton Review*, Volume XV. Philadelphia: John T. Robinson, 1843.

Jones, David, *The Doctrine of the "Laying on of Hands," Examined and Vindicated*, Philadelphia: Francis Bailey, 1786.

Jones, Horatio Gates, *Historical Sketch of the Lower Dublin (or Pennepek) Baptist Church*, Morrisania, New York, 1869.

Lancaster, Robert Bolling. *A Sketch of the Early History of Hanover County Virginia and Its Large and Important Contributions to The American Revolution*. Richmond: Whittet and Shepperson, 1976.

Ledwith, William L. "Six Letters of President Burr." *Journal of the Presbyterian Historical Society*, Vol. I, No. 5. (Sept., 1902).

Lewis, Frank Bell. "Samuel Davies, A Pattern for Preachers in Hanover Presbytery," *Minutes of Winter and Spring Meetings of Hanover Presbytery* (1958).

Lloyd-Jones, D. Martyn, *Knowing the Times*, Edinburgh, Scotland and Carlisle, PA: The Banner of Truth Trust, 1989.

http://www.lowermerionhistory.org/burial/merion/d.html accessed on March 18, 2016.

Marsden, George M. *Jonathan Edwards: A Life*. New Haven, Connecticut and London, England; Yale University Press, 2003.

Meade, Robert Douthat, *Patrick Henry, Practical Revolutionary*, Philadelphia: Lippincott, 1969.

Meade, William. *Old Churches, Ministers and Families of Virginia*, Volume I. Philadelphia: J. B. Lippincott & Co, 1861.

Murray, Iain H. *Jonathan Edwards: A New Biography*. Edinburgh, Scotland and Carlisle, Pennsylvania: The Banner of Truth Trust, 1987.

Myers, Thomas, trans. John Calvin, *Commentaries on the First Twenty Chapters of the Book of the Prophet Ezekiel, Calvin's Commentaries*, Volume XI. Grand Rapids, Michigan: Baker Book House, 2009.

Nelson, William, ed. *Documents Relating to the Colonial History of the State of New Jersey*, Volume XIX. Paterson, N.J.: The Press Printing and Publishing Co., 1897.

Bibliographies

Nelson, William, ed. *Documents Relating to the Colonial History of the State of New Jersey*, Volume XX. Paterson, N.J.: The Press Printing and Publishing Co., 1898.

Newland, Jeremiah. *Verses Occasioned by the Earthquakes in November, 1755*. Boston: 1755.

http://www.newrivernotes.com/other_states_delaware_religion_welshtractbaptistchurch.htm, accessed on March 18, 2016.

Parker, Percy Livingston, ed. *The Journal of John Wesley*. Chicago: Moody Press, n.d.

Pede, George, ed., *Methodist Quarterly Review*, 3rd Series, Volume VI. New York: 1846.

Pennsylvania Gazette, October 9, 1760.

Perry, William Stevens. *Historical Collections Relating to the American Colonial Church*, I. Hartford, Connecticut: The Church Press, 1873.

Pierre, C. E. "The Work of the Society for the Propagation of the Gospel in Foreign Parts Among the Negroes in the Colonies." *The Journal of Negro History*, Vol. 1, No. 4. (1916).

Prince, Thomas. *The Christian History*. Boston: Kneeland and Green, 1743.

Redford, George and James, John Angell, eds. *The Autobiography of William Jay*. Edinburgh, Scotland and Carlisle, Pennsylvania: The Banner of Truth Trust, 1974.

Rice, David. *Slavery Inconsistent with Justice and Good Policy*. New York: Samuel Wood, 1812.

Ryle, J. C. *Five Christian Leaders*. London: The Banner of Truth Trust, 1960.

Ryle, J. C. *Holiness: Its Nature, Hindrances, Difficulties, and Roots*. Cambridge and London: James Clarke & Co., LTD.:1956.

Schaff, Philip. *The History of the Christian Church: The German Reformation*, Volume VII. Grand Rapids, Michigan: Wm. B. Eerdmans Publishing Company, 1980.

Sermons of the Great Ejection, London: The Banner of Truth Trust, 1962.

Smith, Lisa. *The First Great Awakening in Colonial American Newspapers: A Shifting Story*. Lanham, Maryland; Boulder, Colorado; New York, New York; Toronto, Canada; and Plymouth, United Kingdom: Lexington Books, 2012.

Smith, Horace Wemyss. *Life and Correspondence of the Rev. William Smith, D.D.*, Volume I. Philadelphia: S. A. George & Co.,1880.

Smith, J. W. "Devereux Jarratt and the Beginnings of Methodism in Virginia", *The John P. Branch Historical Papers of Randolph-Macon College*, Ashland, Virginia, June 1901.

Spurgeon, C. H. *Lectures to My Students*. Grand Rapids, Michigan: Associated Publishers and Authors, Inc, n.d.

Tankus, Nathan. "Jackpot: For Colonial Slaves, Playing the Lottery was a Chance at Freedom." JSTOR Daily, February 2, 2016. Accessed on October 26, 2016 at: http://daily.jstor.org/jackpot-for-colonial-slaves-playing-the-lottery-was-a-chance-at-freedom/

Tappan, Eva March, ed. *The World's Story: A History of the World in Story, Song and Art*, 14 Volumes, Volume V: Italy, France, Spain, and Portugal. Boston: Houghton Mifflin, 1914.

"The Fight Over Inoculation During the 1721 Boston Smallpox Epidemic," December 31, 2014. Accessed on February 6, 2017 at: http://sitn.hms.harvard.edu/flash/special-edition-on-infectious-disease/2014/the-fight-over-inoculation-during-the-1721-boston-smallpox-epidemic

The Querists. Philadelphia: B. Franklin, 1741.

The General Assembly's Missionary Magazine; or Evangelical Intelligencer: For 1805. Philadelphia: Fry and Kammerer, 1805.

The Works of John Flavel, Volume IV. London: The Banner of Truth Trust, 1968.

Thornbury, John. "David Brainerd," *Five Pioneer Missionaries*. London: The Banner of Truth Trust, 1965.

Tracy, Joseph. *The Great Awakening: A History of the Revival of Religion in the Time of Edwards and Whitefield*. Edinburgh, Scotland and Carlisle, Pennsylvania: The Banner of Truth Trust, 1976.

http://en.wikipedia.org/wiki/Now_I_Lay_Me_Down_to_Sleep, accessed on January 29, 2016.

Virginia Gazette, Williamsburg, VA: William Parks, 1739.

Walker, James. *The Theology and Theologians of Scotland 1560-1750*. Edinburgh: Knox Press, 1982.

Wallace, George R. *Princeton Sketches, The Story of Nassau Hall*. New York: G. P. Putnam's Sons, 1894.

Warfield, Benjamin B. "How Princeton Seminary Got to Work," Journal of the Presbyterian Historical Society, (1901-1930), Vol. 9, No. 6 (JUNE, 1918).

White, Henry Alexander. *Southern Presbyterian Leaders*. Edinburgh, Scotland and Carlisle, Pennsylvania: The Banner of Truth Trust, 2000.

Whitefield, George. *Seventy-Five Sermons on Various Important Subjects* in Three Volumes, Volume I. London: W. Baynes, 1812.

Whitefield's Journals. London: The Banner of Truth Trust, 1973.

Woody, Thomas, *Early Quaker Education in Pennsylvania*, New York: Columbia University, 1909.

Wright, Louis B. *The Cultural Life of the American Colonies*. Mineola, New York: Dover Publications, 2002.

Index

Act of Intineration (1737), Synod of Philadelphia 46
Act of Ministerial Education (1738), Synod of Philadelphia 58
Act of Toleration (1689) 22, 82, 96-9, 108-9, 116-7, 139, 145-50, 152-3, 169, 183, 236, 369-70
Act of Uniformity (1662) 22, 26, 82, 98, 147, 149
Alexander, Archibald 38, 56, 70, 72, 83, 85, 101, 105, 123,
.... 156, 166-8, 176-7, 227, 231, 318, 377, 416-7
Bellamy, Joseph 93, 116, 118, 129, 133, 163-4, 167, 169, 171,
.... 173-4, 182, 245, 264,
.... 321, 336, 354, 365, 371, 387, 394, 417
Blair, James (Commissary of Virginia) 86-88, 93-4, 286
Blair, John (brother of Samuel Blair) 95, 98, 214, 263, 336, 400, 404
Blair, Samuel 38-9, 51, 53, 56, 58-9, 61-6, 68-71, 73, 76-9,
.... 100, 102, 104-7, 121, 124, 151, 155, 175-6, 181, 201, 208-9, 211, 302, 392-3
Bostwick, David 214, 265, 365, 371, 373, 382, 387, 394, 414, 417, 419
Brainerd, David 201, 214, 343-4, 359
Brown, John 215, 290, 281, 290, 299
Burr, Aaron 201, 203, 212-3, 237, 259-60, 293, 305, 362, 380-1, 384, 427
Caldwell, John 121-5
Chandler, Samuel 226-231, 233-4
College of New Jersey (Princeton College) 22, 179-80, 200-4, 211, 213, 222,
.... 228-9, 238, 241, 243-4, 247, 253, 259, 280, 291, 293, 302, 304-5, 316,
.... 350, 353, 361-3, 366, 373-4, 376-8, 380-3, 387, 391-2, 395, 407-8, 410-3, 416
Cowell, David 234, 364-6, 371, 386, 408-9
Craighead, Alexander 62, 287, 290, 356
Cuthbertson, John 207-211
David, Morgan 22-24
Davenport, James 67, 169-171, 182
Davies, David 23, 25, 27, 30, 34, 379
Davies, Jane Holt 135-7, 156, 204-6, 217, 235, 242, 258-9, 304, 414-5
Davies, Martha Thomas 27, 30-33, 39, 104, 415, 418
Davies, Samuel
    Accepts call to Hanover, Virginia 113-4
    Appearances at General Court in Virginia 146-8
    Assurance of salvation 54
    Birth 30

Index

Calling John Todd as an assistant in Virginia 179-83
Chapels of ease 132-3
Charity and Truth 265-75
Childhood- 3-4
Conversion 47-51
Davies and John Rodgers in Virginia 114-9
Death of first wife, Sarah Kirkpatrick, and son 110
Doctrine of Church and state 278-9
Evangelization of African slaves 311-24
Fund Raising at College of New Jersey 221-260
General Assembly of Church of Scotland 241-4
Last sickness and death 41-4
Licensure by New Castle Presbytery 105
Marriage of parents 29-30
Marriage to Jane Holt (second wife) 136-7
Marriage to Sarah Kirkpatrick (first wife) 105-7
Masters Thesis at College of New Jersey 213
Maternal lineage 25-9
Move to Princeton 378-9
Ministerial students at Hanover 177-9
Missionary Society of Hanover Presbytery 345-7
Opposition and persecution in Virginia 143-5
Ordination by New Castle Presbytery 107
Paternal Lineage 22-25
Petition for new meetinghouses in Virginia 114-9
Preaching in Somerset County, Maryland 110-3
Preaching Tour to Hanover, Virginia 108-110
Preaching Tours in Virginia 164-9
Raising militias in Virginia 283-4, 286-7
Seeking Jonathan Edwards as an assistant 171-5
Sermon to New Castle Presbytery 186-94
Sickness in 1756 332-6
Student at Fagg's Manor Academy 69-71
Student at Pencader Academy in Walsh Tract 57
Student at Robinson's school in Hopewell, New Jersey 39-44
The Impartial Trial 121-6
The Virginia Pindar 155-61
View of Samuel Blair 175-7
Views of Anglican clergy of Virginia 150-2
Views of Old Light- New Light Division 76
Visits George Whitefield 225, 229
Visits Mrs. Doddridge (widow of Philip Doddridge) 252
Visits Samuel Chandler 227-30
Visits Thomas Gibbons 232
Visits William McCulloch at Cambuslang, Scotland 246-7
Warning against Rev. John Cuthbertson 208-11
William Robinson's support of education 94
Davies, Sarah Dickinson (David Davies' first wife) 25
Davies, Sarah Kirkpatrick (Samuel's first wife) .... 105-6, 110, 136, 207, 371'

Index

Dickinson, Jonathan 68, 75, 201, 212
Dinwiddie, Robert (Governor of Virginia, 1751-1756) 155, 177-80, 183,
.... 247, 277-8, 283-4, 286, 337, 347, 416
Edwards, Jonathan 18, 22, 44, 48, 60, 67, 102, 124, 162, 170-5, 178-81, 185, 201-2, 226,
.... 248, 275, 293, 336, 343-4, 354, 362, 374, 384, 412, 417-8
Fauquier, Francis (Governor of Virginia, 1758-1768) 355
Finley, Samuel 16, 36, 38, 47, 50-1, 53-4, 64, 70, 73, 99-100, 118, 124,
.... 131, 176, 206-8, 214, 304-5, 353, 362, 364-66, 372, 387,
.... 390, 394, 400-1, 403, 407, 412, 417-8, 420
Franklin, Benjamin 37, 53, 67, 186, 308, 391
Gibbons, Thomas 49, 111, 157, 224, 227, 231-2, 304, 333-4, 361- 376, 413-4
Gooch, William (Governor of Virginia, 1727-1749) 86, 89, 95-7, 99-100, 107, 110, 115-7,
.... 119, 132, 138-9, 144, 146, 180, 197
Great Awakening 44, 55, 57-8, 63-5, 67, 71, 73-5, 77-8, 81-3,
.... 101-2, 124, 128, 130, 143, 228, 233, 238, 337, 344-5, 359-60, 398
Henry, Patrick (Statesman, Orator) 19-21
Henry, Patrick, Sr. (Reverend) 38, 98-102, 108-110, 117, 121, 136, 138, 145, 151-2, 158, 164
Henry, Robert 282, 290-1, 293, 303, 318
John Holt 136, 139-40, 155-6, 187, 411
Hunt, James 88-9, 91, 179, 301, 408
Kirkpatrick, John 106, 207, 280
Makemie, Francis 111, 118
Martin, John 296, 298, 352-6, 360
Mather, Cotton 40, 42, 44, 48, 63, 128, 386
Mauduit, Jasper 257, 346
MacClenachan, William 398-402, 405
McAden, Hugh 210-2
Merion Meeting (Quaker) 24
McCulloch, William 175, 246-7, 346
Moravians 96, 218, 256
Morgan, Joseph 39-40, 42, 45, 48, 54
Morris, Samuel 28, 83-5, 88-95, 97-102, 108, 117, 138, 198, 206, 290, 301
Morton, John 146-7, 166-7, 293
Morton, Little Joe 165-7, 292-3
New Lights, New Side, New Light Presbyterians 57, 58, 71-6, 87-8, 90, 96-100, 102,
.... 109,121-3, 133, 136-8, 143, 146, 149, 152, 163-7, 169-70, 172,
.... 180-3, 194, 198, 201, 208-11, 230, 244, 256, 263, 265, 280, 290-1370, 390-405
Occum, Samson 344-5, 354
Old Hop, (Sachem of Overhill Cherokees) 347, 356-8
Old Lights, Old Side, Old Light Presbyterians 57-8, 71-6, 97-9, 117, 123, 163,
.... 178, 185, 210, 215, 241, 256, 280, 402-5
Old Light- New Light Split (1741) 71-6
Patillo, Henry 177-8, 262-3, 293, 297-300, 323, 332, 367, 425
Pemberton, Ebenezer 201, 203, 214, 216, 263-4, 352
Pencader Meeting (Baptist) in Welsh Tract 27-9, 31-3, 35, 57, 300, 319, 354-8, 360
Randolph, Peyton 19, 115, 146, 148, 165, 236, 265, 347
Rice, David 84, 93, 178, 301-4, 308, 322-3, 392-3
Rice, John Holt 16, 38, 82, 83, 89, 246, 194-6, 319
Richardson, William 319, 354-8, 360

Index

Robinson, William 36, 38-44, 48, 51-3, 70, 90-4, 98- 124-5,
.... 110-1, 113, 132, 164, 167, 169-70, 185, 189, 301
Rodgers, John 38, 64-5, 70, 73, 82, 114-8, 194, 215-7
Rush, Benjamin 38, 43, 93, 140, 385, 388, 392, 411
Savage, Samuel 226, 232
St. George's Presbyterian Church 104, 113, 118, 216-7, 165, 415
Tennent, Gilbert 12, 44-7, 49, 52, 65, 73, 75, 77, 83, 98-100,
.... 102, 121, 123-4, 151, 201-4, 206, 211-2, 214-9, 221-9,
.... 241-5, 250-9, 305, 346, 353, 378, 397, 400-1
Tennent, William, Jr. 67, 69, 100, 201, 205, 353, 400, 403
Todd, John 162-3. 170, 172, 180-3, 206, 235, 262, 284, 290-1,
.... 301-2, 313, 367-8, 370, 372, 393, 404, 414-5
Washington, George 20-1, 277-8, 280, 284, 300, 349, 377, 391
Wesley, John 218, 256, 319
Whitefield, George 53, 64-73, 75 79, 81, 85-6, 100, 104, 124, 138,
.... 143, 154, 185, 197-8, 212, 225, 227-8, 232, 238-9, 243, 250,
.... 262-4, 308-9, 322-3, 327, 336, 346, 400, 405, 418
Wright, John 206, 214, 249, 290, 292-6, 303, 316

Illustration below (a detail) and on the following page (full map):
Reproduction of a map showing the "most inhabited part of Virginia" drawn by
Joshua Fry and Peter Jefferson, 1751, reproduced with the permission of Special
Collections, John D. Rockefeller Library, Colonial Williamsburg Foundation.

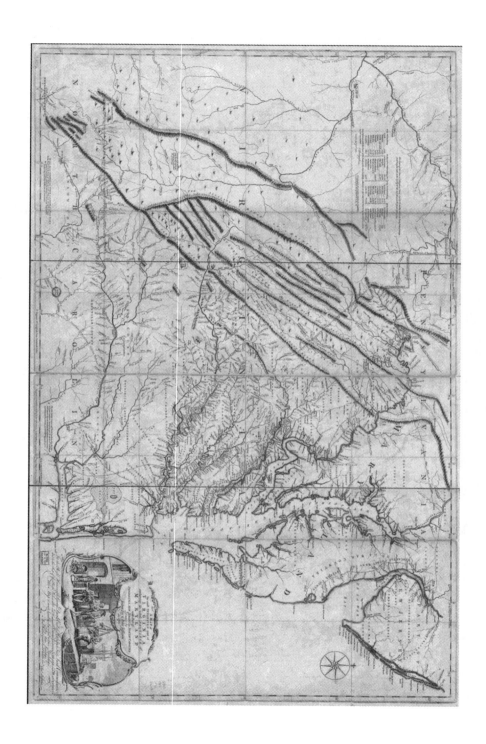

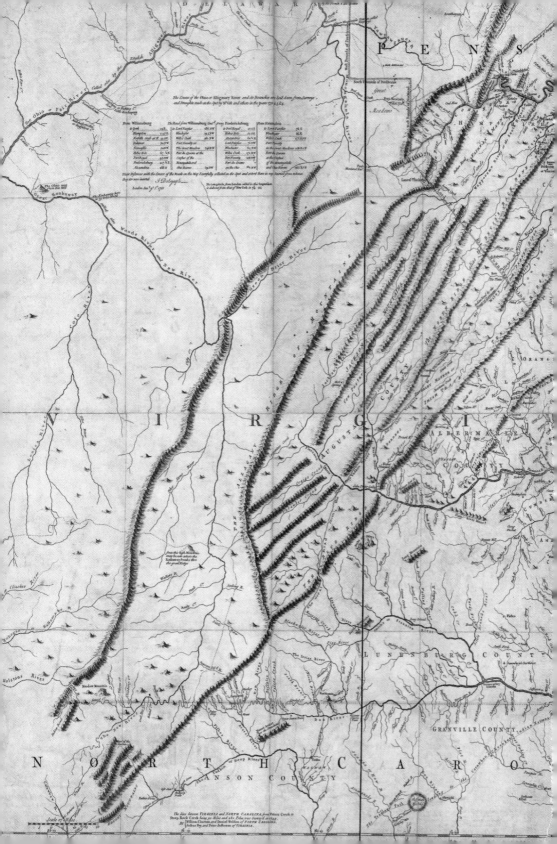